SNAFFLES On Racing and Point-to-Pointing

THE LAMBOURN PRESS

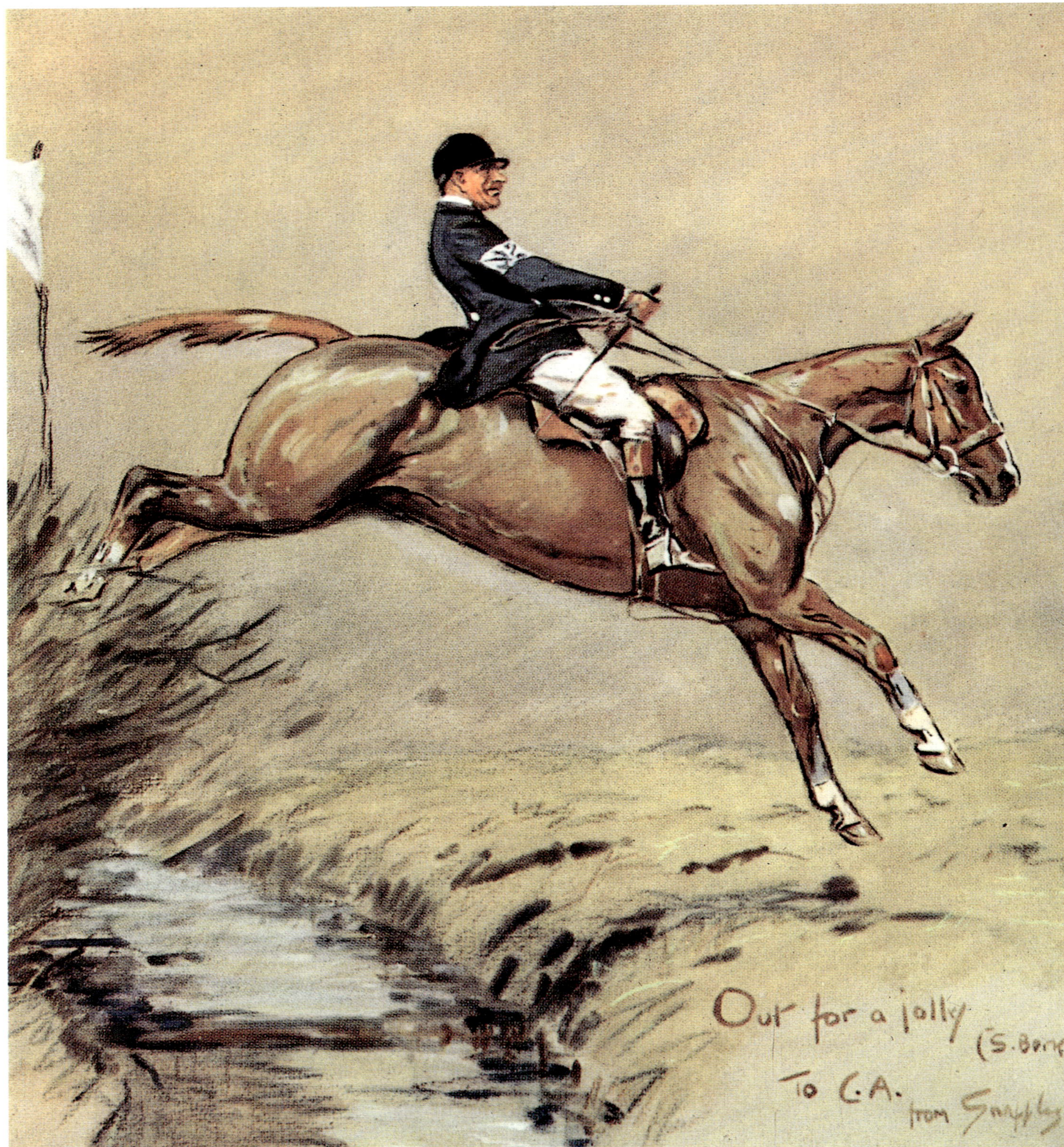

Snaffles gave this watercolour of Cecil Aldin to him. Aldin used it as the frontispiece to his memoirs, *Time I was Dead*

SNAFFLES On Racing and Point-to-Pointing

John Welcome and Rupert Collens
with a foreword by Molly Keane (M.J. Farrell)

THE LAMBOURN PRESS
London·Dublin·Melbourne

THE LAMBOURN PRESS LTD
The Old Forge, 7 Caledonian Road,
London, N1 9DX, England

28 Molesworth Street, Dublin 2, Eire

9 Queen Street, Melbourne 3000, Victoria, Australia

First published 1988

A limited edition of 275 signed and specially bound copies is published
by
The Marlborough Bookshop and Sporting Gallery
6 Kingsbury Street, Marlborough, Wiltshire

Produced by Antler Books
Photography by Charles Chrestien
Jacket design by Peter Hedges
Book from a design by Peter Hedges

Typesetting by TJB Photosetting Ltd
Colour Origination and Printing by Motta, Milan, Italy

ISBN 0 9513697 0 9

Acknowledgments for this series of books

First and foremost, we would like to express a great debt of gratitude to The British Sporting Art Trust for producing the excellent essay and listing of prints in the catalogue for their exhibition of Charlie Johnson Payne's work held in 1981, without these books would have been virtually impossible to produce.

The authors and their research assistant, Annabel Buchan, wish to express their sincere thanks to all those who went to great trouble in answering their letters, returning telephone calls, providing them with information, lending them letters and Christmas cards from Snaffles, photographs or books with pictures of Snaffles in them, granting them interviews and arranging for transparencies to be made of their paintings or prints, and to the occupiers of Snaffles' two main residences after 1918 for allowing access for photographic purposes, and in particular to:

Lieutenant Colonel A.G.S. Alexander, Mrs B. Allen, Mrs Diane Alley, Squadron Leader Pat Biegel, Mrs Peter Biegel, Sir Richard Body MP, Brigadier Lyndon Bolton DSO,DL, Mrs Bowes Daly, Captain W.W.F. Chatterton Dickson RN, Mrs H. Cleeve, Lady Clive, Tim Corballis, Major-General J.G. Elliott, Mrs. J. Gibson, Miss D. Gibson, Miss Daphne Hall-Dare, Lieutenant Colonel W. Harris, Mrs Jean Holt, Major N. Jackson RA, Mrs J. Jackson, Mrs Molly Keane, Harry S. Kenny, Miss Naomi Kerans, George Knowles, Victor Lakin, Lieutenant Colonel Patrick Langford, Mrs Winifred Langford, Mr and Mrs P. Latham, Jack Leonard, Stephen Ling, Major A.C. Lynch-Staunton, Mrs Suzie Monkland, Lieutenant Colonel W.L. Newell DSO, Mrs Norah Pearson, Mr and Mrs B. Rees, Mrs Patsy Scott-Cockburn, Mrs Susan Sloman, Colonel G.B. Thatcher DSO, Mrs. Marjorie Waller, Mr and Mrs Peter Walwyn, Lieutenant Colonel W.G. Watt, Mr and Mrs D. Wyatt, the Curators of the National Army Museum, the Leicester Museum, the Chisolm Polo Gallery of Palm Beach USA, the Masters of Foxhounds Association.

I, John Welcome, would personally like to express my special thanks to Major-General Brian Daunt for his recollections of Snaffles' techniques and permission to publish them; Mrs. Terrence Cleeve for the loan of a charming Snaffles watercolour and permission to reproduce it; Peter Brooke for the help with the relationship of his father, Geoffrey Brooke, and Snaffles, and for the loan of the important "Sandown 1921" watercolour and permission to reproduce it, and to Molly Keane for her kindness in writing the foreword.

I, Rupert Collens, would once again particularly like to thank Mark Flower of The Court Gallery for the hours of time he has spent helping with this book and the unstinting supply of information he has given on both Charlie and Lucy Payne's lives and, of course, on Snaffles' artistic output. I would also like to thank Pam Turnbull of The Countryman's Gallery in Leicestershire for her encouragement, support and, above all else, the loan of material from her private collection; Major Bill Weightman of Yorkshire who has also been remarkably kind with material from his fabulous private collection; and Timothy Cox, who has laboured long and hard over form-books, stud-books and other material to try and resolve many obscure queries raised by Snaffles' more obtuse statements regarding form and breeding.

Both the authors would like to express their gratitude to Annabel Buchan for all the research work which she has undertaken so diligently, and Jan Alexander for her help with typing and proof reading.

Paintings and prints

With a few exceptions, the colour transparencies of original works and prints have been kindly supplied by two specialist dealers in Snaffles' works: The Court Gallery, 8 Lancashire Court, New Bond Street, London W.1; and the Marlborough Sporting Gallery and Bookshop, 6 Kingsbury Street, Marlborough, Wiltshire.

Contents

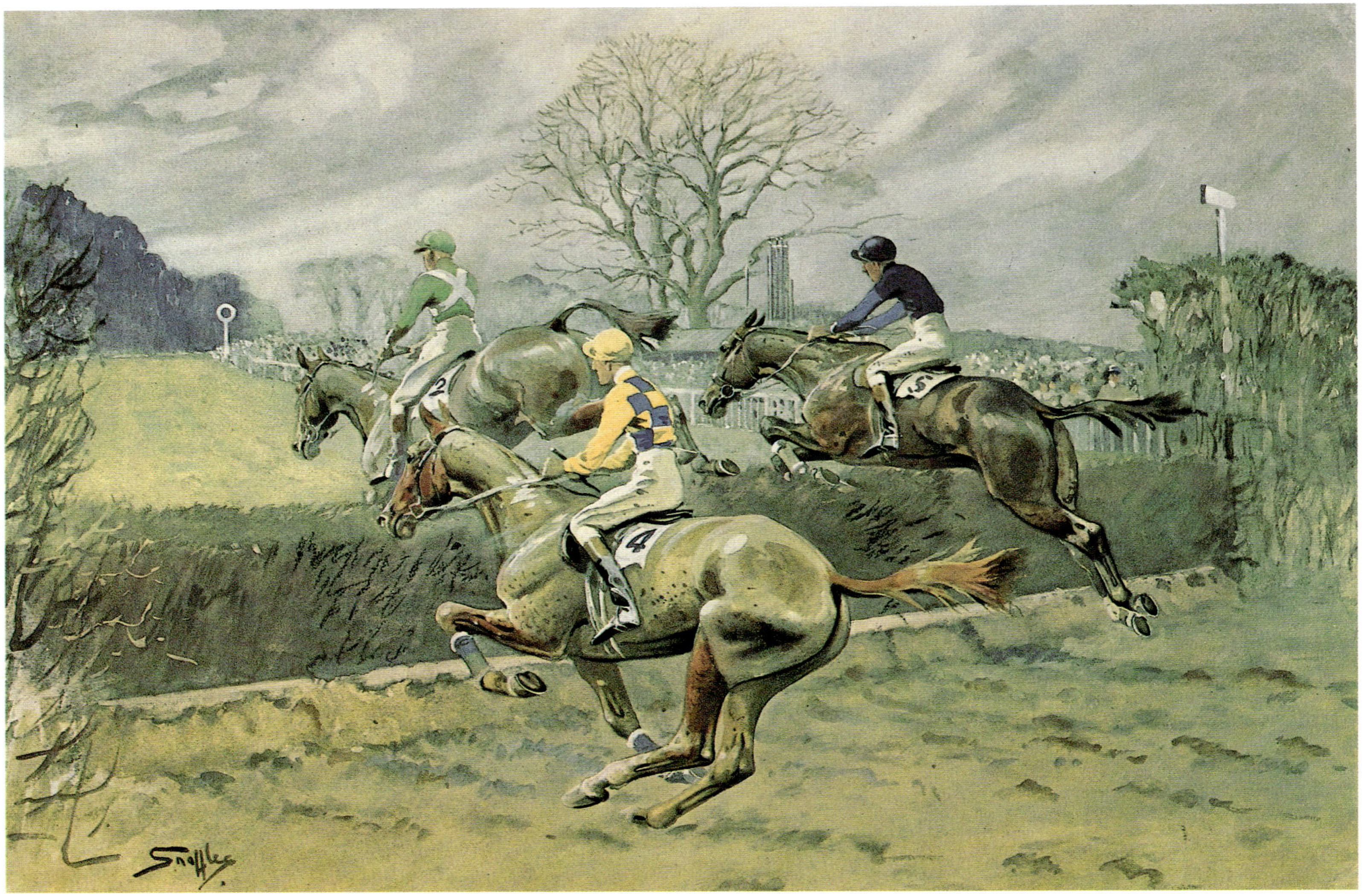

Sandown

– Asking 'em the Question

One of Snaffles' greatest racing prints and almost certainly the finest steeplechasing print ever of Sandown

Foreword

One need not be an addict of Snaffles' pictures to find in John Welcome and Rupert Collens' book a meticulously researched and fascinatingly interesting history of steeplechasing and point-to-pointing since the early years of this century. The background this supplies adds a wonderful interest to these pictures that will always quicken memory in their intimate reality, a perception closer than any television picture or commentary can ever create.

The authors catch the character of Snaffles that is behind all his prints and drawings. In his way Snaffles was a visionary with ecstatic pleasure in achievement and a knowing sympathy with failure. Situations difficult, funny, dangerous or triumphant are seen with an unsurpassed eye and understanding.

Snaffles caught truth at its flying moments, and the authors tell us how he did it, and it was not achieved through any easy craftsmanship, but by intense and continuous work and observation, aided by his ability to store in memory and transfer to his pictures the exact moment of drama that lived for him and lives in them.

I have never waited beside such silent and absolute concentration as on the day when the embryo of the great Sandown print was in his mind. He did not have the shadow of a notebook or pencil about him when we stood at the fence, only a knife-sharp concentration maintained in an unbreakable and lasting silence, intense as a prayer, then reality was stored away far from any of the flippancies of life for he was a great chatterer and always ready to amuse or be amused.

The memories we share here of the greatest – whether horse or jockey – their triumphs or disappointments are delightfully leavened by the inclusion of the risks and chances and sometimes miraculous successes achieved by indifferent horses ridden by lesser jockeys. The book is a treasury of names, amateur and professional, many of their owners are still actively with us – others, ghosts to a younger generation, are summoned back so clearly in John Welcome's spare descriptions, one might be trembling on the rails watching his race beside a deeply concerned owner and trainer of other unforgettable days.

John Welcome and Rupert Collens hold the right key to Snaffles' work and life, never under-rating, never over-praising, yet the quality of glory and venture that is behind all the drawings shines through the writing.

Molly Keane.

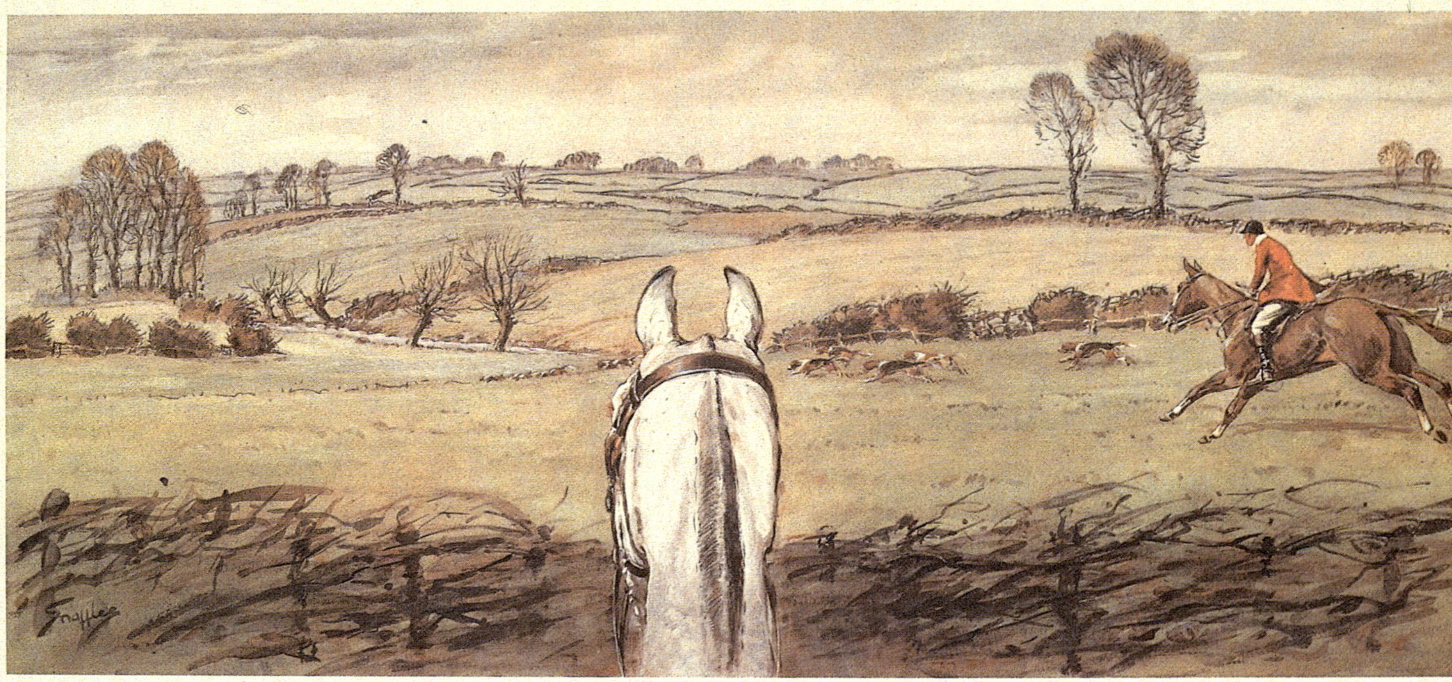

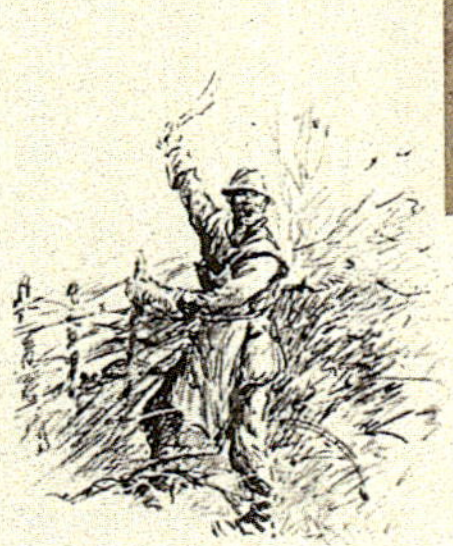

THE FINEST VIEW IN EUROPE

Although the first of Snaffles' great pair of prints, 'The Finest ...' and 'The Worst View in Europe', was set in the hunting field, the grey horse in the picture being ridden by the artist, was Rifle Brigade, on whom HRH The Prince of Wales won his first point to point at the Pytchley meeting in 1922. He was, in fact, a bay gelding, not a grey, but Snaffles changed his colour to enhance the contrast

1 The Start

'I have been mixed up with steeplechasing for the last half century', so wrote Snaffles in 1950, when looking back on his memories. Passionately devoted as he was all of his long life to every form of equestrian sport, along with hunting, steeplechasing and point-to-point racing were very much to the fore.

As he said himself in another brief recollection, his recall, if his memory served him rightly, went back further than fifty years, since he referred to an occasion in 'the mid nineties' when he heard Lord Willoughby de Broke despatch a point-to-point field with the words: 'There's your point, Gentlemen. Go! And Heaven be with you!.' 'The point referred to', he went on to say, 'was Chesterton Windmill in the Warwickshire country. It was such a long haul back to those bygone days that I am afraid the scene is somewhat blurred in my memory. But I do remember it was very unlike the point-to-point meeting as we know it today. The riders all wore top hats, there were quite a few cock-tailed horses entered, and unless one was mounted it was not possible to see the contest or pounding match for such it was. The riders were shown a point some four miles away, usually a church steeple or windmill, and they had to get there the best they could. The only condition was that no rider was allowed to open a gate, to ride along a road or to walk the country prior to the race. A breach of these rules disqualified him.'

That first meeting which Snaffles attended in the 1890's was almost certainly that known as 'The Midland Sportsmen's Races' founded in 1888 in Warwickshire by Lord Willoughby de Broke. The races were always run over a strongly fenced course, of at least four miles, and were described as 'fences of fair and proper hunting type'. Whether the participants always agreed with this description is very doubtful, as well under twenty five per cent used to complete without a fall, although participants were limited to members of five good hunts, the Warwickshire, North Warwickshire, Pytchley, Bicester and Heythrop.

The House of Commons point-to-point was run at this meeting for five years from 1888 to 1892, but in the last year double tragedy befell the meeting when two well-known competitors, who were keen hunting men, both met their deaths. One riding in an open race, was the famous Captain Bay Middleton, who had piloted The Empress of Austria out hunting in both England and Ireland and the other was the seventy-year-old member for Cheshire, the Right Honourable James Thomkinson.

Snaffles, as we have seen, confessed that his memory on occasions was 'somewhat blurred' as it well may have been, for in 'the mid nineties' he would have scarcely have reached his teens, having been born in early 1884 at Leamington Spa in Warwickshire, where his father ran a boot-making business. He was duly christened Charlie Johnson Payne although in later life, when not signing himself 'Snaff' or 'Snaffles' he took to signing himself 'Charles' rather than Charlie. So far as can be ascertained, since records of his early life are scanty, there was no sporting tradition in the family, but a great uncle had served in the Cavalry and ridden with the Light Brigade at Balaclava. It is entirely probable that it was this great uncle who fired the boy's imagination with stories of 'hard riding sojer h'officers' and brought him to that early Warwickshire point-to-point which was to inspire his lifelong enthusiasm for the sports of point-to-pointing and steeplechasing and all who took part in them, whether human or equine.

Leamington had ceased to hold proper steeplechase meetings at the time of Snaffles' birth, but in the early records of steeplechasing it was one of the most important venues. The Leamington Grand Annual Steeplechase in the 1830's and 1840's was often the most valuable race in the calendar with more added money than the Grand National. The immortal Lottery, the winner of the first Grand National in 1839, won a four mile race there the following year, carrying 12 stone ridden by Jem Mason. Grand Military meetings were held at Leamington Spa, the last one being in 1848. Only two of the eleven starters who sallied forth in the most atrocious conditions, with driving snow and gale force wind, completed the course and it was unlikely that either did so without at least one fall.

Warwickshire itself during the last twenty or so years of the 19th century was an equestrian sportsman's paradise. There were many packs of foxhounds, the Warwickshire was considered to be one of the leading packs outside the Shires, and the Midlands were then the stronghold of steeplechasing. Warwick Steeplechase Course, only a few miles from Leamington Spa, was well established and, in fact, played host to the second most important race, the four-mile National Hunt Chase, in 1902 and 1903, and 1906 to 1910 inclusive, before it found a permanent home at Cheltenham in 1911, hence founding the festival of steeplechasing we now know as The National Hunt Festival. (see Table A)

Table A
NATIONAL HUNT CHASE
Conditions Steeplechase for Amateur Riders 4 Miles.

Venue		*Winning Horse*	*Rider*
1880	Liverpool	New Glasgow	Capt. Smith
1881	Birmingham	Pride of Prussia	Mr. E.P.Wilson
1882	Derby	Llantarnam	Mr. E.P. Wilson
1883	Melton	Satellite	Mr. E.P. Wilson
1884	Leicester	Equity	Mr. E.P. Wilson
1885	Lincoln	Lady Tempest	Mr. W. Beasley
1886	Malton	Why Not	Mr. C.J. Cunningham
1887	Derby	Monkshood	Capt. E.R. Owen
1888	Sandown Park	Glen Thorpe	Mr. Geo. Lambton
1889	Cardiff	Nap	Mr. C. Thompson
1890	Irvine	Innisfail	Mr. T.G. Arthur
1891	Hurst Park	Impeyan	Mr. Crawley
1892	Derby	Royal Buck	Mr. Yorke
1893	Sandown Park	Van der Berg	Sir C. Slade
1894	Derby	Philactery	Mr. Ricardo
1895	Sandown Park	Finma-Coul II	Mr. F.B. Atkinson
1896	Hurst Park	Ludgershall	Mr. H.M. Ripley
1897	Newmarket	Nord Ouest	M. Morand
1898	Gatwick	Real Shamrock	Mr. E.P. Gundry
1899	Hurst Park	Glen Royal	Mr. J.J. Fergusson
1900	Kempton Park	Eoos	Mr. A. Gordon
1901	Melton Hunt	Friar John	Mr. H. Sidney
1902	Warwick	Marpessa	Mr. Persse
1903	Warwick	Comfit	Capt. R.H. Collis
1904	Cheltenham	Timothy Titus	Mr. Ivor Anthony
1905	Cheltenham	Miss Clifden II	Mr. H.M. Ripley
1906	Warwick	Count Rufus	Mr. A. Gordon
1907	Warwick	Red Hall	Mr. H.G. Farrant
1908	Warwick	Rory O'Moore	Mr. P. Whitaker
1909	Warwick	Wychwood	Mr. P. Roberts
1910	Warwick	Nimble Kate	Mr. P. Roberts
1911 Onwards always run at Cheltenham			
1911		Sir Halbert	Mr. A. Smith
1912		The Rejected IV	Mr. G.E. Cotton

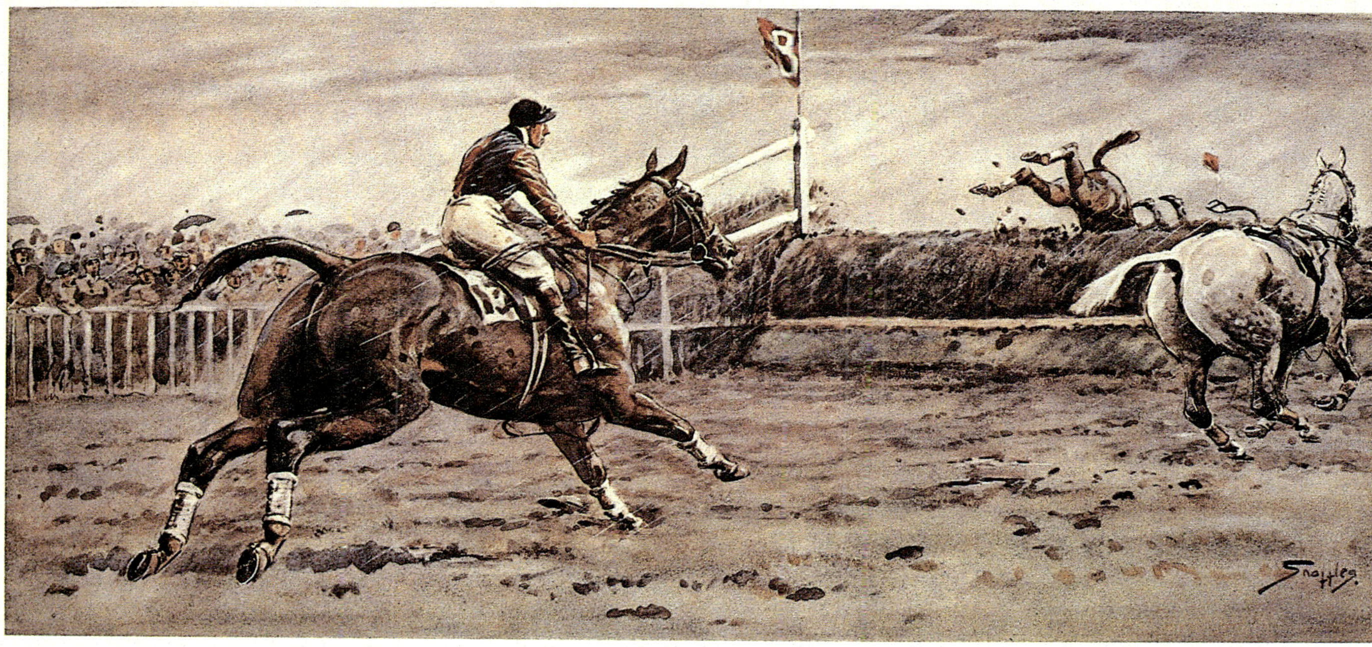

THE WORST VIEW IN EUROPE

"Oh murther! The dhrink died out of me and the wrong side of Bechers."

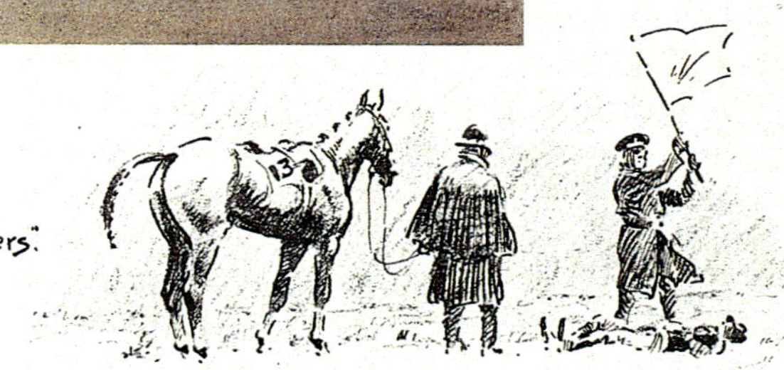

Snaffles executed the watercolour from which this print was produced some twenty years after Grudon won the 1901 Grand National

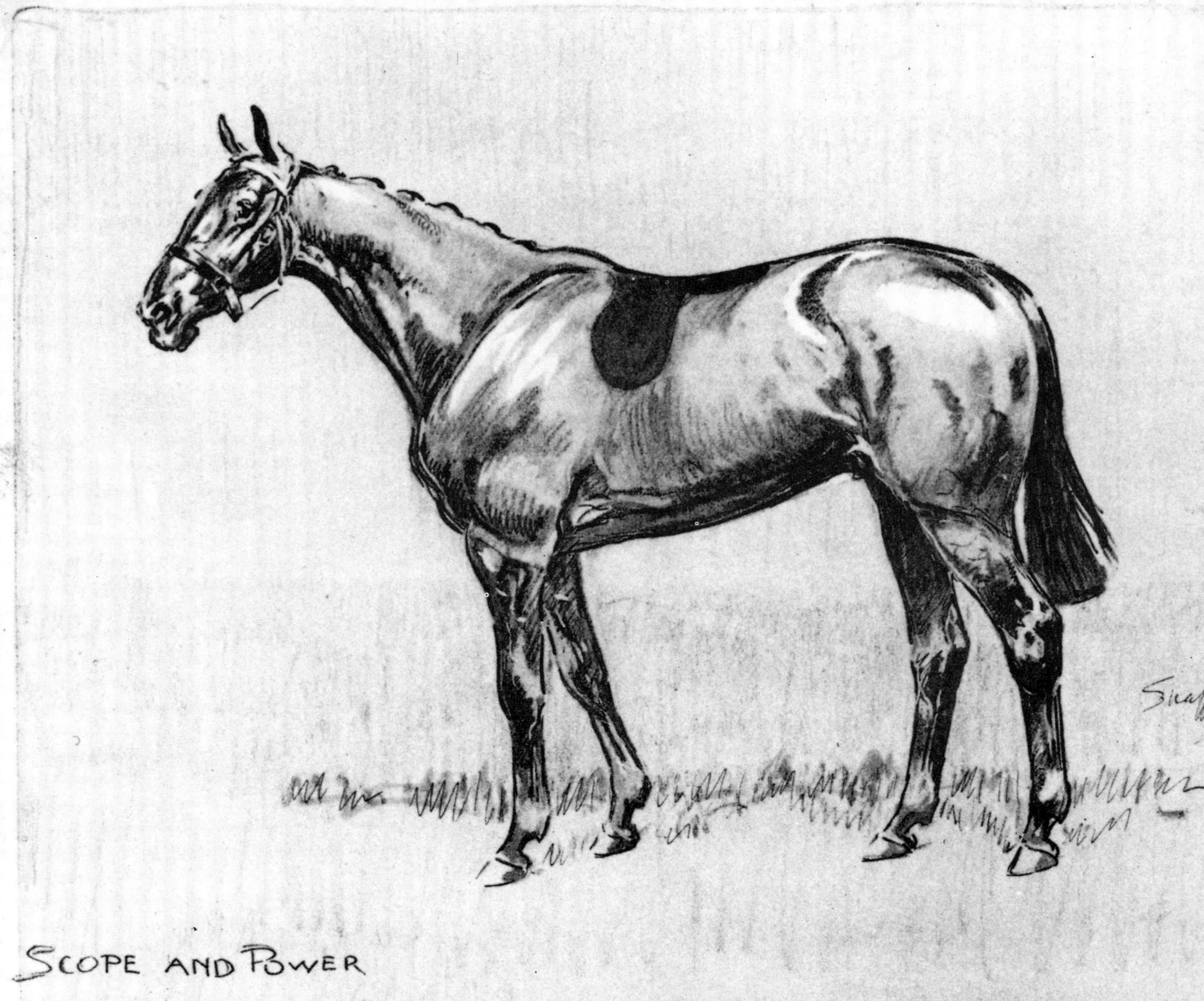

The Right One to carry thirteen stone

Slap bang over

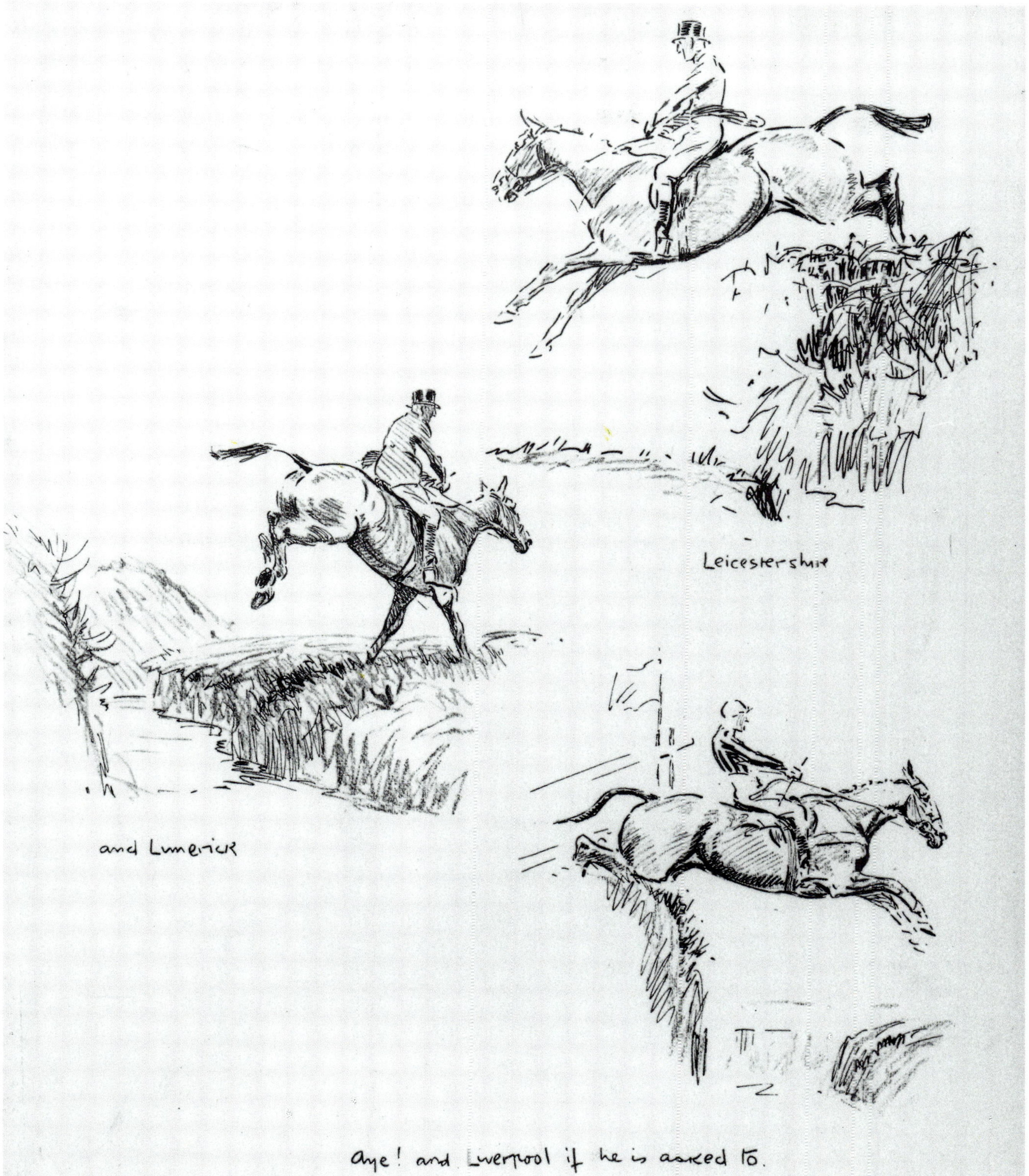

Snaffles always favoured a big, strong, blood horse who, as he said, would go slap bang over Leicestershire, Limerick or Liverpool

From a very early age Snaffles was possessed with the urge to draw and, more particularly, to draw horses, sometimes with hunt staff, sometimes with soldiers, but often on their own; and he liked to draw the horses in action. There can be no doubt too that, consciously or unconsciously, he was storing, in that receptive memory of his, incidents, often humorous by flood and field as it were, which were to reappear in his sketches many years later.

Snaffles' schooling, as he recalled it, was cursory and spasmodic. Apart from some rudimentary instructions from an art master, who commended his early efforts, he never had a lesson in art or drawing in his life, although his natural talent was apparent even in his early teens and that master, perceiving it, promoted him to the sixth form for 'drawing'. Snaffles tells us he learned much of his drawing technique from copying the fashionable sporting artists of the day such as Finch Mason and John Sturgess. It is safe to assume that one reason his schooling was so scanty was that he played truant to watch the Yeomanry on parade, of which he left records in his later books and prints, and to see his heroes – he was a hero worshipper of men and horses all his life – performing prodigies of derring-do over the natural obstacles they faced in their point-to-points about the turn of the century.

He records that at that time the point-to-point was changing; 'it was then that the point-to-point race entered a new phase and emerged from the pounding match to an organised meeting under the rules of the Masters of Hounds Association. The course and the fences were flagged, which ended between a double row of carriages and wagons which served as a grandstand for spectators. For some years the competitors were genuine hunters and the fences retain all the natural characteristics of the countries hunted over.' Snaffles depicted all of this with a wealth of humour and incident within a few years.

The Payne family's circumstances did not prosper and they moved to Banbury, where Snaffles' father became the tenant of a small hotel. On leaving school at sixteen Snaffles found employment as a clerk in the Hook Brewery, of which his father was a tenant. Fascinated as ever by racing, it was whilst in this employment that in 1901 he heard the romantic story of Grudon's Grand National win. This was to form the subject of one of his most famous pictures some twenty years later – 'The Worst View in Europe'.

Grudon was one of the few stallions to win the National. His sire, Old Buck, had been bought by Grudon's owner, Mr. Bernard Bletsoe for 'a few sovereigns out of a plough'. The race was run in a snowstorm so thick that the jockeys protested it was unsafe and should be abandoned. The Stewards over-ruled this and decreed that the event should go ahead. Immediately he heard the decision, Mr. Bletsoe somehow obtained a large quantity of butter which he packed into Grudon's feet to prevent the snow balling in them. It was the opinion of Arthur Nightingall, Grudon's rider, that this made all the difference between victory and defeat. Nightingall, who had already won the National twice was then regarded as the finest jockey riding. He was one of the leaders of the petition to the Stewards, signed by those due to participate in the race, asking for a postponement and he was not too pleased at the Stewards' decision to go ahead. 'No doubt', he wrote, 'it reminded them of their own grand old days of derring-do when they rode after the fox through snow and over tremendous obstacles just as though they had a spare neck in their pocket and were not afraid to produce it in the nick of time.' Once he knew he had to face the elements on a horse, who in his words, 'had a will of his own' and a reputation for being a far from perfect jumper, Nightingall took the precaution of fortifying himself well with whisky.

In the event Grudon never put a foot wrong and won comparatively comfortably, but grief there was in plenty. Only eight finished from the field of twenty four and the race so impressed itself on Nightingall's mind that twenty years later, having struck a friendship with Snaffles, and on seeing his picture 'The Finest View in Europe', he told the artist that he should draw a companion. The result of this conversation was 'The Worst View in Europe', aptly captioned 'Oh Murther, the dhrink died out of me and the wrong side of Bechers'. It may be of some interest too that Finch Mason, an earlier sporting artist, whose work Snaffles used to copy, attended the same race and did a number of paintings of it which were widely reproduced in various sporting magazines. No doubt Snaffles copied some of them, little knowing that twenty years later he was to make Grudon's race one of the most famous Nationals of all time due to the immense popularity of 'The Worst View in Europe'.

It was not to be expected that Snaffles' roving and adventurous spirit would remain long confined to a clerkship in a brewery. He had tried to enlist when aged only fifteen or sixteen to go to the Boer War, but was told to 'Go back to the Nursery'. But in May 1902, at the age of eighteen, he enlisted in the Royal Garrison Artillery for 'Three Years with the Colours and Nine Years with the Reserve'. He was soon posted to Fort Widgely at Portsmouth where he learned to ride or, to be more precise, he learned the rudiments of equitation as laid down in the relevant Army manuals; which Snaffles later translated in his own inimitable way, adopting the diction of one of his fellow Gunners 'Six days to learn Equitation and four months of blooming well Trot!'

As luck would have it, Portsmouth then had a flourishing steeplechase course. It was one of the leading dozen or so in the country and held five or six meetings a year; most of these were two-day affairs, often with racing on a Saturday, so we can assume that Snaffles and the other horse-mad young Gunners attended on a regular basis. The racing was, by the standards of those days, good and all the leading riders, whether amateur or professional, rode there regularly. F. (Tich) Mason, the Champion Jockey every year between 1901 and 1907, except 1903, seemed to farm the races there. At the November 1902 meeting, run on Friday 21 and Saturday 22, he rode four winners, while other eminent professionals to ride winners at that meeting were Will Dollery (two wins), and Ernie Piggott. Will Dollery had already won the Grand National of 1893 on Cloister while Ernie Piggott was to be Champion Jockey in 1910, 1913 and 1915, and win the National on Jerry M in 1912, and twice on Poethlyn, in 1918 at Gatwick and 1919 at Liverpool.

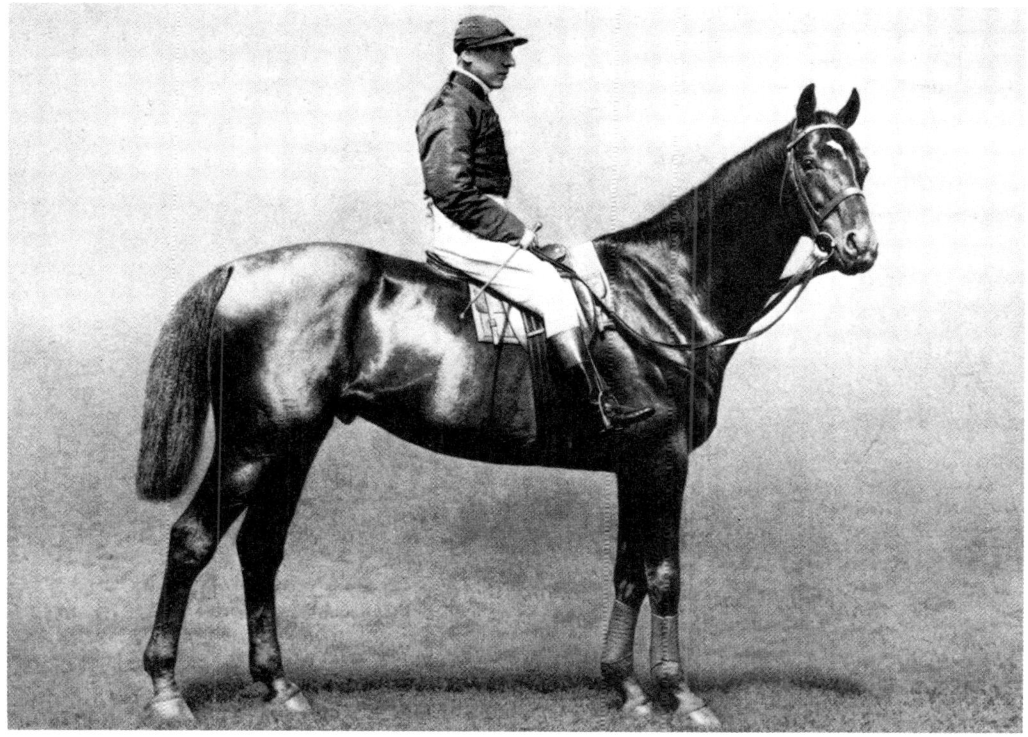

Grudon, Arthur Nightingall up

The card for the May 1903 meeting was equally distinguished. The first race was won by the five-year old Rubio, ridden by Mr. H. Bletsoe, the son of Grudon's owner Mr. B. Bletsoe, who went on to win the 1908 National as a professional; the second winner was ridden by Arthur Nightingall, and the fifth race went to Percy Woodland, the 1903 Champion Steeplechase Jockey who had just ridden the Grand National winner of that year, Drumcree. Certainly Snaffles could not have gone to a better station than Portsmouth. He learnt to ride and saw many of the best steeplechase riders and horses on a regular basis. He joined the Army for excitement and he had started to find it.

It was at Fort Widgely, too, in the barrack rooms, that Snaffles began his life-long love affair with Kipling's verse. From somewhere he had acquired a copy of *Barrack Room Ballads* and, fascinated by their rhythms and the true picture of Army life they contained, retained them in his memory, quoting and misquoting them as captions to his pictures throughout his painting career. Though never subscribing to his more jingoistic moods, he worshipped Kipling as a man and a poet. Oddly enough the Kipling quotations of which he made such use, some would say misuse, as indeed he wryly confessed himself on occasions when he prefaced them with apologies, appear confined almost entirely to his army pictures and drawings and not to his racing or hunting scenes. Either he overlooked or forgot that Kipling, too, knew a thing or two about racing and horse-coping, and that certain of his verses concerning them would have made splendid subjects for his pencil and brush. Take for instance two couplets from 'Certain Maxims of Hafiz':

> As the thriftless gold of the babul so is the gold that we spend
> On a Derby Sweep, or our neighbour's wife, or the horse that we buy from a friend.
> The ways of a man with a maid be strange, yet simple and tame
> To the ways of a man with a horse, when selling or racing the same.

Or again:

> Stopped in the straight when the race was his own –
> Look at him cutting it – cur to the bone!
> Ask ere the youngster be rated and chidden
> What did he carry and how was he ridden!

Perhaps the omissions may be explained by the fact that, after Kipling's death in 1936, Snaffles' relations with his daughter, Mrs. Bambridge, who so jealously guarded her father's reputation and his copyright, were not always entirely easy. Be that as it may, his reverence for the poet remained with him throughout his life and one of his last colour plates, depicting amateur riders in a fanciful re-creation of a National Hunt chase at Cheltenham, with Cleeve Hill in the background, was entitled with yet another Kipling adaption and misquotation 'Gentlemen Bumpers Out on the Spree. (R.K. Transcribed).'

During Snaffles' three years in the ranks, besides reciting Kipling aloud in the barrack rooms, to the admiration and astonishment of his room-mates, Snaffles was sharpening his pencil and practising his art with caricatures of his officers and their horses and of his Gunner friends, none of which appear, unfortunately, to have survived. His military duties prohibited him from going racing as much as he would have wished, although he did steal more than the odd day to see his already embryonic heroes such as Arthur Nightingall or Tich Mason at Portsmouth Park. Snaffles was always an avid reader and he read every racing report in such papers as he could lay his hands on, and spent many hours in his barrack room copying the early action photographs of racehorses.

From the very beginning Snaffles' liking and admiration for the good, old-fashioned stamp of hunter-cum-steeplechaser that, as he said, would carry you over Leicestershire, Limerick or Liverpool, best described by Harry Brown, one of the greatest gentlemen riders of all time, as 'big, rangy horses with long backs and two good ends', remained with him for all time and he was to portray them time and time again, mostly in action.

By early May 1905, Snaffles' three years with the Colours were up and that part of his military career was over. He appears to have distanced himself from his family and henceforth, at the age of twenty-one, he was very much on his own, determined to make a living with his pencil and brush. His subjects were to be those nearest to his heart – horses, steeplechasing, point-to-pointing, fox hunting and, in the early days, particularly the Army. But it was going to be uphill work to make a proper living.

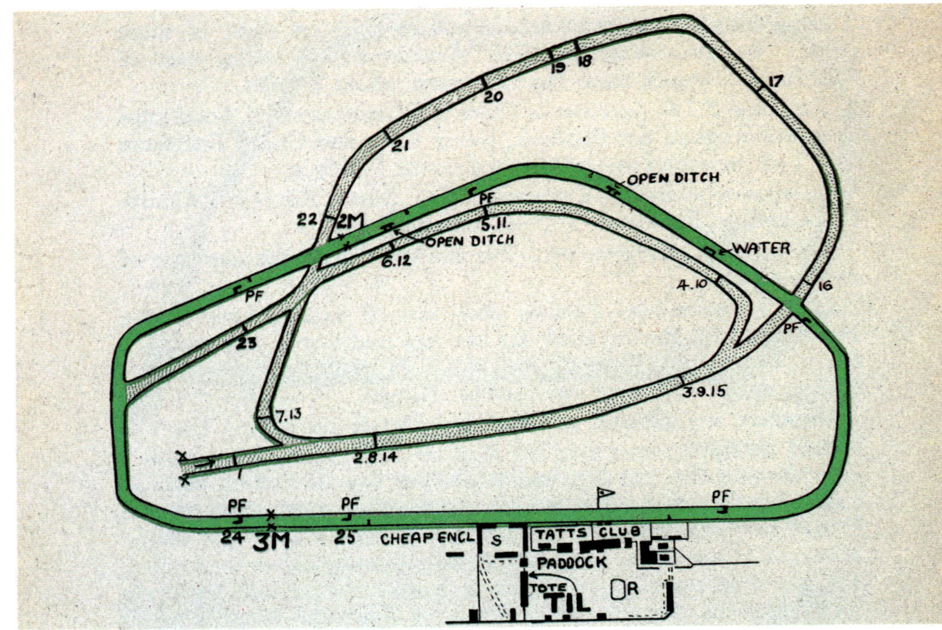

Between the years 1900–39, Hawthorn Hill was one of the most sporting and smartest National Hunt courses

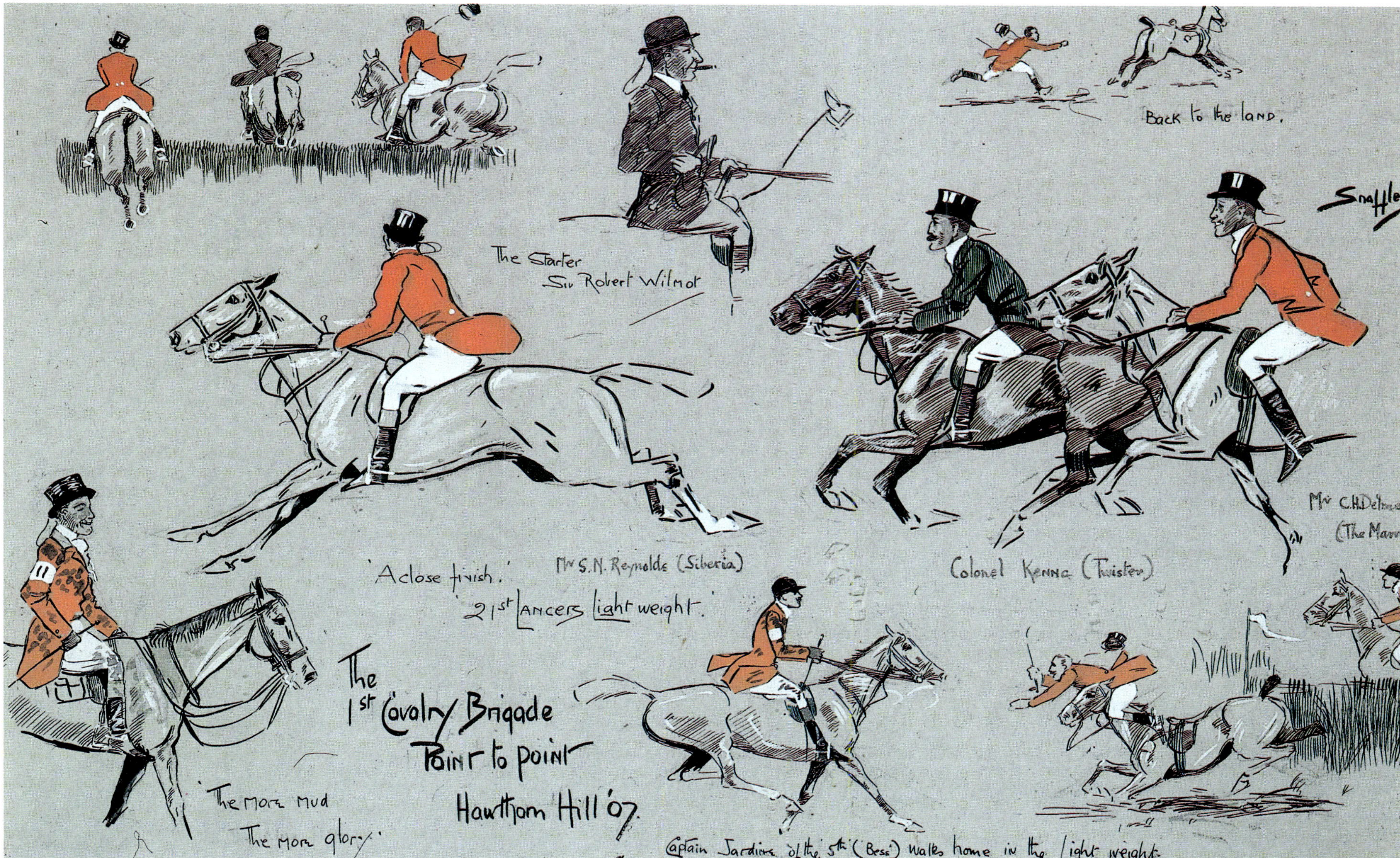

Snaffles' earliest racing and point to pointing pictures were drawn at Hawthorn Hill, where there were two steeplechase courses and a point to point course. There could have been no finer place for the artist to learn his craft

This, and the drawing opposite were done for the magazine market which, in the period 1907–14, was a major source of income for Snaffles

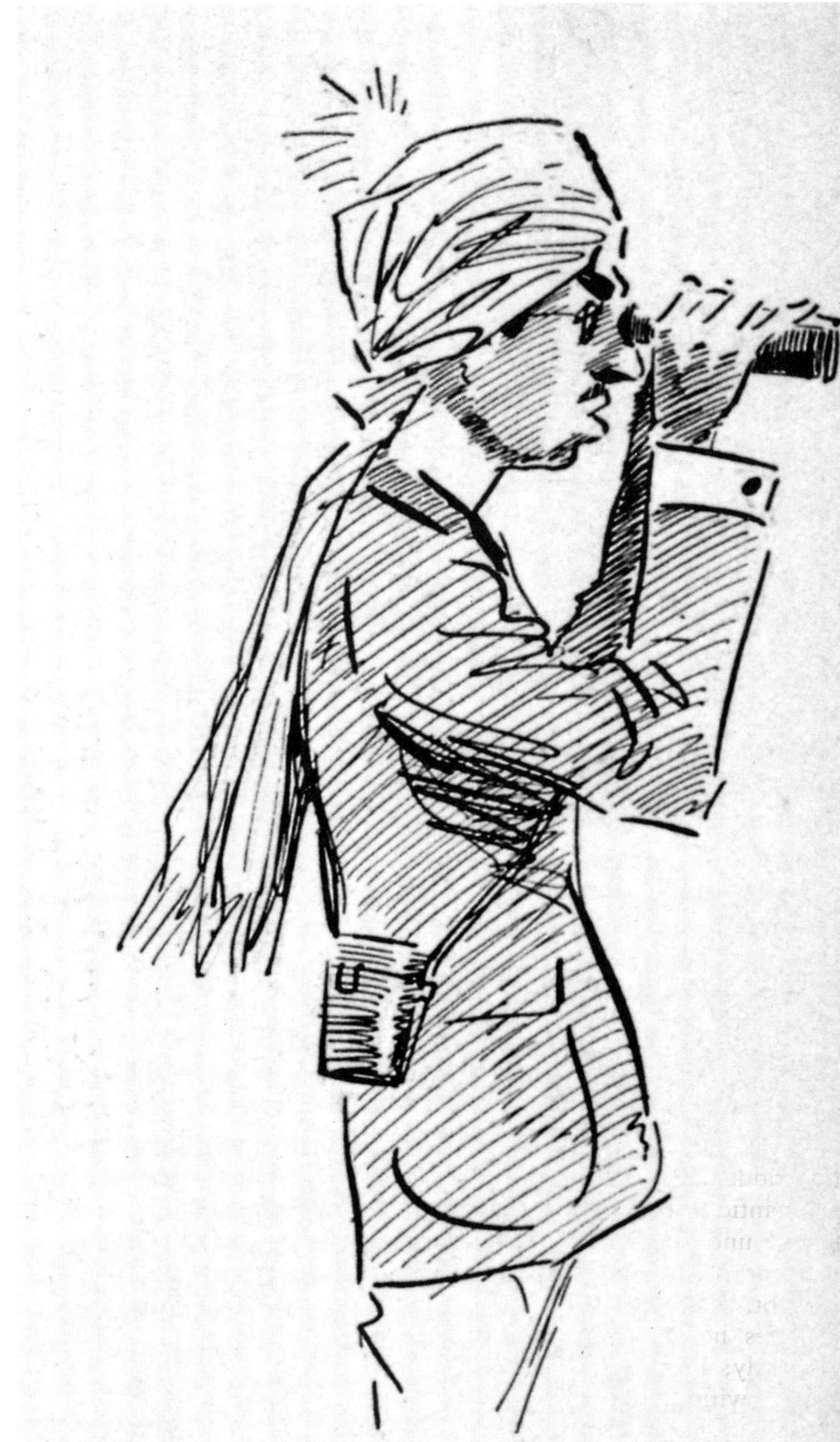

2 The First Obstacle

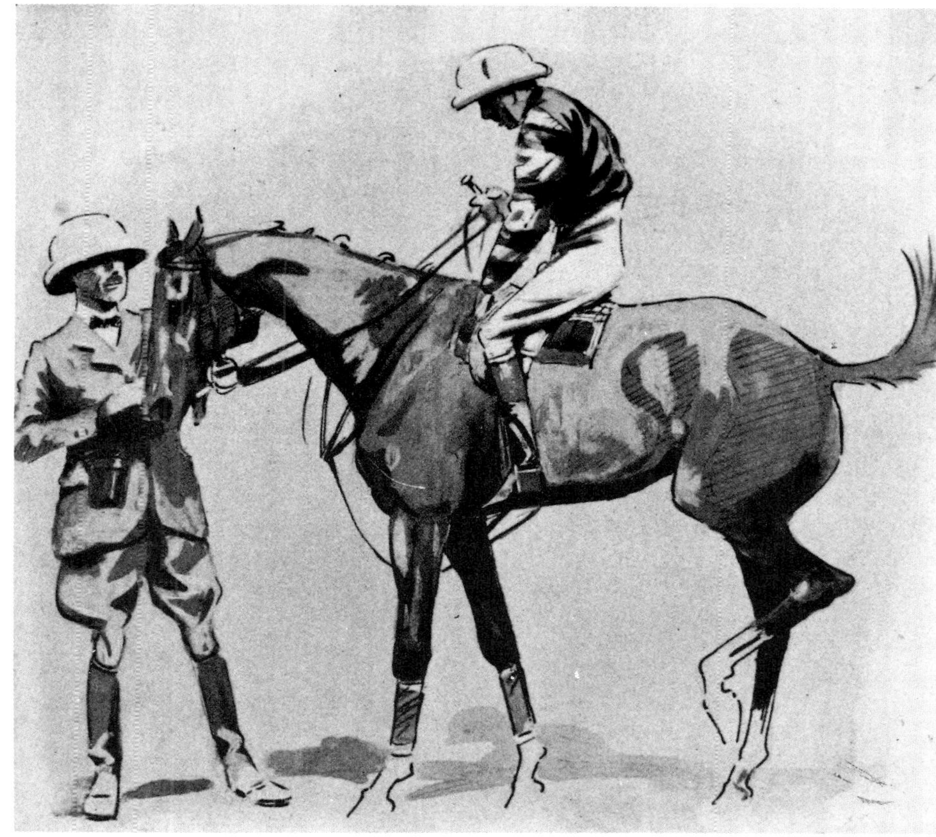

Snaffles never rode in a race himself; financial considerations precluded that. In this period of his life, during his twenties, when others more fortunately placed than himself were having their 'jollies' round the course or cutting out the work against each other on blood horses, he was poor and struggling; and just as financial matters were easing in 1913/1914, the world that he so gaily set off into as an artist in 1905 came to an abrupt halt, with the outbreak of World War One.

Years afterwards Snaffles was rather wistfully to confess 'this chase riding must be a grand game when one has acquired the art of swinging along in perfect rhythm of movement with one's horse over fences'. The fact that he hadn't ridden races increased his admiration for those who had and did, and his romantic enthusiasm for the racing game remained constant, though it was put under considerable strain during those early struggles. In his endeavours to obtain recognition, he haunted military meetings around Aldershot, sketching all the time, with the materials he could afford and sometimes he even had to sleep rough. All the time he was reading voraciously; Kipling, of course, but also Surtees, Somerville and Ross, together with the sporting poets Egerton Warburton and Bromley Davenport, all of whose works he was to quote and misquote as captions at one time or another.

Few, if any of his early sketches, dated between 1905 and March 1907, have survived, though there are two, from the military meeting near Aldershot, of one of his benefactors, Captain Jardine, of the Fifth Lancers, which are now in the possession of his daughter, Mrs. Charles Allan. The reason why little datable survives between the end of his three years with the Colours in May 1905 and March 1907 is probably because Snaffles was out of the country. It now appears clear, from recollections supplied to the authors, that, soon after his discharge in May 1905 from the Gunners, Snaffles went on a major trip to India, via West Africa and the Cape. Exactly in what capacity he went is unknown, but it was probably as a groom or civilian clerk to the Army or shipping line. Certainly he spent some time in India, since there is, amongst his early works, an authentic print of chasing in India, the detail of which cannot be faulted and which bears the same stamp of authenticity that characterizes all that he did from life.

When Snaffles was out in India he must, as was his custom, have filled his notebook with sketches and ideas for further work, so, when a little later, having broken into publication, we find *The Illustrated Sporting and Dramatic News* asking him to illustrate 'A Forced Hand', a story of racing in India, he was able to fulfil the commission with his accustomed verve and accuracy.

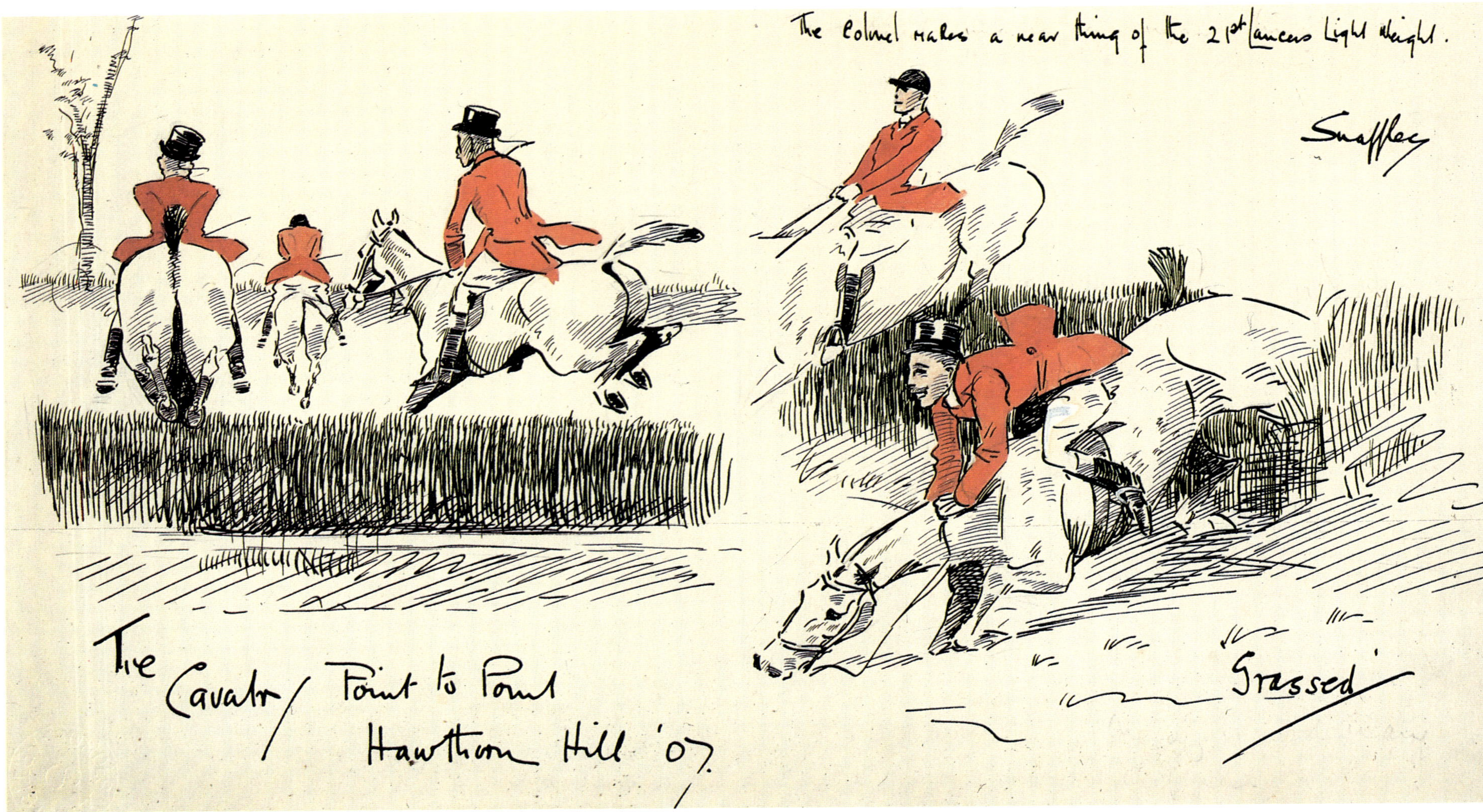

Another of the many watercolours of Hawthorn Hill executed by Snaffles in the period 1907–10, before he moved to Leicestershire

In 1909 came the first known of his full and detailed racing pictures in the style he was to make his own – a centrepiece of a point-to-point surrounded by smaller, humorous vignettes and characters of the race and the day. It is interesting to note that here we hark back to his earliest recollections, since almost all of the competitors were wearing red coats, top hats and jumping natural fences. The first Point-to-Point print, which he produced, in 1909 is the only one where the horses in the central portion of the print, which was entirely hand coloured, were going right to left. In all of the rest they are going from left to right. Over the years he developed this theme of a point-to-point and the 1925 edition is one of his most sought after and valuable prints.

This print was soon to be followed by a similar painting, portraying the Grand Military at Sandown. He entitled its centrepiece 'Only two of 'em in it over the Last Fence'. It showed Mr., as he was then, Dermot McCalmont on his Vinegar Hill in the lead at the last before going on to win his race from Captain Springfield, 'Springer of the Bays, possibly our best man on a bad horse', riding his own horse, Viz.

In 1913 Dermot McCalmont was to be the owner of The Tetrarch – commonly known as 'The Spotted Wonder' and probably the fastest horse ever seen on English turf, remaining unbeaten in all his seven races. The Tetrarch was trained by McCalmont's cousin, Atty Persse, who, before becoming one of the great gambling trainers of the period 1905–1939, was a top class amateur rider in both England and Ireland.

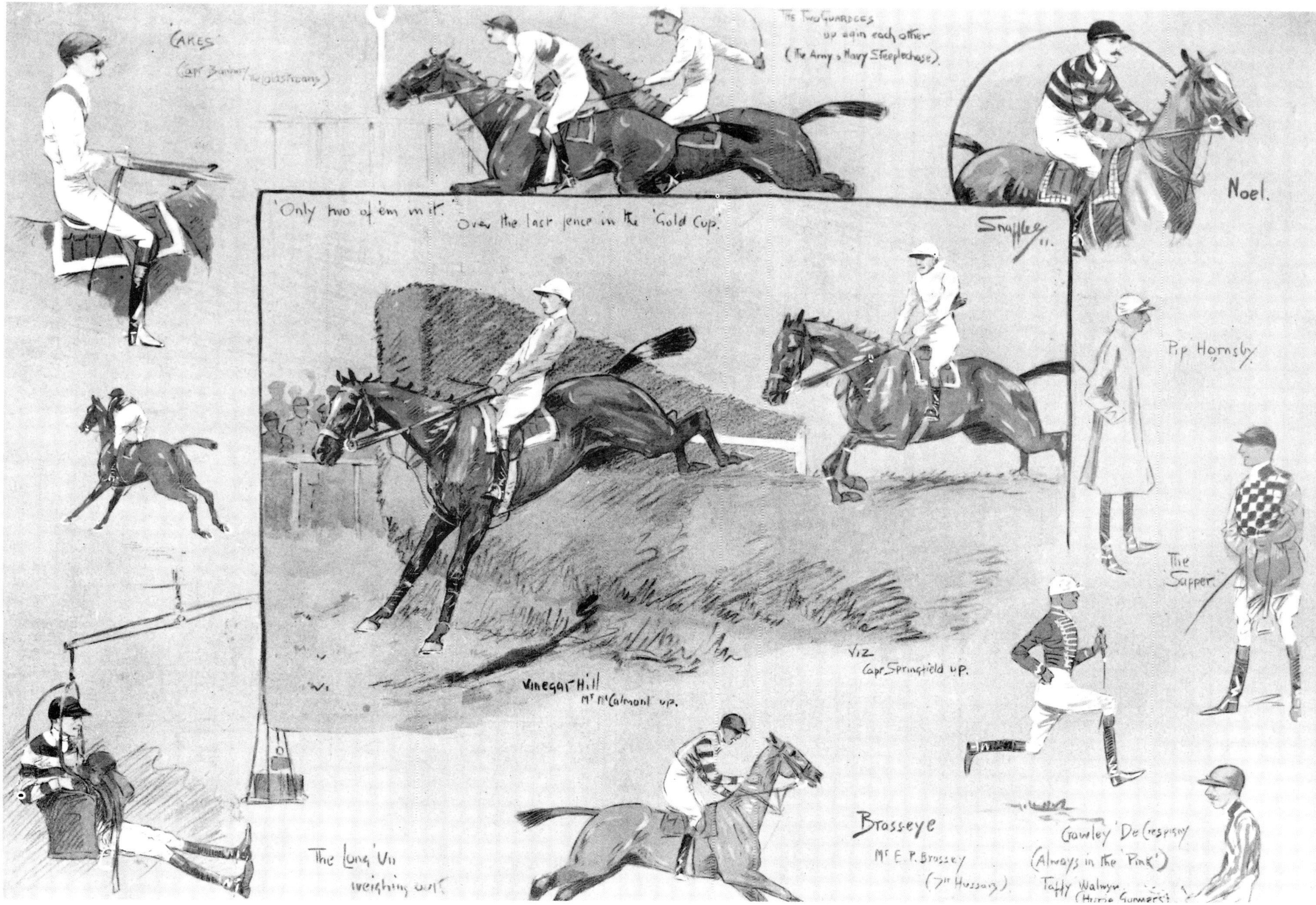

Dermot McCalmont winning the Grand Mili:ary on Vinegar Hill

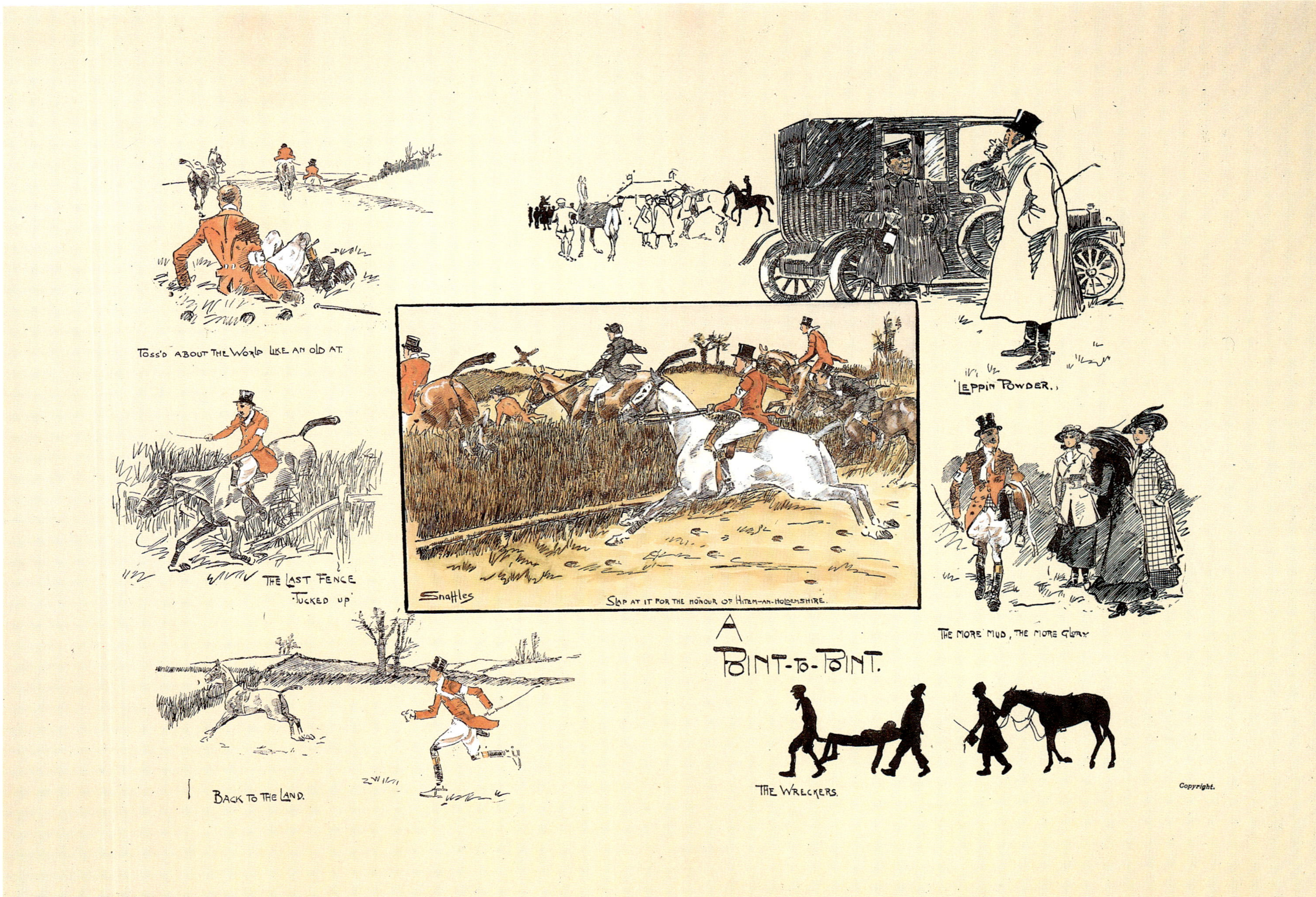

This is the first example of Snaffles' Point to Point prints, and the only one where the horses in the centre panel are running from right to left. It was first sold in 1909

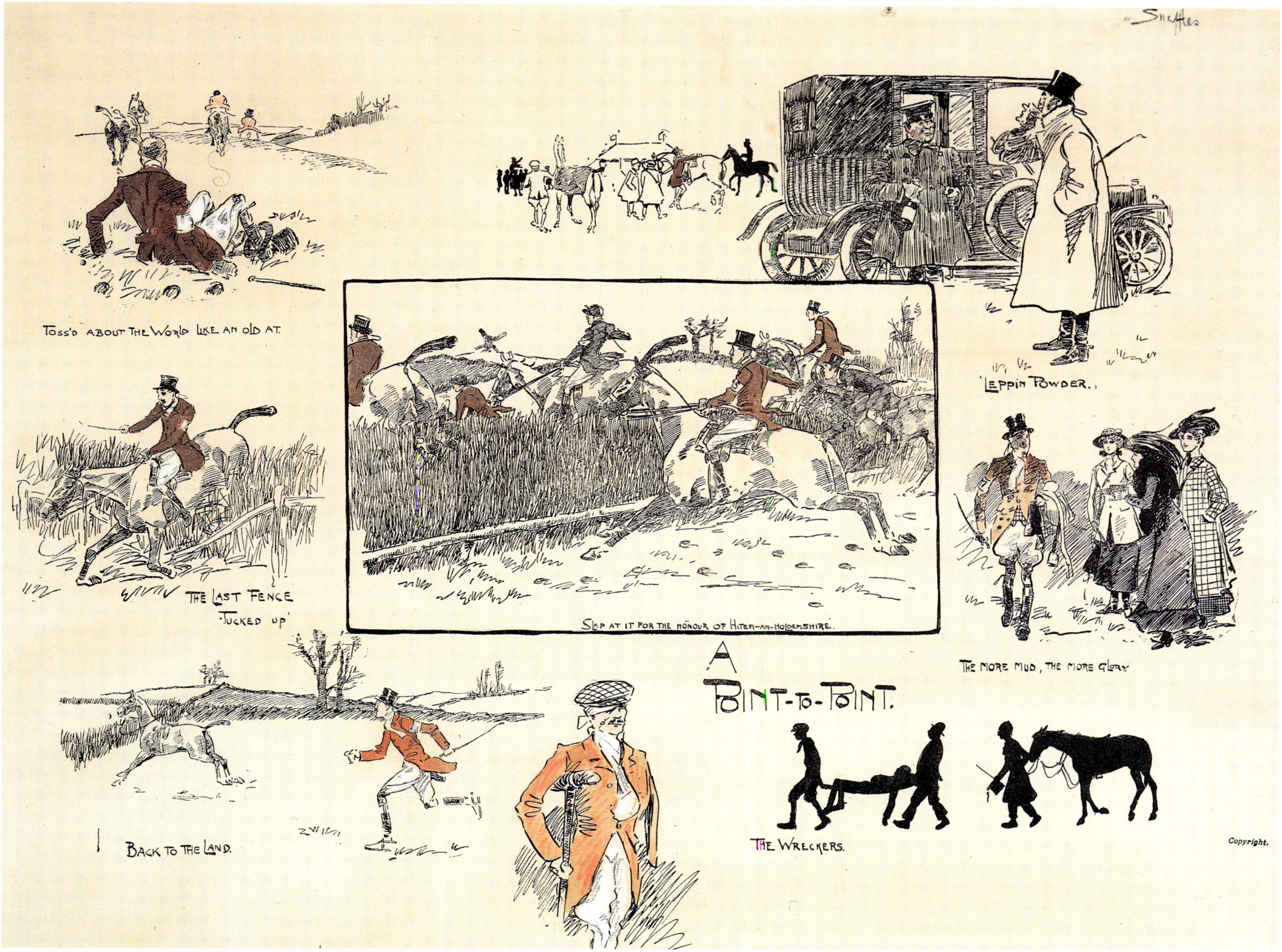

The same print as that opposite, but Snaffles has done an original watercolour of a gent on crutches, which he incorporated in subsequent editions of the print and entitled 'The Glutton'

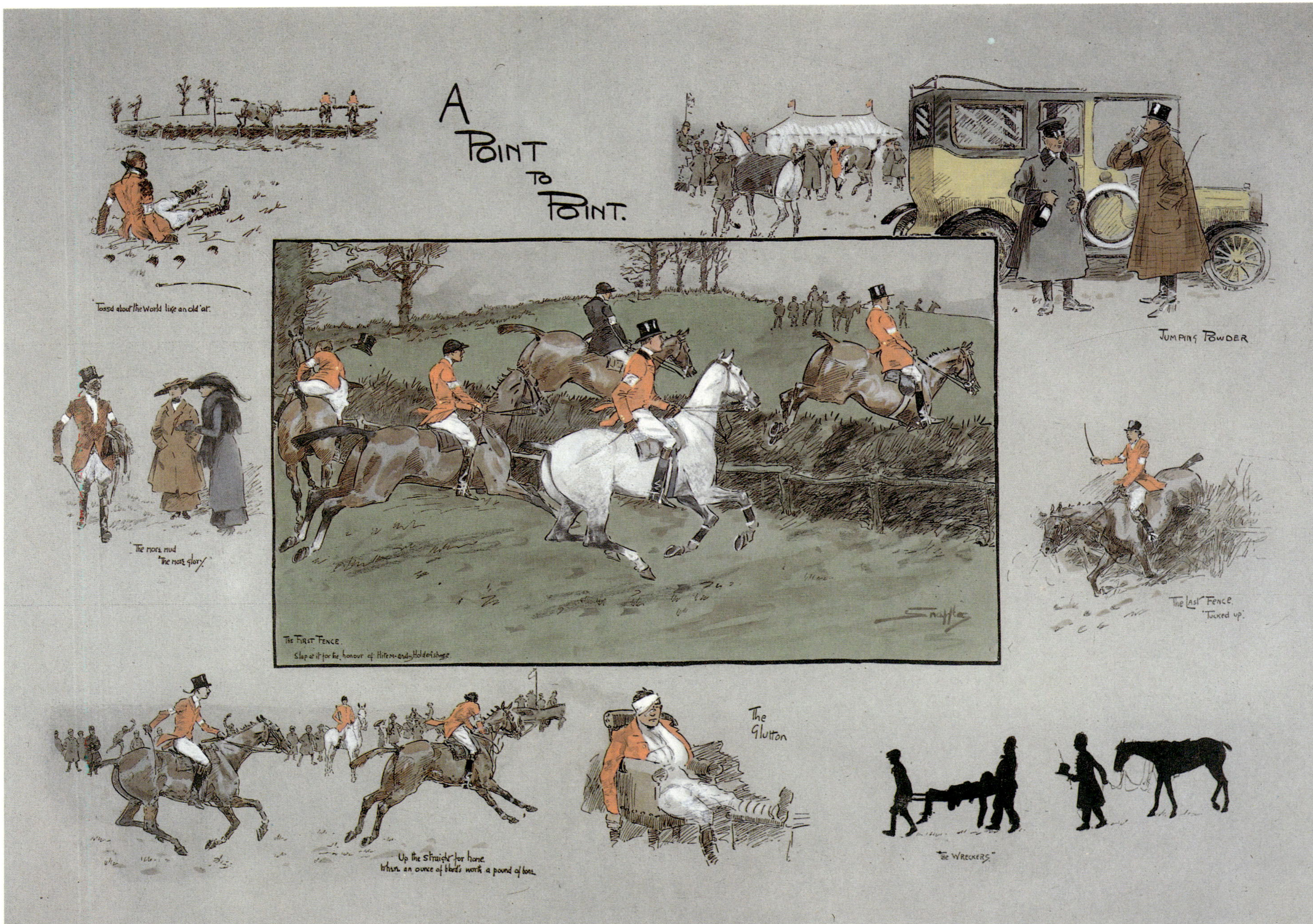

This is the 1911 edition of A Point to Point; a great advance visually and technically from the 1909 edition. The Rolls Royce is always yellow in this edition

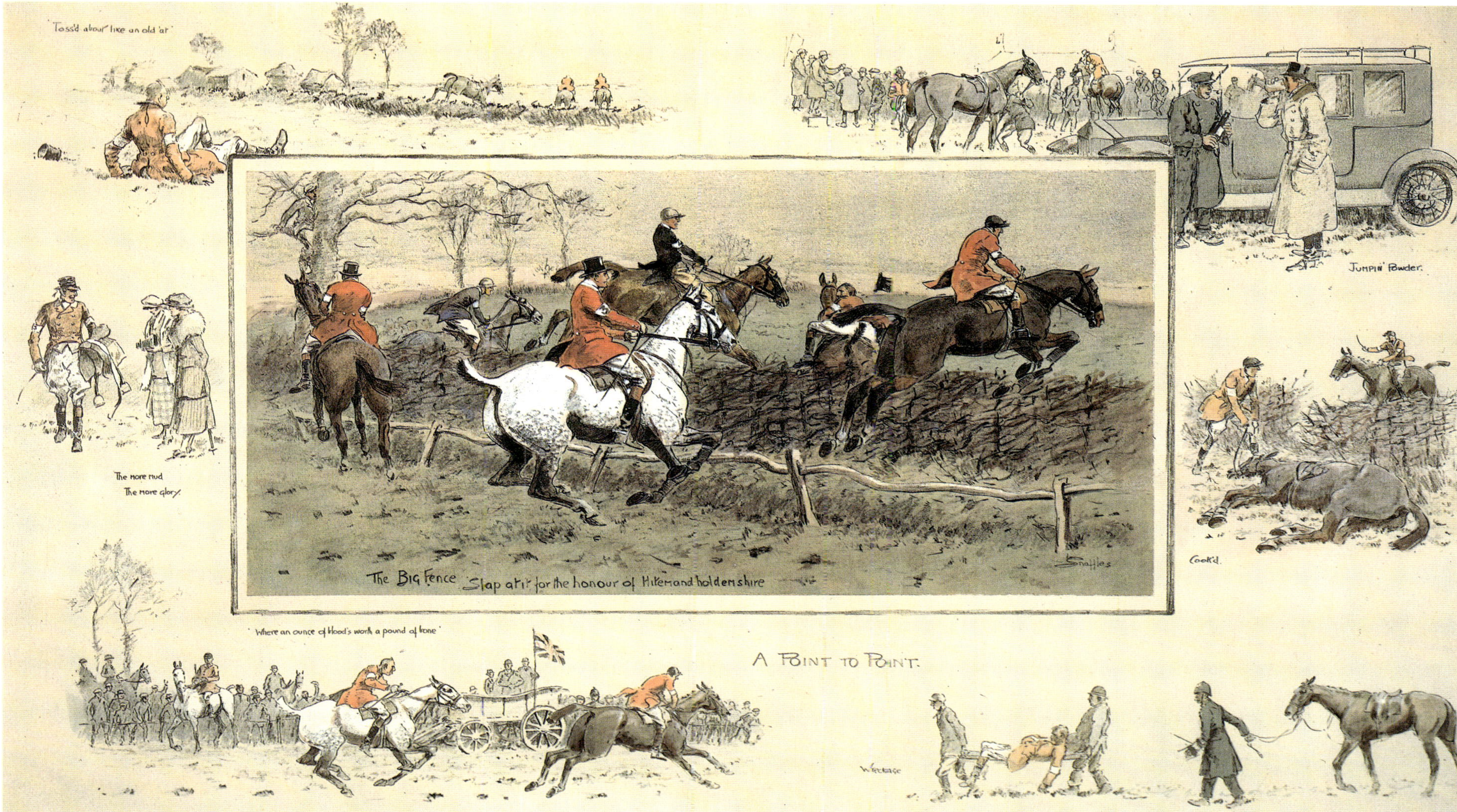

This edition came out soon after the First World War. Snaffles sold it for several years, up to 1925

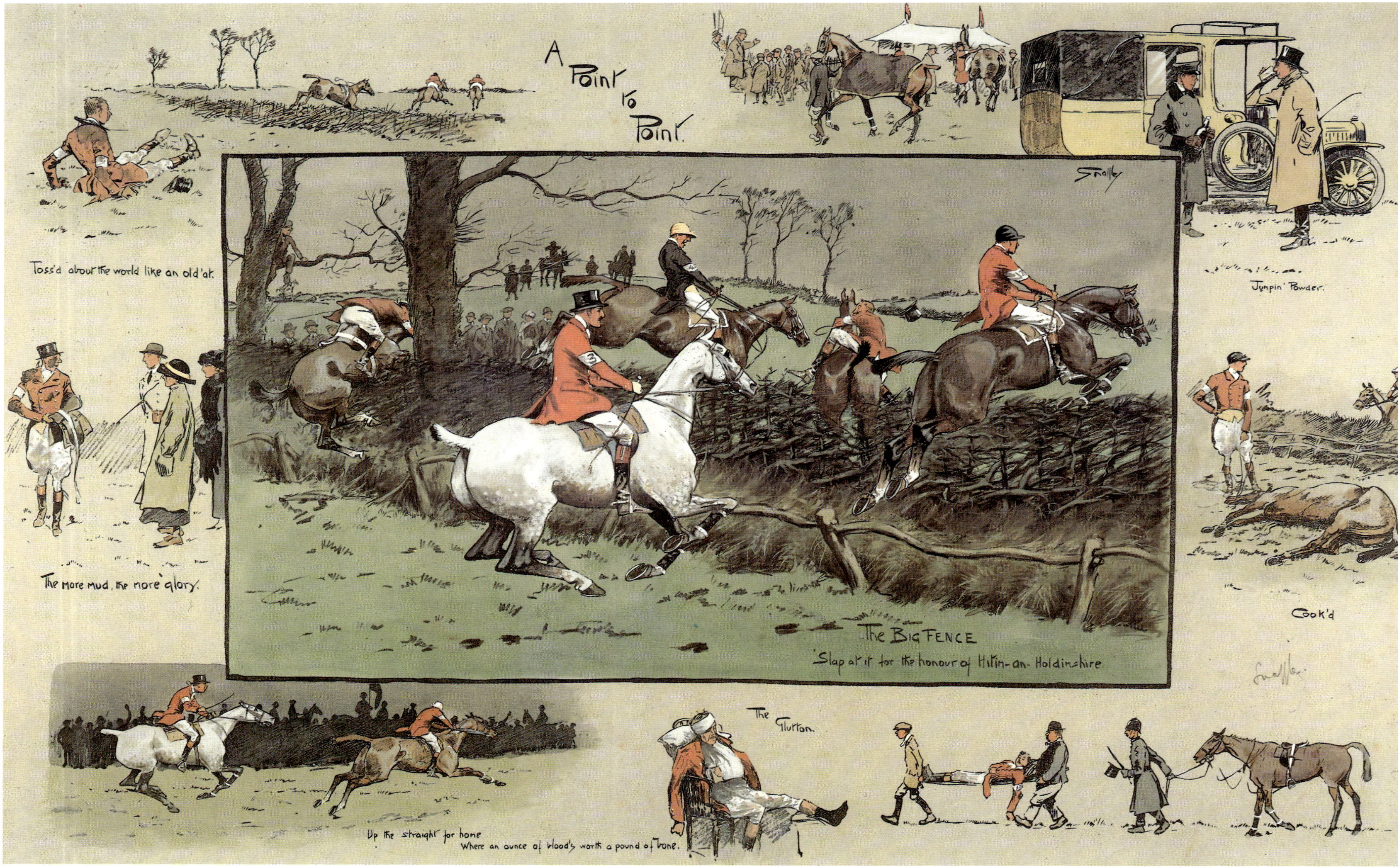

This is the final version of Snaffles' A Point to Point, the most sophisticated. It was first produced in 1925. Normally the Rolls Royce is black or grey; there are few known examples such as this where the car is yellow

The Grand Military and Royal Artillery meetings would have then been the highlight of Snaffles' racing year and he was to attend them on a regular basis from around 1905 to well into the 1950's. In the ten years leading up to the First World War, though it would be wrong to say that the Grand Military was one of the six most important steeplechases in the calendar, it would certainly be fair to say that it was amongst the top dozen. The four or five 'acceptable' social meetings to be seen at then, to a certain extent even between the wars, were Liverpool's Grand National meeting, the two military meetings at Sandown, the National Hunt at Cheltenham and the Household Brigade meeting at the now sadly defunct Hawthorn Hill course.

Snaffles was to submit another full page for *The Illustrated Sporting and Dramatic News* of the 1912 Grand Military which was won by Mr. E.H. Wyndham's Another Delight. The same combination won the Grand Military the next year, but apparently Snaffles did not submit any illustrations as he was probably in Ireland that year. The last race before the War, in 1914, went to Captain George Paynter riding his own horse, Jack Symons, and Snaffles submitted a rather muddled painting of the race to *The Illustrated Sporting and Dramatic News* entitled 'The jostle by the Big Fence'.

Captain Paynter, as he was then, deserves more than a passing mention. A tremendous sportsman and, despite his heavy weight, a keen and successful gentleman rider; a Scots Guardsman, he won their regimental point-to-point three years in succession and their steeplechase twice, as well as having won the Grand Military. He and Lord Manners were the only members of the then National Hunt Committee to have won the Grand Military on their own horses. After a gallant war spent 'leading from the front', he ended up a Brigadier General, was made Crown Equerry to King George V, and was knighted. We shall meet him again.

It was in 1911, that Snaffles, with increasing income from both the periodical and print market, was encouraged to take himself off to Oakham in Rutland, a centre of the hard-riding fraternity he so much admired. Even then, however, lack of funds prevented him from fulfilling his ambition to mount himself well enough to join them, although at least he was never amongst those 'large paying subscribers', whom he observed with that all-seeing eye of his, 'riding with great determination in the first flight of second horsemen'. Around 1908 he had started hunting with the provincial packs near Aldershot, such as the Knaphill and Ripley Harriers, the Garth and HH Foxhounds firstly on borrowed mounts, and then on his beloved mare Connie. Connie naturally accompanied him to Oakham. Although he was to say she 'was nearly as slow as a man', her prodigious jumping ability allowed him to see a hunt, if not to lie up with the leaders.

A year or two after his arrival at Oakham, the one occasion when he did try to put himself in a position to take on 'the top sawyers' and 'the visiting soldiers', whose pounding matches he had observed from the rear, ended in disaster. He bought an ex-hurdler called The Colonel out of a racing stable. The Colonel was a failure on the racecourse and had been cast off cheaply, since he made a noise, but he was certainly very handsome. Snaffles became his proud new owner and at the same time, with a sense of humour that was never far absent from him, christened his smart new horse 'Flash Harry'.

Snaffles says in his reminiscences that a veterinary friend, almost certainly 'Doc' Gibson, operated on The Colonel and passed him fit to go hunting. Snaffles does not specify what this operation was, but since Professor Hobday only began his eponymous operation in 1906, and according to Colonel 'Mouse' Townsend, RAVC, who followed him, 'performed it very exclusively', it is unlikely that Flash Harry was 'hobdayed'. More probably the veterinary friend took the usual course of those days and 'stuck a tube in'. Snaffles, however, was filled with enthusiasm for his new acquaintance and spent some of his increasing funds on the purchase of a smart new hunting outfit, which included a top hat, to go with his smart new horse. He then sallied forth to the opening meet of the Cottesmore, with every intention of showing how a sporting artist of thrusting taste 'should o'er a country go'.

Unfortunately for Snaffles, Flash Harry was more accustomed to the flat trajectory of jumping hurdles at speed than to taking on stiff timber, and stiff timber was the very first fence they encountered, with Snaffles, for the first time in his life, in the very first flight of a smart hunt on its opening day. Flash Harry took off at least a stride too early and smashed into the top rail, turning himself over and depositing his owner on his new and last top hat. Snaffles, of course, being Snaffles, saw the humorous side of the incident and, as usual, stored it away in his memory for later use. We reproduce it here on pages 152 and 153. In fact the 'top hat trick' appeared regularly in vignettes of many of his early point-to-point and racing pictures and he was to use this caption before and after he was subjected to it himself, over and over again in different settings.

When Snaffles left Surrey in 1911, to move to Oakham, his drawings of horses in races were very much at what he termed 'the rocking horse stage'. The centrepiece of the 1909 Point-to-Point certainly shows the influence of Finch Mason and no-one would want to describe many of Finch Mason's horses, as other than 'animated rocking horses'. During the three years he was based in Oakham, Snaffles' observation and technique in the drawing of horses greatly improved.

The crack amateur riders of the day were mostly drawn from the Military, and nothing fascinated Snaffles more than the combination of the Army and a proficient cross-country rider. In 1911 Snaffles was to start a series of prints of these leading military amateurs, and in Appendix A we have listed seven, numbers 34 to 41 inclusive, although there could have been more. All were painted with little background, carefully hand coloured by Snaffles himself, and it is doubtful, even in the case of the most popular subject, whether Snaffles would have done more than twenty or thirty, so nowadays they are all very rare.

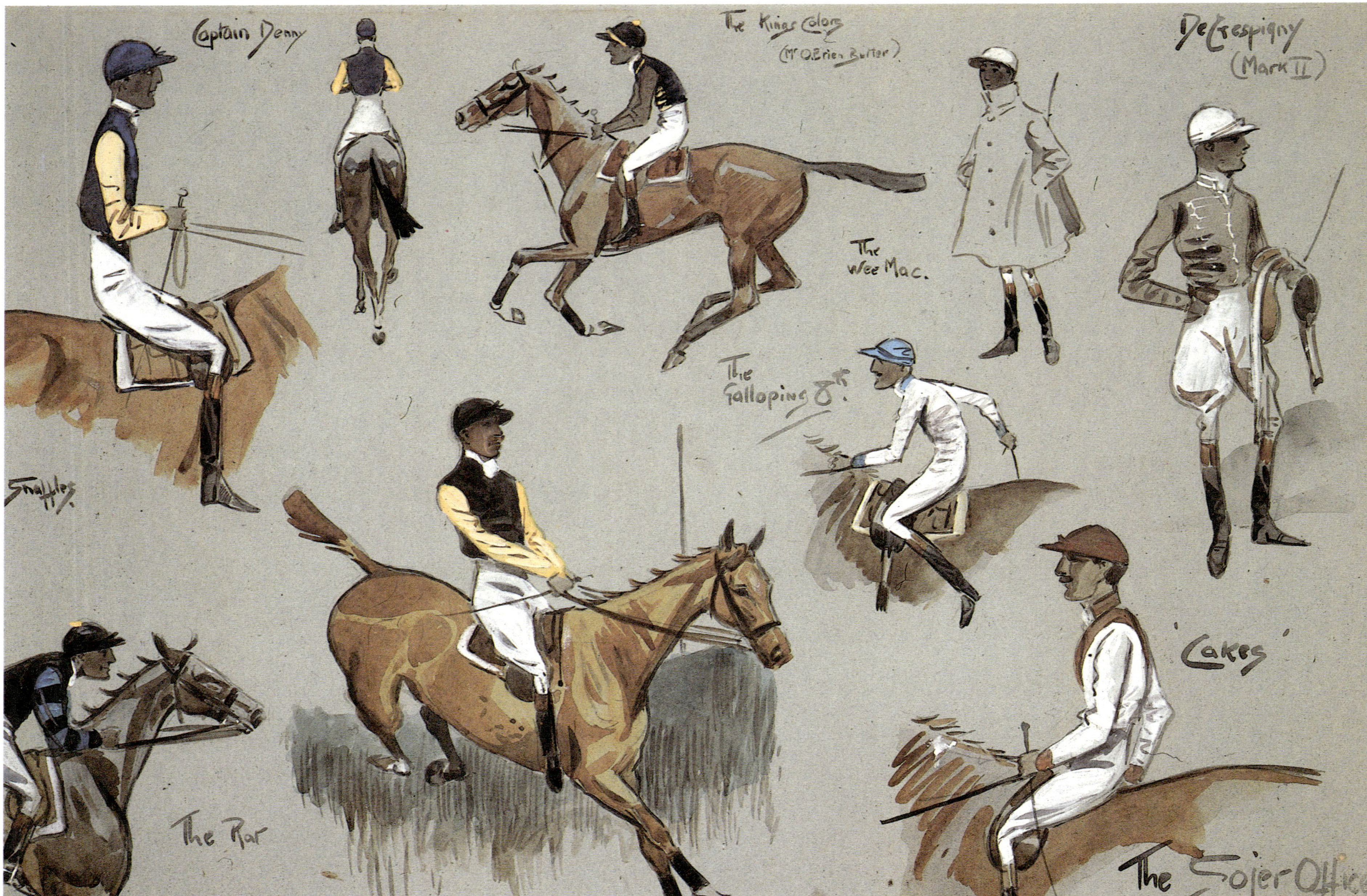

The Sojer Officers

The Grand Military meeting in 1910

It was in the Grand Military, run on 4 March 1910, that King Edward VII's colours were carried for the last time in a steeplechase. His Majesty's Bahadeur was third to Captain E. Christie-Miller's Sprinkle Me, ridden by Captain C.W. Banbury, and Mr. McCalmont's Vinegar Hill, the following year's winner. King Edward VII died on 6 May 1910.

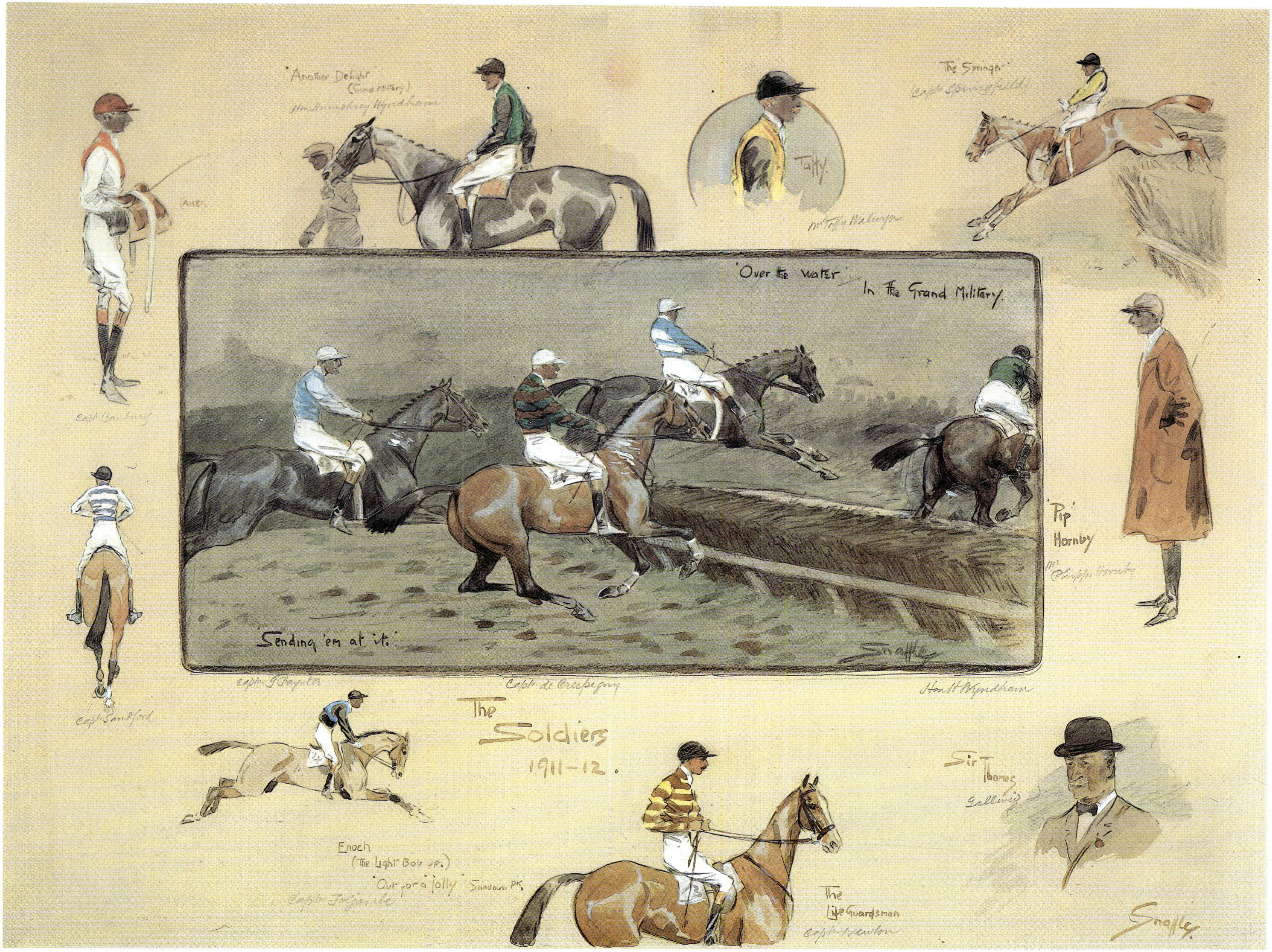

The 1912 Grand Military meeting at Sandown. This was Snaffles' most successful racing painting before the First World War

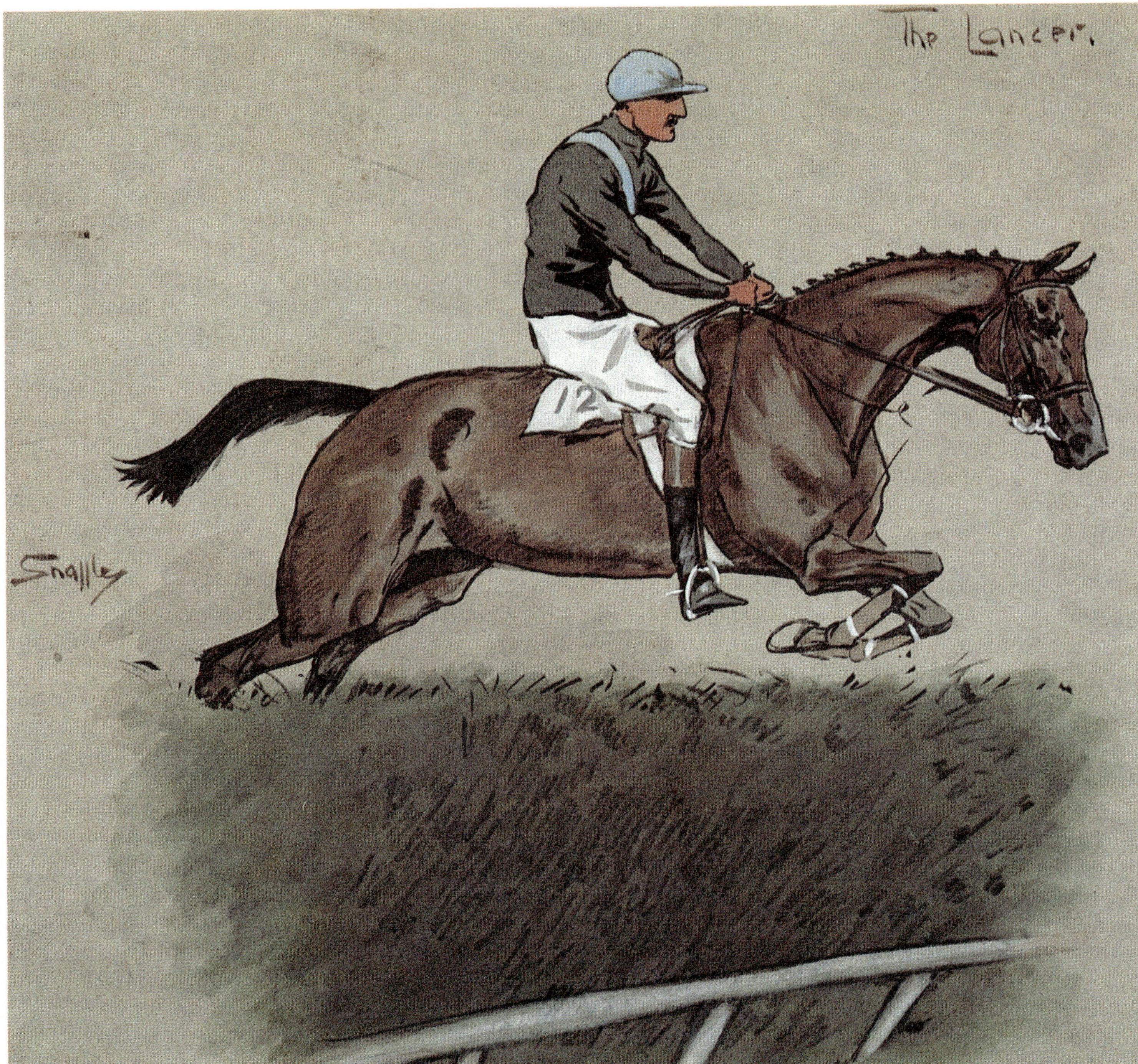
The Lancer.
Snaffles

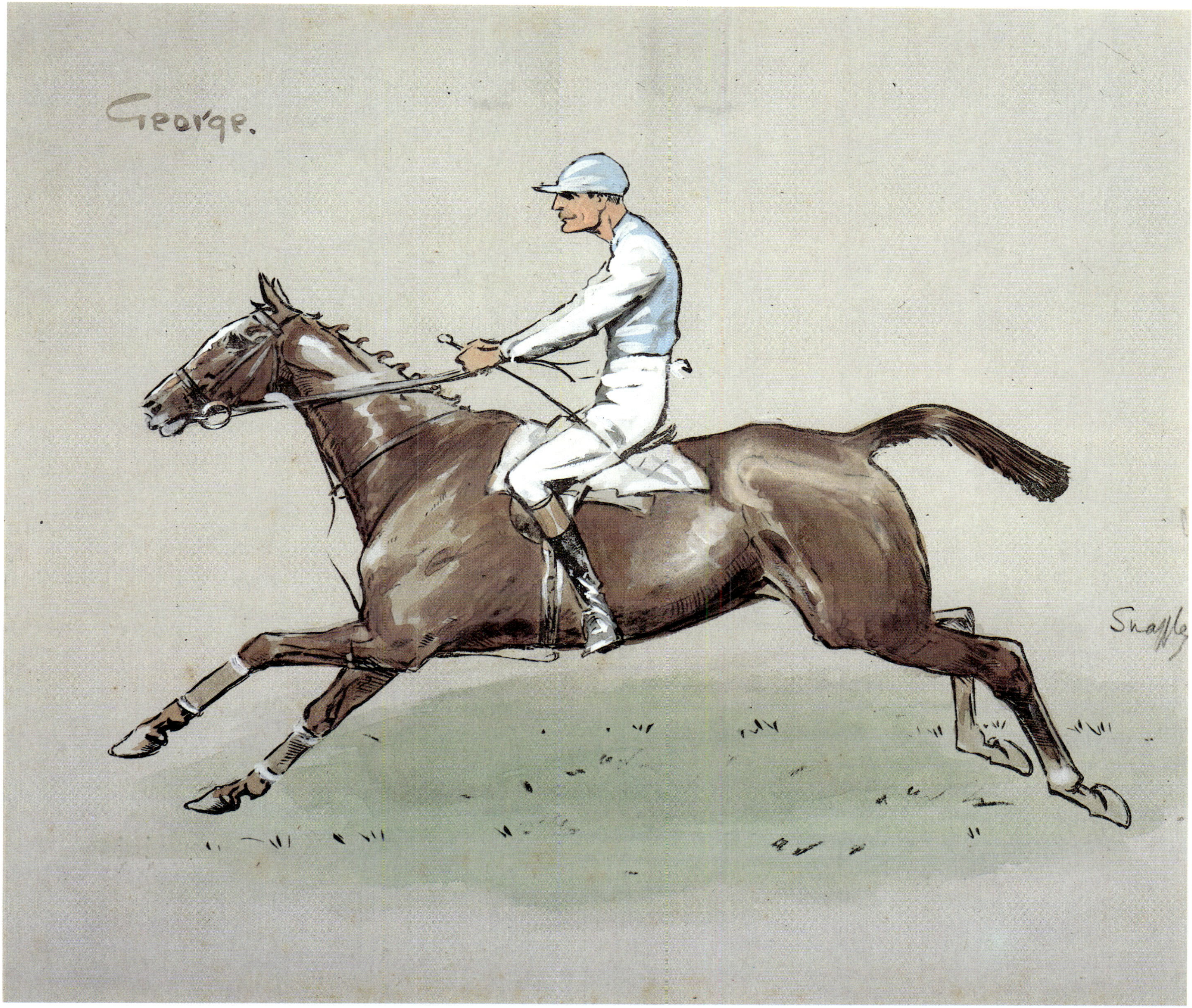
George.
Snaffles

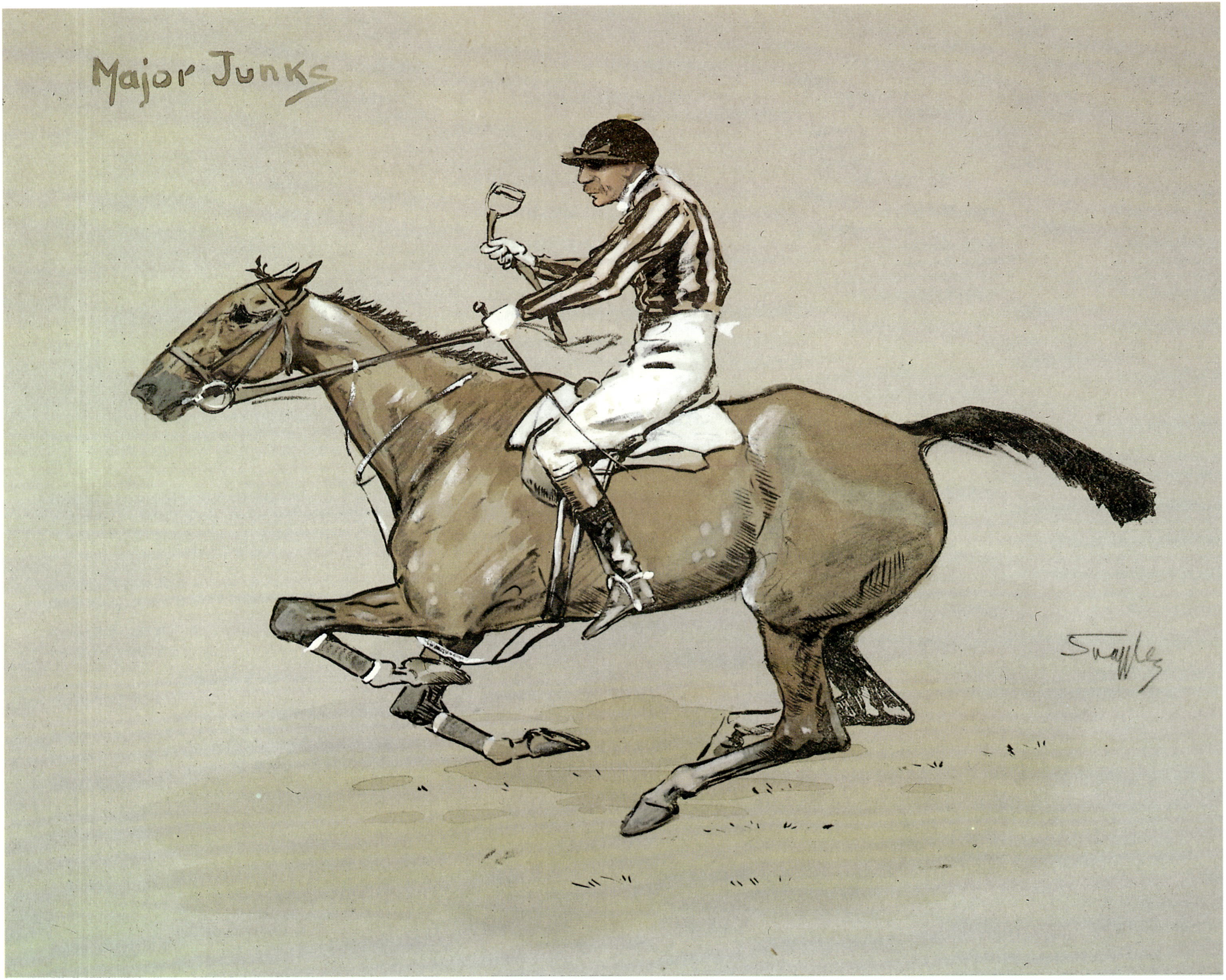
Major Junks
Snaffles

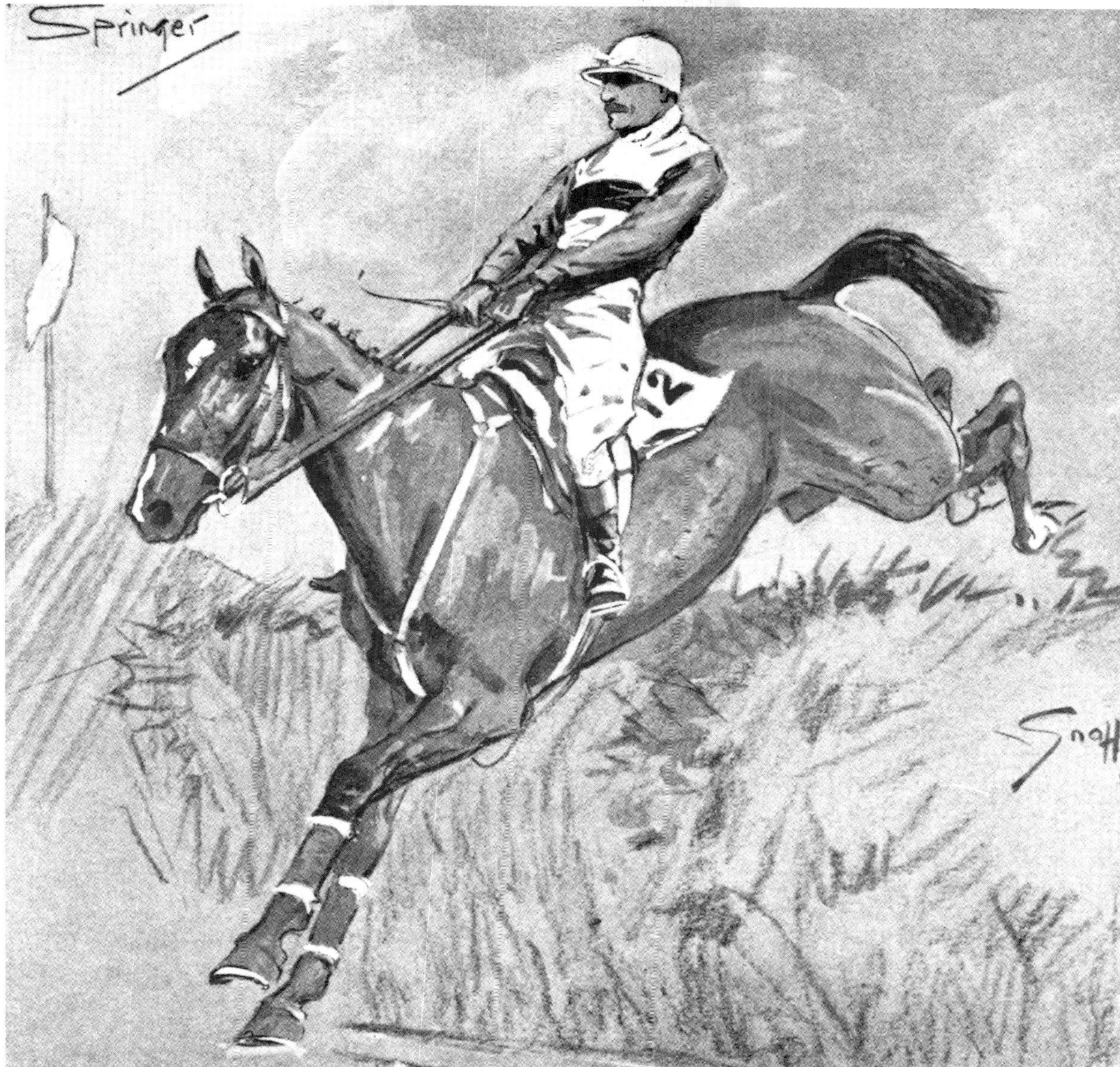

Capt G.P.O. Springfield (The Bays)

'The Springer' was Captain Springfield who was, as we have said previously, a great man on a bad horse and 'George' was the then Captain George Paynter who Snaffles drew on many occasions and who in fact won the Grand Military twice, in 1908 and 1914. Paynter was a very big man and it was the sort of thoroughly sporting effort which so appealed to Snaffles, for on both occasions he carried the welter burden of 13 stone, yet rode in a 3 lb saddle. The best known amateur amongst the set was 'Major Junks', who was Arthur Hughes Onslow of the Tenth Royal Hussars, and when Snaffles depicted him winning a race carrying a stirrup he must have been at least fifty years of age. Known everywhere as 'Junks' for no apparent reason, Arthur Hughes Onslow, although now forgotten perhaps, because he was one of the first to die in the carnage of World War One, must have been one of the greatest gentleman riders ever to grace the turf. His record is a truly formidable one and it is worth mentioning some of its highlights.

Table B
GRAND MILITARY GOLD CUP
Conditions Steeplechase for Serving Officers. 3 Miles 180 yards

Horse	*Owner*	*Rider*
1900–02 *No Race*		
1903 Marpessa	Maj. E. Loder	Maj. Onslow
1904 Dunboyne	Mr. H.E. Brassey	Maj. Richardo
1905 Ruy Lopez	Rear-Admiral Lambton	Capt. Stacpoole
1906 Royal Blaze	Mr. R.F. Eyre	Capt. L.S. Denny
1907 Old Fairyhouse	Mr. C. Bewicke	Owner
1908 Mount Prospect's Fortune	Capt. G. Paynter	Owner
1909 Sprinkle Me	Capt. E. Christie-Miller	Capt. C.W. Banbury
1910 Sprinkle Me	Capt. E. Christie-Miller	Capt. C.W. Banbury
1911 Vinegar Hill	Mr. D. McCalmont	Owner
1912 Another Delight	Mr. E. H. Wyndham	Owner
1913 Another Delight	Mr. E. H. Wyndham	Owner
1914 Jack Symons	Capt. G. Paynter	Owner
1915–19 *No Race*		
1920 White Surrey	Admiral of the Fleet Sir Hedworth Meux	Maj. Walwyn
1921 Pay Only	Mr. W. Filmer-Sankey	Owner
1922 Pay Only	Mr. W. Filmer-Sankey	Owner
1923 Annie Darling	Mr. R.L. McCreery	Owner
1924 Lee Bridge	Mr. R.G. Shaw	Owner
1925 Ruddyglow	Mr. W. Filmer-Sankey	Owner
1926 Foxtrot	Capt. H. Lumsden	Owner
1927 Scotch Eagle	Capt. A.F.W. Gossage	Owner
1928 Dash o' White	Mr. P.S. Ackroyd	Capt. R.L. McCreery
1929 Drin	Capt. A.F.W. Gossage	Owner
1930 Drintyre	Mr. C.N. Brownhill	Owner
1931 Slieve Grien	Capt. R.B. Moseley	Owner
1932 Castledown	Sir P. Lawson	Owner
1933 Backsight	Mr. R.B.T. Daniell	Owner
1934 Crafty Alice	Mr. T. Wallis, jun.	Owner
1935 Young Cuthbert	Mr. R. Courage	Owner
1936 Misdemeanour	Sir P. Lawson	Owner
1937 Buck Willow	Mr. M.G. Roddick	Owner
1938 Kilstar	Capt. M.G. Roddick	Owner
1939 Fillip	Maj. M.D. Roddick	Owner
1940–48 *No Race*		
1949 Demon Vino	Maj. J.W. Phillips	Owner
1950 Klaxton	Mr. W.D. Gibson	Owner
1951 Klaxton	Capt. W.D. Gibson	Owner
1952 Klaxton	Capt. W.D. Gibson	Owner
1953 Atom Bomb	Maj. P. Fielden	Owner
1954 Pointsman	Maj. C. Blacker	Owner
1955 Skatealong	Maj. P. Fielden	Owner

Home from India, where he had won the Indian Grand Military at Meerut, Junks won his first Grand Military at Sandown in 1888 at the age of twenty six. He won it again in 1898 and for a third time in 1903. A record of his other minor wins would be too numerous to list, but in 1908, at the age of forty-five, he out-rode George Thursby the leading flat race amateur, and Otto Madden, a top and tough professional, to win a hotly contested race on the flat which will give some indication of his strength and skill. In Ireland with his regiment he won the Military Maiden Plate at Punchestown no less than five times and, riding Major Eustace Loder's good mare, Cover Hack, the Conyngham Cup, then the chief race in the Irish calendar, on three occasions.

Major Loder, the owner of the peerless mare, Pretty Polly, thought Junks the 'best of the soldier riders' as he almost certainly was, though the competition in those days was fierce indeed. Two of his Conyngham Cups were won under the top weight of 13 stone 5 lb – steeplechasers, horses and men, were asked stern questions then, for the Conyngham Cup was run over four miles of banks and semi-natural country of turns and undulations. Hughes Onslow always held that along with the National it comprised one of the two severest tests to which any horse could be put. Comparing the two, his opinion was, that although Aintree required a greater effort from the horse, his hardiness and intelligence were more highly tried at Punchestown, where hardly two fences were alike, and sharp left and right turns presented other problems to horse and rider.

Major Junks was a forthright character who disliked, as most experienced riders do, being tied down with lengthy instructions and declared that the best instruction he could ever receive were from Major Loder's groom as he went out to ride in one of his Conyngham Cups: 'Take a dangerous tight hold of her head, Captain, and knock hell's blazes out of the fences!' It was a pity that Snaffles never heard this remark, for he would have made good use of it had he done so, as it was in this period that he paid his first visit to Ireland, duly making the pilgrimage to Punchestown and walking out to see its most famous fence 'The Old Double'.

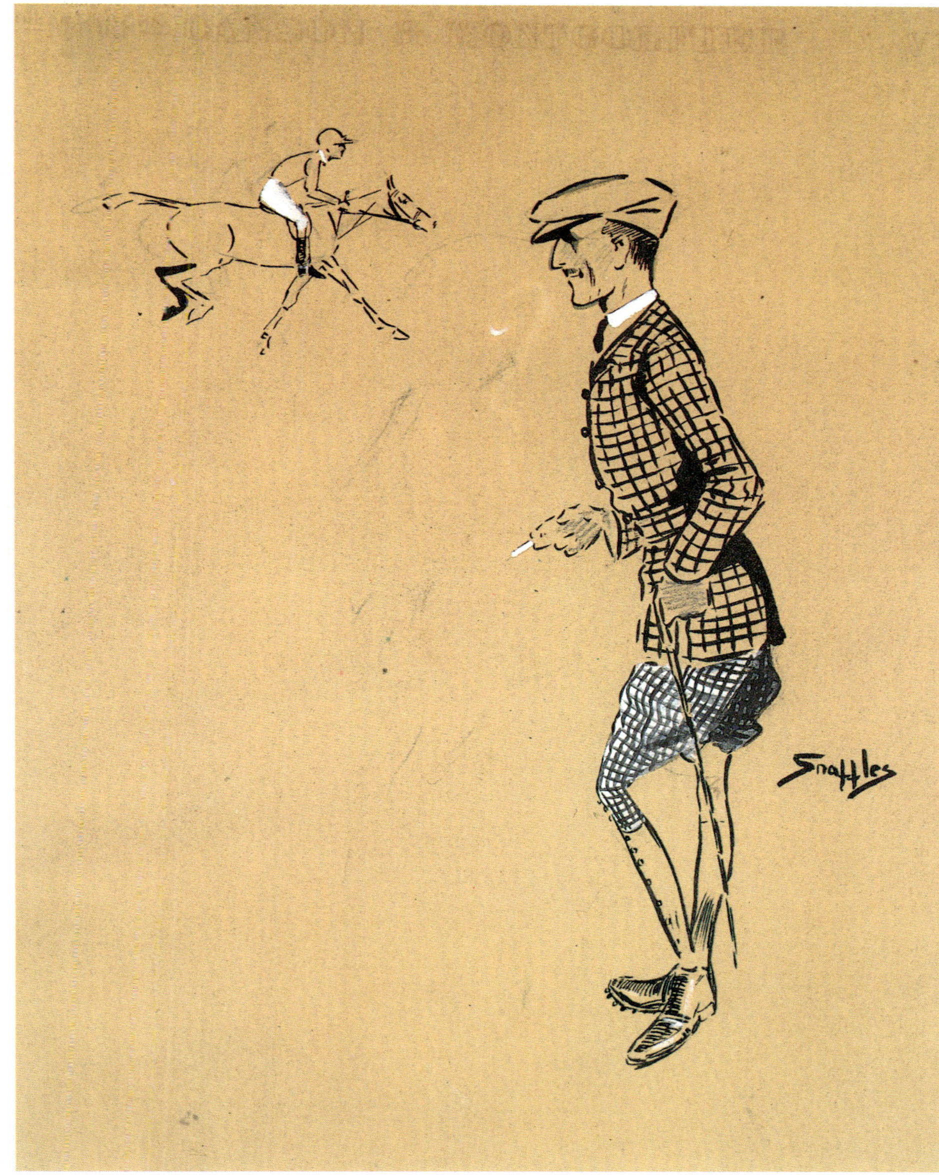

This sketch is obviously of a trainer, probably one who trained for soldier officers, and dates from around 1910. It is very similar in style to Snaffles' print of the comedy actor, George Grossmith Jr, which he entitled Gee-Gee

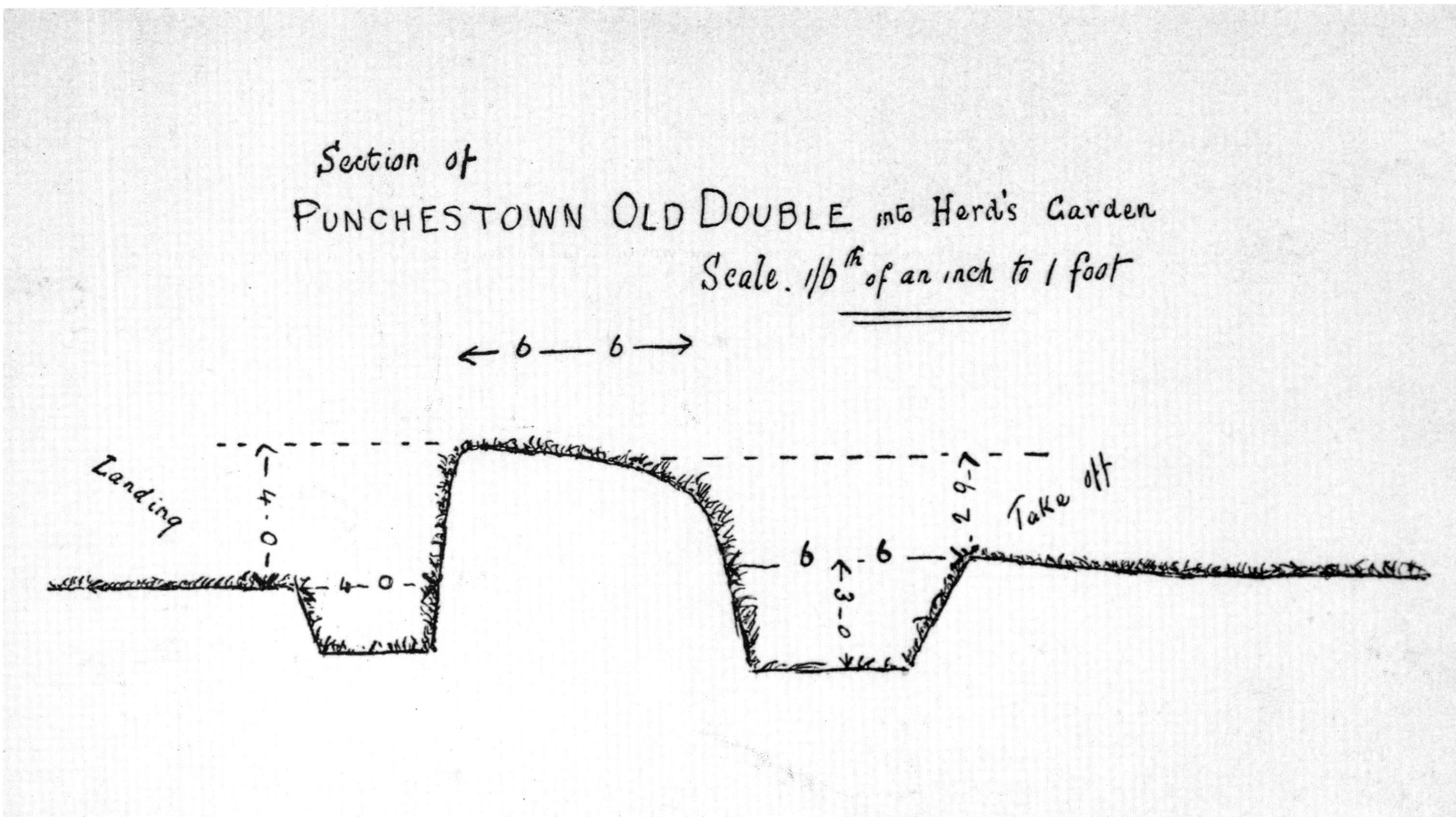
Section of
PUNCHESTOWN OLD DOUBLE into Herd's Garden
Scale. 1/6th of an inch to 1 foot
← 6 — 6 →
Landing
4-0
4-0
6 - 6
3-0
2-9
Take off

3 Irish Banks

Punchestown, when Snaffles first visited it in 1913, was then at its supreme best. It was the apogee of the Irish social and sporting calendar and well and truly deserved the epithet 'Peerless Punchestown'. Behind the stands were regimental and club tents for entertaining. The Lord Lieutenant arrived at the course in a procession of carriages preceded by outriders; morning dress was *de rigueur* for gentlemen and all their finery for ladies. 'I have been many places', wrote Harry Sargent, a chronicler of the times, 'where women do most congregate, but commend me to the ladies' lawn on a fine afternoon for a display of beauty and elegance which I have never seen equalled, much less excelled. Neither Royal Ascot nor Glorious Goodwood can produce lovelier specimens'. Altogether it was Ireland's answer to Ascot and Goodwood, the show piece of its natural and national sport – steeplechasing.

Unlike England where, in the period leading up to the First World War, steeplechasing was very much a third rate cousin to flat racing, in Ireland the reverse was true. The two most important race meetings held every year, Punchestown and Fairyhouse, were both steeplechase meetings and in reality the Irish Derby, now one of the most important European three-year-old weight-for-age races, was what its historians call a 'glorified handicap' right up to 1946. From the 1880's Irish steeplechasers had dominated major English races, and the Curragh, close to Punchestown, was the major training centre of steeplechasers for the whole of Europe. The Prince of Wales, soon to become Edward VII, had his 1900 Grand National winner Ambush II trained there.

Some idea of the importance of racing in Ireland can be gleaned from King Edward VII's and Queen Alexandra's spring visit to Ireland in 1904. Arriving on Tuesday 26 April, accompanied by their daughter Princess Victoria, they went straight to Punchestown, where the King's Grand National winner of four years previously ran disappointingly. The following day the King attended Punchestown without his wife or daughter. On Thursday 28 the whole royal party went to Phoenix Park and on Friday 29 they were racing once again at Leopardstown.

As an obstacle 'The Old Double' at Punchestown was then a far more formidable fence than now. It consisted of a large broad bank with wide ditches or 'wide gripes' as they were called, on either side. Harry Sargent, who had ridden over it, took the trouble to go out and measure the spread a horse would have to jump were he to try to clear it 'field to field', a course strongly not recommended; horses in the usual way changing legs on the top of the bank. 'To clear from field to field the old Bank in the Herd's garden', he wrote, 'requires a horse to cover at least 20 foot in an arc of at least 26 foot. This has been attempted by many horses, but very few have accomplished the feat without a fall and some have been killed themselves in the attempt. The only horses I remember to have landed it safely without laying an iron on it are Redman, Lord George (an English Horse) and Charity Boy, but others, no doubt may have done so. I need not say that when these aerial eccentricities were performed, it was not usually with the consent of the jockeys ... its dimensions are, as nearly as possibly, grip (sic) on take-off six foot six inches wide, three foot deep. Height of the fence from take-off two foot nine inches; width on top six foot six inches; drop four foot; grip (sic) on landing side four foot wide' and he drew a diagram to illustrate this. Snaffles too drew it and watched the Conyngham Cup field taking it on. From that came one of his more spirited drawings showing 'Grief a-plenty' which *The Illustrated Sporting and Dramatic News* was delighted to publish. A later one, recollected in tranquility, forty years later, was captioned with an echo of a countryman's comment in the crowd behind him: 'Thim' jockey lads don't waste much time over that one!'. In 1913 the year Snaffles first saw the Conyngham Cup, it was won by Shaun-N-Scuab.

As we have commented when talking of Major Junks in the previous chapter, the Conyngham Cup was then the most important race in the Irish calendar and it was not until after the First World War that the shorter Irish Grand National became a real rival to it. Incidentally, although Fairyhouse was normally considered an easier course to negotiate than Punchestown, the great upbank at the far end of the course, called Ballyhack, was held in almost as much awe as the Double at Punchestown, as the height the horse had to jump to gain the top was nearly 5 foot.

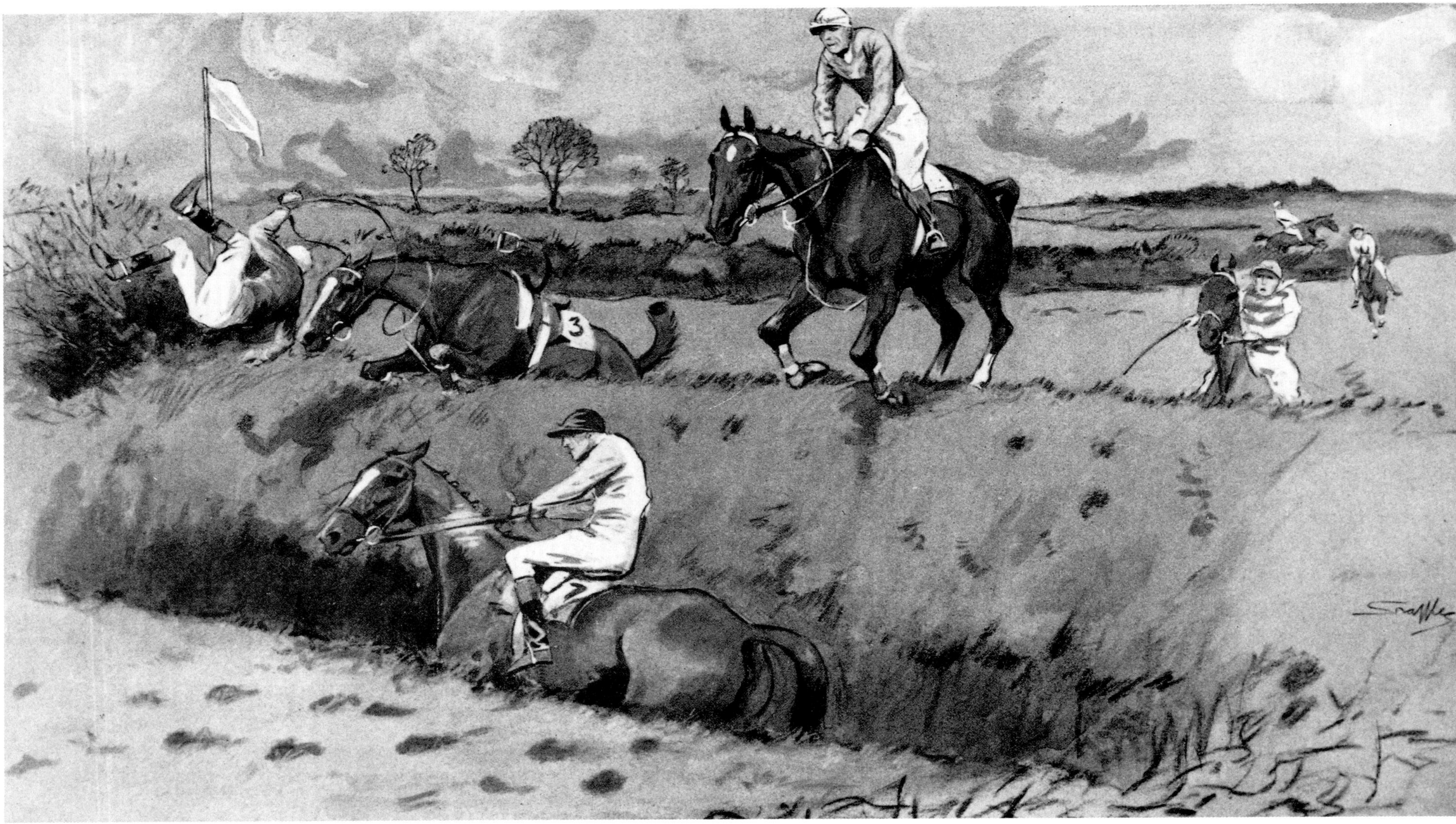

Grief! The Old Double at Punchestown

Snaffles drew this scene in 1913 or 14

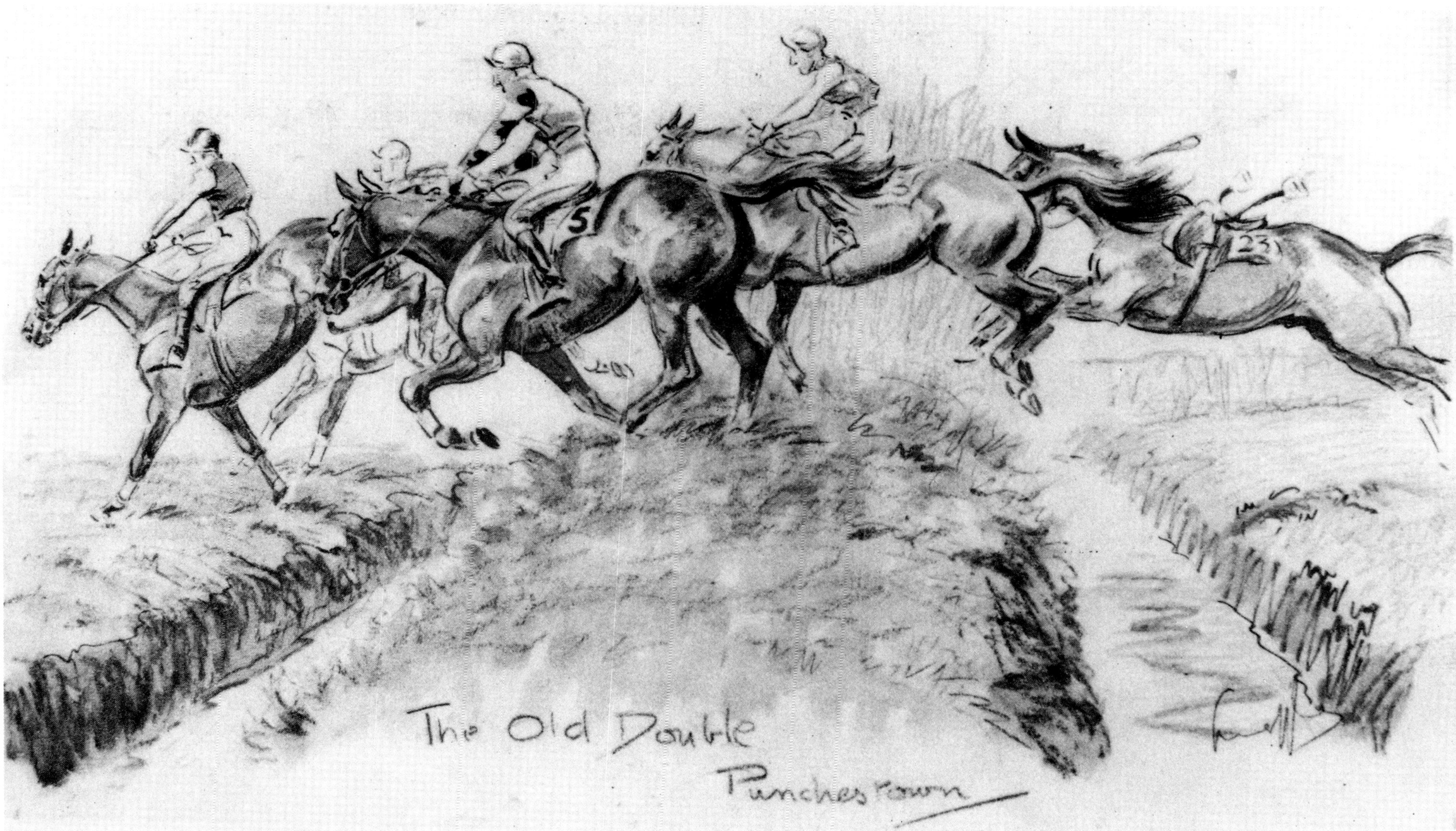

This drawing was made in the late 1940s or early 1950s, and it is possible that Snaffles hadn't seen the Old Double for fourteen or fifteen years; although we know he was in Ireland for social visits at about that time. The development of the artist's style is clearly demonstrated by these two pictures

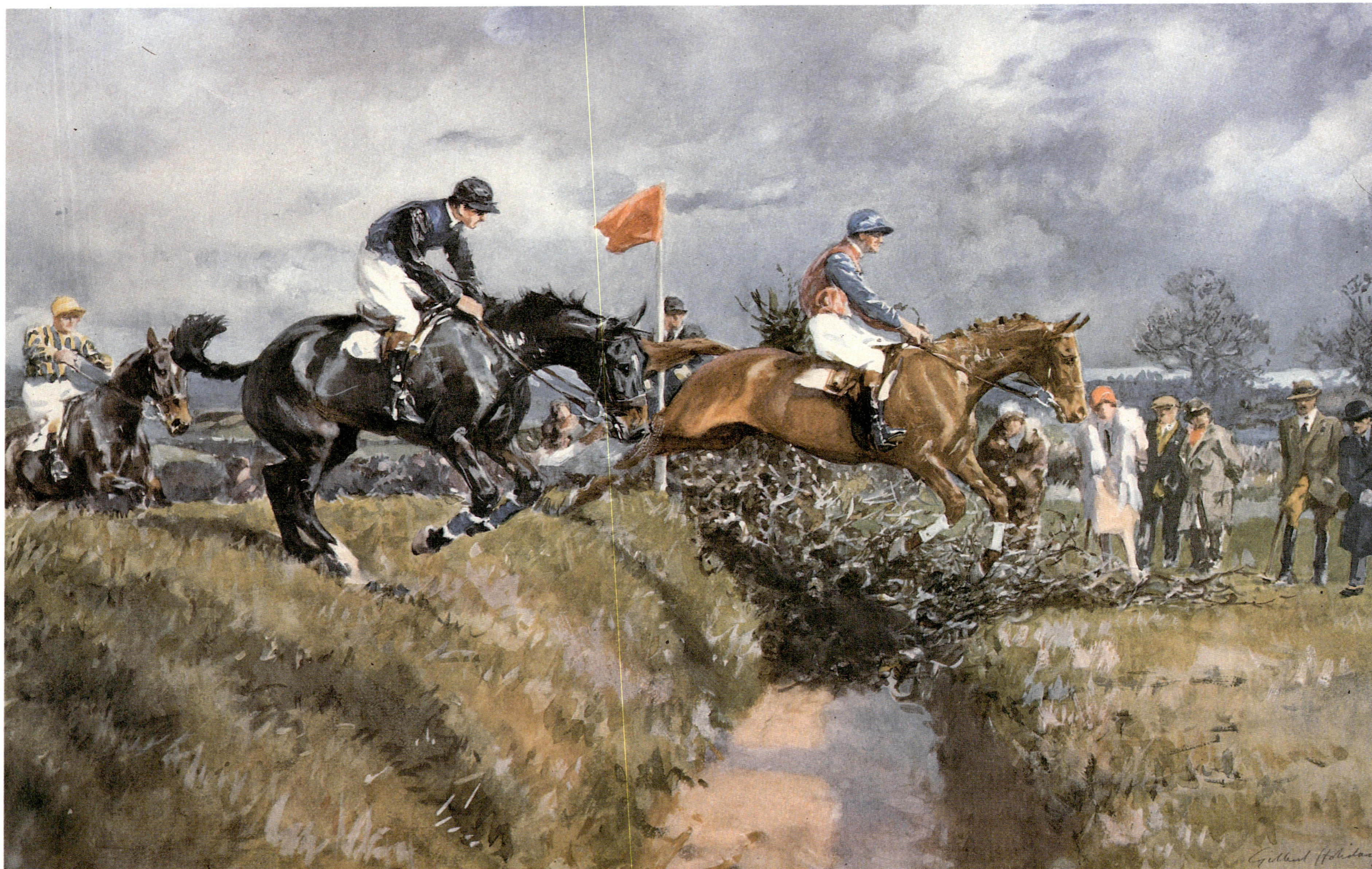

This pair of paintings was executed in the 1920s by Snaffles' fellow Gunner and close personal friend, Gilbert Holiday. They are considered the greatest ever paintings of Punchestown. Holiday was the great pastel painter of the coterie of artists which included Snaffles, Lionel Edwards and Cecil Aldin

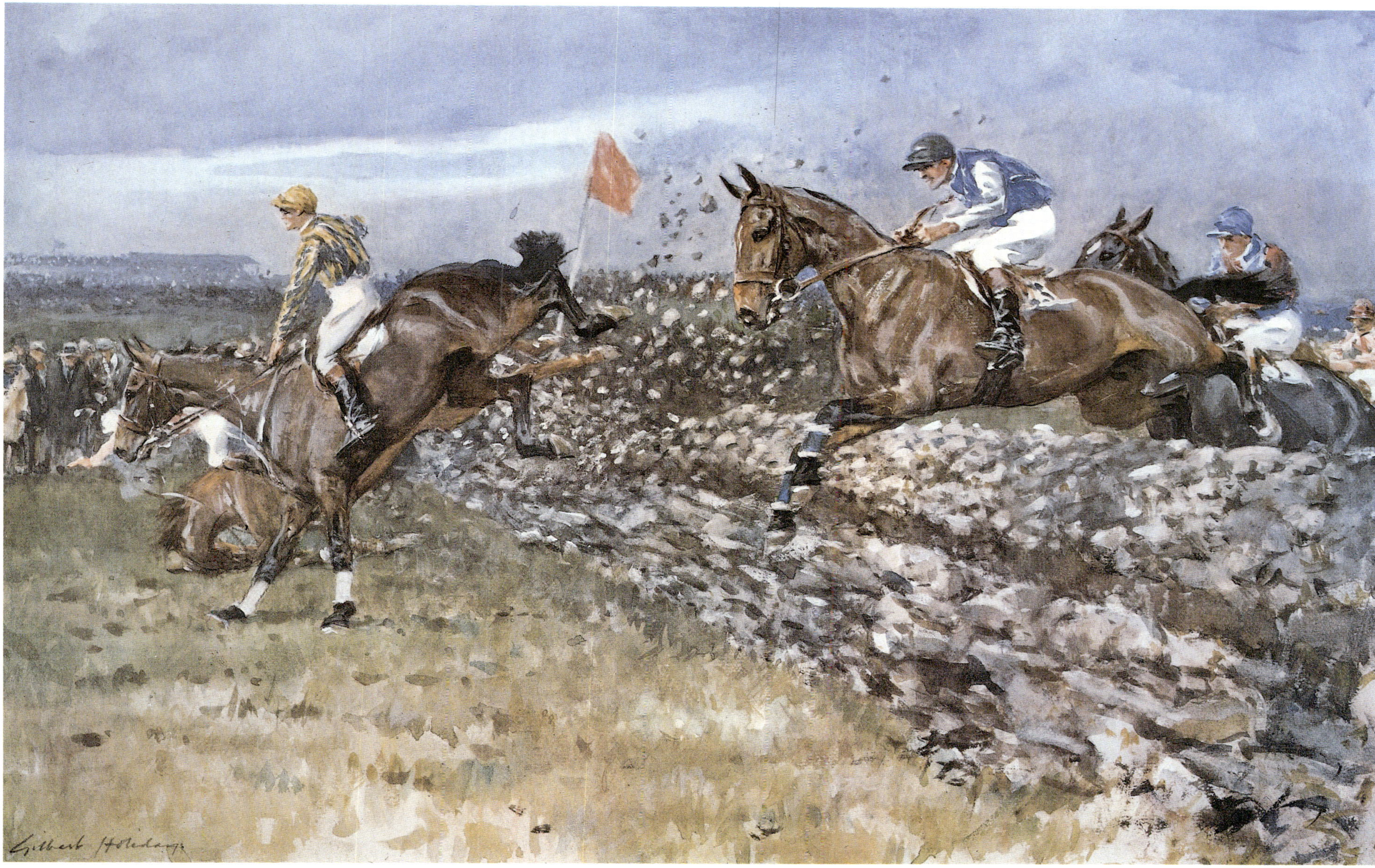

At Punchestown Snaffles found, before the First World War and again in the 1930s, the strong, bold, blood horses he so admired and which Holiday has depicted so brilliantly in his pair of prints

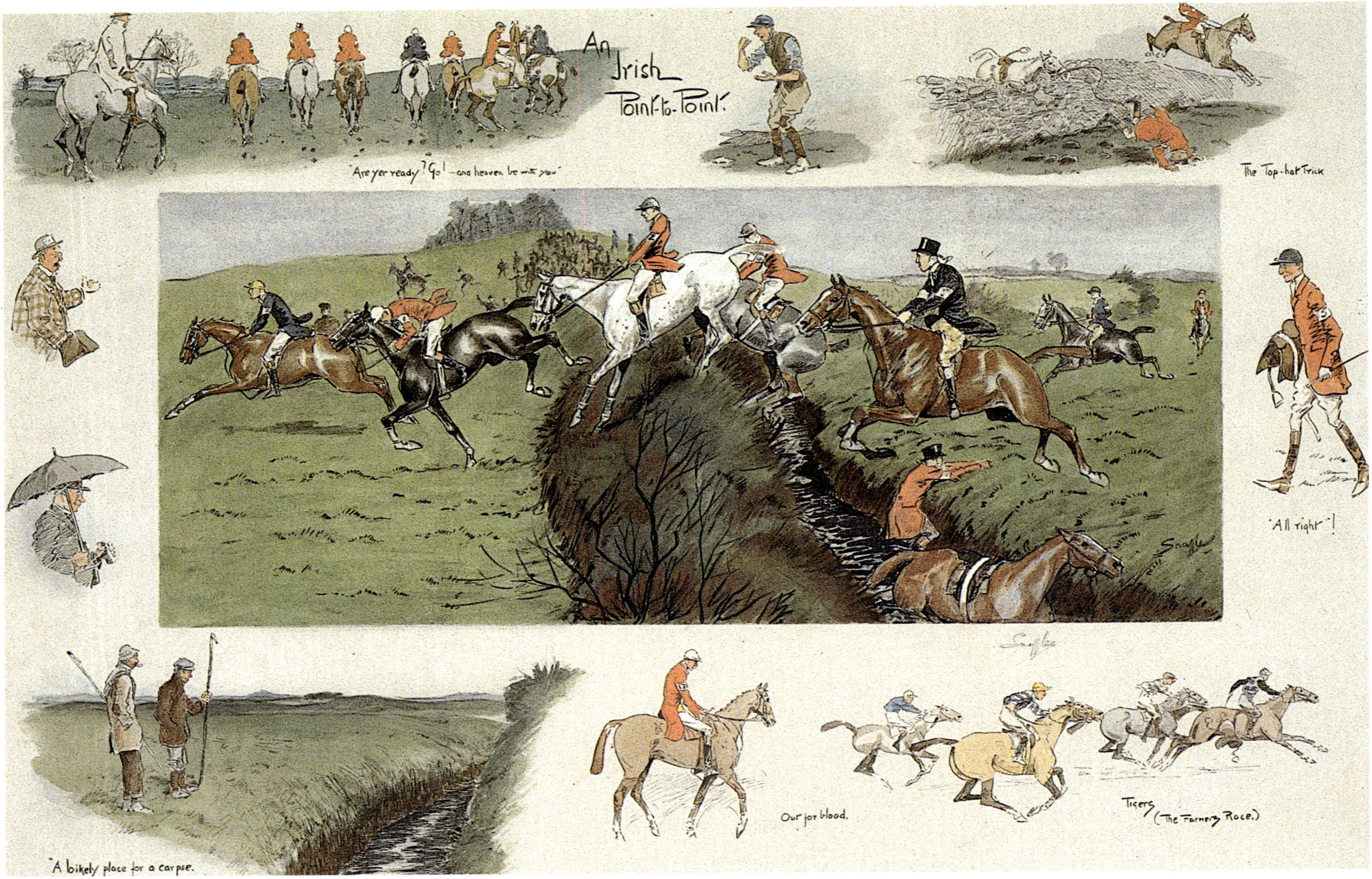

This was Snaffles' greatest work from his pre-First World War visit to Ireland. It is one of his rarest and most valuable prints

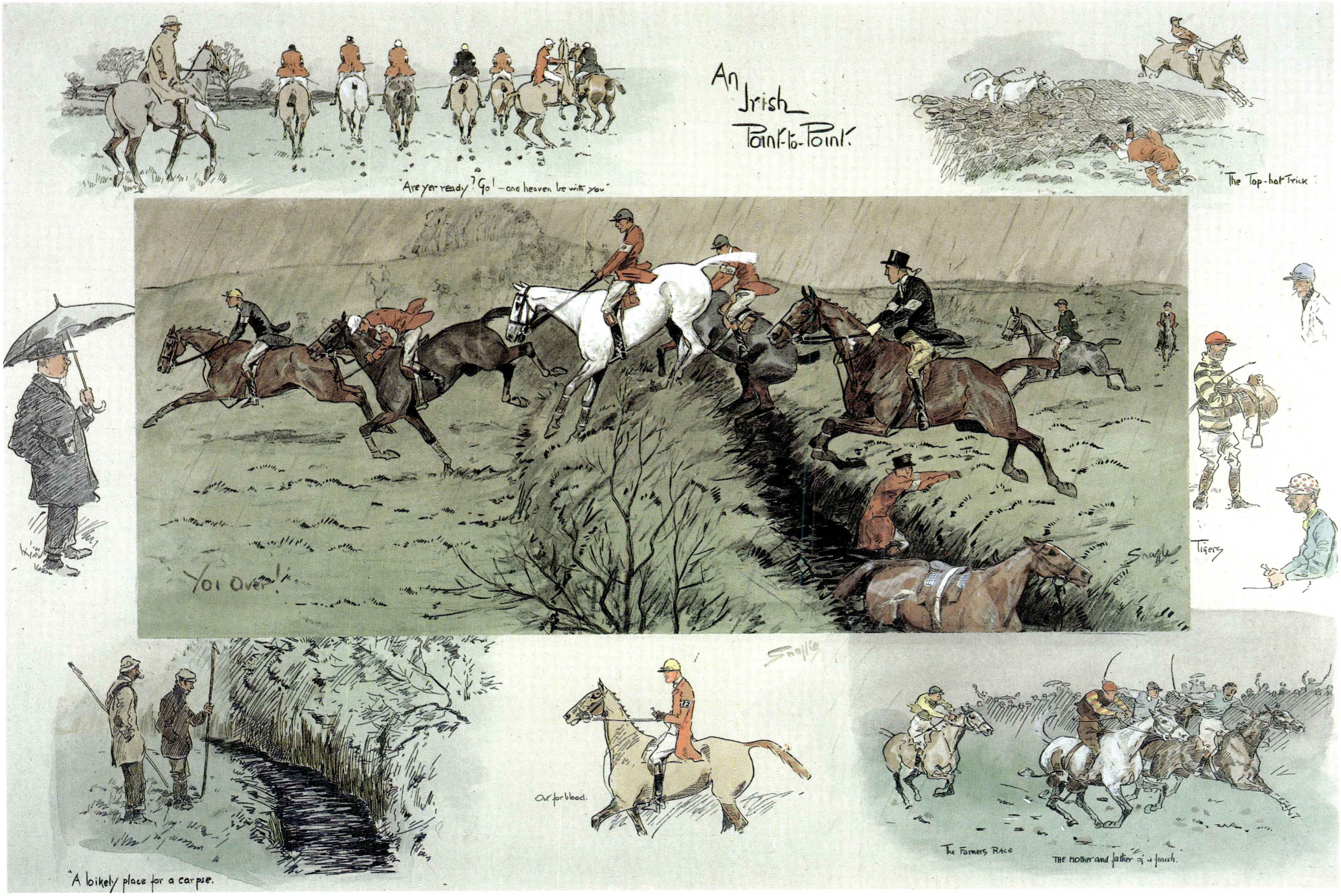

There are two main versions of An Irish Point to Point, both produced in 1913–14. It is thought that the one above is the later of the two as it is slightly more sophisticated

Table C

IRISH GRAND NATIONAL
Handicap Steeplechase 3¼ miles run at Fairyhouse

Year	*Value Sovs.*	*Horse*	*Rider*
1895	245	Yellow Girl II	Mr. J. Ennis
1896	245	Royston Crow	Mr. Parsons
1897	245	Breemount's Pride	Hopper
1898	242	Porridge	T. Collier
1899	245	Princess Hilda	Mr. J. Clarke
1900	166	Mavis of Meath	J. Kelly
1901	166	Tipperary Boy	T. Moran
1902	165	Patlander	J. Cheshire
1903	165	Kirko	J. Scully
1904	164	Ascetic's Silver	Dowdall
1905	160	Red Lad	C. Kelly
1906	164	Brown Bess	J. Bresname
1907	164	Sweet Cecil	Mr. T. Price
1908	164	Lord Rivers	Mr. R.H. Walker
1909	167	Little Hack II	Mr. R.H. Walker
1910	216	Oniche	Mr. F. Malone
1911	245	Repeater II	Mr. J.A. Trench
1912	245	Small Polly	Mr. R.H. Walker
1913	245	Little Hack II	S. Mathews
1914	245	Civil War	Capt. P.O'B. Butler
1915	167	Punch	Mr. R.H. Walker
1916	197	All Sorts	J. Lynn
1917	197	Pay Only	Mr. W.F. Sankey
1918	197	Ballyboggan	C. Hawkins
1919		NO MEETING	
1920	640	Halston	D. Colbert
1921	640	Bohermore	D. Colbert
1922	640	Halston	J. Maloney
1923	640	Be Careful	J. Maloney
1924	690	Kilbarry	W. Horan
1925	840	Dog Fox	Jos Doyle

CONYNGHAM CUP
Conditions Steeplechase 4 miles run at Punchestown

Year	*Value Sovs.*	*Horse*	*Rider*
1895	345	Surveyor	Mr. J.F. Croome
1896	271	Oldtown	Mr. L. Sheil
1897	271	Sweet Lavender	Mr. Persse
1898	267	Acrobat	Capt. Bidgood
1899	271	Covert Hack	Major Hughes-Onslow
1900	271	Covert Hack	Mr. G.S. Davies
1901	271	Covert Hack	Major Hughes-Onslow
1902	271	Grange	Mr. J.F. Croome
1903	271	Covert Hack	Major Hughes-Onslow
1904	469	St. Corinne	Mr. M. Hayes
1905	269	Lively Lad	Mr. H. Beasley
1906	271	Famous	Mr. J.W. Widger
1907	271	Teddie III	Mr. W.P. Hanley
1908	271	Paddy Maher	Mr. P.O'B. Butler
1909	271	Wild Fox III	Capt. W.A. Pallin
1910	271	Repeater II	Mr. C. Brabazon
1911	271	Victor Olympic	Count Stolberg
1912	276	Noble Grecian	Mr. L. Brabazon
1913	276	Shaun-Na-Scuab	Mr. J. Manley
1914	346	Ruddygore	Mr. M.C. McCarthy
1915	246	Minden Rose	Mr. B.B.Bellew
1916	246	Merri Merri	A. Hogan
1917	196	Awbeg	Mr. T. O'Rourke
1918	216	Abou Ben Adam	Jos Canty
1919		NO MEETING	
1920		NO MEETING	
1921	346	Mark-On	M. Colbert
1922	356	Halston	Mr. L.L. Firth
1923	331	St. Jago	W. Horan
1924	331	Halston	J. Meany
1925	330	Pop Ahead	Mr. F. O'Brien

Returning to Punchestown, the other fence which was unique to it was the stone wall which was 'a formidable 4½ foot in height' according to Harry Sargent. Since this was met after the Old Double with a sharp left turn and two single banks intervening, Punchestown and its fences fully lived up to Hughes Onslow's dictum that 'horse and rider had to know what they were about before tackling it'. Later the wall was modified and reduced in size. Its top consisting of a layer of loose stones through which a horse could brush. Snaffles' close personal and artistic friend, and fellow war artist, Gilbert Holiday, was later to produce two of his finest racing pictures showing a field crossing these two formidable obstacles.

Snaffles was entranced by his visits to Irish race courses. The informality behind the dressing up, the gaiety, the roguery and the fun all made an enduring impression on him and his ear for a phrase, coupled with his eye for a scene and incident, enabled him to portray the people and their sport without a trace of condescension or stage Irishness. From his visit he was to produce one of his largest, greatest and rarest prints, 'An Irish Point-to-Point', which shows a field tackling a nasty looking narrow bank with a 'grip' on the take-off side and a red-coated top-hatted gentleman in it. The scene is almost certainly set in either Kildare or Meath, as we know that he followed the Meath Hounds on foot on that visit. There are two or three versions of the print, all very rare, all carefully hand coloured and, if one may say so, the most valuable of his prints. Around the centrepiece there were humorous vignettes including another version of the 'top hat trick'. It seems that Snaffles could not do a major point-to-point picture without this little scene and it has to be admitted that at times Snaffles did repeat himself. Always a modest and self deprecating man, at no time would he have imagined that he was drawing for posterity or that his work would be some of the most sought after produced by any twentieth century sporting artist in the British Isles. We have taken the opportunity of showing the vignettes at aproximately the size Snaffles drew them to show at that stage of his career he was certainly able to draw faces with considerable skill.

It is a pity we do not know who was the model for one of his most successful racing prints of the period, 'The Tiger', but Snaffles obviously admired him and the feeling is that he was probably an English Cavalryman stationed on the Curragh. There is a possibility that it could have been George Paynter, as Snaffles used him again for an illustration later on in 1921. We have included two colour plates of the print to show how on many occasions the hand colouring varied. Snaffles would have had a number of black and white bases run off, probably by Gale & Polden in Aldershot, who did much of his black and white work after the First World War, although as he was living in Leicestershire at the time, it could just as easily have been a jobbing printer in Oakham or Melton Mowbray. A master copy, or perhaps two master copies, were then coloured by Snaffles and, when he received an order, he would take out his watercolours and colour up one of his black and white bases or, conversely, write to his sisters who were then working with him in this 'cottage industry' and ask them to do so.

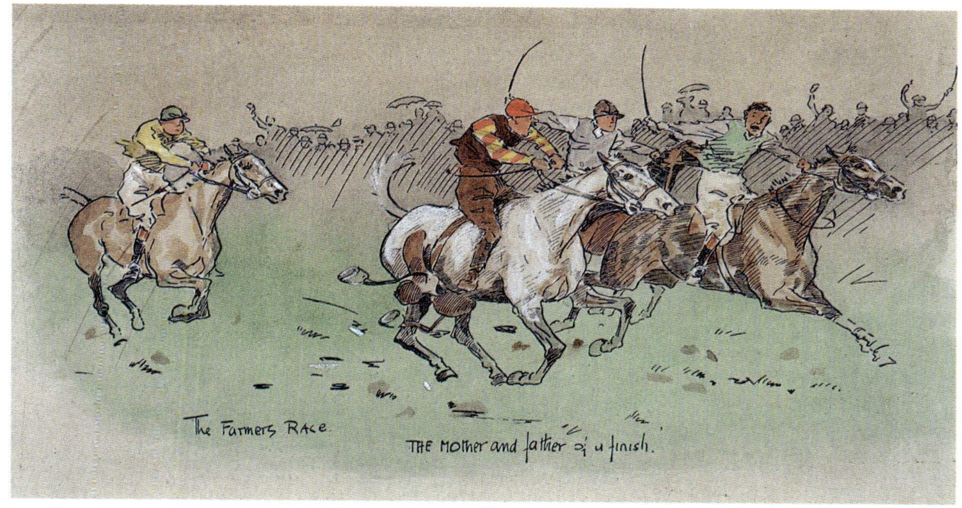

These vignettes, from An Irish Point to Point, are reproduced here approximately the same size as Snaffles drew them

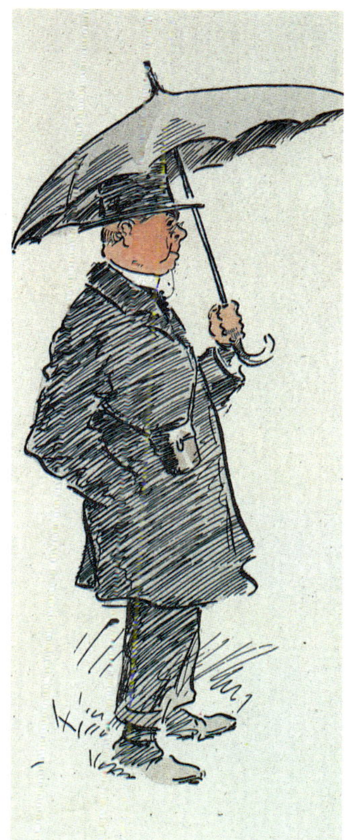

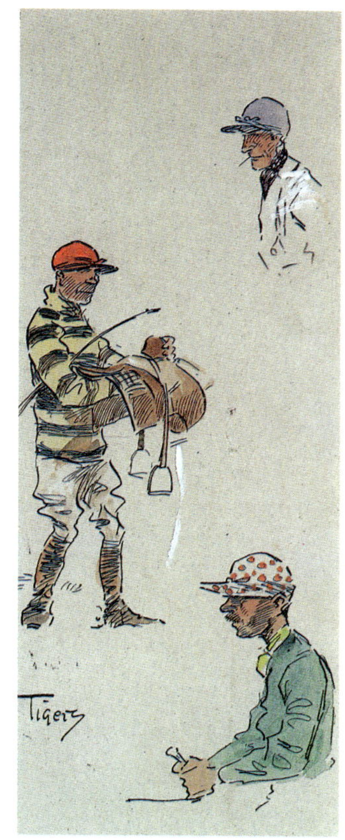

This print, like An Irish Point to Point, is very rare and entirely hand coloured. It is almost certainly an English soldier winning a point to point or small steeplechase in County Kildare or Meath, around 1913

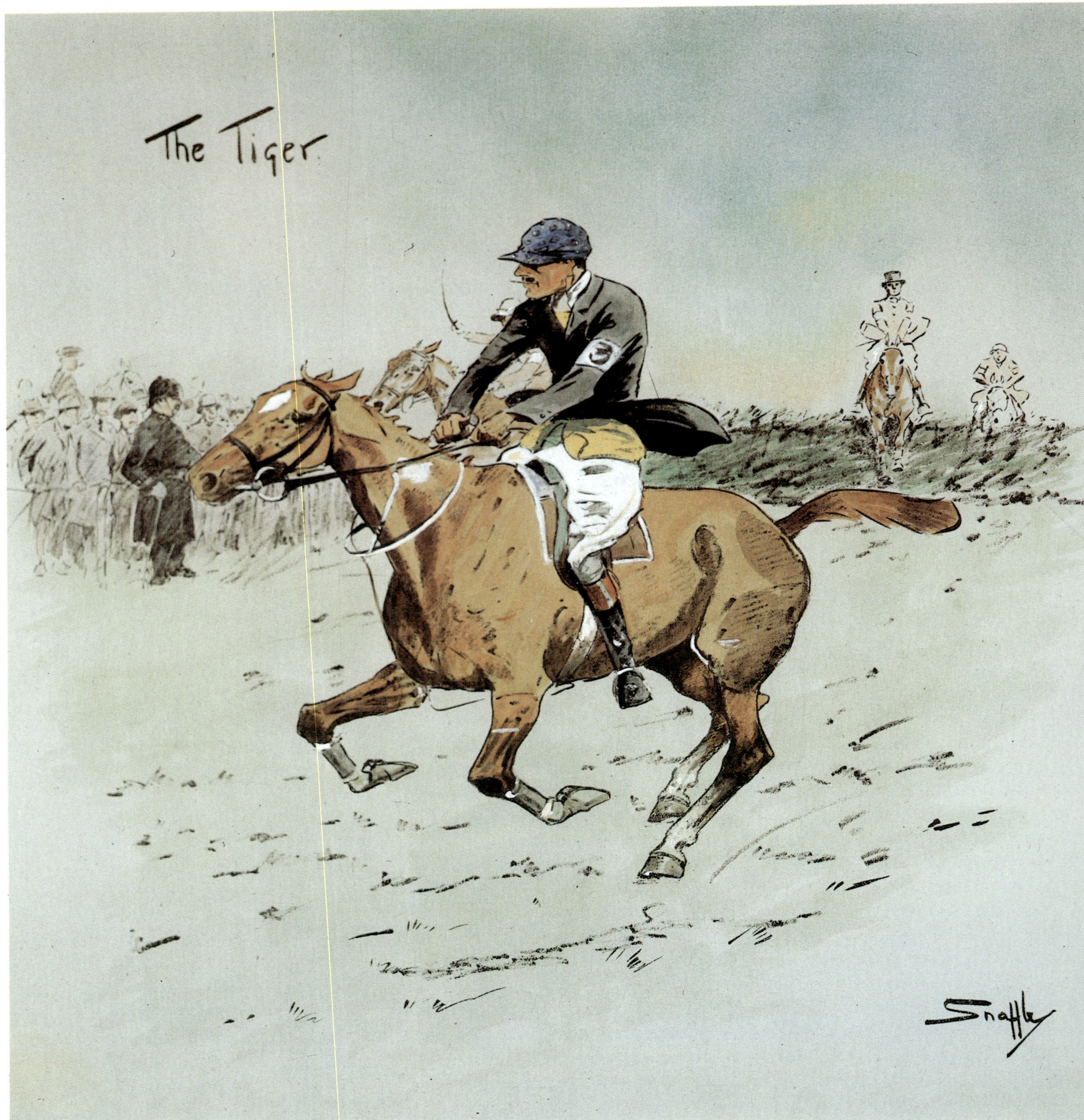

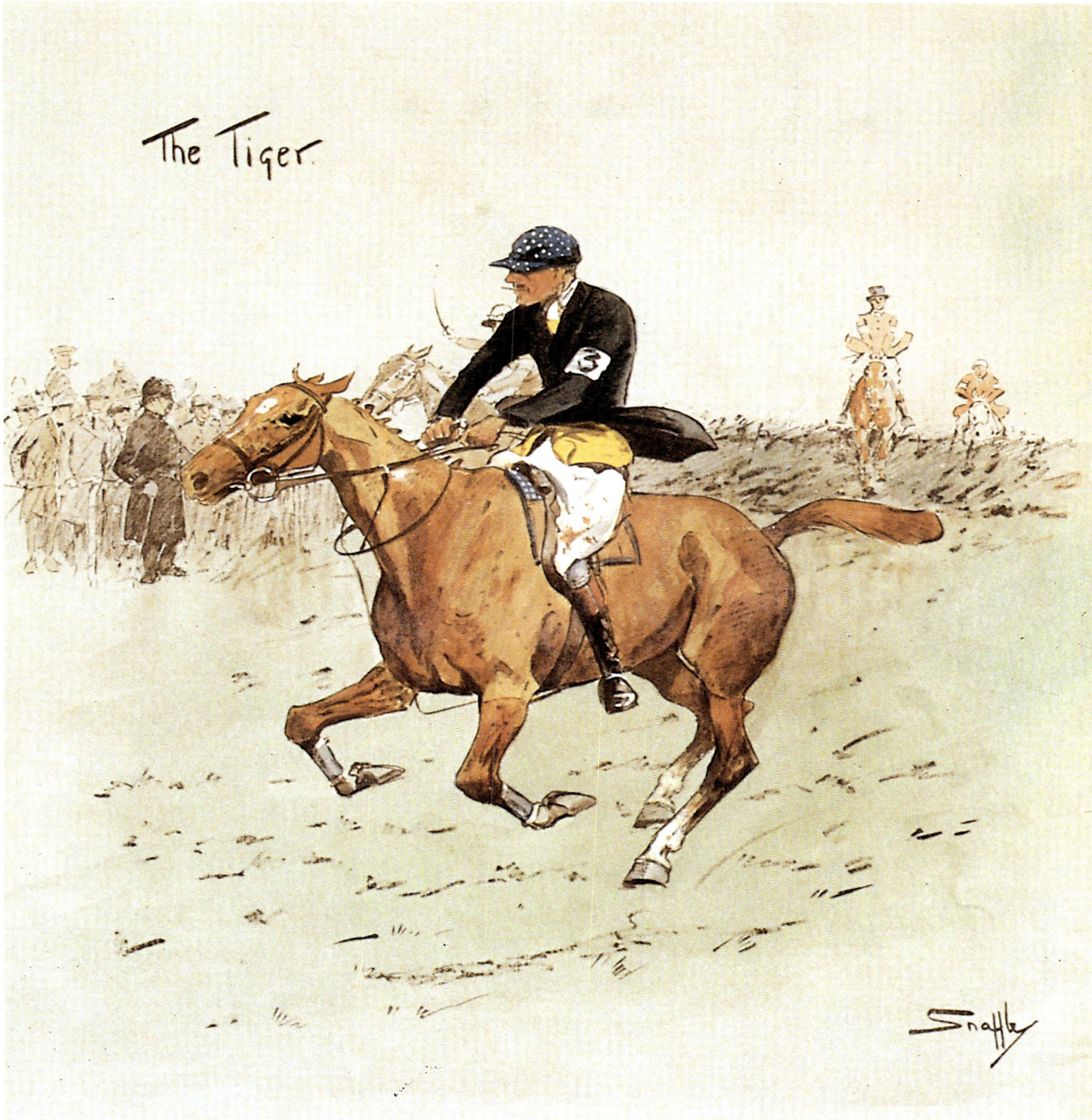

It is doubtful if Snaffles issued more than forty of these prints, hand coloured to order by Snaffles or his sisters. These two examples show how the hand colouring varied. On the left the horse has a webb girth, on the right he has a leather one – and there are other small differences in the colouring

Snaffles early work, such as that mentioned here, was mainly for the ephemeral magazine market, quickly done for quick returns to finance his travels and his sport. In fact it is unfair to say that his work was done quickly at this stage, as he laboured over each and every drawing he submitted to the publishers of such magazines as *The Tatler* or *The Illustrated Sporting and Dramatic News*. It was not until he went to France with Gilbert Holiday that, working under tight press and time schedules, he became even half proficient at working quickly. During the years 1911 to 1914, Snaffles was struggling with the sale of his prints many of which were worked up from his sketches for periodical publications. Either the prints were published by Fores, who became his agents in 1908, and with whom he remained right to the end of his working life, or they were published by himself. In most cases the print runs were very small and it is now very hard to find his pre-War racing work.

By that stage in his career, Snaffles was very much in love with phrases and quotes, some from his favourite authors, others which he heard and memorized. They rang and re-rang in his head, and he could not help repeating them. His use of 'the top hat trick' is an instance which we have already quoted. Another is the repetition of the valediction he first heard as a boy, delivered by Lord Willoughby de Broke, to a Warwickshire point-to-point field, 'Go! and Heaven be with you', which he used again and again in his vignettes of point-to-pointing. Yet another of his favourites was 'Up the straight for home when an ounce of blood is worth a pound of bone'. Ireland, then and later, was for him to be a treasure house of phrase and story.

During his visit he was invited to dine at a Cavalry mess in the Curragh Camp, the then Headquarters of military life in Ireland. Irish stories were bandied about over the port and pigeon-holed by him in his retentive memory for re-use. From one of them came, much later, a sketch which, although it did not affect racing, is worth reproducing here to demonstrate his attention to and retention of detail and his command of idiom. Everything about it is just right; it is, in fact, a little classic of humorous composition; its background of barrack building, dog-cart driving away and the soldier in a forage cup saluting, all lightly and accurately sketched in, leading to the figures in the foreground which give life to the caption.

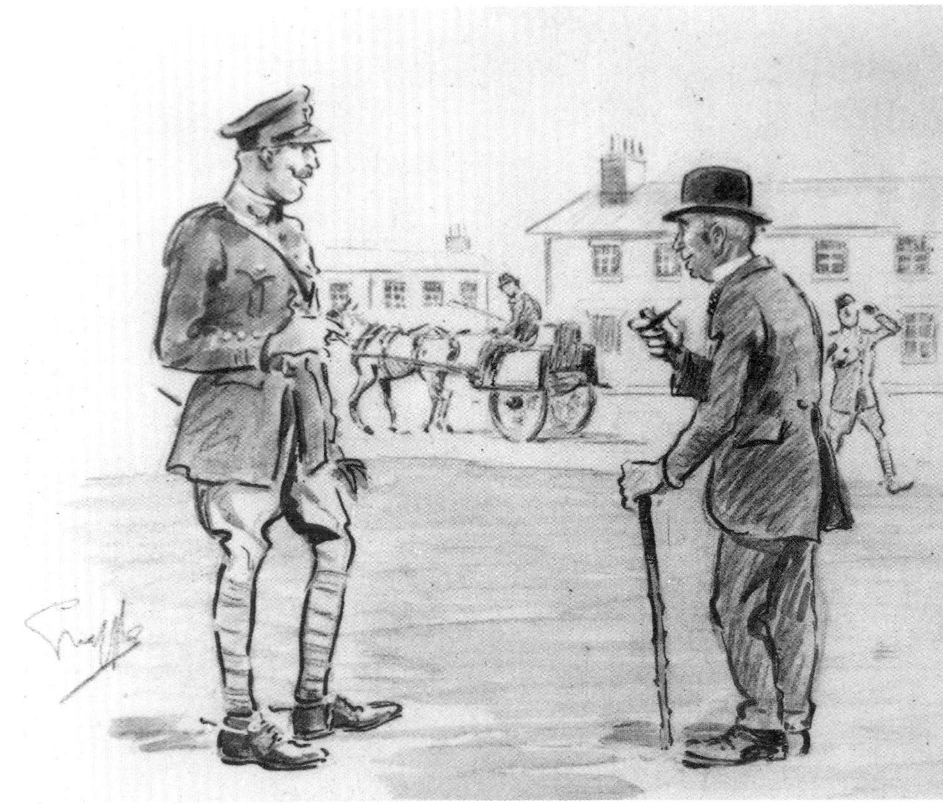

The introduction of the puttee to the Curragh

'Good morning, Paddy'
'The top of the morning to yerself, Meejor. Becripes! them's grand little thwisty trousies ye're wearin'.'

4 The Yeomanry and World War I

Snaffles had finished his three years with the Colours in May 1905 and terminated the nine years on the Reserve with a payment of £25.0s.0d. in early September 1911. Exactly why he chose to buy himself out is unknown as, although money was easier by 1911, £25.0s.0d. was still a considerable figure for him. The reason could have been that he wished to join the Leicestershire Yeomanry, along with his great friend Bill Gibson. His Yeoman career was fairly short, as he had a bad fall which resulted in his being invalided out, but he maintained his close association with the regiment, went every year to watch the Yeoman race at the local meeting and regularly attended camps, with his notebook always at the ready.

On returning home to Oakham after his very enjoyable trip to Meath and Kildare, which included visits to Punchestown Races and the Curragh Camp, he was busy again with his pencil at the Melton Hunt meeting at Burton Lazzard in 1913 where the Master of the Quorn, Captain Forester, rode two winners and Major Junks another. In the same season, he was present to witness and record a milestone in the history of jumping. A friend of his owned Brantingham, 'A cock-tailed chestnut gelding, and if the ass who had cut his tail off had left it alone he would have been as good-looking a horse as ever had a saddle on his back.'

In that season, the then aged Brantingham had to his credit a total of forty nine wins, or so Snaffles claims, and it was his friend's ambition to achieve his fiftieth in his twentieth year. However, the friend was very hard up and when they arrived at the course for the Burton Hunt Meeting, they found to their dismay that a hot thing called Bagpipes was in their race. The friend told Snaffles he had to get into money somehow and he doubted if he could beat Bagpipes, who had a 7 lb pull in the weights. He instructed Snaffles to put £10 each way on Bagpipes as a saver.

Watching the race Snaffles was horrified to see that the pressure of finance had overcome the call of fame and his friend was all but blatantly making no effort on the old horse. 'You blighter', Snaffles, who had backed Brantingham to win, said to himself 'you deserve to be warned off!' Then something happened. The old horse knew where he was, he knew all about a finish and what he was expected to do. He caught hold of his bit and ran on. Inspired by his mount his rider forgot about his finances and his overdraft. He sat down and kicked for home; no more was needed. Brantingham did the rest. He caught Bagpipes on the run-in and went on to win by two lengths. It was a jubilee win – his fiftieth in his twentieth year. 'Never have I found any horse who could even approach his wonderful record', Snaffles wrote in the fifties, and the manner of his doing it, together with the scene in the paddock beforehand, he set down in one of his books.

Our research into Brantingham's record differs from Snaffles recollection. Perhaps he meant his friend wanted to ride his twentyfirst winner in his twentyfirst year, and not his fiftieth winner.

Brantingham's Racing Record

Year	*Runs*	*Wins*	*Placed*
1904	7	2	5
1905	9	3	4
1906	9	3	2
1907	16	2	7
1908	16	4	7
1909	6	2	–
1910	5	2	2
1911	4	2	1
1912	4	1	1
Total	76	21	29

He won at the following courses: Wetherby, Hooton Park (2), Nottingham, Wye (4), South Wold (2), Brocklesby (2), Chelmsford, Totnes, Shirley Hunt (4), Market Rasen (2), Cambridge University. Of the winning races eighteen were three mile chases (two were selling races), two were two mile chases and one was over two and a half miles.

How Snaffles must have loved Crudwell, whose fifty wins, seven flat, four hurdle and thirty-nine steeplechases, spanned the fifties and no doubt Snaffles would have seen him winning open races at the Grand Military meeting, although by the time Crudwell was winning his fiftieth race, Snaffles had laid down his professional pencil. Crudwell's toughness and tenacity after the Second World War would have taken Snaffles back to the questions which his soldier friends asked their horses thirty or forty years earlier and which so often they answered.

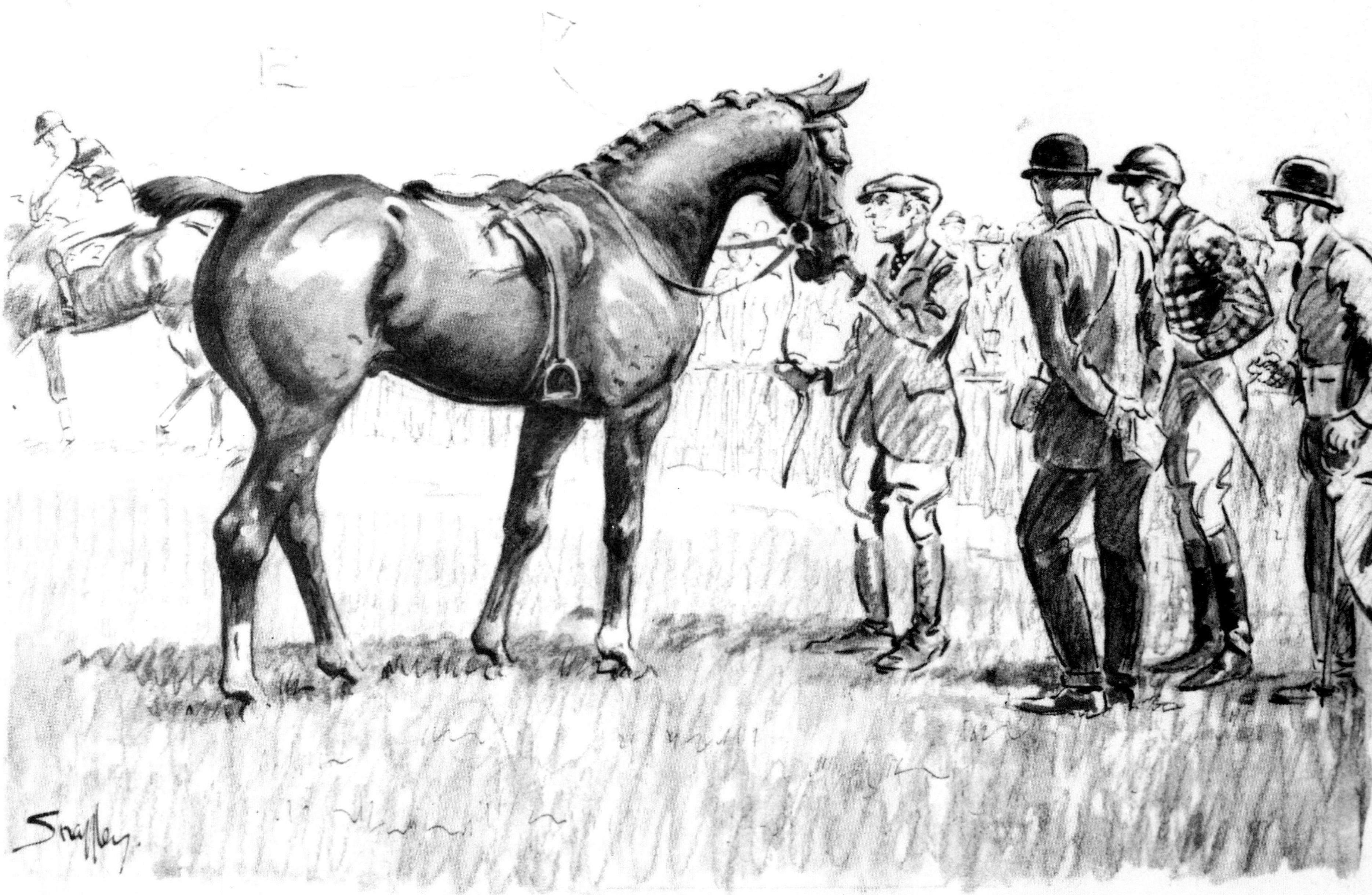

He asked us in a whisper to put a tenner each-way on Bagpipes

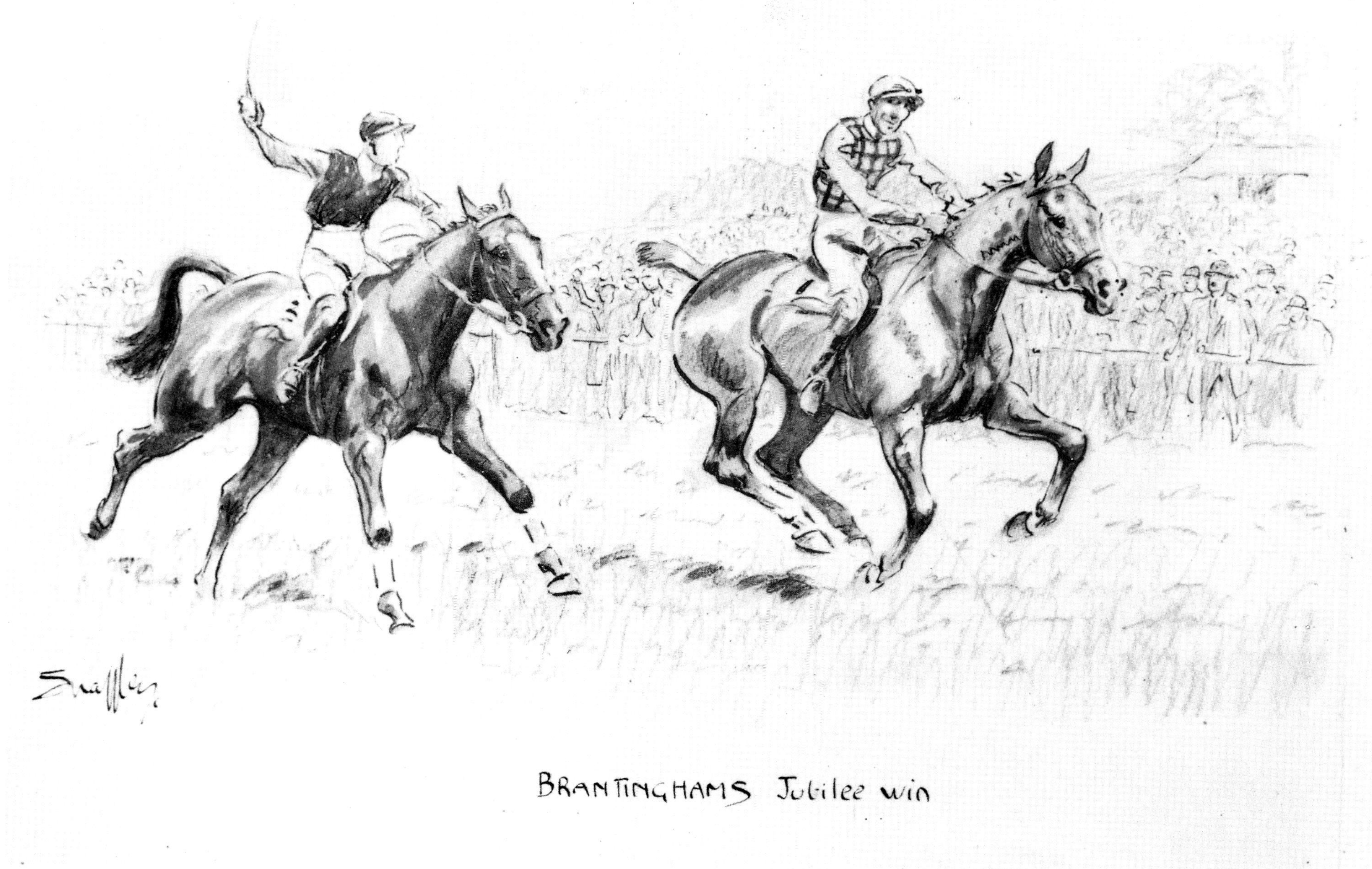

Opposite: The gent in the bowler hat, with a shooting stick, is a self portrait of Snaffles. There are more such self-portraits than photographs. He disliked being photographed

Above: *Erantingham's Jubilee win*
Exactly what jubilee? Fiftieth or twenty first?

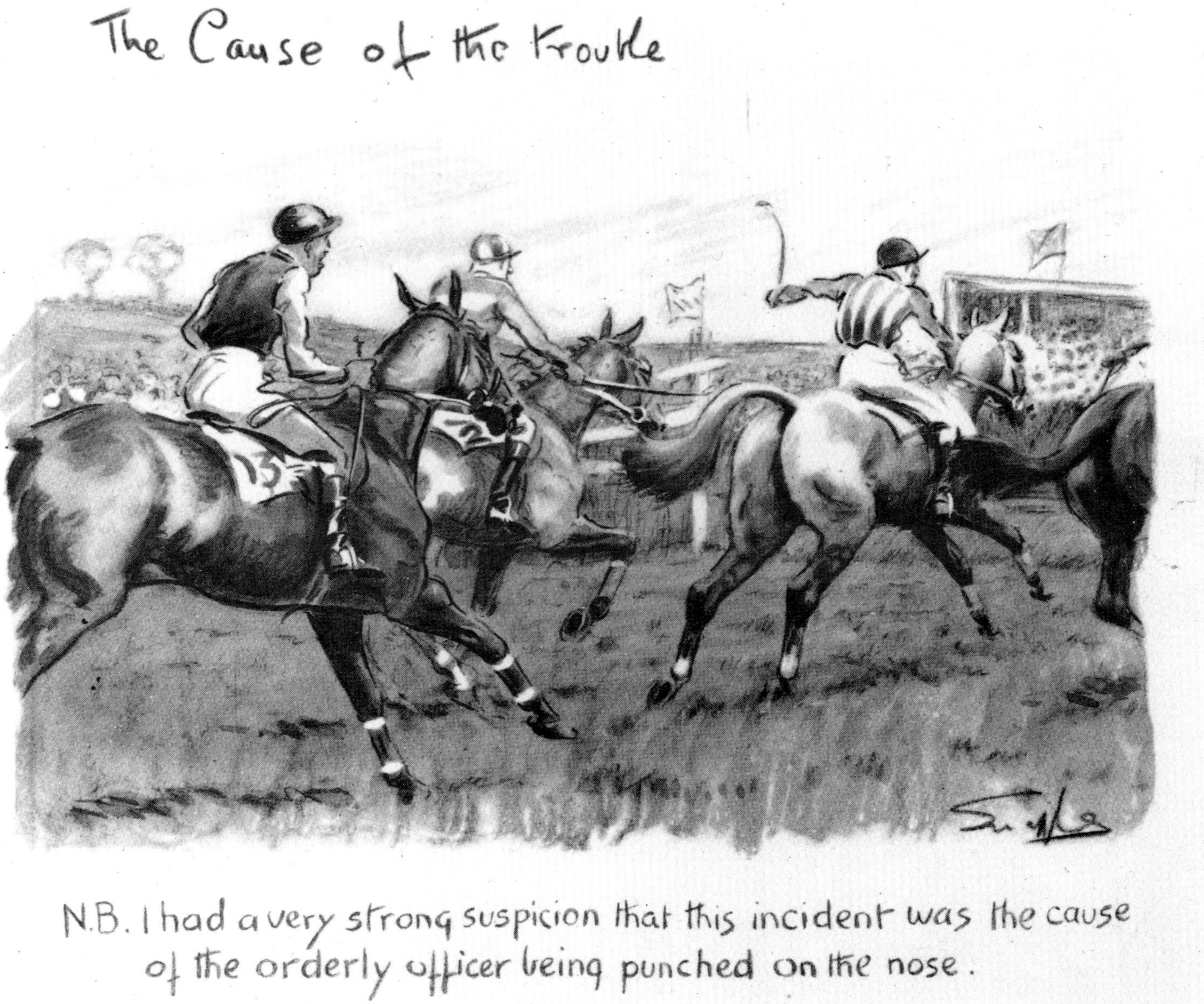

Another interesting race Snaffles was to view in 1913 or 1914 was the Leicestershire Yeomanry Cup. He attended the meeting as always and was particularly interested to see how a young friend of his was to progress. Snaffles doesn't say who this was, but it was almost certainly his close friend Bill Gibson. He was going the best coming to the last and he thought he had his race won, but the two leaders, experienced and well known 'gentlemen' riders, were determined to foil the youngster's chances. As they came to the fences there was room for him to go up between the two leaders but they closed the gap, so that he had to check and come round. As a result of this deliberate interference the youngster lost several lengths and the race.

Snaffles said that he also witnessed the sequel which took place in the Yeomanry horse lines in November of 1914, while the regiment was waiting to go to France. When he set down the story it was in his old age and his memory had become unreliable. Old men forget and so did Snaffles. He was not with the Yeomanry in November 1914, being in France with Gilbert Holiday, so it is more likely that he heard the story from his friend. In any

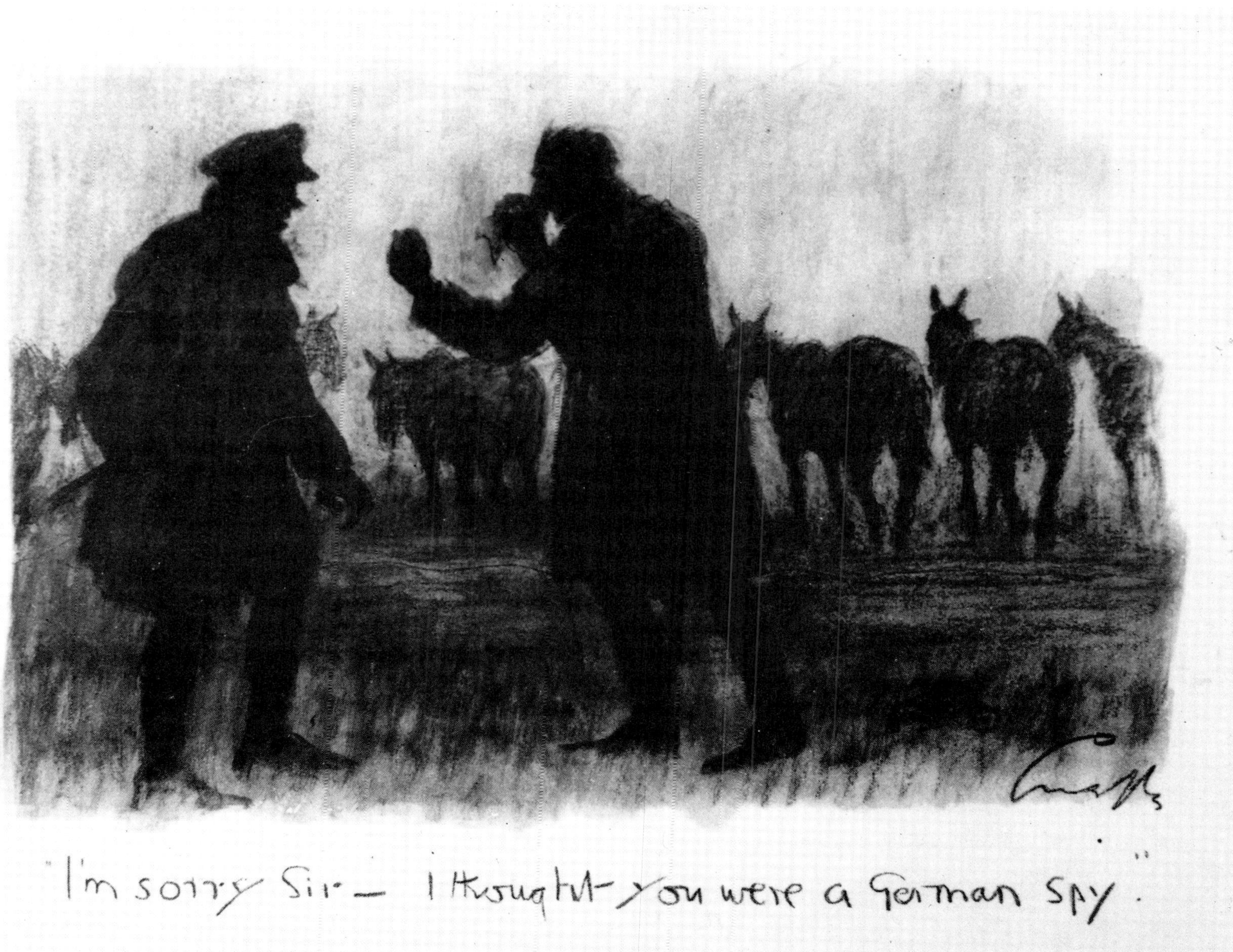

event, that November night the friend was on guard with the piquet in charge of the horse lines. The Orderly Officer was one of the two 'gentlemen' riders who had out-manoeuvred him. Since horses had escaped the night before through piquets sleeping, the Orderly Officer decided to check up by stealth and take the guard unawares. Snaffles' friend, seeing a strange figure suddenly looming up out of the darkness, and thinking it must be up to no good, decided, as he claimed afterwards, to strike first and challenge later. This he did and landed a straight left on the Orderly Officer's nose. A burst of pure, unadulterated vituperation informed him of his error, whereupon he exclaimed 'Oh, I am sorry sir. I thought you were a German spy!'.

Yeomen were, and are, unconventional soldiers of sporting tastes and the officer, to his credit, accepted the explanation. No court martial followed, but Snaffles remained convinced that his friend knew very well who was making the rounds and the losing of that race was paid for in the blood which poured from the officer's nose. All was more grist to Snaffles' mill and he illustrated it in two sketches.

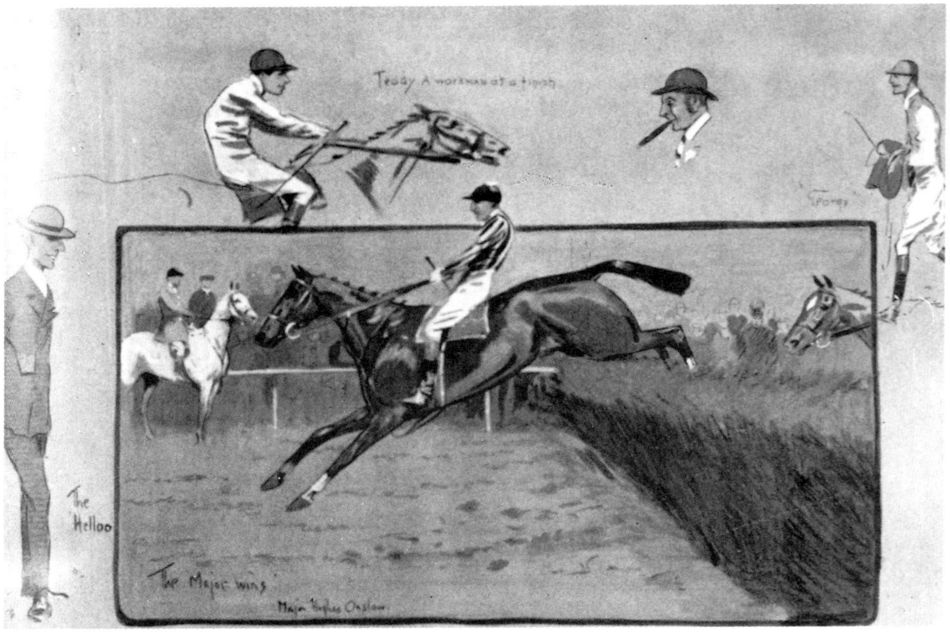

A sketch from the Melton Hunt meeting in 1913, showing 'Junks' winning his race

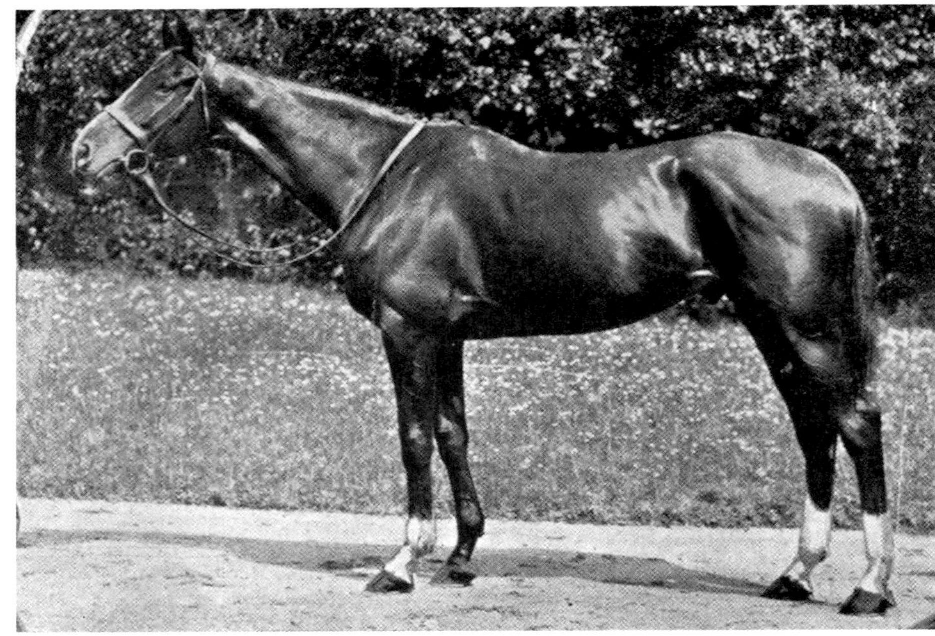

Sunloch

Snaffles tells us that in 1913 he saw the 1914 Grand National winner, Sunloch, at the Leicestershire Yeomanry camp ridden by his owner/trainer, the sporting Leicestershire farmer, Tom Tyler. Sunloch carried 9 stone 7 lb to victory the following year and was one of the few National winners who won from in front. At one time he was some forty lengths ahead and won easily in the end. The other horses gave him too much rope and it is of interest to note that the second and third horses were both French, Triannon and Lutteur.

Right up until the First World War, Snaffles' work was still somewhat immature and he was to remain in many aspects mainly a caricaturist. The humour in the story or situation was normally uppermost, certainly when he was working for periodicals. But of two things the editors who employed him, and the sporting public who enjoyed him could be sure – he was never unkind and he was never inaccurate. All of his work, whether racing or military, was stamped with authority. Every item of uniform, regalia, military harness or sporting equipment had to be correct to the last detail so that none of them could be faulted by the experts and the experienced, of whom we know there were many among those who viewed his work.

Moreover, in his action portraits of such as 'George' (Paynter), 'The Lancer' and 'Junks' he now showed that he could catch a likeness in horse and man and, perhaps more important to their riders, in styles of horsemanship. He was also in the last year or two before the War starting to produce some very proficient watercolours and the watercolour of Glenfinder at the Cottesmore point-to-point showed how much improvement he had made over the last five years.

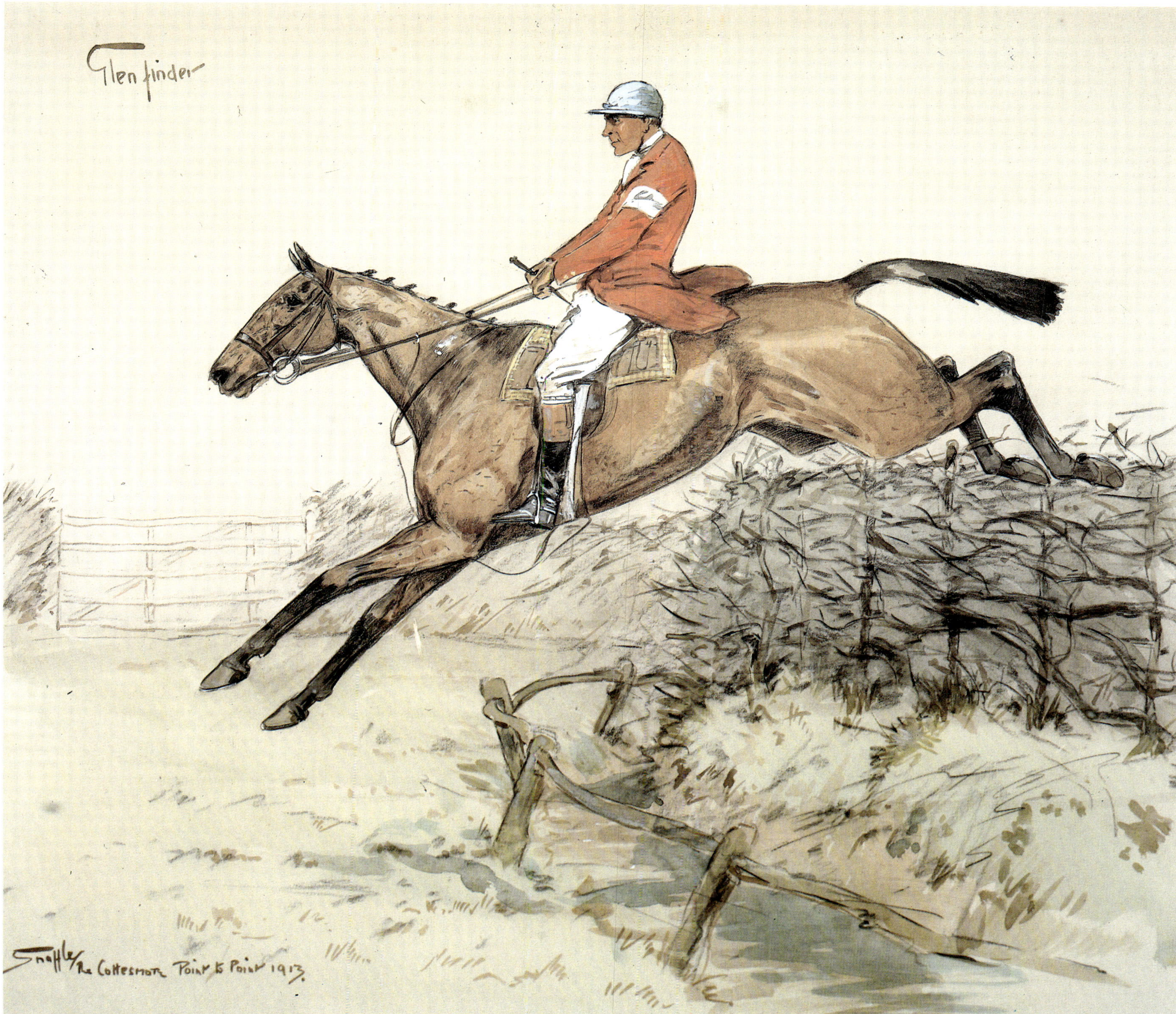
Glenfinder
Snaffles/The Cottesmore Point to Point 1913.

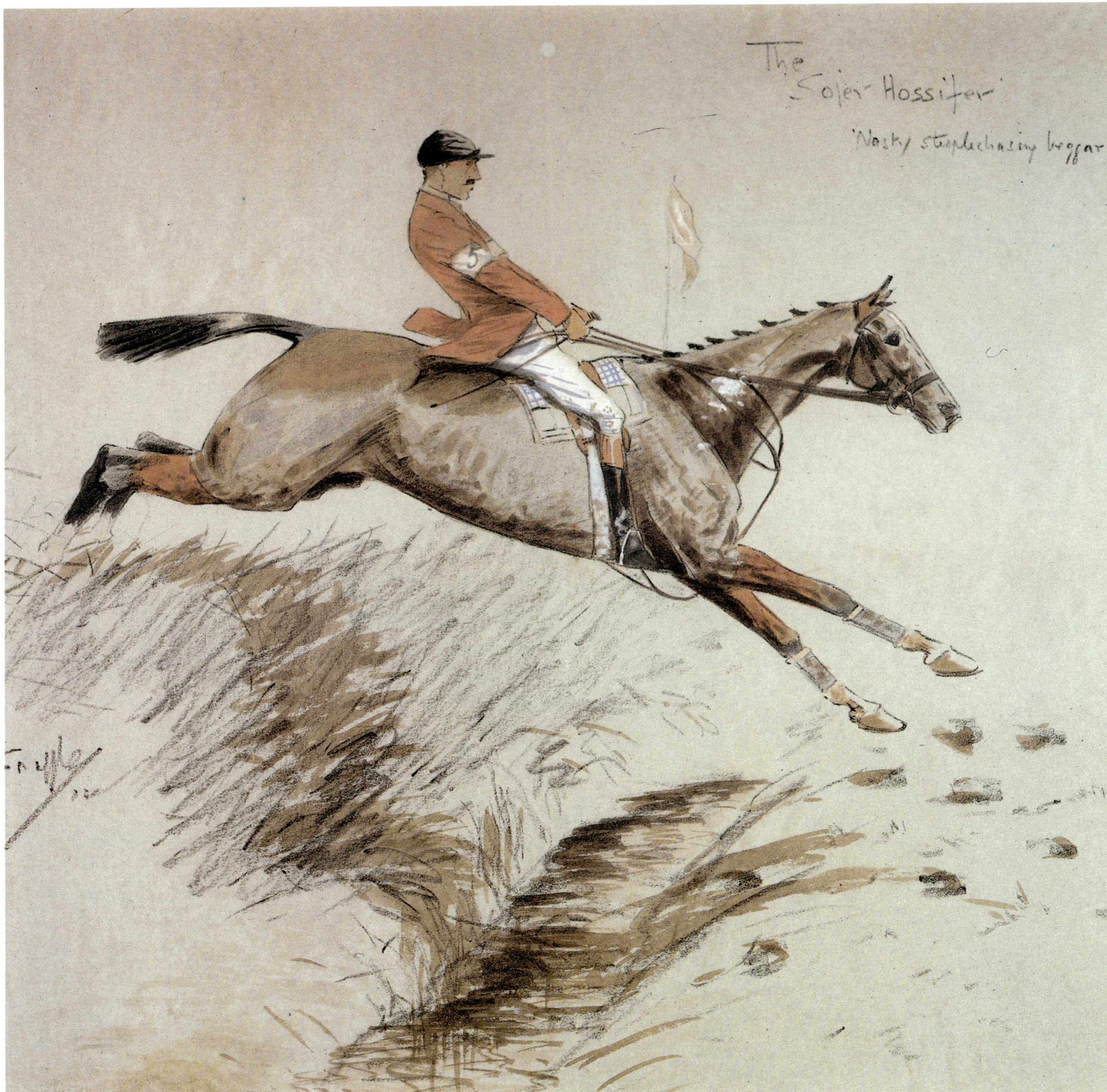
The Sojer Hossifer
'Nasty steeplechasing beggar'

The last print Snaffles produced before the outbreak of the War was a racing one. The 'Sojer Hossifer' shows the rider taking a natural hedge and ditch in fine style for those days; the rider leans back, giving the horse plenty of rein, so he jumps naturally and without interference. Snaffles subtitled it 'Nasty steeplechasing beggar'. As so often with his prints, it first appeared as a small illustration on the 28 February 1914 in *The Illustrated Sporting and Dramatic News* as No. 5 of a series of 'Hunting Types'. The relationship between hunting, point-to-pointing and steeplechasing was much closer then and the divides far smaller. By the artistic standards of the day, this print is outstanding as it gives a fairly accurate picture of what the actual horse and jockey looked alike. There is much less of the 'rocking horse' in this work, even if compared to the 1911 sketch of Vinegar Hill winning the Grand Military. Of Snaffles pre-World War prints, this is one of his most highly acclaimed and sought-after.

Racing was, of course, severely curtailed during the First World War. Aintree was closed in 1915 after the running of the Grand National, won by Ally Sloper, ridden by Jack Anthony, and substitute races were held at Gatwick for three years, where the fences were strengthened to make them as much like the real thing as possible.

Snaffles himself saw little or no racing during those years, since almost immediately after the outbreak of hostilities, he was employed by *The Graphic* as a member of a team of war artists, headed by his friend Gilbert Holiday, and sent to France. No record exists of his having attended any type of race meeting during the hostilities or drawn any racing pictures, for he was busily engaged elsewhere. After his stint in France as a war artist, where he perfected the art of drawing heavy horses which he saw pulling up the guns of his old arm, the Garrison Artillery, and matured his technique both in draftsmanship and colour, he enlisted in the Royal Navy Air Service as a mechanic, where his main duties were to help rescue crashed aeroplanes from the Thames Estuary and the Channel.

From there he was gazetted Temporary Lieutenant in the R.N.V.R. and posted to HMS *President*, which was a department of naval equipment. Here he was to serve under the distinguished marine and fishing artist Norman Wilkinson on Navy camouflage. During his time in the Navy, he made sea-faring sketches and paintings and conceived an undying admiration for all that pertained to those who go down to the sea in ships, especially destroyers.

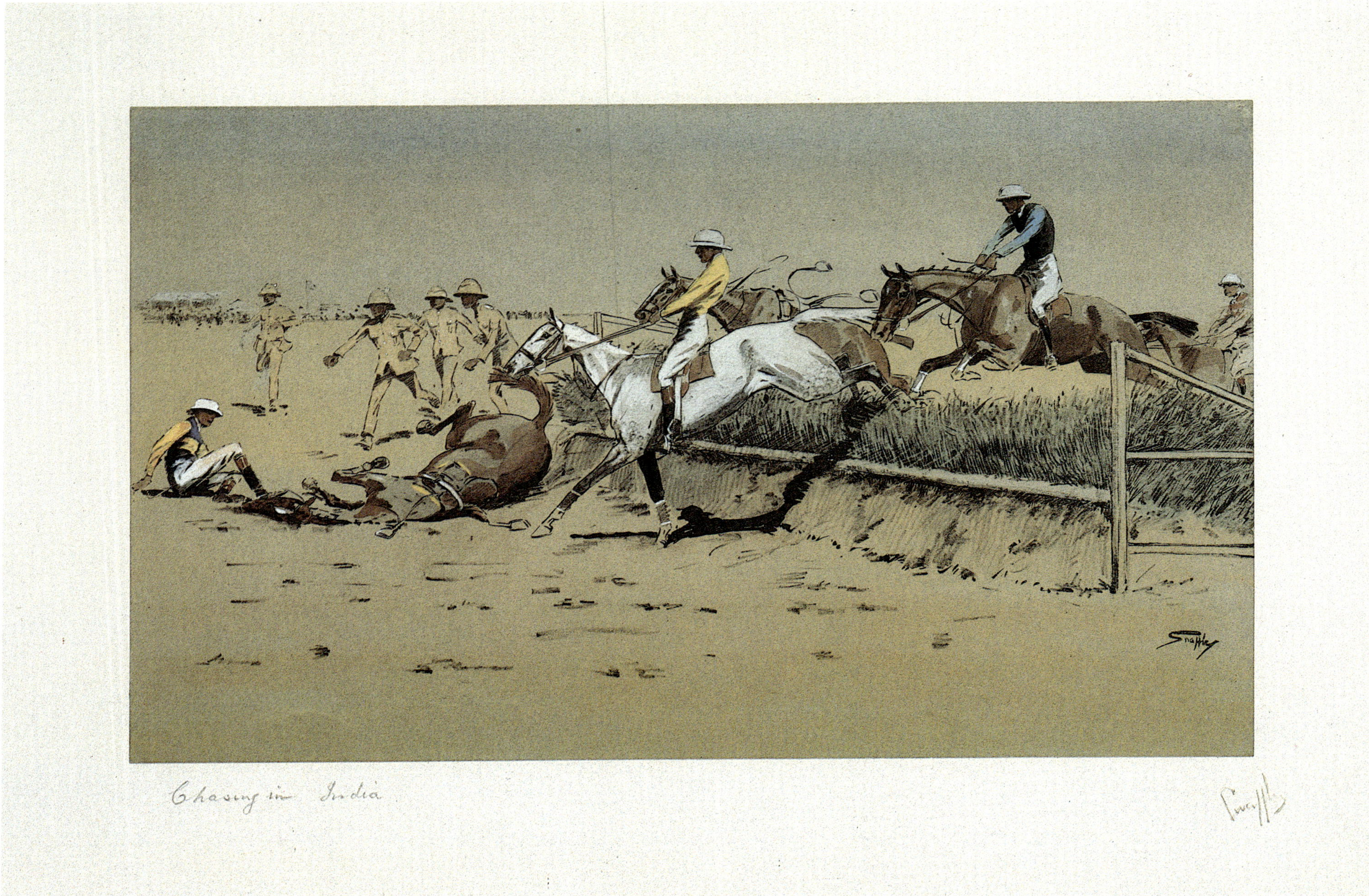

At the same time as he was producing his famous pre-First World War series of prints of individual soldiers he also produced a number of Indian and African subjects, including the one above

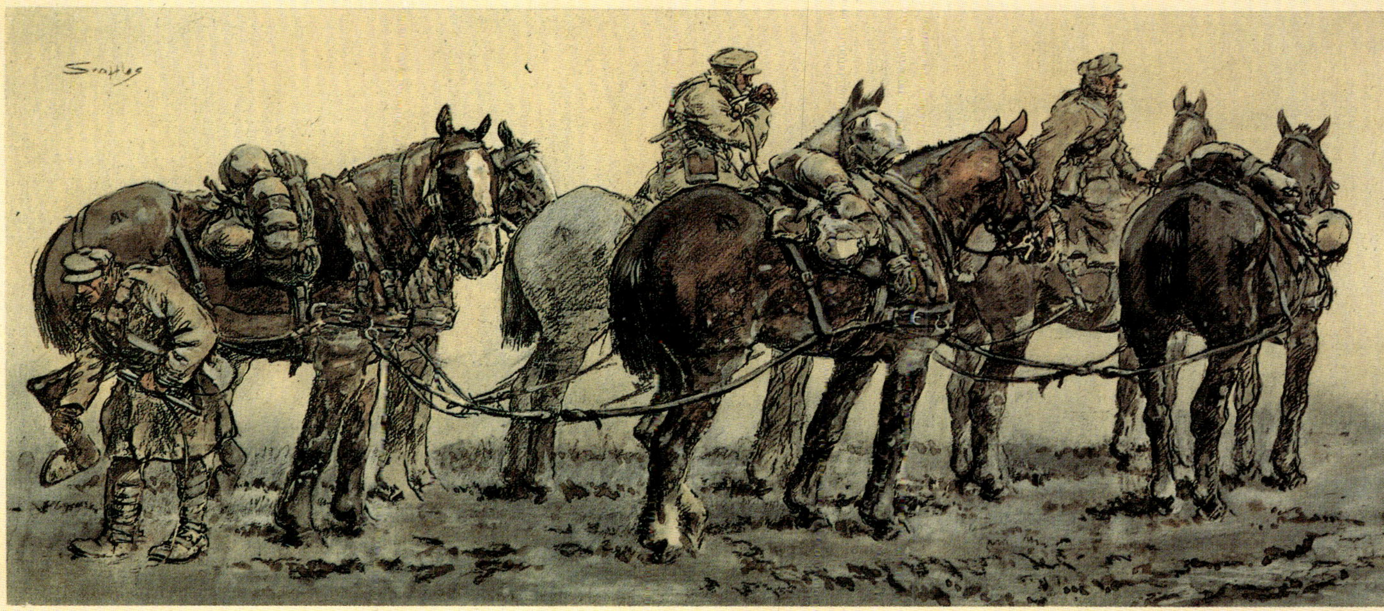

'Gunners'

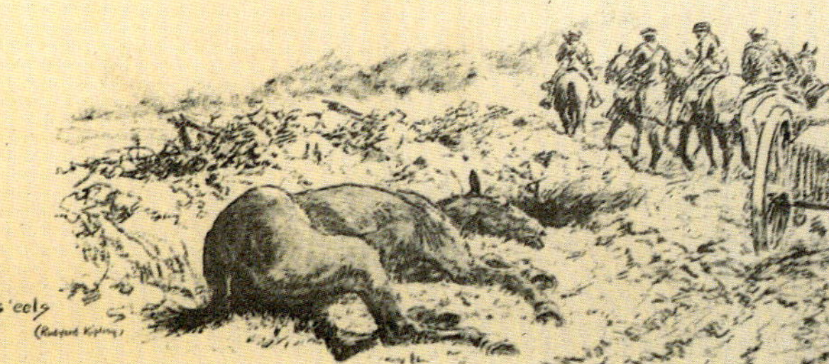

'There lay the driver's brother
with 'is 'ead between 'is 'eels
(Rudyard Kipling)

Snaffles perfected his drawing of heavy horses during the First World War, often in horrendous conditions

5 Peace

Perhaps the most important thing which happened to Snaffles during the years 1914–1918 was his marriage, on the 8 November 1915, at Exmouth, to Lucy Georgina Lewin. Lucy was petite, charming and attractive to all, but underneath this gentle exterior was a will of iron. She soon took Snaffles over, managed and mothered him, controlled his fecklessness and, more importantly, his finances, encouraged him in his work and stabilised his life. The marriage, a happy union of opposites, lasted over fifty years, until Snaffles' death in 1967, after which Lucy survived for several years.

The Paynes, Snaff and Lucy, set up home in Surrey, not far from Aldershot – the home of the British Army – and as soon as peace was declared Snaffles was back racing, frequenting point-to-points, 'bona-fide' meetings, and the smart and grand occasions at such courses as Aintree and Sandown. Many of his pre-war heroes were gone, claimed by the holocaust, Major Junks and Springer amongst them; although George Paynter had survived serious wounds to continue his riding career, and there was a new breed of Corinthians to take their place – Geoffrey Brooke, Taffy Walwyn, Mead Dennis, Paddy Doyle and Tuppy Bennett to name but a few. 'Nasty steeplechasing devils' he may have called them again and again, following Jorrocks, as he portrayed their style and dash, but they and his public knew that the quote was used in admiration and affection, not in deprecation and vituperation, as old Jorrocks had used it when they rode over his hounds.

As soon as the war was over, Snaffles started his love affair with the Grand National at Liverpool. He tells us that he visited the great race on nineteen occasions between the two wars, so he can only have missed two runnings between 1919 and 1939. He never wrote of attending pre-war races or submitted any illustrations to the glossy magazines, so we can assume that he was never there before 1919.

Snaffles could not have chosen a better year to attend his first National than 1919, or for that matter 1920 for his second, as the two winners of the races those years were not only individual horses of the stamp he so admired, but very, high class steeplechasers. The 1919 winner was the powerful bay gelding Poethlyn, owned and bred by Major Hugh Peel. Major Peel was one of the few people to land the Liverpool double, which then consisted of the Grand National and the Waterloo Cup – the blue ribands of steeplechasing and coursing respectively. In the years 1918/1919 Poethlyn won ten chases on the trot, including two Grand Nationals, the 1918 one over the reinforced fences at Gatwick and the 1919 one at Liverpool, the Lancashire Chase twice and the Prince of Wales Chase at Sandown; five major prizes and every time he carried over 12 stone. He was favourite for the 1920 National, but fell at the first and was promptly retired to Major Peel's Shropshire home where he had been bred. For the record he was trained down at Lewes by Harry Escott.

As we noted earlier, Poethlyn was ridden by Ernie Piggott in the 1918 Gatwick Grand National and the 1919 Liverpool Grand National. Snaffles would have been familiar with this top-class jockey for a long time, as he would have seen him when he was a young Gunner around 1903 at Portsmouth. Incidentally, Ernie Piggott was father of Keith Piggott, the well known National Hunt jockey, whose biggest triumph was the Champion Hurdle on African Sister in 1939. Although Keith Piggott never won the National as a jockey, he was successful in 1963 as the trainer of Ayala and was indeed Champion National Hunt Trainer that season. Keith Piggott is the father of Lester Piggott, whose greatness as a jockey needs no emphasis here.

The 1920 winner was an equally good steeplechaser, the enormous Troytown. Troytown was all of 17 hands and a great, fine, strong stamp of a horse with a tremendous front and great depth of heart. In fact he was so strong in front of the saddle he tended to look weak behind. This is brilliantly caught in the set of prints Snaffles' close friend Cecil Aldin did of the 1920 National. Troytown's first really major win was the most important steeplechase in France in 1919 – the Grand Steeplechase de Paris – when he made all the running and won under a beautiful ride from Anthony (Tony) Escott, the son of Harry Escott who had trained Poethlyn. In 1920 at 6 to 1 Troytown slammed the Grand National field and won by twelve and six lengths from The Turk and The Bore. Not only did he slam his field, he slammed quite a large number of the fences. He was one of the few high calibre horses who had the physique and agility to hit the Aintree fences hard and keep galloping. His whole performance in the National was sensational. He must have given his rider, Mr. Jack Anthony, a thrilling, but hair raising ride as he went straight to the front, pulling like a steam engine, made a series of mistakes, at two fences he hardly seemed to rise at all, and as Jack Anthony said afterwards 'he seemed to be trying to kick the fences out of the way'. He was still pulling like a steam engine when he passed the post for the second time and it took Jack Anthony nearly half a mile to stop him.

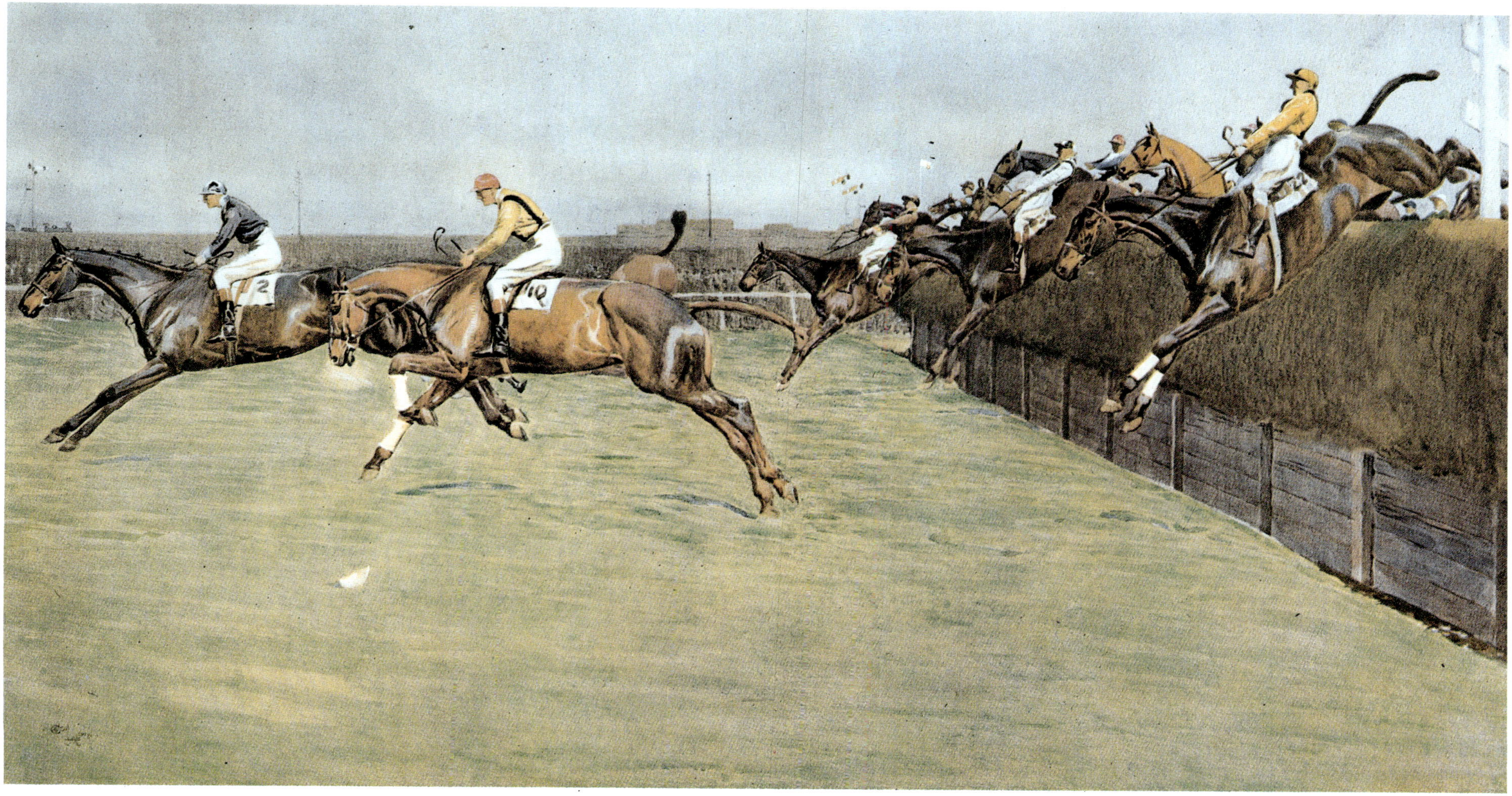

This print is from Cecil Aldin's great series of four of the 1920 race.
In all probability Snaffles went to the meeting with Aldin; certainly they would have met at Liverpool that year as Aldin spent a week there before, during and after the racing

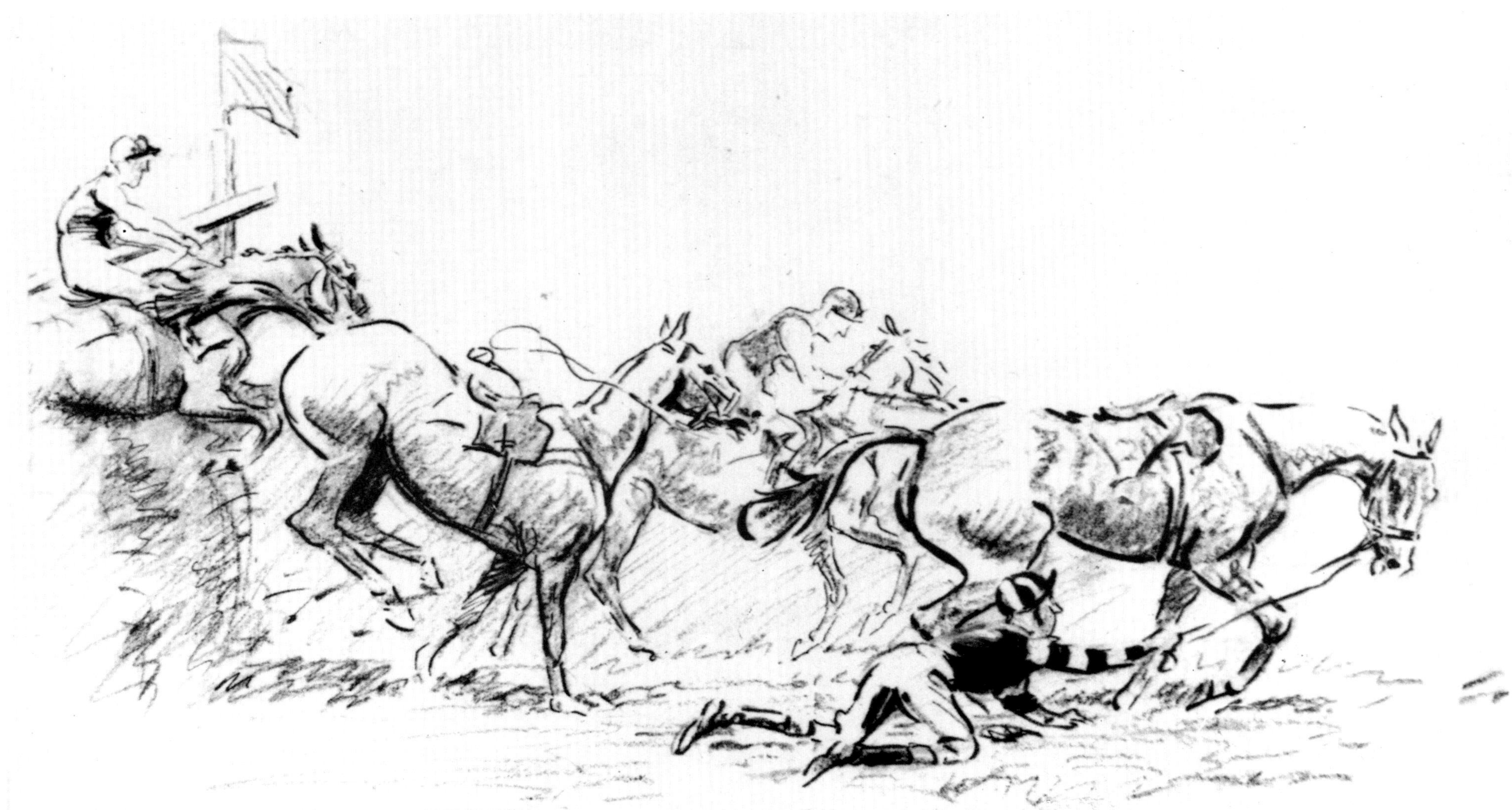

Styles in Falling

The Amateur

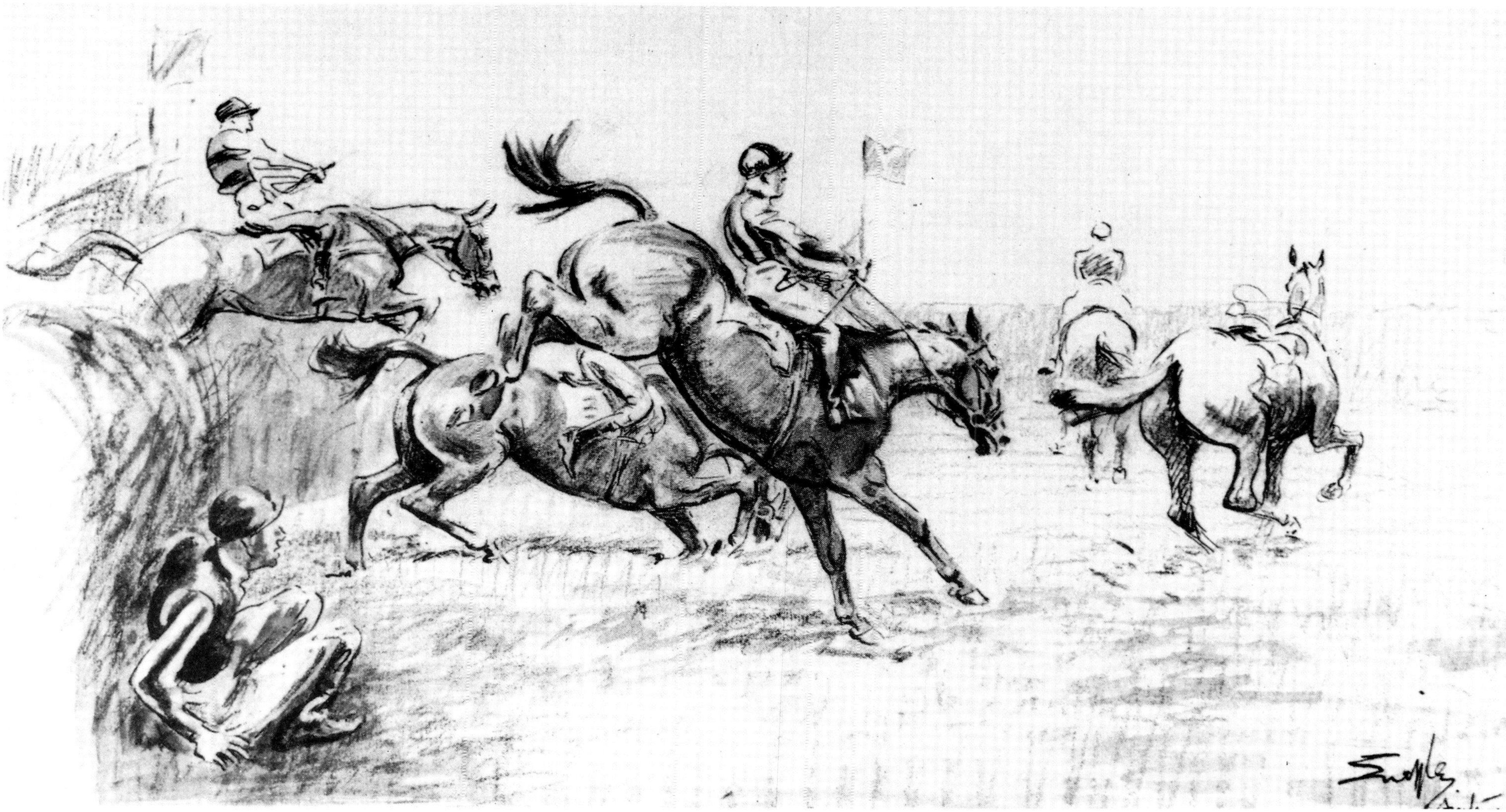

Styles in Falling

The Professor: 'Goodbye and a soldier's farewell to you!'

This pair of sketches from Liverpool sums up Snaffles' complete understanding of the Winter Game

Table E

GRAND NATIONAL			GOLD CUP			NATIONAL HUNT CHASE		
Year	*Horse*	*Value*	*Year*	*Horse*	*Value*	*Year*	*Horse*	*Value*
1924	Master Robert	£ 8,240	1924	Red Splash	£ 685	1924	Patsey V	£ 1,285
1925	Double Chance	£ 8,120	1925	Ballinode	£ 850	1925	Ardvasar	£ 1,360
1926	Jack Horner	£ 7,635	1926	Koko	£ 880	1926	Cloringo	£ 1,500
1927	Sprig	£ 8,215	1927	Thrown In	£ 780	1927	Fine Yarn	£ 1,545
1928	Tipperary Tim	£11,255	1928	Patron Saint	£ 780	1928	Cryptical	£ 1,460
1929	Gregalach	£13,000	1929	Easter Hero	£ 776	1929	Big Wonder	£ 1,403
1930	Shaun Goilin	£ 9,805	1930	Easter Hero	£ 670	1930	Sir Lindsay	£ 1,266
1931	Grakle	£ 9,385	1931	No Race		1931	Merriment IV	£ 590
1932	Forbra	£ 8,165	1932	Golden Miller	£ 670	1932	Robin-a-Tiptoe	£ 1,249
1933	Kellsboro' Jack	£ 7,345	1933	Golden Miller	£ 670	1933	Ego	£ 1,063
1934	Golden Miller	£ 7,265	1934	Golden Miller	£ 670	1934	Crown Prince	£ 1,142
1935	Reynoldstown	£ 6,545	1935	Golden Miller	£ 670	1935	Rod and Gun	£ 1,122
1936	Reynoldstown	£ 7,095	1936	Golden Miller	£ 670	1936	Pucka Belle	£ 1,155
1937	Royal Mail	£ 6,645	1937	No Race		1937	Hopeful Hero	£ 590
1938	Battleship	£ 7,598	1938	Morse Code	£ 720	1938	St. George II	£ 1,251
1939	Workman	£ 7,284	1939	Brendan's Cottage	£ 1,120	1939	Litigant	£ 1,284
1940	Bogskar	£ 4,225	1940	Roman Hackle	£ 495	1940	No Race	
1941	No Race		1941	Poet Prince	£ 495	1941	No Race	
1942	No Race		1942	Medoc II	£ 495	1942	No Race	
1943	No Race		1943	No Race		1943	No Race	
1944	No Race		1944	No Race		1944	No Race	
1945	No Race		1945	Red Rower	£ 340	1945	No Race	
1946	Lovely Cottage	£ 8,805	1946	Prince Regent	£ 1,130	1946	Prattler	£ 1,036
1947	Caughoo	£10,007	1947	Fortina	£ 1,140	1947	Maltese Wanderer	£ 835
1948	Sheila's Cottage	£ 9,103	1948	Cottage Rake	£ 1,911	1948	Bruno II	£ 1,115
1949	Russian Hero	£ 9,528	1949	Cottage Rake	£ 2,818	1949	Castledermot	£ 921
1950	Freebooter	£ 9,314	1950	Cottage Rake	£ 2,937	1950	Ellesmere	£ 977
1951	Nickel Coin	£ 8,815	1951	Silver Fame	£ 2,784	1951	Cushendun	£ 858
1952	Teal	£ 9,268	1952	Mont Tremblant	£ 3,233	1952	Frosty Knight	£ 1,085
1953	Early Mist	£ 9,330	1953	Knock Hard	£ 3,258	1953	Pontage	£ 2,226
1954	Royal Tan	£ 8,571	1954	Four Ten	£ 3,576	1954	Quare Times	£ 2,245
1955	Quare Times	£ 8,934	1955	Gay Donald	£ 3,776	1955	Reverend Prince	£ 2,148
1988	Rhyme 'n Reason	£85,881	1988	Charter Party	£61,960	1988	Over the Road	£13,812

Obviously the Grand Nationals of 1919 and 1920 fascinated Snaffles and the race dominated his racing paintings for the whole period between the wars, rather as the Grand Military had in the few years leading up to the First World War.

Back in Snaffles' early racing days, between 1903 and 1914, the Grand National was by far the most important race. This was followed in prestige by the four miles Amateur Riders National Hunt Chase which moved from course to course as we have commented earlier in the book (see Table A). In fact, right through the twenties and, to a lesser extent, through the thirties, the Grand National stood unrivalled as the blue riband of steeplechasing. It was not until 1924 with the introduction of the Cheltenham Gold Cup over three miles and two furlongs that there was anything approaching a championship weight-for-age race for steeplechasers. Even then for years the Gold Cup was regarded as a superior National trial, the prize money remaining below that of the National Hunt Chase (see Table E), for some time and for people such as Snaffles, the National Hunt Chase would have taken pride of place at Cheltenham. As Clive Graham of The Daily Express was to write some years later, 'A bustle of wives and others and girl-friends surround the riders in the paddock. The paddock rails are thronged with tweed-clad critics ... the rush to cheer the winner as he comes back to the unsaddling enclosure is evoked by a sincere and genuine sentiment quite unconnected with pecuniary gain'. And Snaffles would have been one of the most enthusiastic and knowing of those 'tweed-clad critics'.

These inter-war years were the time of Snaffles greatness as a sporting artist. The grandees on the flat at the time may have castigated steeplechasing as an occupation for 'the needy and the greedy' and indeed one of them, when asked if he had been to the National Hunt meeting at Cheltenham, offered the opinion that he would have preferred to go dog-racing, but to Snaffles, the soldier-riders and their like, steeplechasing was where, in the words of Molly Keane in another context, 'the real blood and bones of the sport lay'.

The years 1921/2 saw the publication of Snaffles' two most famous prints which, in truth, are two of the most famous sporting prints produced this century, 'The Finest View in Europe' and 'The Worst View in Europe'. The genesis of the first of these has been dealt with in some detail in the first book of this series [*Snaffles – The Life and Work of Charlie Johnson Payne 1884–1967*] and of the second in an earlier chapter of this book, but it may be of interest to note that Rifle Brigade, the horse which gave Snaffles the splendid hunt that he says inspired 'The Finest View' was not a grey as in the print, but a bay. Snaffles no doubt changed the colour to heighten the effect of the print by contrast, as indeed it does.

Soon after completing this pair of prints, his eye and affection were caught by another horse who was to become the first of his inter-war equine heroes. This was Sergeant Murphy, a big raking chestnut, a real Aintree type who he painted in action again and again and who is said to be the model, some ten years later, for the picture of 'A National Candidate', one of the set of prints published under the title 'Osses and Obstacles' in 1932. Ridden by Captain Tuppy Bennett, after running promisingly the year before and winning the Scottish Grand National, Sergeant Murphy won the big one at Aintree in 1923 at the age of thirteen, the oldest horse ever to win. Captain Bennett, one of the most popular of the soldier riders and the leading amateur that year, died some months later from injuries received to his head after a fall at Wolverhampton, an accident which led to the compulsory wearing of crash helmets.

Sergeant Murphy carried the colours of the well-known polo playing American, Laddie Sanford, and was just the sort of gallant old campaigner to catch Snaffles' imagination. Snaffles painted him twice in that winning National, once as 'The Game Old Sergeant', and once as he and his rider attacked Becher's with such dash as to make a member of the crowd cry out 'Ba goom, canna that old chestnut horse jump!', a phrase which Snaffles eagerly seized on and used as his caption.

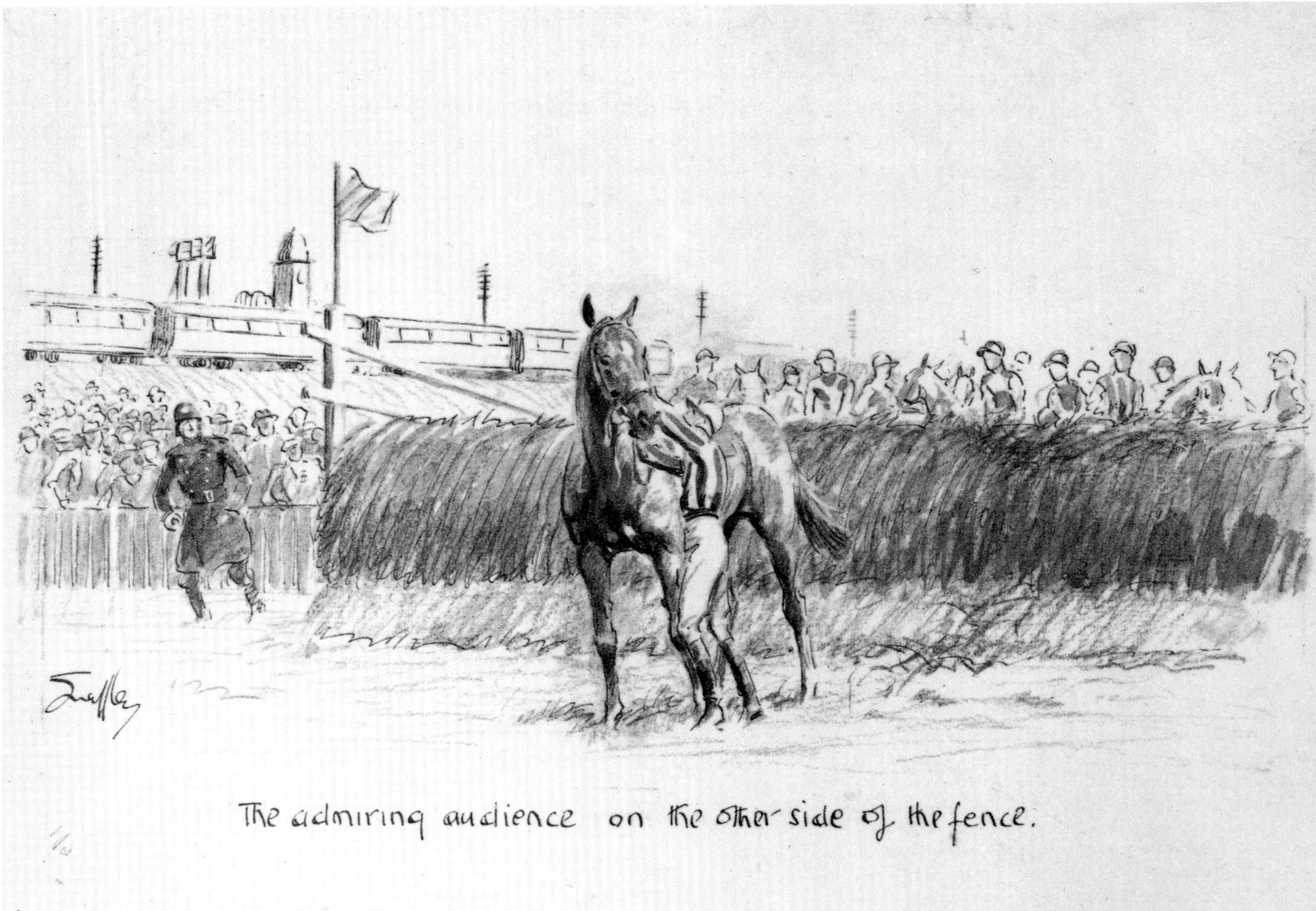

These two pictures were drawn nearly thirty years after the events depicted, for one of Snaffles' autobiographies

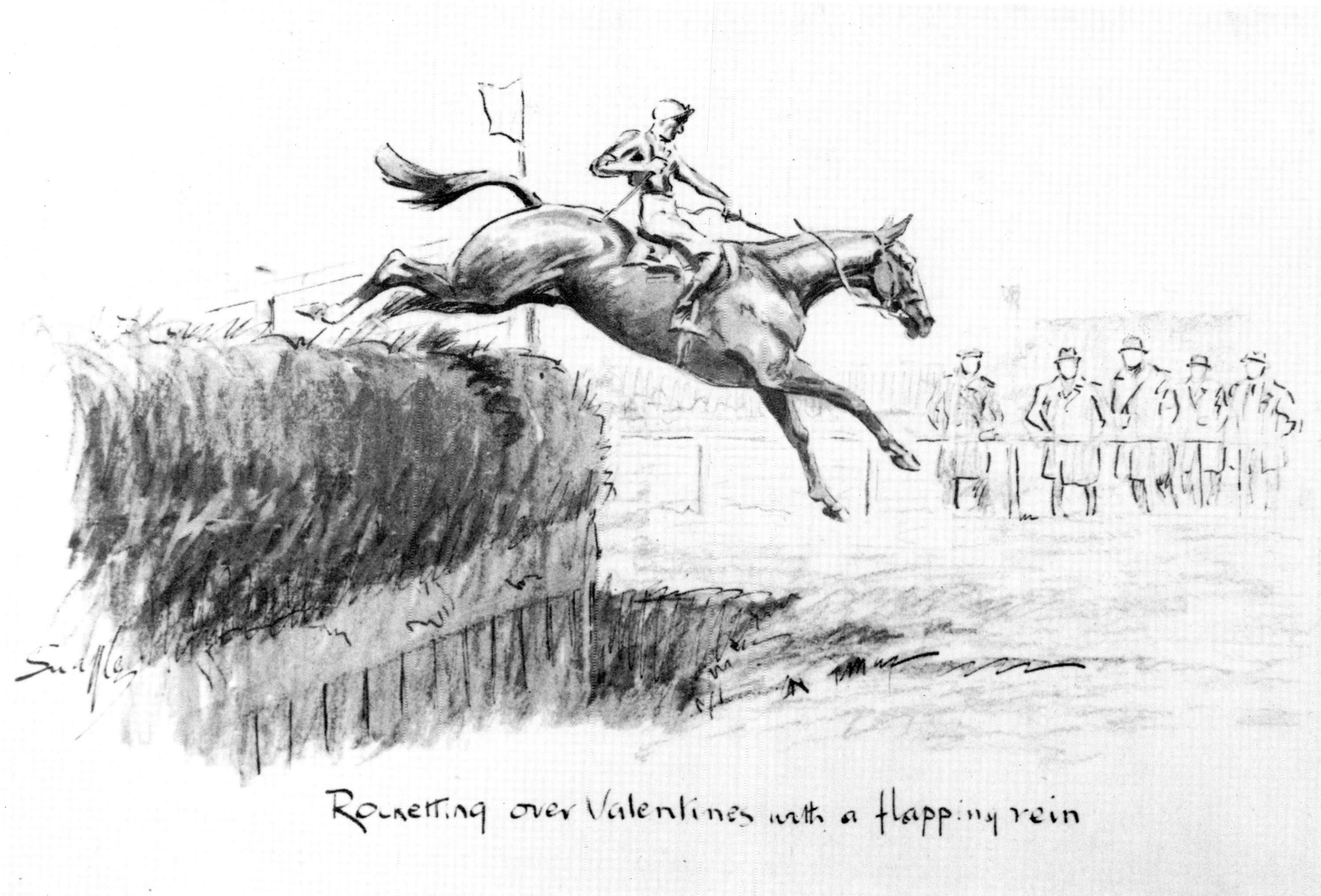

Snaffles probably fell in love with Sergeant Murphy in the 1922 Grand National when the great horse stood and let his jockey rebridle him after they parted company, and then finished the course with only one rein.

This print was produced nearly ten years after Sergeant Murphy's Grand National win as part of a set of prints entitled ''Osses and Obstacles'. It is clearly based on 'the old sergeant' as Snaffles used to refer to him

Opposite is the centrepiece of the print blown up. The authors both consider this to be Snaffles' greatest print of a horse in repose as opposed to in action

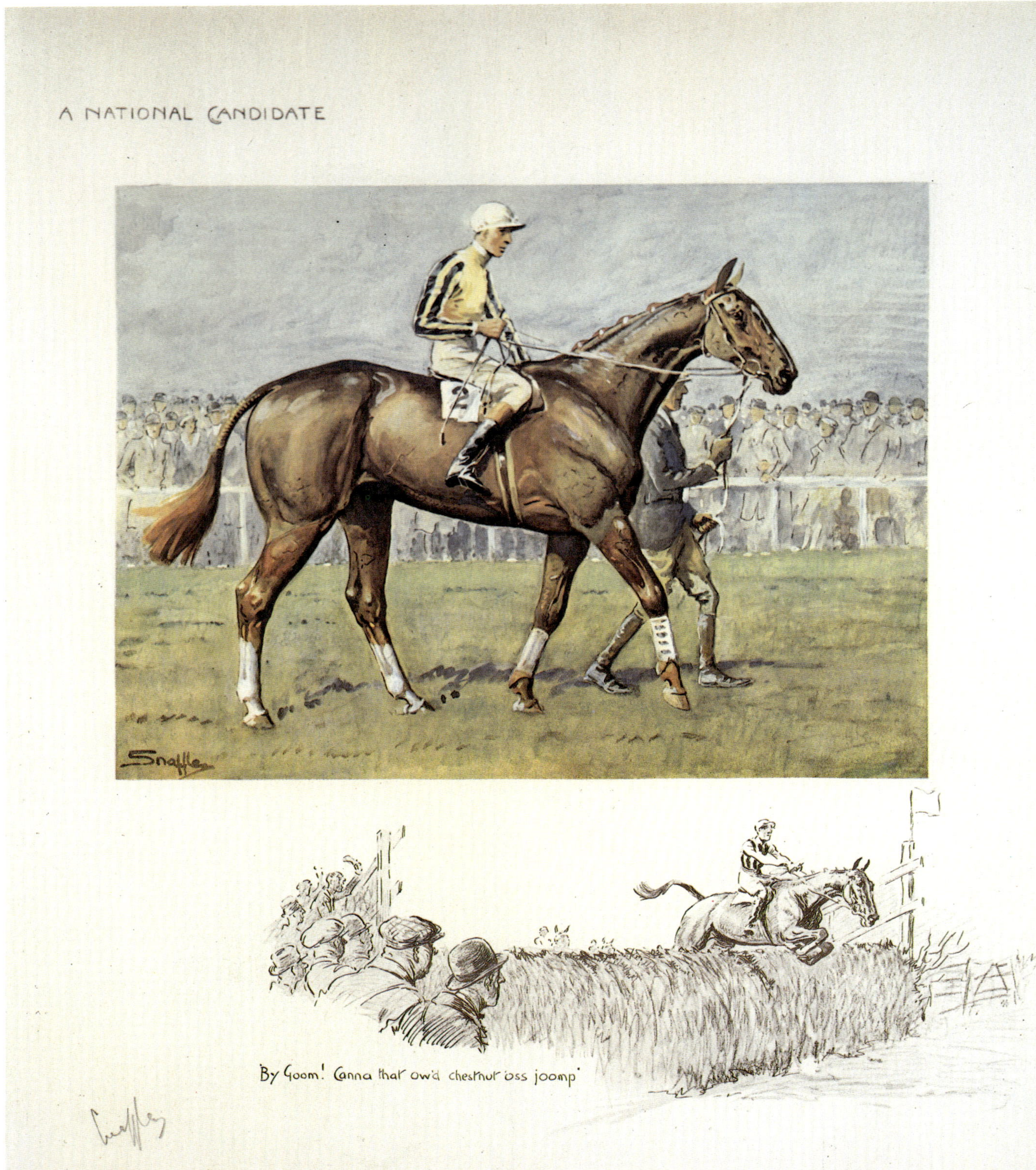

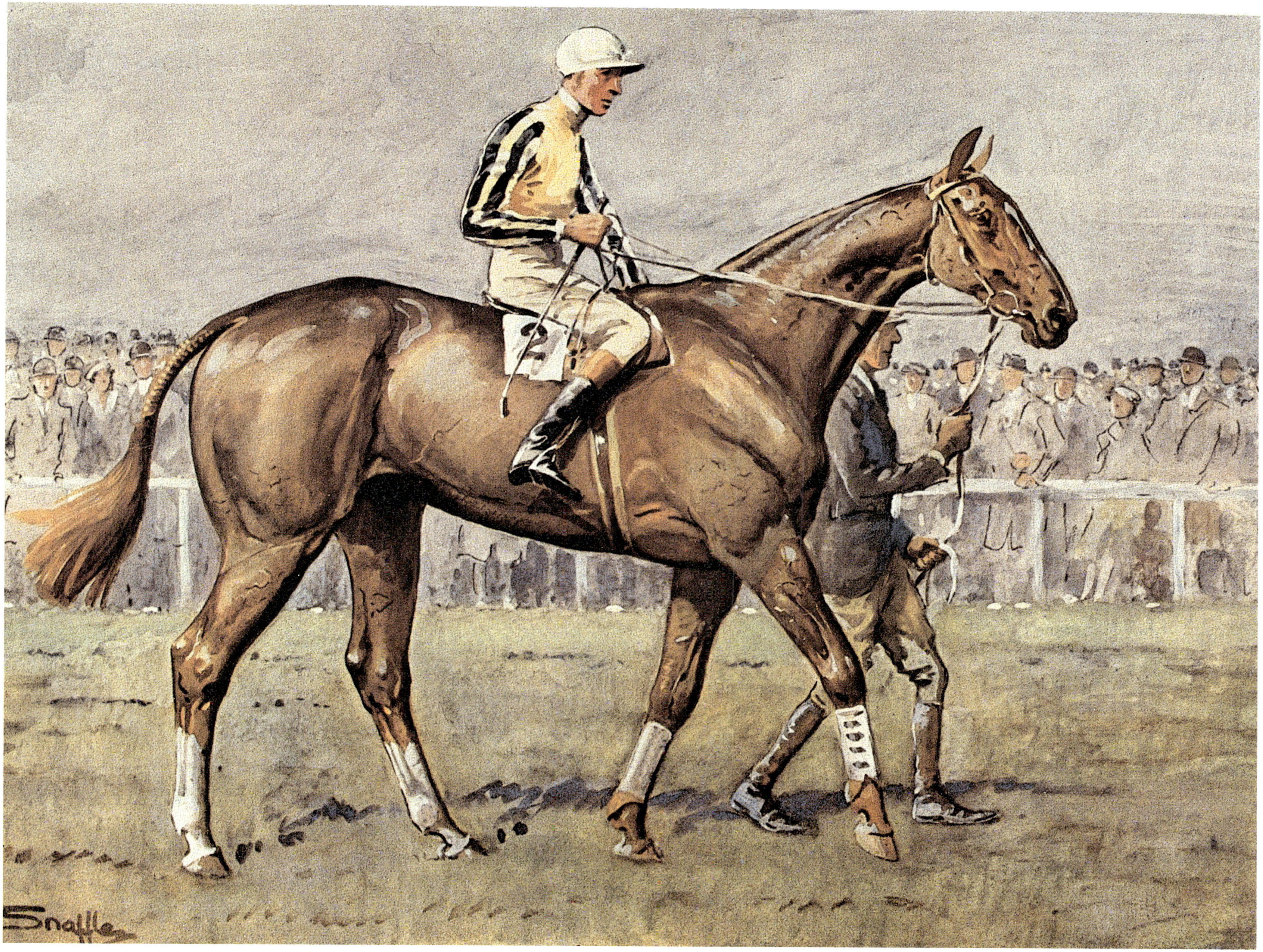
Snaffles

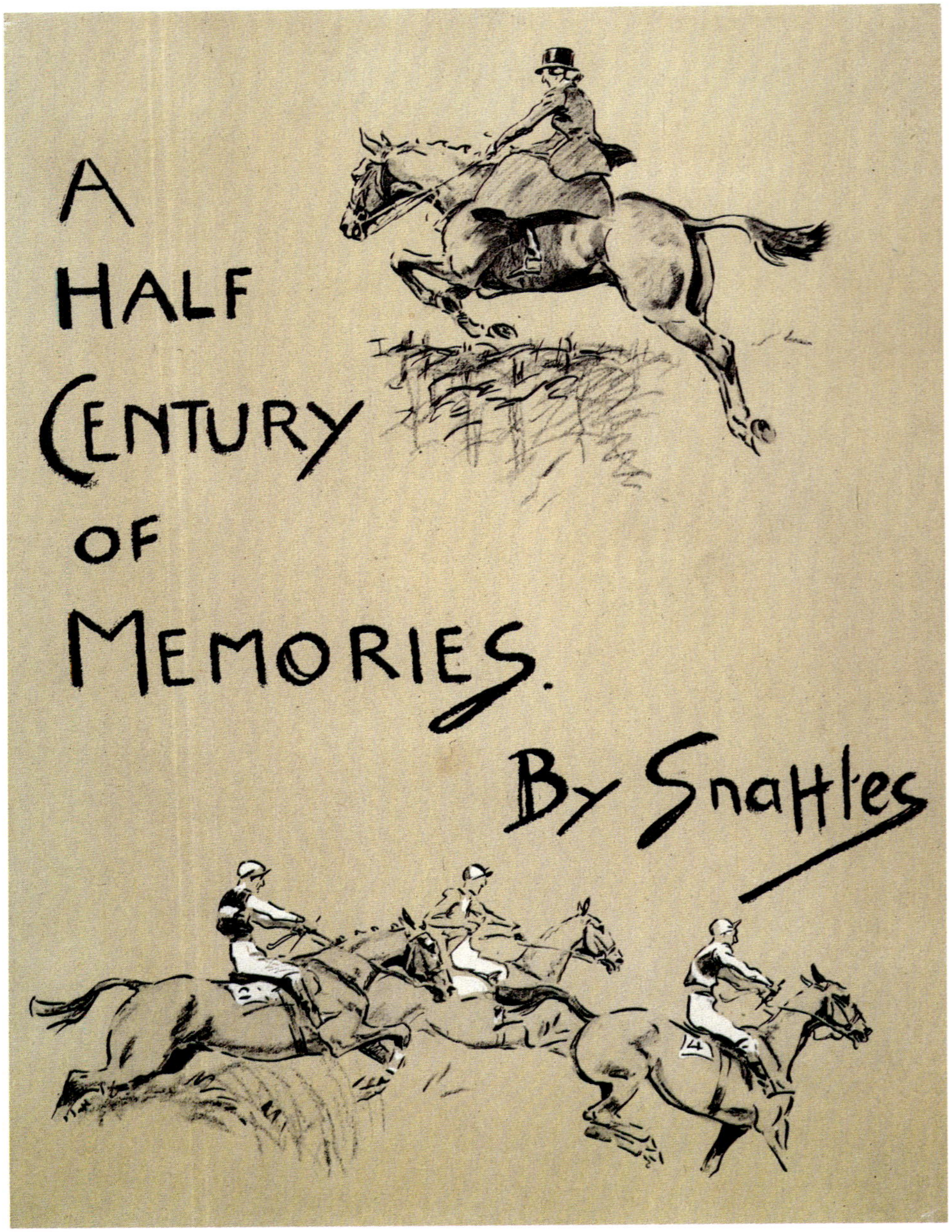

Snaffles' drawings on buff paper, highlighted with white, for the dust wrappers of his books, were very effective. He used steeplechasing only once, as above, which is obviously a scene from Liverpool

As Sergeant Murphy, along with Connie were undoubtedly Snaffles' two favourite horses, perhaps we should pause a little longer before moving on. Sergeant Murphy was bred by Mr. G.L. Walker, by General Symonds from the good chasing mare Rose Croft who was by Ascetic. Ascetic dominated National Hunt breeding from around 1888 to 1904, and sired three National winners in Cloister, Drumcree and Ascetic's Silver, and was the maternal grandsire not only of Sergeant Murphy, but also Troytown. Sergeant Murphy won ten chases in total. His major win, other than the National, was the Scottish Grand National at Bogside in 1922, but it was for his performance in the National that he was to become so well known. He ran in the first two Nationals which Snaffles watched, finishing sixth to Poethlyn in 1919 and fourth to Troytown in 1920.

Sergeant Murphy was fourth again in 1922, having unshipped his rider at the Canal Turn. He waited patiently for his jockey, C. Hawkins, to put the bridle back on and then carried Hawkins safely on to finish the course. After parting company at the Canal Turn, more commonly known as the Canal Ditch then, Hawkins was purely a passenger as he found the reins had been broken in the fall. Only three horses finished without a fall, and when Sergeant Murphy and Hawkins set off in pursuit they were some minutes behind the leaders who were out of view, so it must have taken some determination for both horse and rider to jump the last six fences in cold blood with no effective method of control.

The following year Sergeant Murphy went on to win as already described. He was trained by George Blackwell, who had won the 1903 Derby with Rocksand, thus becoming the third trainer to have a winner of both the Derby and the Grand National. The previous trainers were James Jewitt and Richard Dawson. Since then this select group has become five, as Willie Stevenson and Vincent O'Brien have both achieved the double.

Sergeant Murphy's Grand National Record

Year	*Age*	*Jockey*	*Weight*	*Result*
1919	9	S. Walkington	10.7	Sixth
1920	10	W. Smith	10.1	Fourth
1921	Did not run			
1922	12	C. Hawkins	11.0	Fourth (re-mounted)
1923	13	Capt. G.H. Bennett	11.3	Won
1924	14	C. Hogan	11.10	Fifth
1925	15	A. Escott	11.7	Tenth (re-mounted)

Sergeant Murphy also ran in substitute races at Gatwick during the First World War.

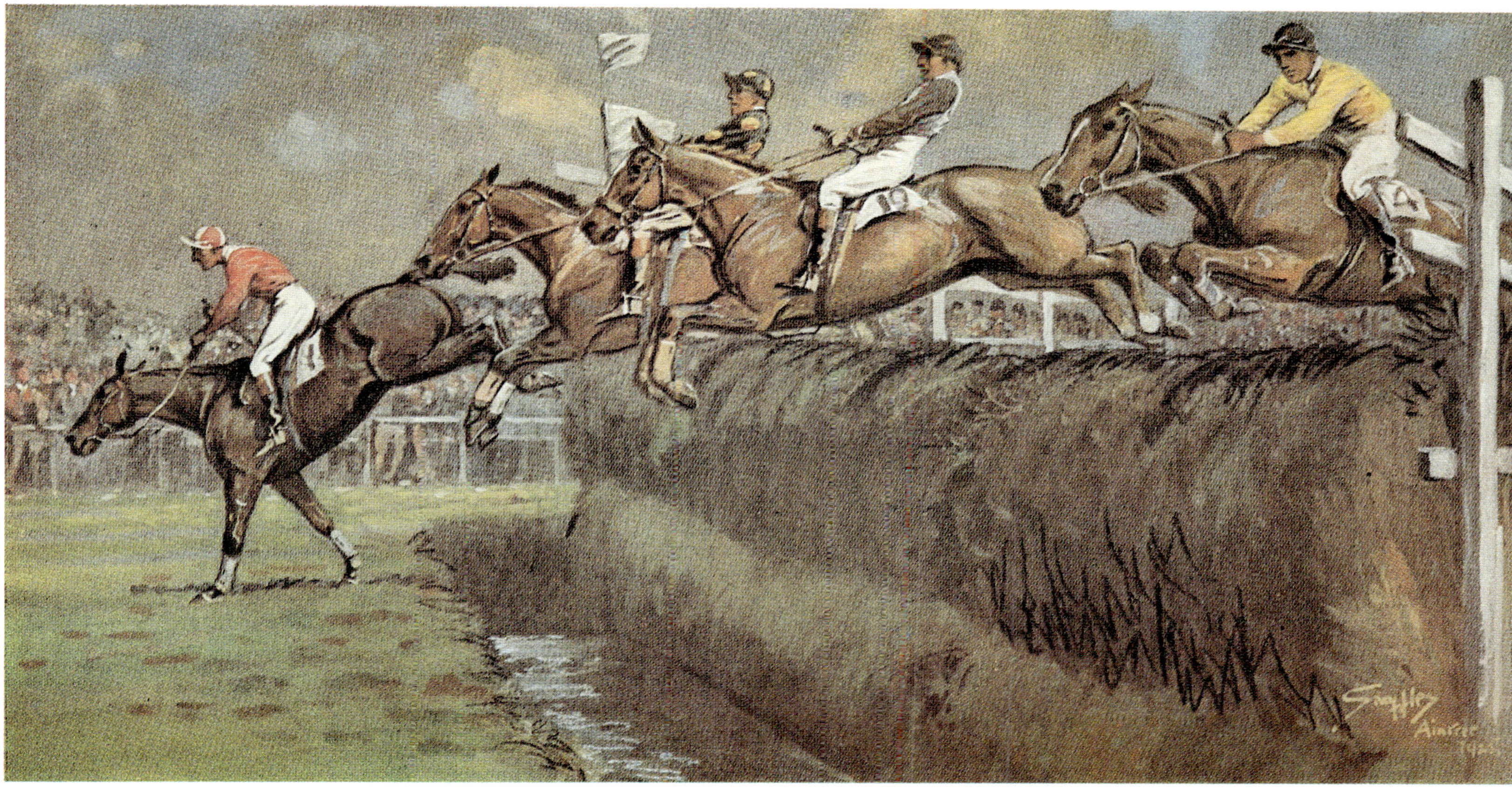

The Grand National, 1925

Evens on the field at Valentines the second time round;
left to right: Silvo (F.B. Rees), Fly Mask (Paddy Doyle), Double Chance (Major Wilson), Old Tay Bridge (Jack Anthony)

We stay with Snaffles and the Grand National, as soon were to follow two of his most effective racing pictures, the second, being his greatest, and it makes Snaffles undoubtedly one of the best artists ever to paint the great race. The first, 'Valentines the second time round', is a representation of the field in 1925 at Valentines. Snaffles has himself named the horses and riders whose styles he has caught with his accustomed accuracy. Paddy Doyle and Major Wilson, who rode Double Chance, the eventual winner, are leaning well back, while Jack Anthony, who had turned professional by that time and was one of the first of the 'professors' to adopt the modern semi-forward seat, is 'sitting up his neck' on old Tay Bridge.

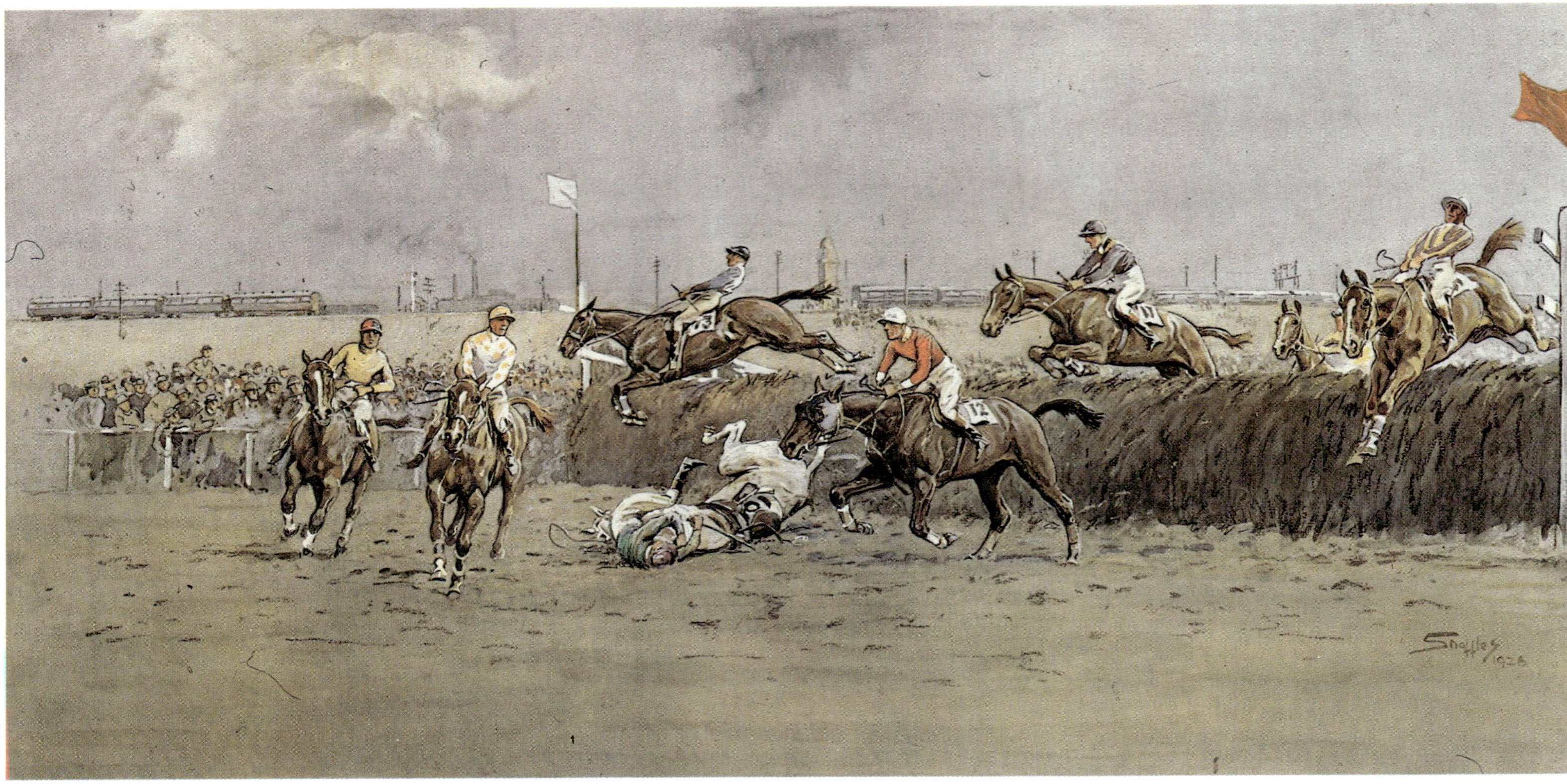

The Grand National

The Canal Turn

Left to right: Sprig (fourth after starting favourite), Jack Horner (the winner), Master Willie (sixth), White Surrey (falling), Darracq (fifth), Thrown In (eighth), Old Tay Bridge (second), and Bright's Boy (third)

The second painting, 'The Canal Turn', in the 1926 race won by Jack Horner and ridden by W. Watkins, first appeared in *The Illustrated Sporting and Dramatic News*. It is clear that his love remained always for the kind of horse that could handle 'Liverpool, Leicestershire and Limerick' if asked. Snaffles had the watercolour turned into a print and inscribed it 'in memory of the Old Sergeant and Geoffrey Bennett' and added a colour remarque of a steeplechaser jumping a fence, obviously based on Sergeant Murphy.

The grey horse and rider falling in the foreground are sometimes wrongly identified as White Surrey and Taffy Walwyn, as in the first book of this series on Snaffles. That is incorrect, since Taffy Walwyn never rode White Surrey in the National, although he did win the Grand Military on him in 1920. In that year, 1926, White Surrey was ridden in the National by a professional, Farragher, for Sir Hedworth Meux. Major Walwyn, by the mid-twenties, was becoming one of Snaffles' closest friends and his son, Peter, now a leading flat race trainer, was to become Snaffles' godson. Taffy Walwyn had however ridden in the National back in 1911 on Great Cross and taken a heavy fall. So when Snaffles presented him with a copy of his print of the 1926 race, he did, as he so often did for Taffy Walwyn, a special remarque. This time it was of Walwyn being helped into an ambulance and Snaffles inscribed the remarque 'To Taffy from Snaffles a memory (rather a sad one) of Glenside's year', all of which may have helped to give rise to the misidentification of White Surrey's rider in the 1926 race. So that further misconceptions do not arise, Glenside was the winner of the 1911 race! He was a one-eyed unsound horse, but the only horse to get round without a fall in the very bad conditions of 1911.

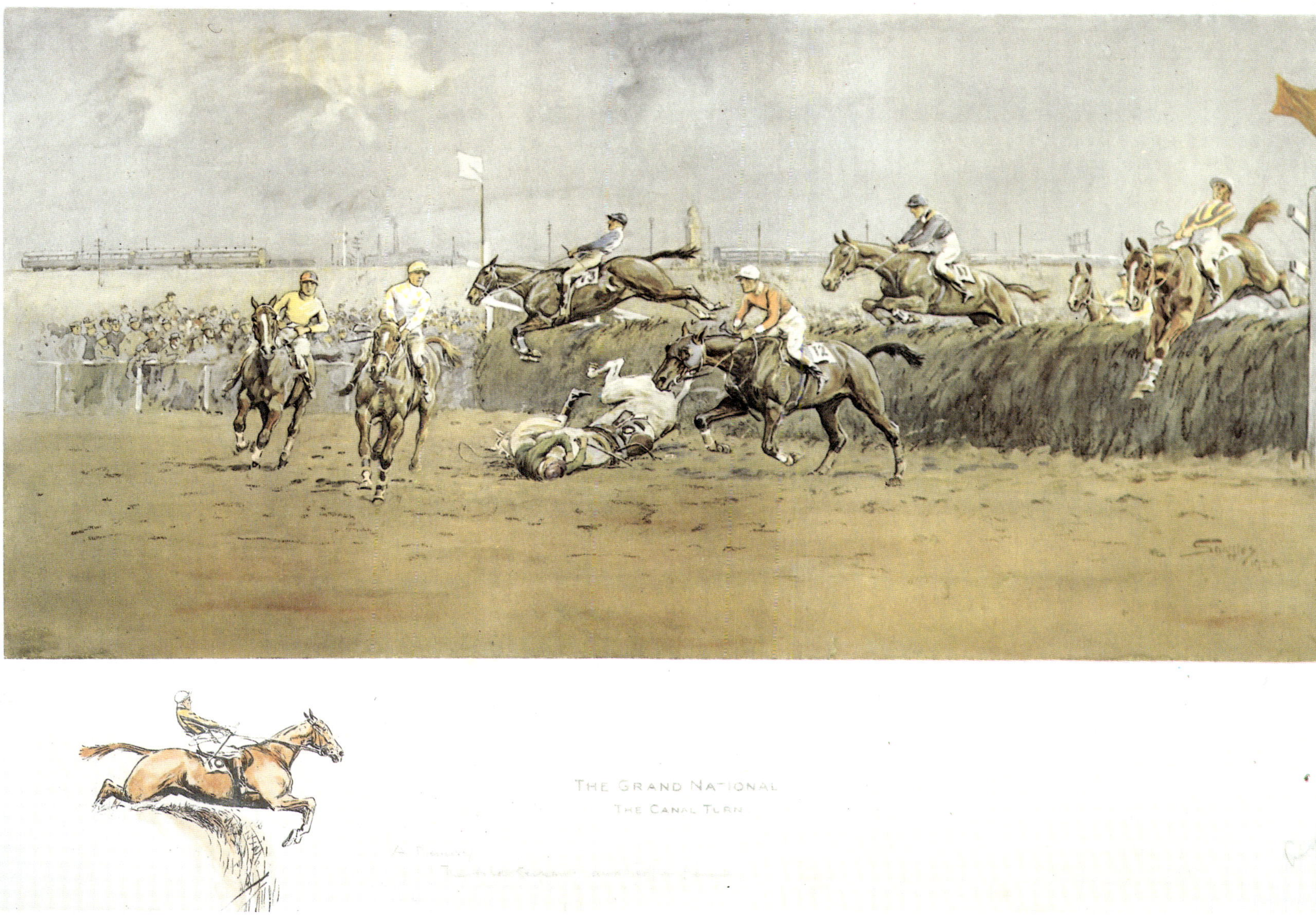

This print is one of the most popular ever produced of the Grand National, and avidly collected the world over. The horse jumping the right hand corner is Bright's Boy who was third, running in the colours of the famous polo player, S Sandford. The same colours were carried to victory in 1923 by Sergeant Murphy, the horse in the remarque

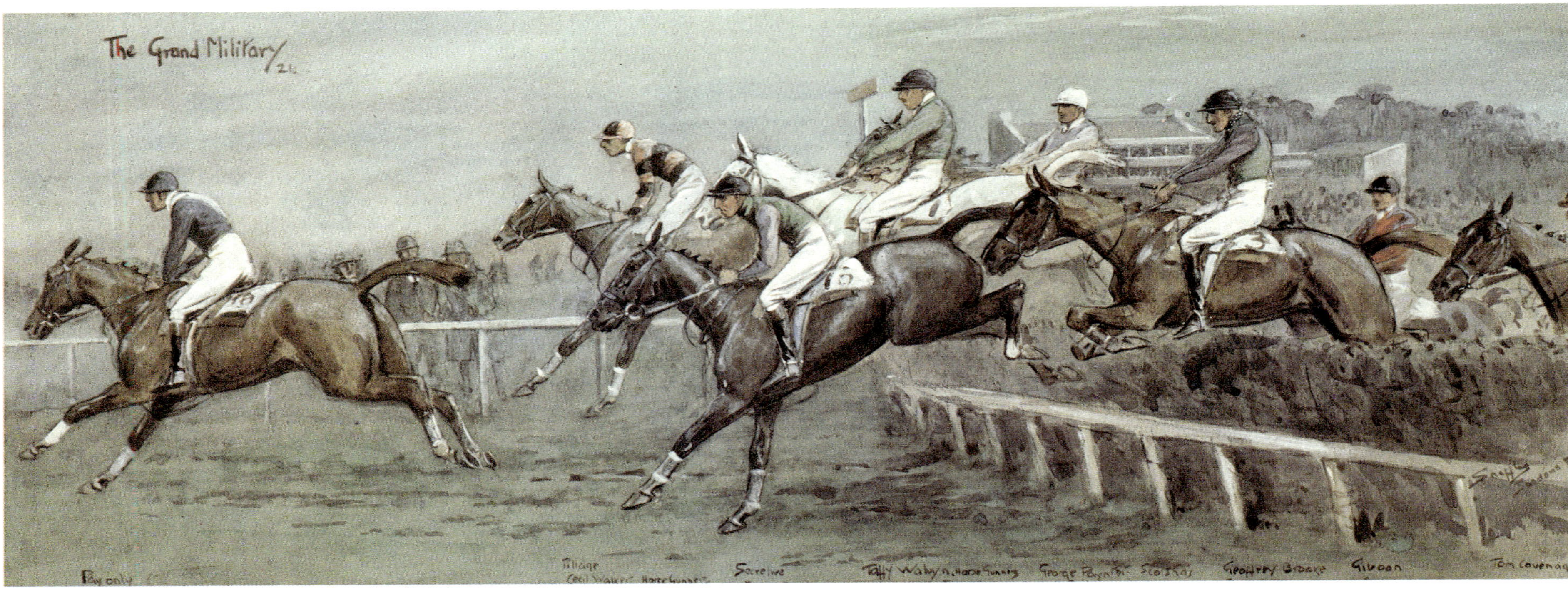

The Grand Military 1921

At Sandown Snaffles was busy too. 1921 was a vintage year for soldier riders. There was a tremendous camaraderie and sporting spirit amongst those who rode and raced and Snaffles was there to record that spirit and their races. He immortalised that band of brothers in his picture of the Grand Military in 1921 'A Sheet would cover 'em'. This first appeared as part of 'Pages from a Chasing Artists Sketchbook' in *The Illustrated Sporting and Dramatic News* in April 1921. Afterwards Snaffles worked on it, and having perfected it, presented the original to Colonel, later Major-General, Geoffrey Brooke, who in turn gave it to his son, Peter Brooke, in whose possession it remains today. No prints were ever made of this picture which is one of Snaffles' finest.

Moreover, not only is it a particularly fine steeplechasing picture, it is of historical interest since it shows the field crossing one of the three railway fences at Sandown, with the old stands and the King Edward Stand in the background. In the original picture which Snaffles presented, he has brushed in the names of those he portrayed and it is worth recording them since they constitute what might have been called a roll call of the best and bravest of the military riders of the day. They are: Pay Only (Filmer Sankey) the ultimate winner, landing about two lengths clear of his field. Behind Pay Only in a bunch are Pillage (Cecil Walker), Secretive (E.C. 'Paddy' Doyle), White Surrey (Taffy Walwyn), Delirium (George Paynter), Rufus (Geoffrey Brooke) and Colonel Gibbon and Tom Cavenagh on their horses which Snaffles did not name. Not only were the riders of the highest calibre and able to hold their own with the top professionals of the day, the horses themselves were very nearly in the highest class. Pay Only had already won an Irish Grand National and White Surrey was decidedly useful.

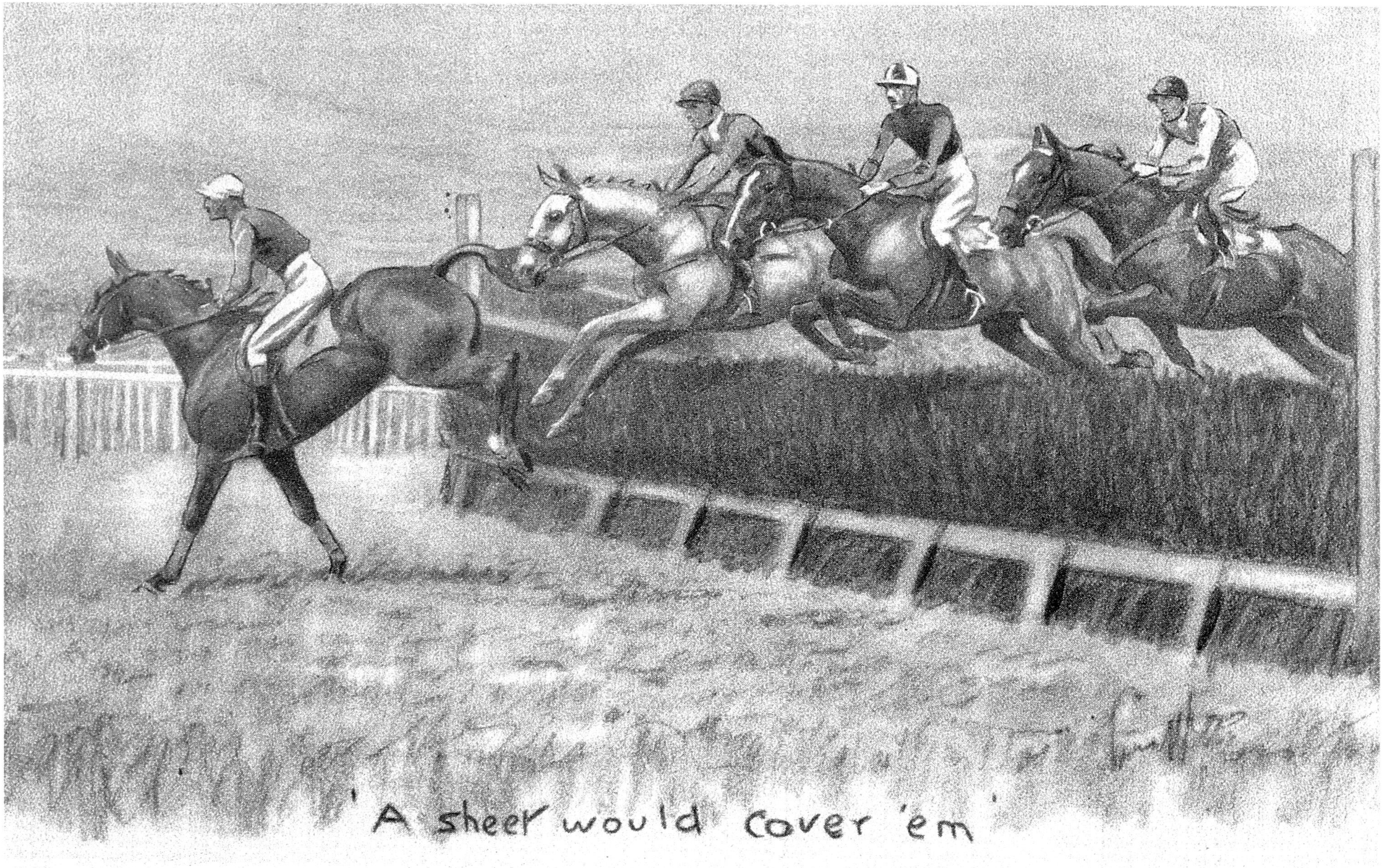

This drawing, done in the late 1940s or early 1950s was based on Snaffles' great watercolour of 1921, but here he has selected four of his favourite riders.

Leading the group is George Paynter (though some say it is Geoffrey Brooke); on the grey is Taffy Walwyn, third is Pippin, ridden by Mead Dennis (not Bill Bedford as we said in the last book), and fourth is Paddy Doyle

Geoffrey Brooke, arguably the best all round horseman ever to be produced by the British Army, whose ambition it was to win the Grand Military, probably went as near to winning it that year as he was ever to do – with the wrong horse! 1921 was a splendid year for him. He won the King George V Cup, show-jumping at Olympia, on his charger Combined Training, who had been badly wounded twice in the war and nursed back to health and fitness by him. In accomplishing this feat he became the first Englishman ever to do so. At the Staff College Drag Point-to-Point he won three out of the six races on Secretive, whom he had bought cheaply in Ireland on the recommendation of his Uncle Heremon Lindsey Fitzpatrick, and he had many other winners, both under Rules and in point-to-points, but his luck was out in the Grand Military.

In those days, if you ran more than one horse in a race you had to declare to win with one or the other. Brooke entered Rufus XXI and Secretive, electing to win with Rufus whom he chose to ride himself, putting up Paddy Doyle on Secretive. In Brooke's memoirs, he says that he was knocked over at the second last when he was sure he was going like a winner, and Paddy Doyle only failed by a neck to catch Pay Only. Secretive, incidentally, after losing by a neck in a gruelling finish in the big soldiers' race, was pulled out the next day and, ridden by Doyle, won his race by eight lengths. As Peter Brooke comments 'They either bred or trained tougher horses in those days!'

In his recollections, Snaffles, who was standing at his accustomed position down the course, records what happened to Brooke's two horses rather differently from the account given by Brooke in his memoirs. Snaffles states that Brooke did not fall but, landing over the second last fence and getting no response from his horse, knew he was beat so called out to his second string, as he was entitled to do, 'Come on Paddy'. It is, however, more probable that once again in old age Snaffles' memory betrayed him and that it was from the ground after his fall that Brooke called out the encouragement, but it makes a nice sketch, Snaffles having caught the action of a tired and struggling horse with his usual accuracy. It makes, too, a good story which he always relished, as does his picture of the young Sapper, Tubby Simon, winning his race at the same meeting with a slipped saddle 'underneath the horse's belly'.

When Brooke took to writing, it was to Snaffles he turned to illustrate his novel *Horse Lovers*. Snaffles was not at his best as a book illustrator, but the head of Crusader, the chief equine character in the book, which appears as the colour frontispiece is effective. The racing scenes too are spirited and give life to Crusader's race and its aftermath. Many are very similar to the great illustrator, Cecil Aldin's, work when he was illustrating the Poet Laureate John Masefield's *Right Royal*, and one feels that Snaffles may have discussed his work for *Horse Lovers* with his close friend Aldin. Geoffrey Brooke, with his superb accomplishment in every aspect of horsemanship and his versatility with the pen, as well as the racing whip, was fully entitled to enter into Snaffles' pantheon of heroes and, if the bond between them was never so close as that with Taffy Walwyn, Peter Brooke has summed it up well by saying 'they were both masters of their art and I feel the relationship was one of mutual admiration'.

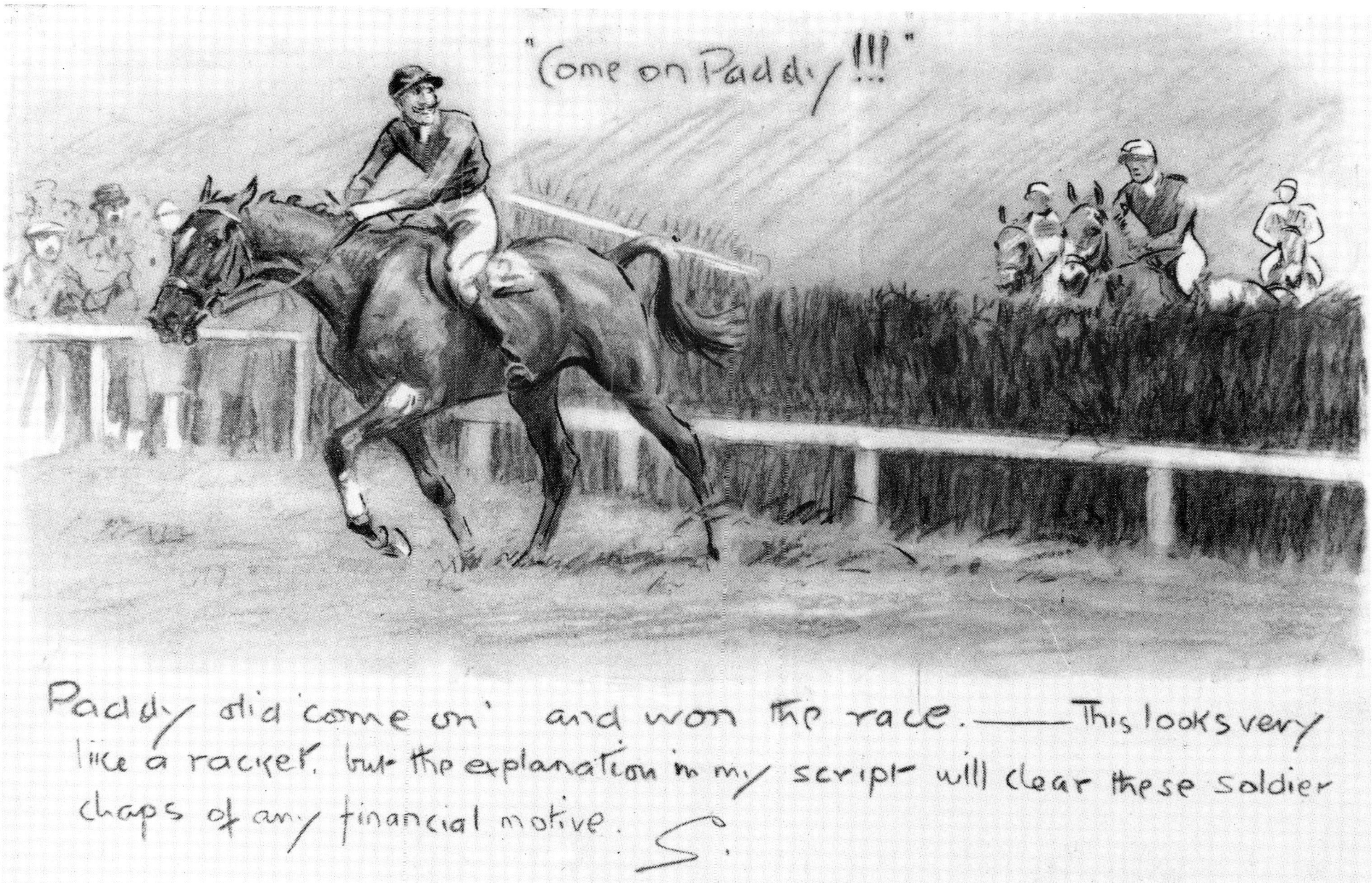
"Come on Paddy!!!"
Paddy did 'come on' and won the race. —— This looks very like a racket, but the explanation in my script will clear these soldier chaps of any financial motive.
S.

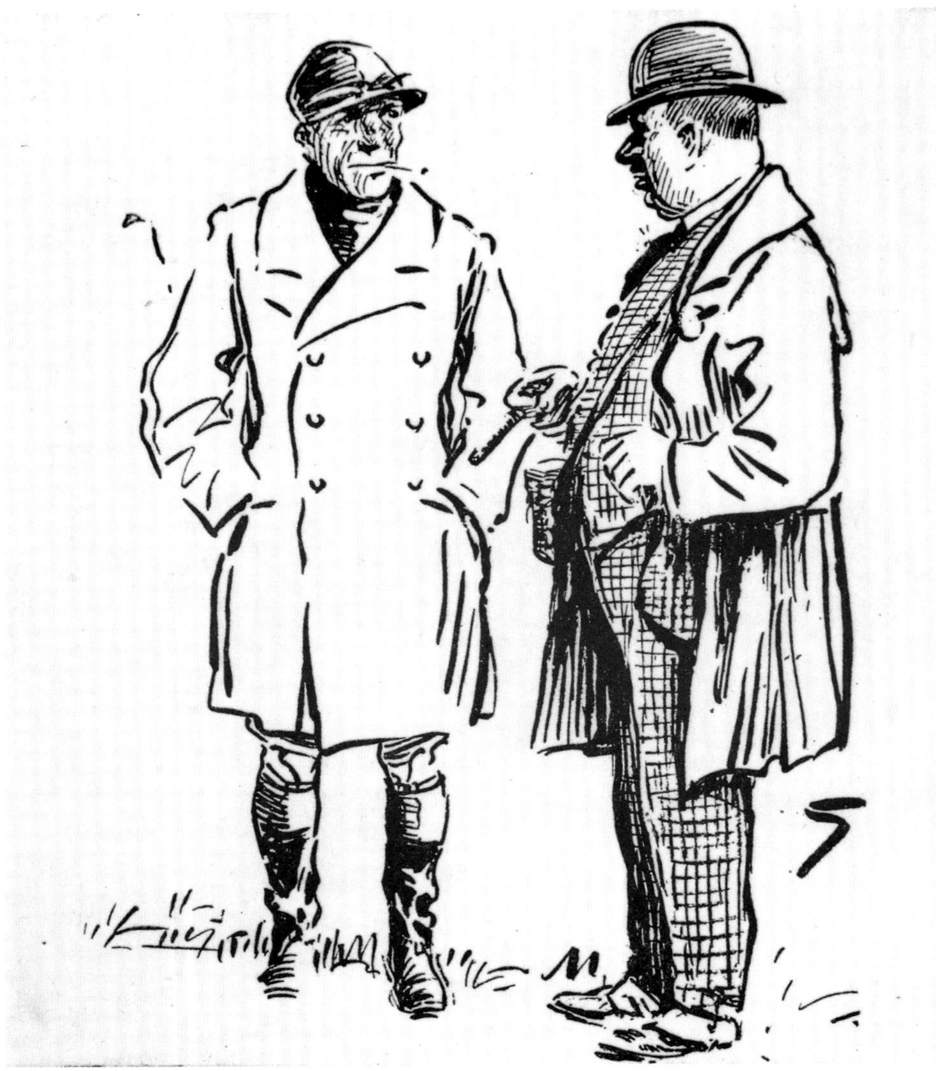

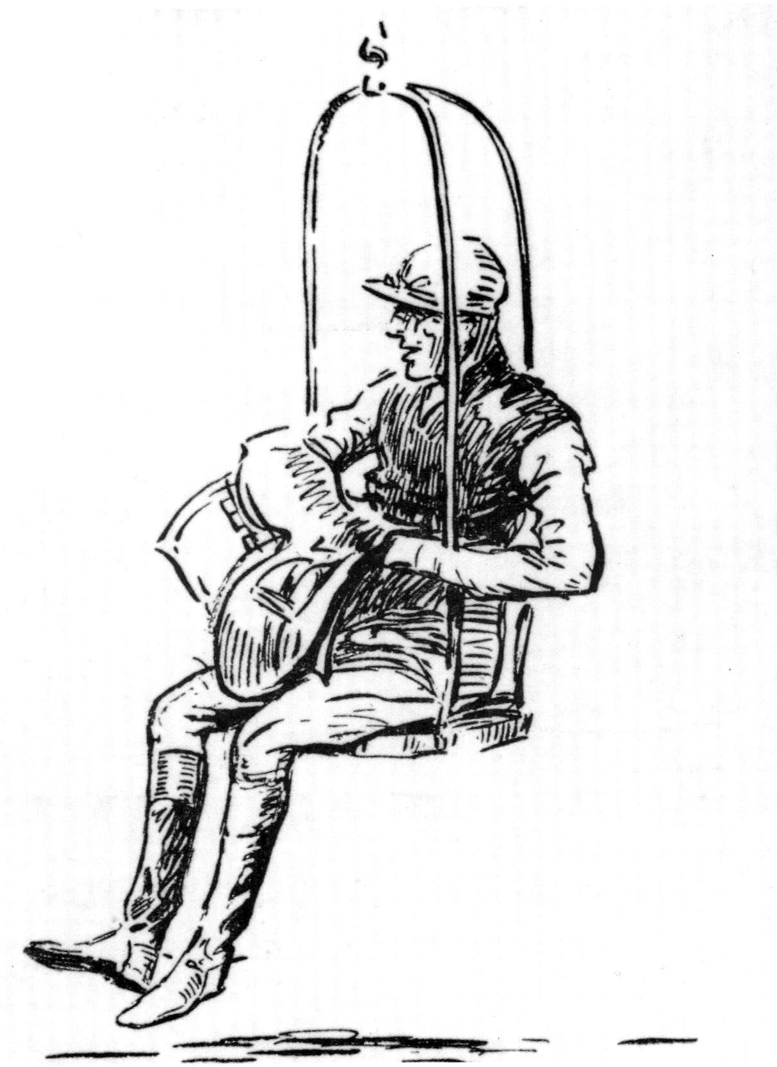

These drawings were done for Geoffrey Brooke's *Horse Lovers*. They demonstrate Snaffles' ability to catch character instantly

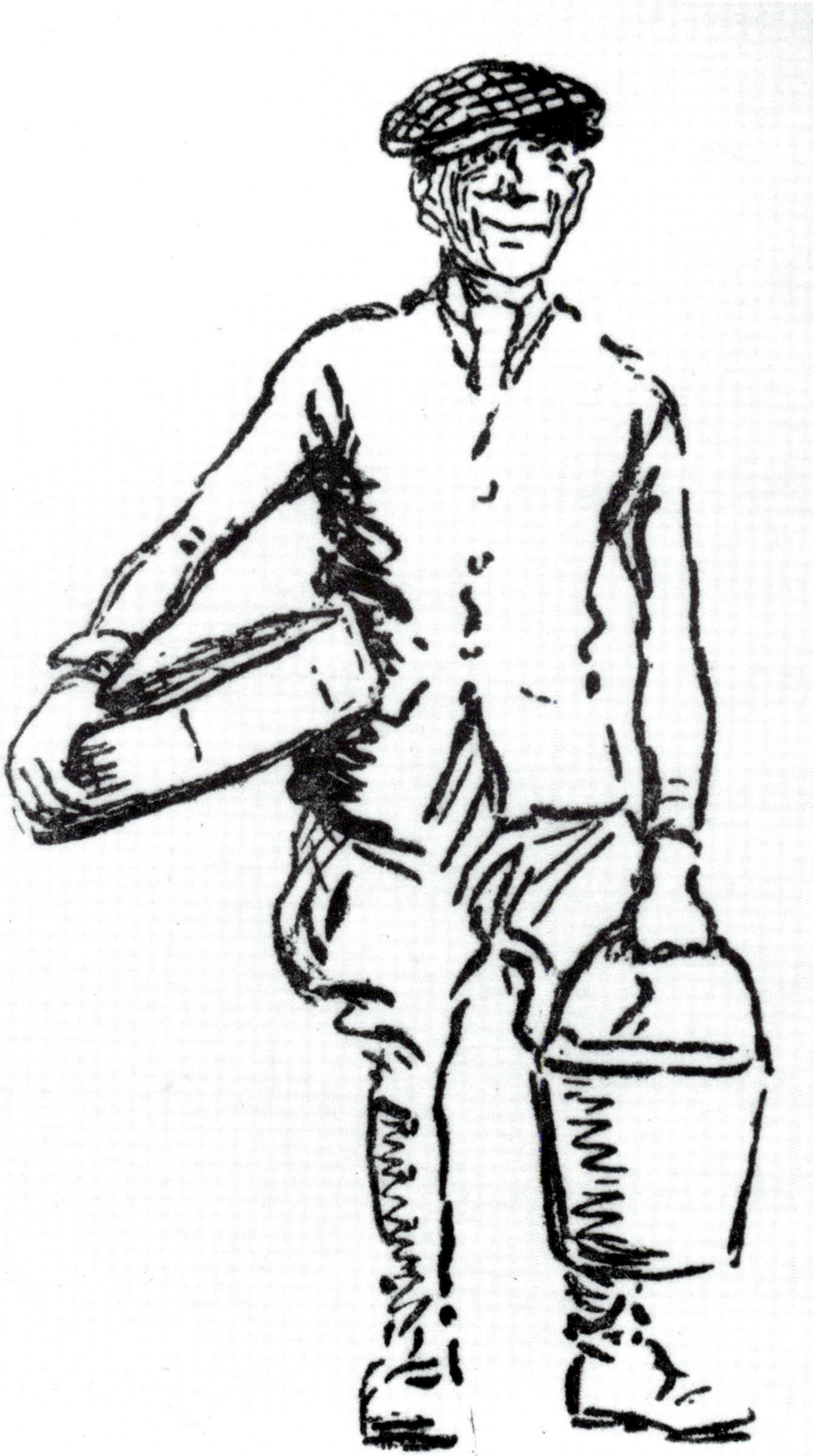

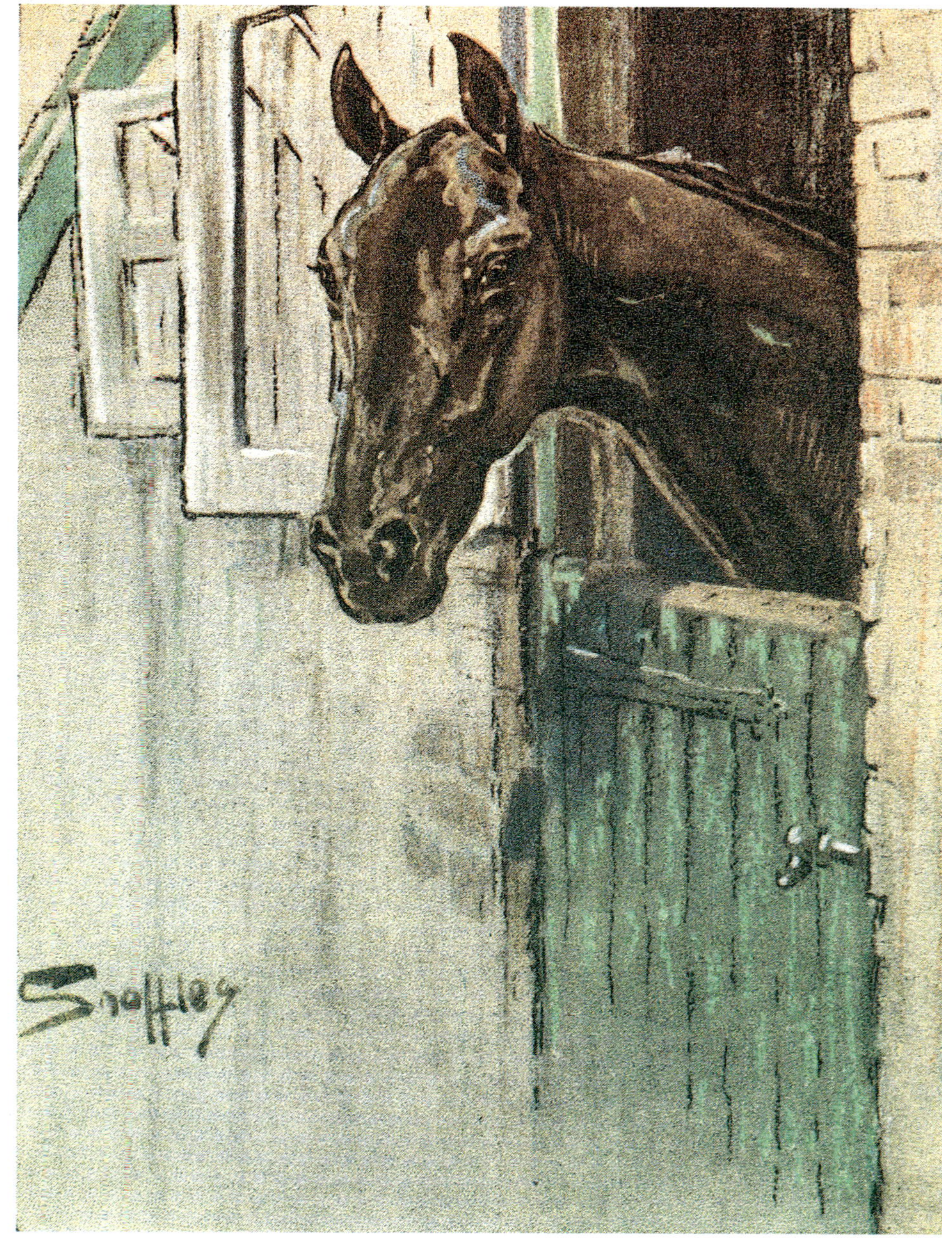

Snaffles' frontispiece of Crusader, which he did in colour, was by far the most successful illustration in the whole book

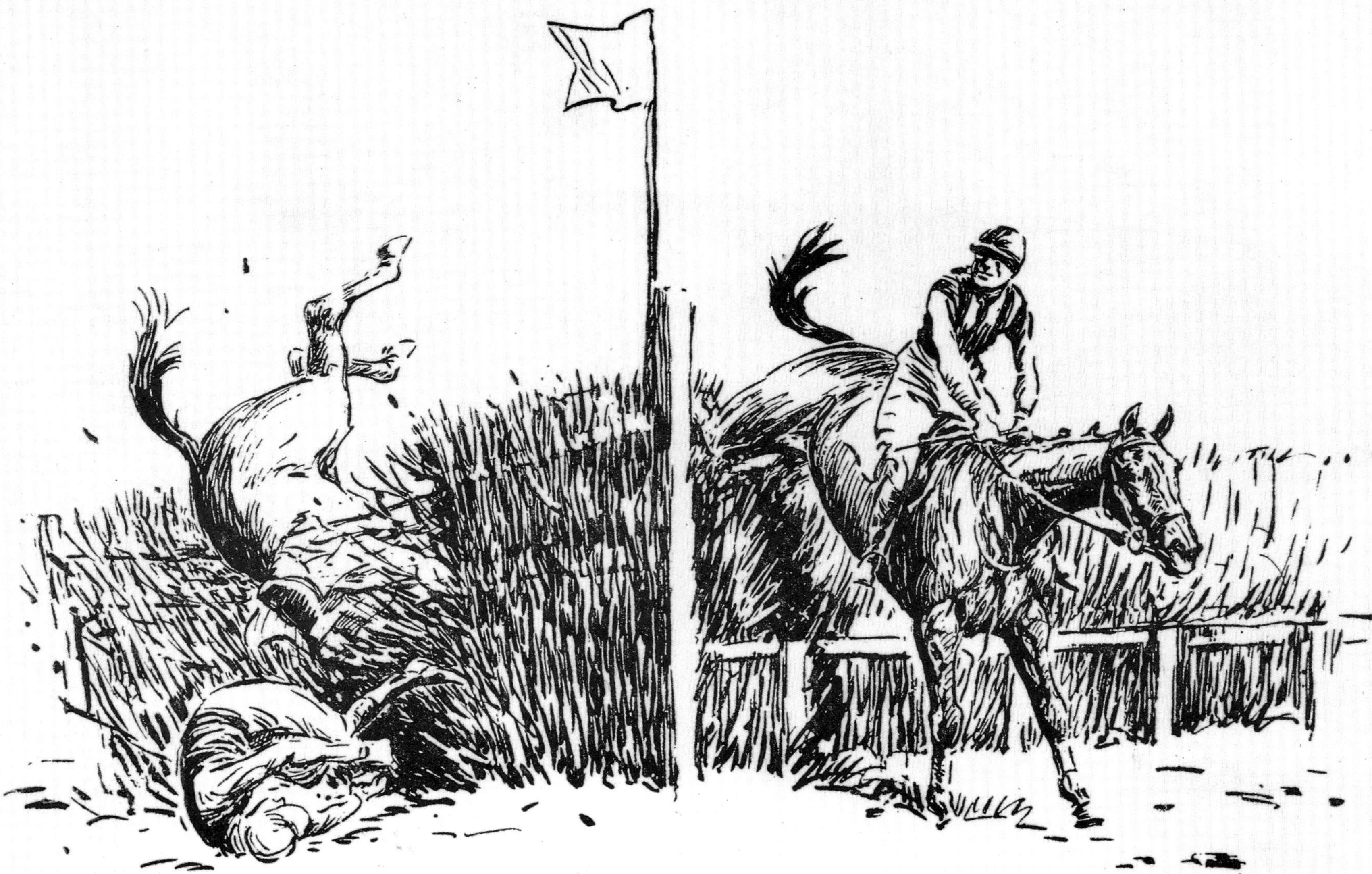

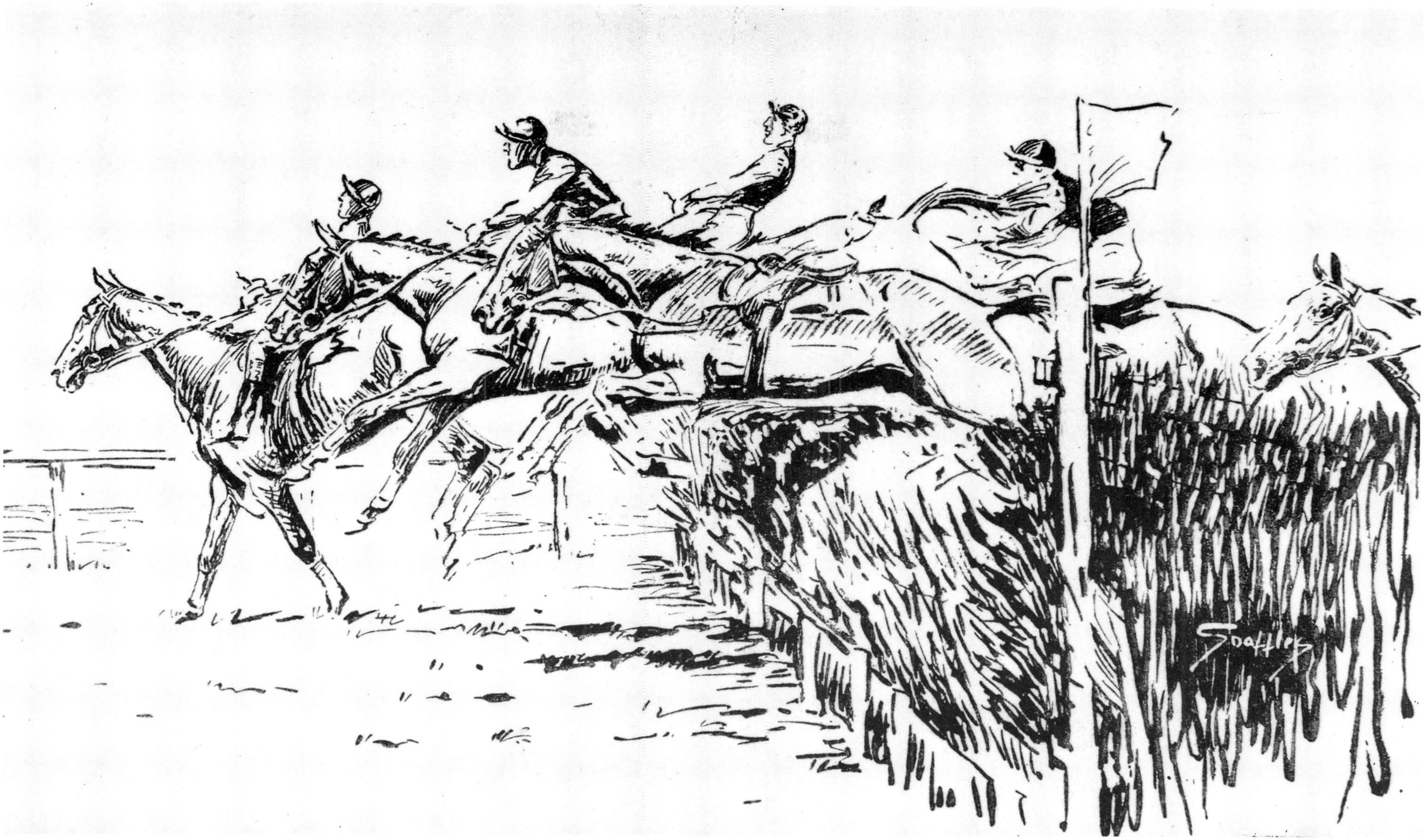

This pair of racing drawings from *Horse Lovers*, showing horses in action were relatively successful but do not have the quality of Snaffles' work for *Red Letter Days* which were scenes drawn from real life

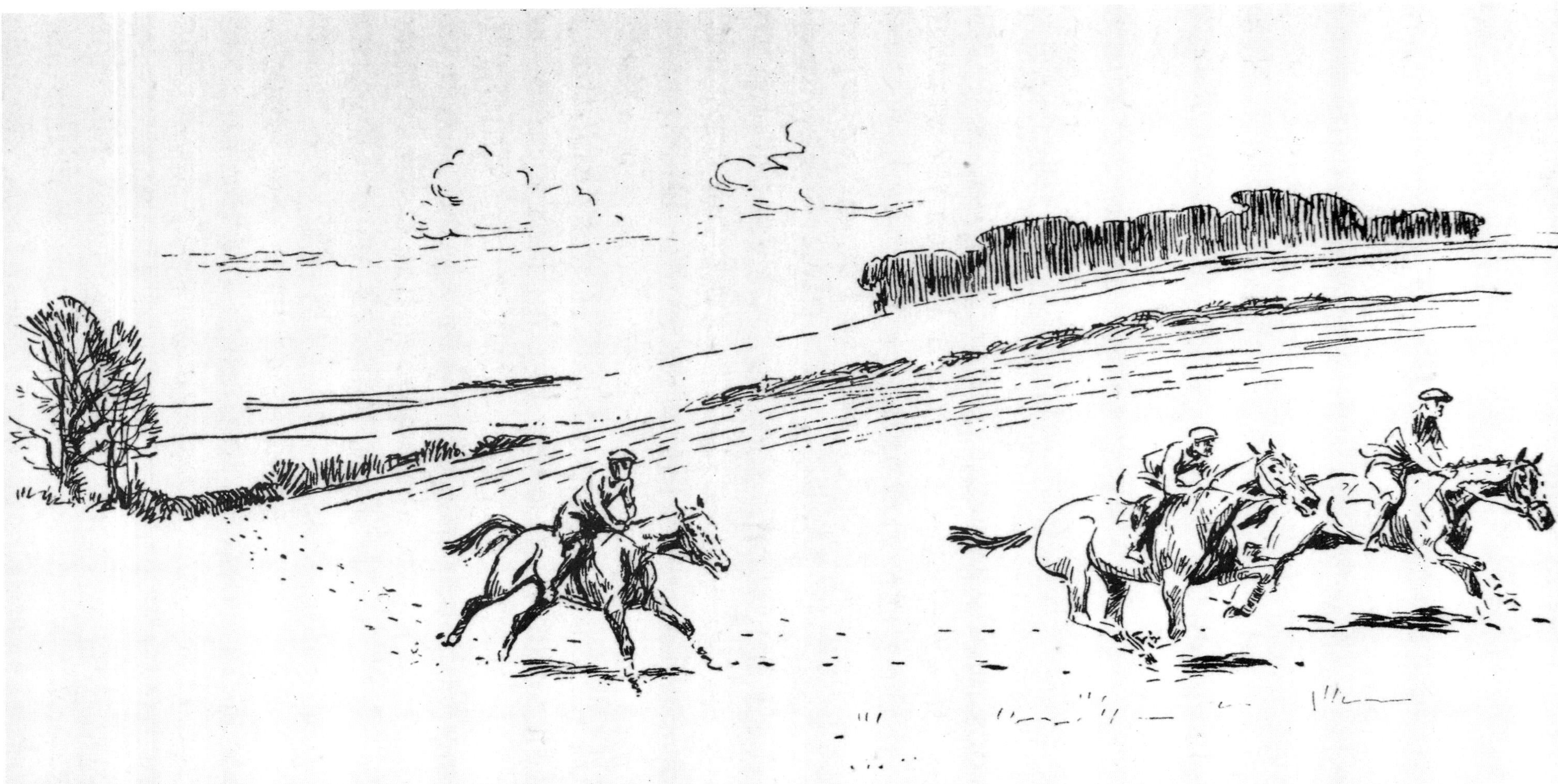

By no means can this drawing be considered successful, and landscapes were certainly not Snaffles' metier as they were Lionel Edwards'

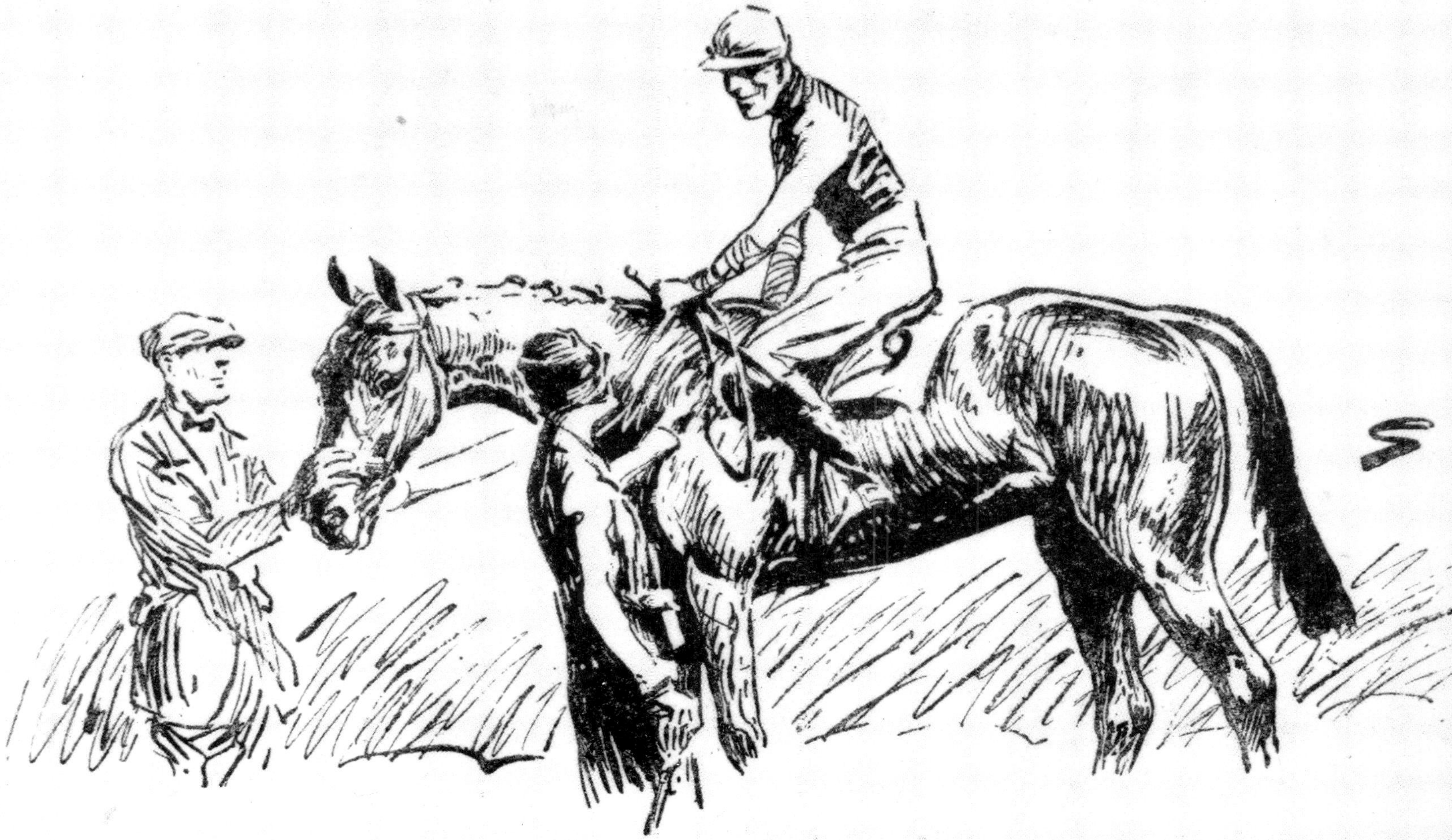

This drawing, if compared to those on pages 80 and 81, lacks spontaneity and is technically not brilliant

The Foxhunters' Maiden Chase
(21 started 16 fell)

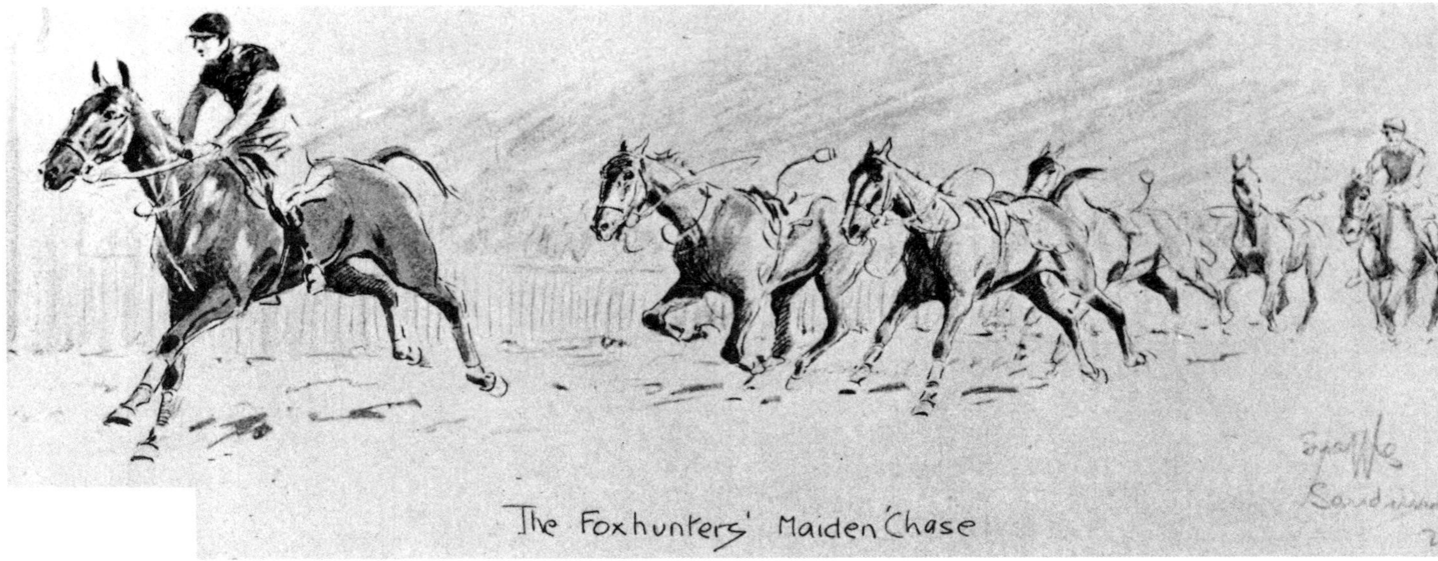

'Pay Only'
Top weight for the Grand Military but as fit as a flea

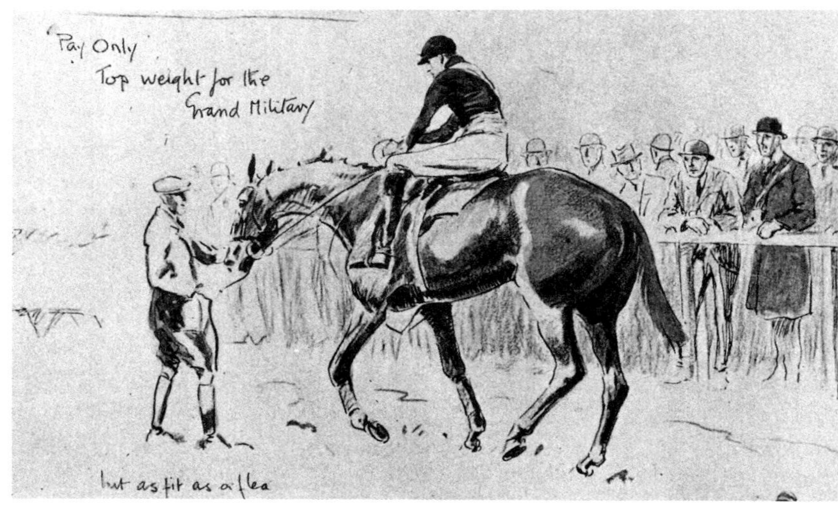

'Thats a Gentlemans 'oss'

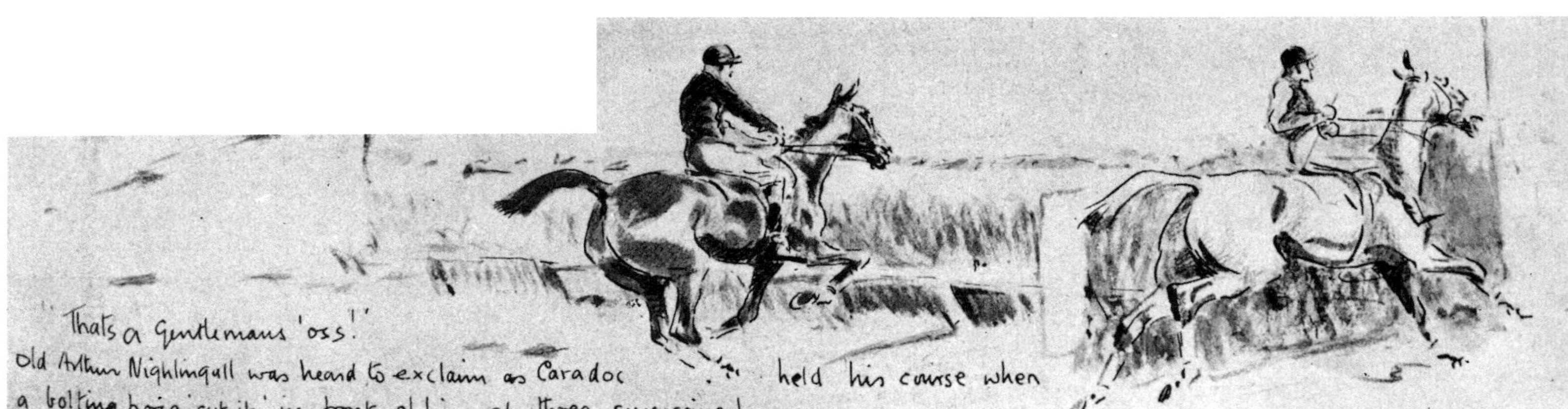

Pay Only, again ridden by his owner, Mr. Billy Filmer-Sankey, won the Grand Military for the second time the following year. 'Top weight but as fit as a flea' Snaffles recorded as he sketched him being led in. He watched that day's racing with Arthur Nightingall who gave him another quote to match 'The Worst View!'. 'That's a gentleman's 'oss', Nightingall exclaimed as he saw Caradoc, ridden by a soldier, hold his course when a bolting horse refused in front of him at three successive fences. It was a great day's racing which produced plenty of material, including the Foxhunter's Maiden Chase where '21 started. 16 fell'.

Much later Snaffles was to produce from memory another Grand Military drawing in which he looked back to those great days of soldier racing between the wars and which again he entitled 'A Sheet would cover 'em'. Snaffles himself named the leading rider as George Paynter, although there are some who claim it was Geoffrey Brooke. The grey, White Surrey, is ridden by Taffy Walwyn, the third horse is Pippin, ridden by Mead Dennis, later Major General Mead Dennis, Field Marshall Montgomery's MGRA. Monty was not renowned for his liking or admiration of the Horse Gunners with their mystique of 'ball buttons' and 'the jackets', believing them to be a throwback to the days of the *arme blanche* and the amateur tradition of soldiering which he so detested. He wrote of them in general, 'none of the artillery colonels in the Eighth Army were fit to command the whole artillery of a corps and only about fifty per cent of the divisional artillery chiefs were fit to hold that appointment. Many of the Lieutenant Colonels were out of their depth ...', but he went on, 'Luckily we had in Mead Dennis a really first class CCRA of the 30 Corps. He was magnificent and is a high class gunner'. So that even in Montgomery's estimation there was at least one of the band of brothers whose devotion to the horse had not unfitted him for his military trade.

Mead Dennis, as he was to show with Pippin, was in the very highest class of gentleman rider of his time. Pippin had a romantic and extraordinary history. Standing only 15.1½ hands high, originally he had been something of a bad character. Another Horse Gunner, Bill Bedford, had had him as his charger and reformed him. With him he had won fourteen point-to-points, including the Army Cup, out of fifteen starts, but he never rode him under Rules. When Bedford went to India he bought him out of the Army and passed him to Mead Dennis, who rode him to win the Foxhunters Steeplechase at Aintree when aged fifteen in 1928, then ran over the full Grand National distance, as well as the Foxhunters at Cheltenham the following year. He came within an ace of winning the Foxhunters at Aintree for a second time. Carried out by a loose horse at Becher's second time round, Mead Dennis brought him round, jumped the fence 'almost out of the Stand', caught and passed his field and only just failed to catch the winner by half a length. As well as these two major and much coveted prizes for amateur riders, the little horse won other good races for his owner-rider. Snaffles was so taken with them both that he drew a sketch of Major Dennis with his saddle over his arm, wrote 'Pippin' on it and presented it to him.

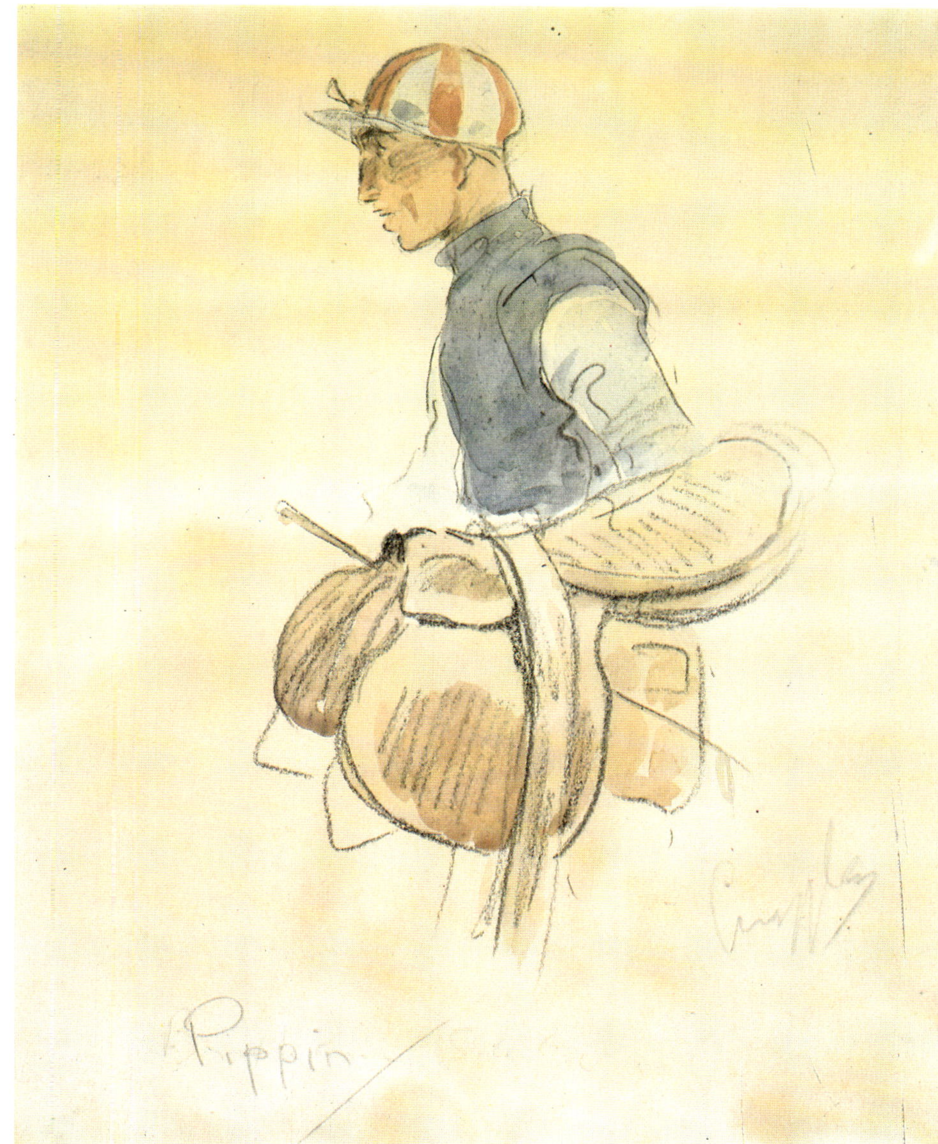

This delightful watercolour was a sketch Snaffles gave to the highly successful soldier, amateur rider, Mead Dennis

The late twenties were to be a brilliant period for Snaffles as one of England's leading sporting artists. 1927 saw the publication of the print 'The Grand National', commented upon earlier as being one of the all time great paintings of Liverpool. Also in that year he published the ever popular hunting print 'Merry England' and 1928 was to see the production of his great racing print 'Sandown'. Like so many of his best prints, it is a composite depicting three horses being driven up the hill into the last by amateur military riders. The view was painted from where Snaffles preferred to watch the races and from where he had heard some years previously Brooke call out encouragement to his second string ridden by Paddy Doyle.

If the 1926 Grand National is to rate as one of the best prints ever produced of this race, Snaffles' print of Sandown is a clear winner when it comes to judging the prints produced of steeplechasing at Sandown. It is a very rare print and little known, but eagerly sought after, not only by Snaffles collectors, but also by lovers of Sandown.

By the late twenties, when Pippin was winning the Foxhunters at Cheltenham and Liverpool, Snaffles was happily settled in his new home, White Cottage, 1 Treehill Road, Guildford, where he was to continue to live until 1940. It wasn't really a cottage, but a substantial house by anyone's standards and, financially life for Snaffles, probably due to Lucy's careful management, had become much easier. He was still an avid attender of point-to-points and bona-fide meetings, as well as full blown National Hunt meetings and although after the First World War he never owned a horse, he continued to hunt regularly on borrowed mounts. In 1923 he saw his old friend Brantingham, then aged thirty, out hunting with the Pytcheley and still going as gallantly as the years would let him, reviving memories of the fun of pre-war days. But it was, naturally enough, the point-to-points and bona-fide meetings around Guildford and Aldershot or on Salisbury Plain which attracted most of Snaffles' attention as a viewer rather than a participant where he could see his civilian and soldier friends competing.

One of the features of racing between the wars was the popularity of 'bona-fide' meetings. These were first started in 1912 and abolished in 1947. They were run either by hunts or military units and the profits had to go to the hunt or to supporting racing in the military unit. Their rules were very similar to point-to-points. The minimum distance of all races was three miles, all had to be steeplechases and no hurdle races were allowed; only amateurs could ride and prize money, like that at point-to-points, was limited to twenty sovereigns. The main difference was that the executive could charge for admittance which was forbidden at point-to-points; also the course had to be inspected and passed by one of the official inspectors of steeplechase courses, and returns of the races were published in *Steeplechases Past* by the National Hunt Committee. In reality they were neither fish nor fowl as they were neither point-to-points nor proper steeplechases, as winners at a bona-fide meeting remained maidens under proper steeplechasing rules. The 1920's saw their heyday, but they continued right through the thirties and a few were even held after World War II.

The owners, riders and horses were very much the same as one would have found at the better class point-to-points rather than those associated with racing under proper National Hunt Rules. Snaffles was a regular attender at these bona-fide meetings within forty or fifty miles, especially those run by the Army, including the RA Harriers down on Tidworth Plain. For instance, in 1936, there were a number of such meetings in the vicinity and among those which he probably attended were the Southdown Hunt, the East Sussex Hunt, Eridge Hunt, West Kent Hunt, Old Surrey Hunt and Burstow Hunt, where Ryan Price, later to become a great National Hunt and flat trainer, rode the winner of the Adjacent Hunts Maiden Chase of three miles and sixty yards, carrying 12 stone 7lb on the six-year-old Gaickster. It is absolutely certain that Snaffles attended the bona-fide military meetings held at Aldershot where on the 28th and 29th February 1936 Neville Crump won races on two consecutive days on Kings Cross II.

At the risk of confusing matters it is worth drawing readers' attention to the fact that some hunts ran proper National Hunt meetings, where hurdle races, races under three miles and professional jockeys were all permitted. Taking 1936 as an example once again, the meetings held by The Beaufort, Quorn and West Norfolk were all proper meetings and not bona-fide meetings.

As soon as point-to-points got going again after the Great War, Snaffles attended them throughout the length and breadth of the country, sketching and submitting illustrations regularly to the periodicals which often featured his work. Although we have devoted considerable space in this chapter to racing under National Hunt Rules, it would be fair to say that for every meeting under Rules which Snaffles attended, he spent at least one day at a point-to-point. In 1921 he was in the west country watching a point-to-point over banks and was to submit an amusing page to *The Illustrated Sporting and Dramatic News*. It is worth noting that, like the famous pair of prints, 'The Finest' and 'Worst Views', the 'rocking horse' stage had not entirely been outgrown. The same year he was to submit a very good illustration entitled 'Soldiers' showing two determined military amateur riders taking each other on over a stiff cut and laid fence in a point-to-point. As with so much of his best work, this was reproduced as a print showing one of the soldiers remounting after a fall. He was to use here the caption 'Nasty steeplechasin' devils', as opposed to the caption 'Nasty steeplechasing beggar' in the 'Sojer Hossifer' print of 1914. Like the previous Point-to-Point print of 1914, the 1922 one became, and has remained, a firm favourite with collectors.

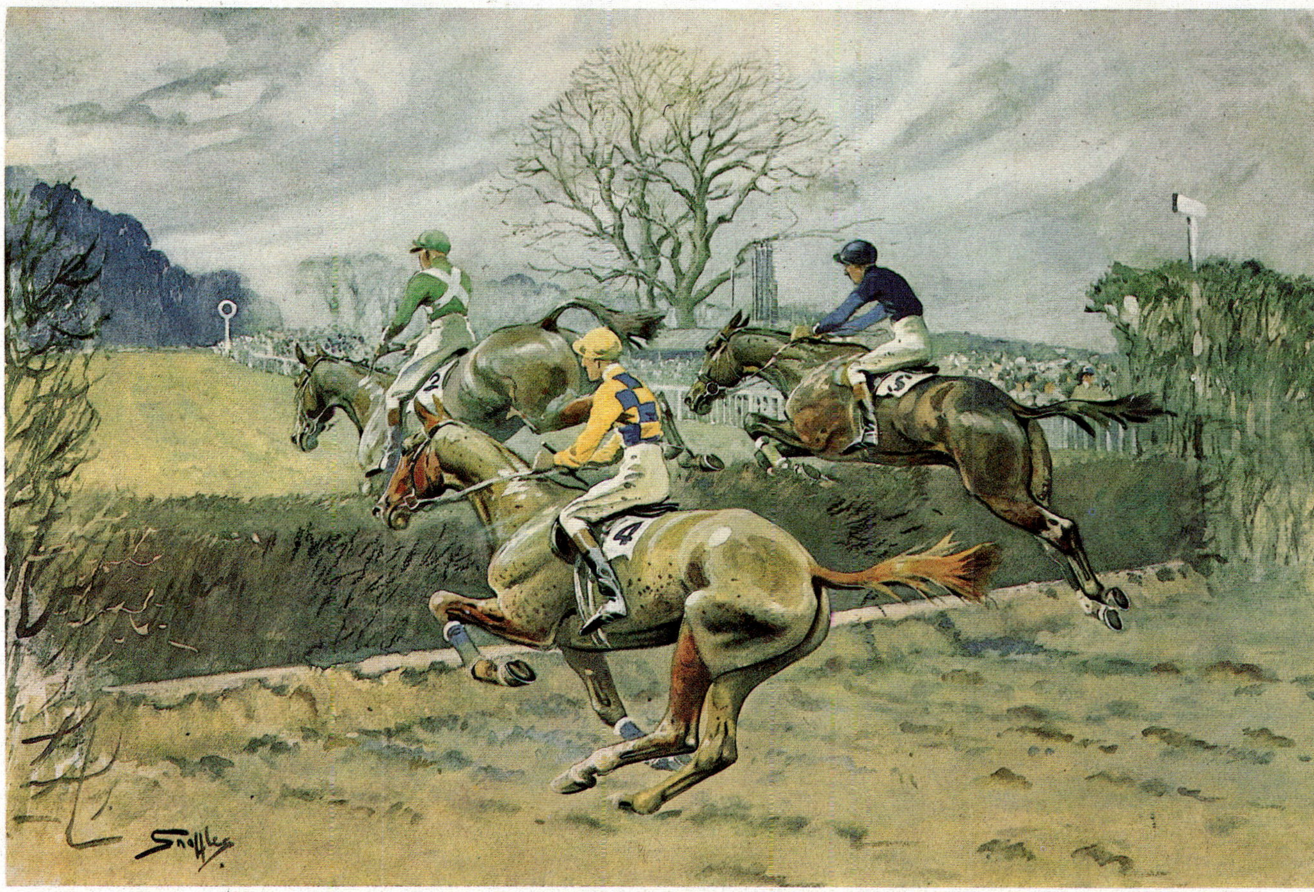

SANDOWN

ASKING 'EM THE QUESTION

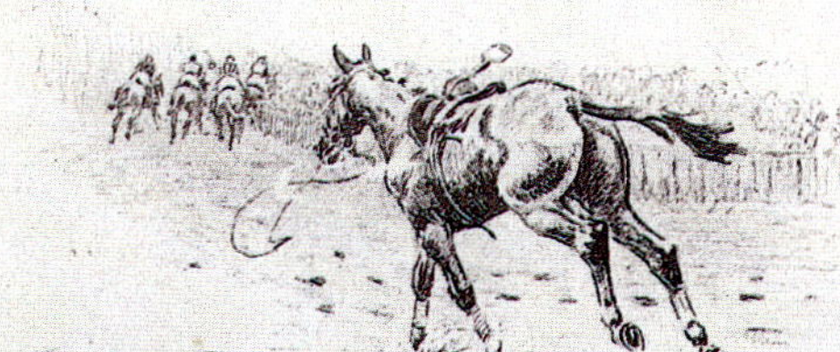

THE EMPTY PLATE

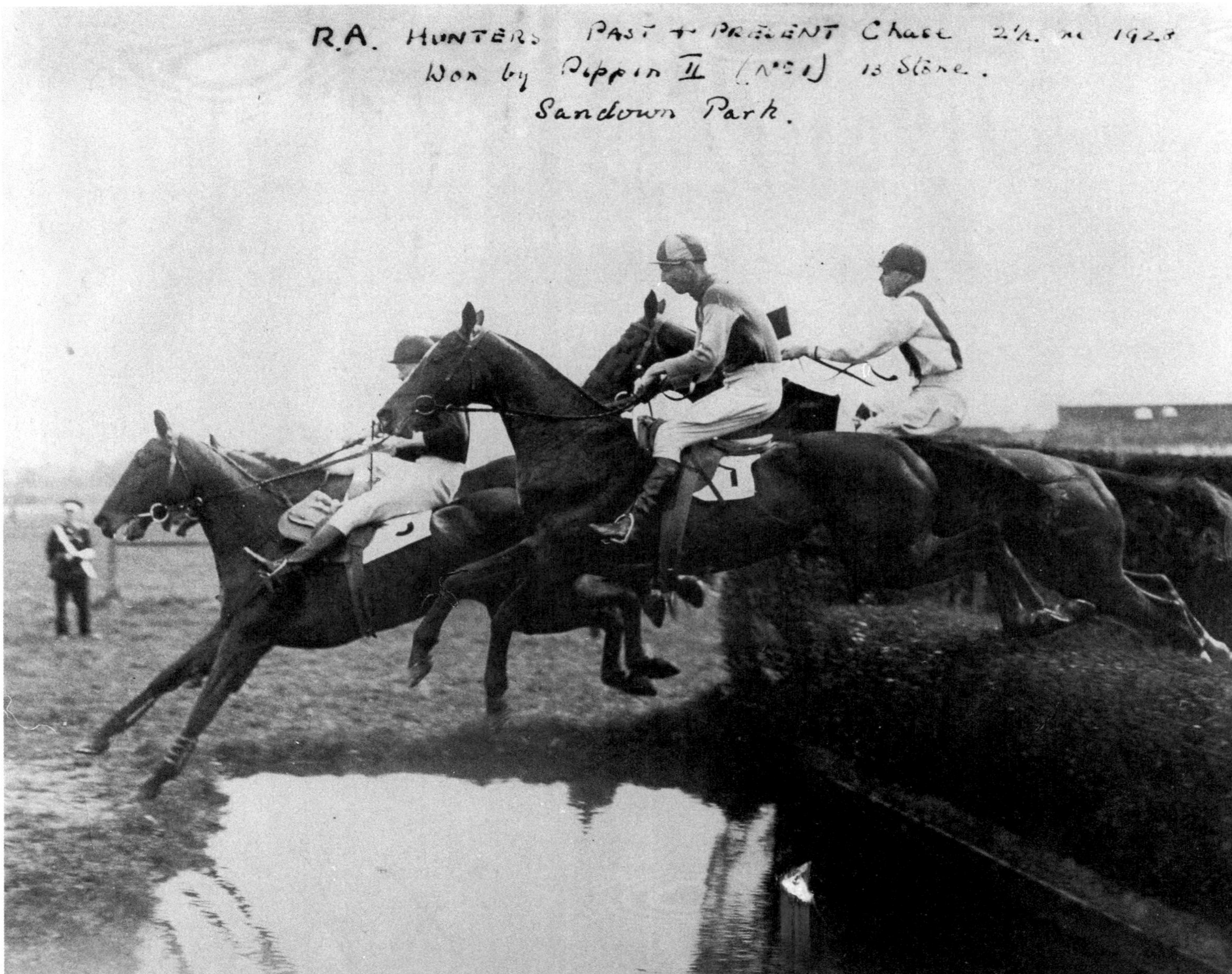

Pippin on the way to win under 13 stone at the Gunners meeting, Sandown 1923.
Some performance seeing how small Pippin was!

This print dates from 1922. The amateur rider in the pink coat is probably Geoffrey Brooke, author of *Horse Lovers*

SOLDIERS.

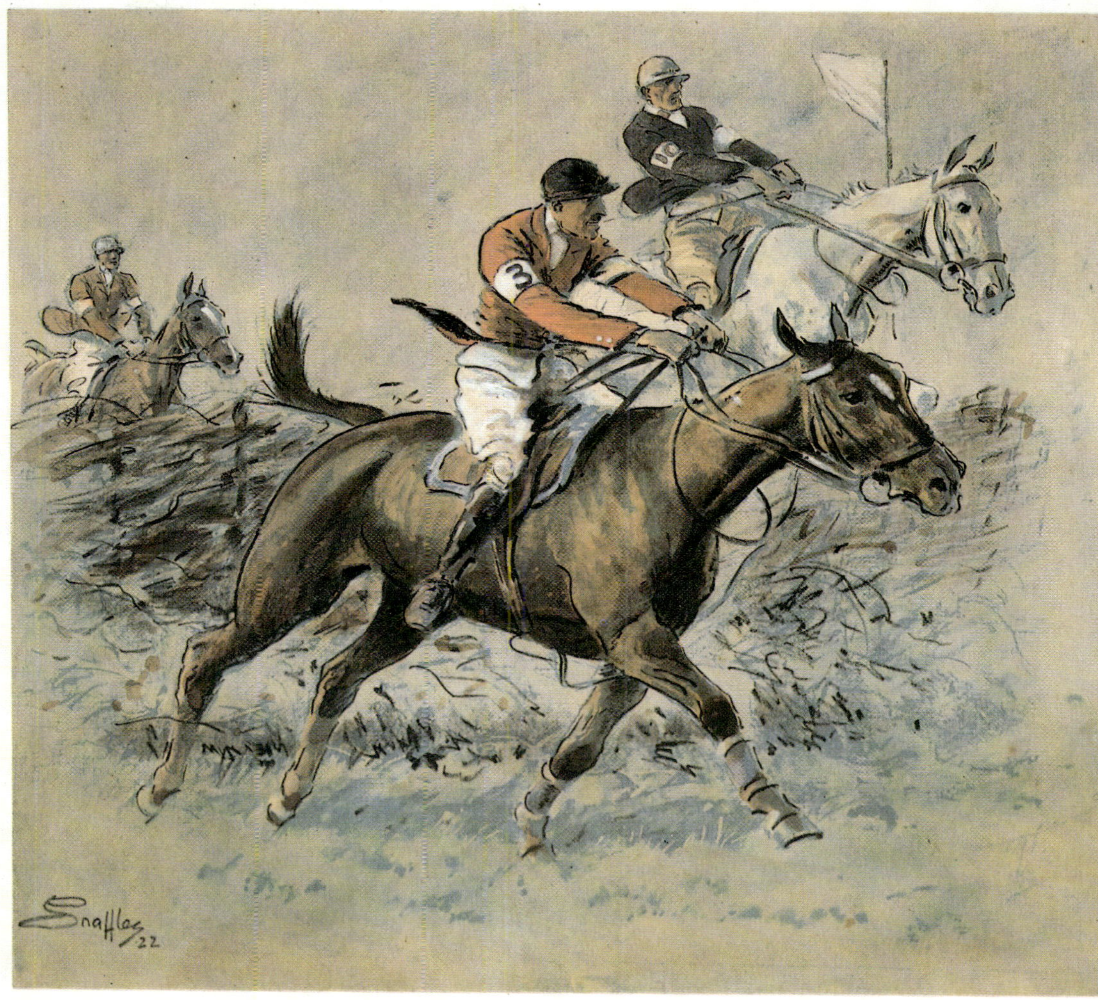

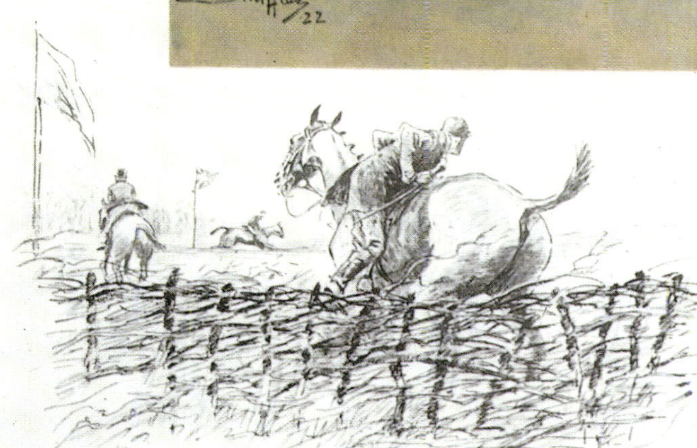

'Nasty steeple chasin' devils'

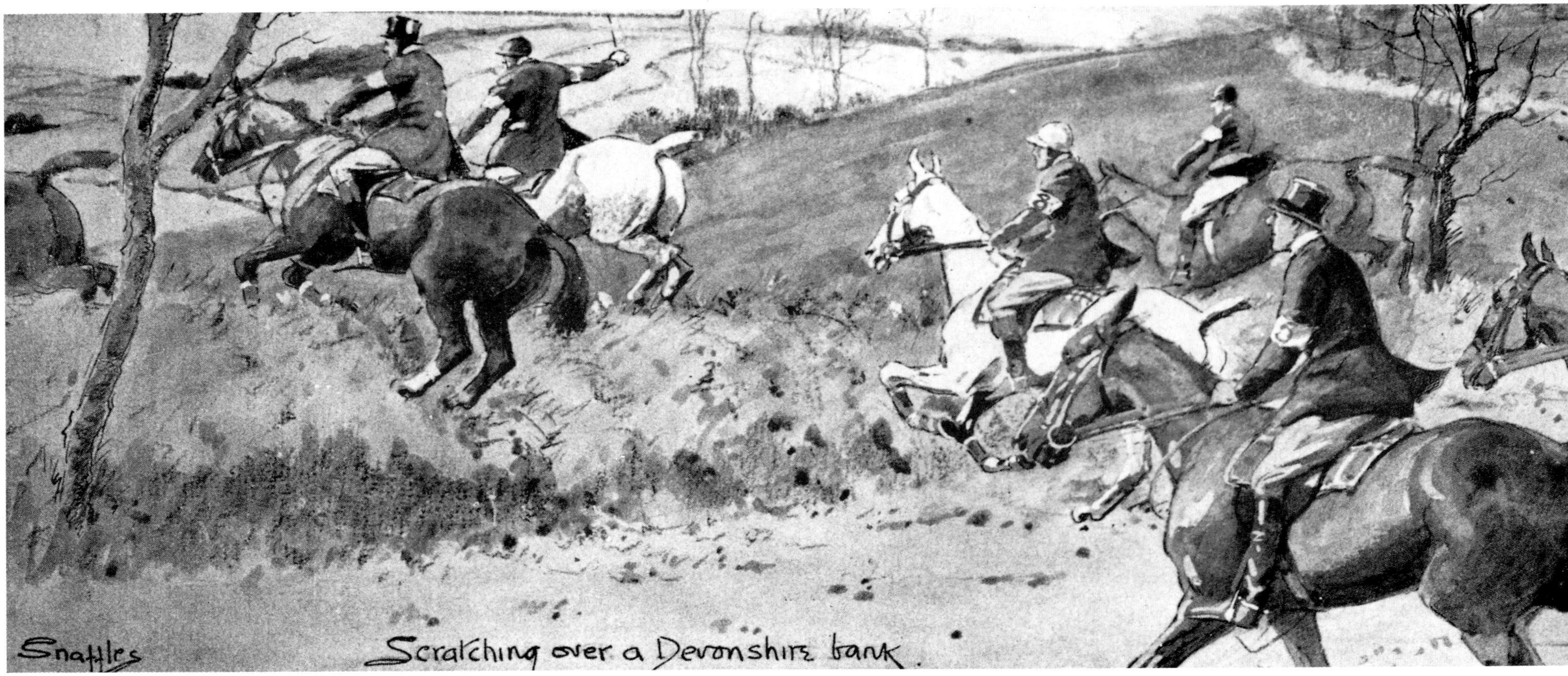

Snaffles attended point to points avidly for sixty or seventy years, throughout the length and breadth of the British Isles. In his later years, when he was becoming frail, they were the only racing he regularly attended, as he found the trip to Sandown too much for him

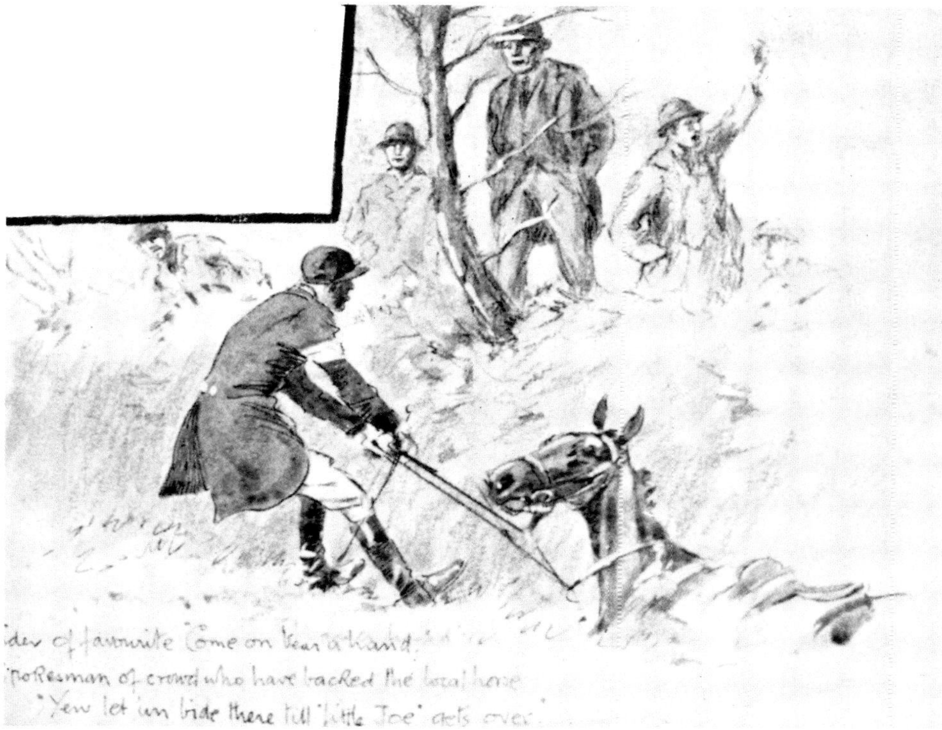

Rider of favourite 'Come on bear a hand',
Spokesman of crowd who have backed the local horse
"Yew let 'un bide there till 'Little Joe' gets over"

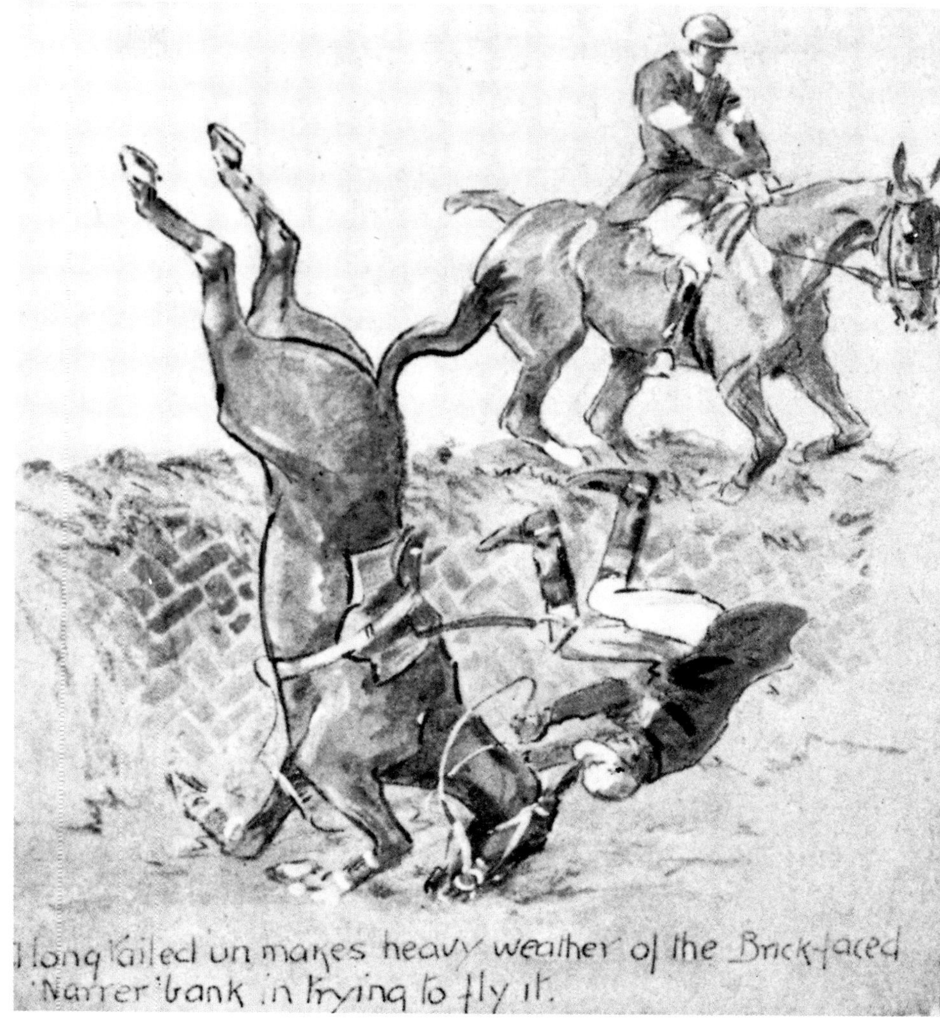

Snaffles' way with words when it came to captioning his drawings and prints was, at times, pure magic

At the Aldershot point-to-points Snaffles' usual position was in or about the Arborfield Brook. This was jumped twice, once as an open ditch and the second time at another place with a 'wattle topped bank' in front of it. 'That shallow imposter, the steeplechase pan' he christened one of his drawings, misquoting once again, this time from another of his favourite sporting poets, W. Bromley Davenport, who in his 'Dream of The Old Meltonian' actually wrote:

> No shallow-dug pan with a hurdle to screen it,
> That cock-tail impostor the steeplechase brook!
> But the deep broken banks tell us plain, if we mean it
> The less we shall like it the longer we look.

Bromley Davenport was referring to the even more famous Whissendine Brook in the Shires – 'The Whissendine Brook runs deep and wide and I wish I was safe on the other side,' as the doggerel went. But the spirit of that doggerel couplet together with the 'deep broken banks' was as true of the Arborfield as of the Whissendine. They claimed their casualties and Snaffles recorded them.

In 1928 Snaffles was to produce the ever popular point-to-pointing print 'Prepare to Receive Cavalry' based on the Arborfield Brook. Once again he used, in the vignettes, the catchphrase 'Go! and heaven be with you', which if one comes to think of it, really isn't the happiest of valedictions that a nervous rider can hear as he sets off towards the first fence, probably half out of control on some brute about whose jumping ability he has grave doubts!

The print 'Prepare to Receive Cavalry' could be said to be the first print of what we now term as Snaffles' mature period. Gone has any influence of the 'rocking horse style' which he acquired by copying artists such as Finch Mason and John Sturgess. He was becoming less and less of a caricaturist when painting racing and point-to-point scenes, although as a printmaker, it was the caption and remarque which made him so successful and his work so eagerly sought after today. As we commented in the first book of this series, Snaffles was the great sporting printmaker of the period 1918–1939, Lionel Edwards the greatest watercolourist, Gilbert Holiday supreme with pastels and Alfred Munnings, at one time President of the Royal Academy, the greatest handler of oil paints amongst sporting artists then living.

At the same time, in the twenties, Snaffles borrowed Taffy Walwyn's blood horse, Viking, and asked the then Miss Norah Roy to ride him over a substantial post and rails again and again on the Twesledown racecourse so he could get the exact image in his mind. The result was the print 'Handing it out to 'em'. Miss Roy later became Mrs. Pearson, the mother in law of Fred Winter, who as a jockey and trainer captured the Grand National, and grandmother of one of the best amateurs of the last few years in Jim Wilson, who rode his brother's and his own Little Owl to victory in the Gold Cup in 1984.

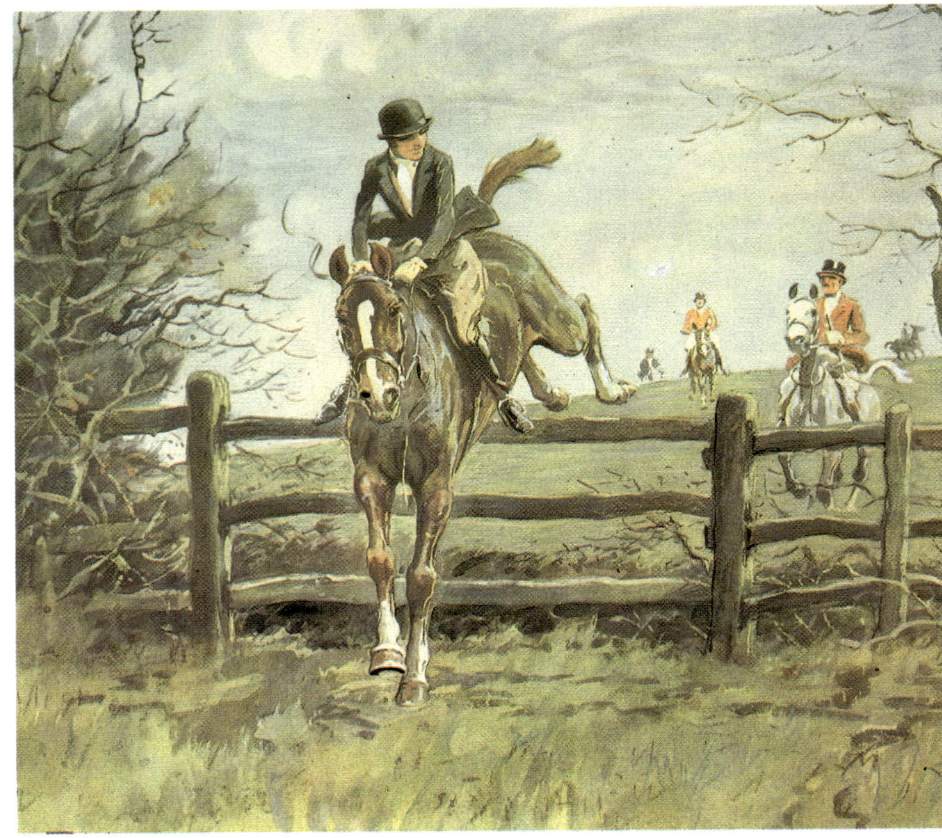

In this picture the horse is Viking, belonging to the Walwyn family. He is ridden by the then Miss Norah Roy. Viking was by the great racehorse Barcaldine and was placed in open point to points and in a hunter chase at Sandown, but failed to gain winning brackets either on the racecourse proper or between the flags

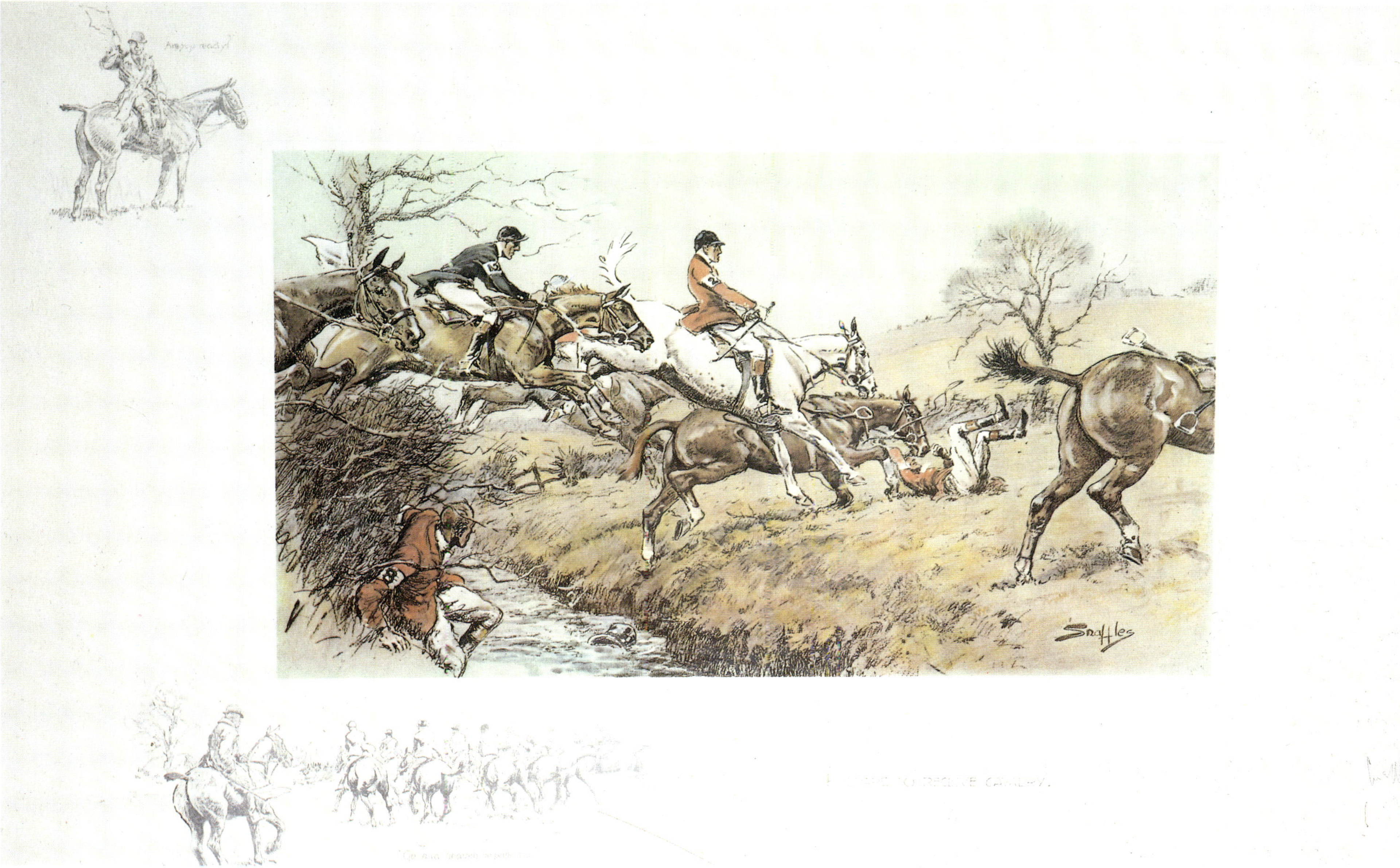

This print, first produced around 1925, shows the Arborfield Brook claiming two victims. Snaffles did a large number of drawings of the brook, both point to pointing and hunting

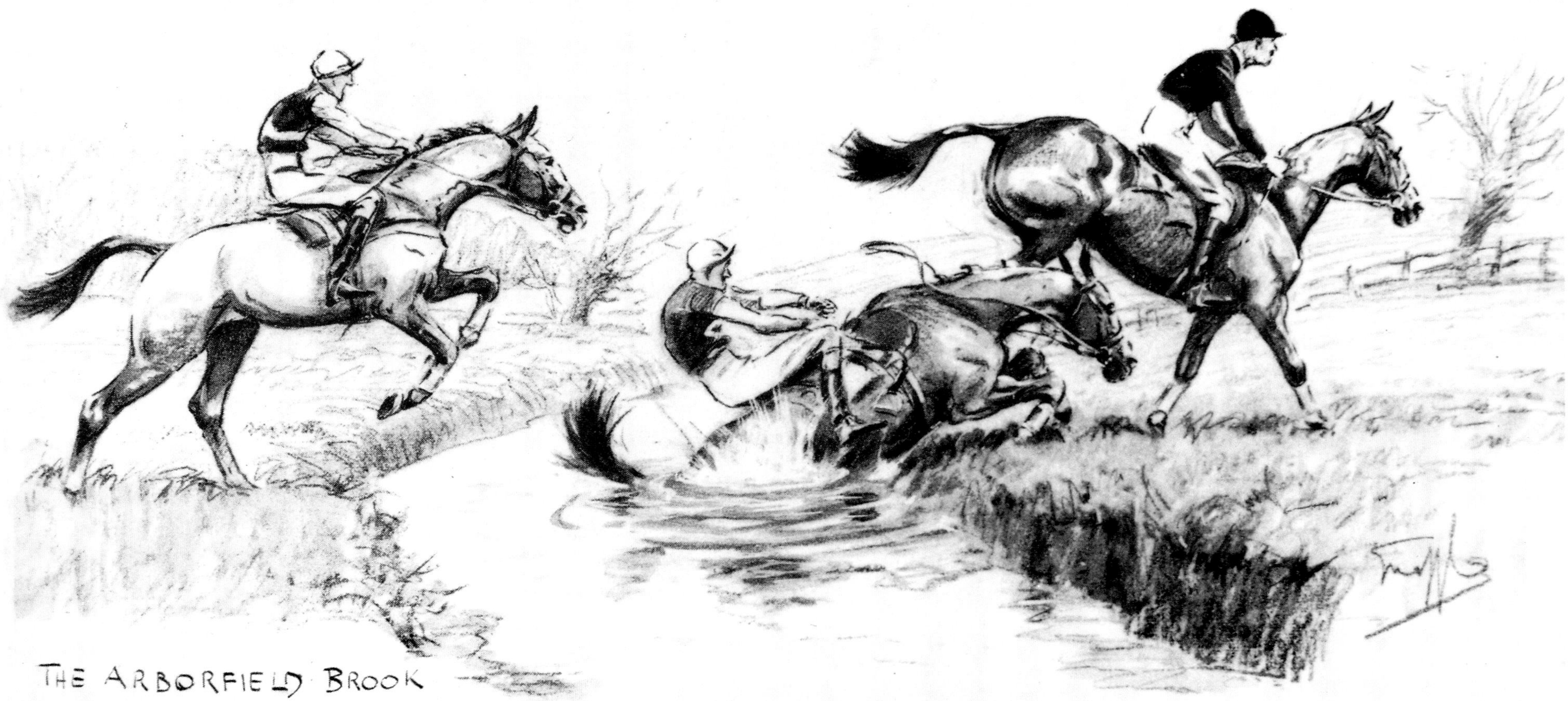

Snaffles seldom drew the Arborfield Brook without some soldier getting a ducking

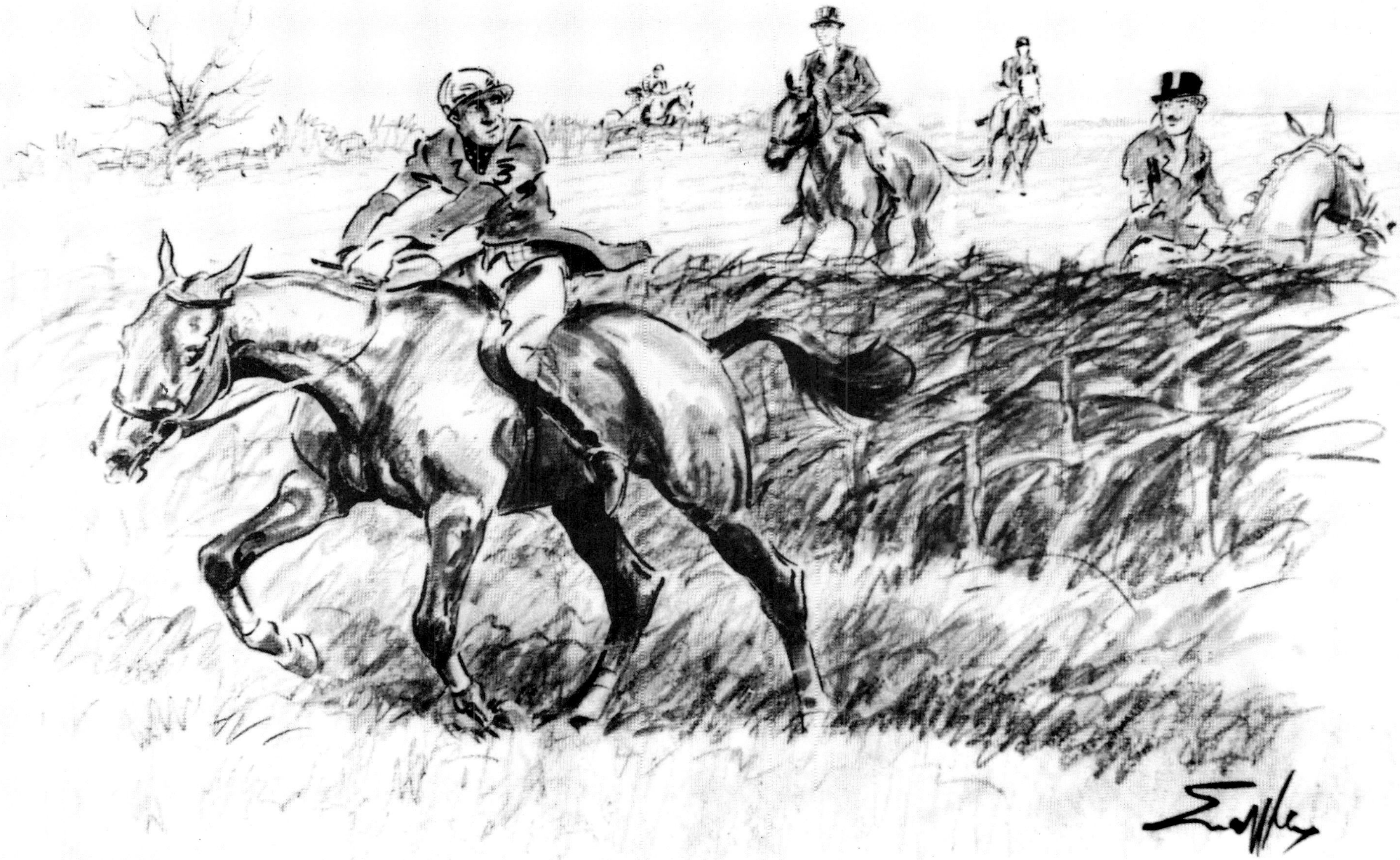

Throughout the 1920s point to point courses and fences were often very stiff, but regulation brush fences became more common in the 1930s. Nobody today would relish riding over the fences shown in these pictures

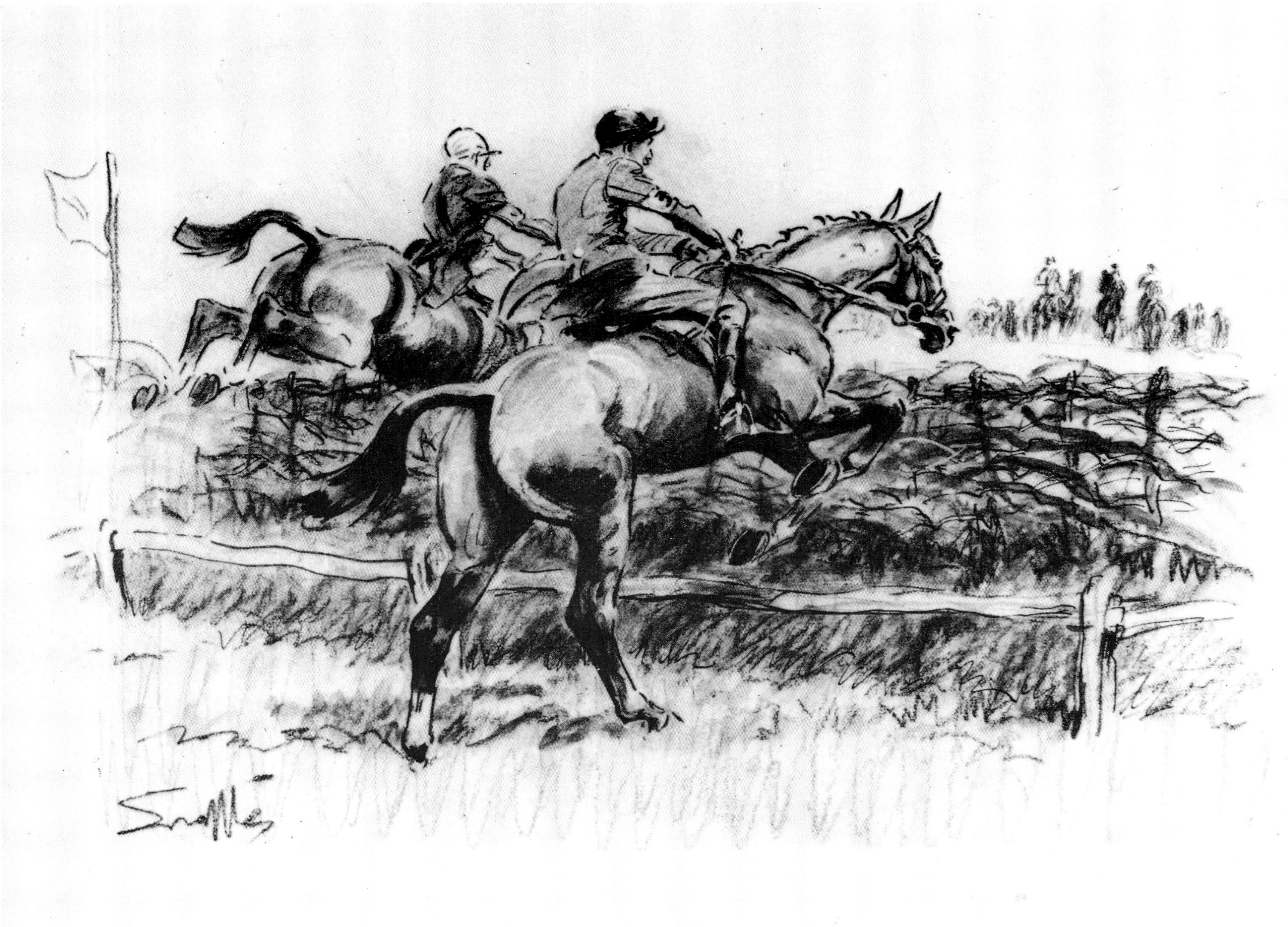

This drawing, although done in the late 40s or early 50s, harks back to Snaffles'
1911–14 days with the Belvoir or Cottesmore

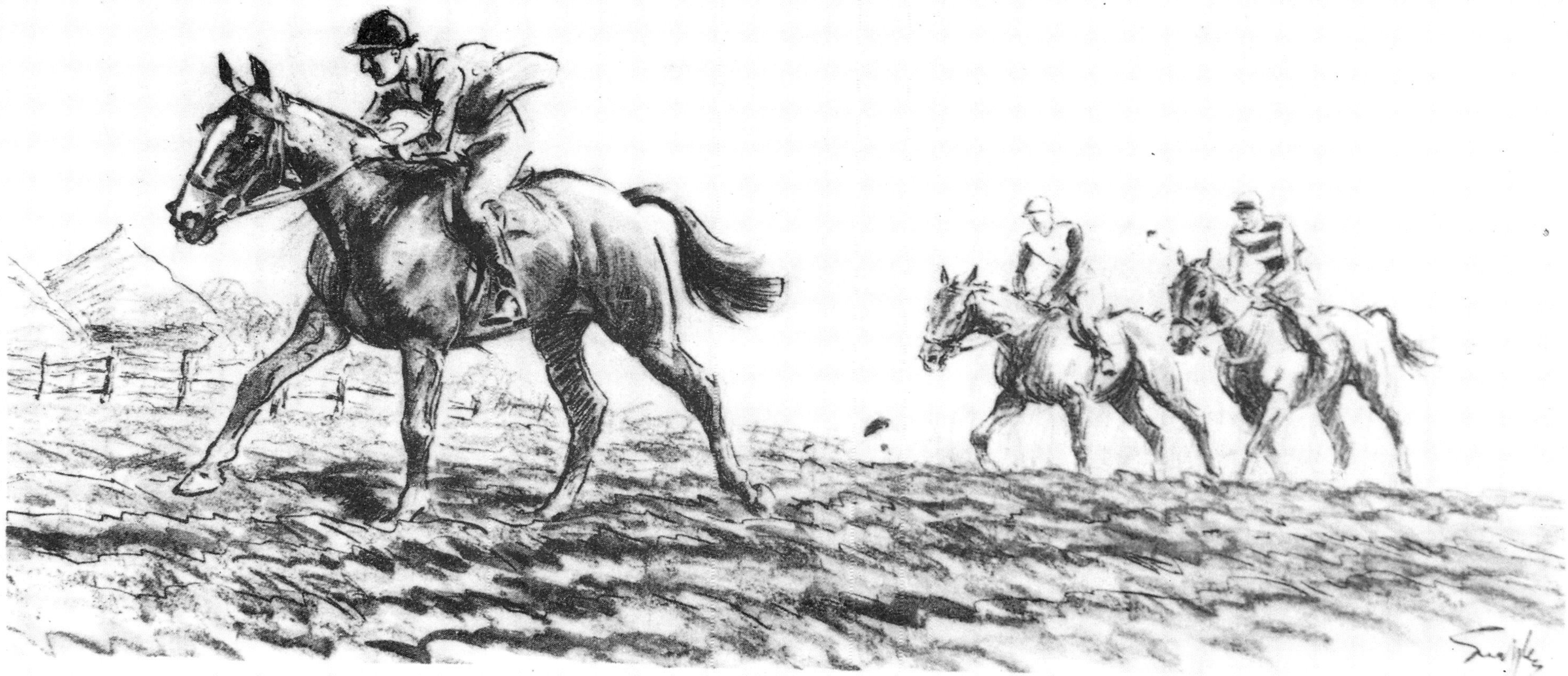

Snaffles entitled this drawing 'The one to dance over the plough'. Not all the winners of point to points over some of the severe courses to be found in the '20s were in the book. Few owners would fancy this plough nowadays, with 12 stone or 12 stone 7 lb in the plate, let alone 13 stone or 13 stone 7 lb as these horses were probably carrying

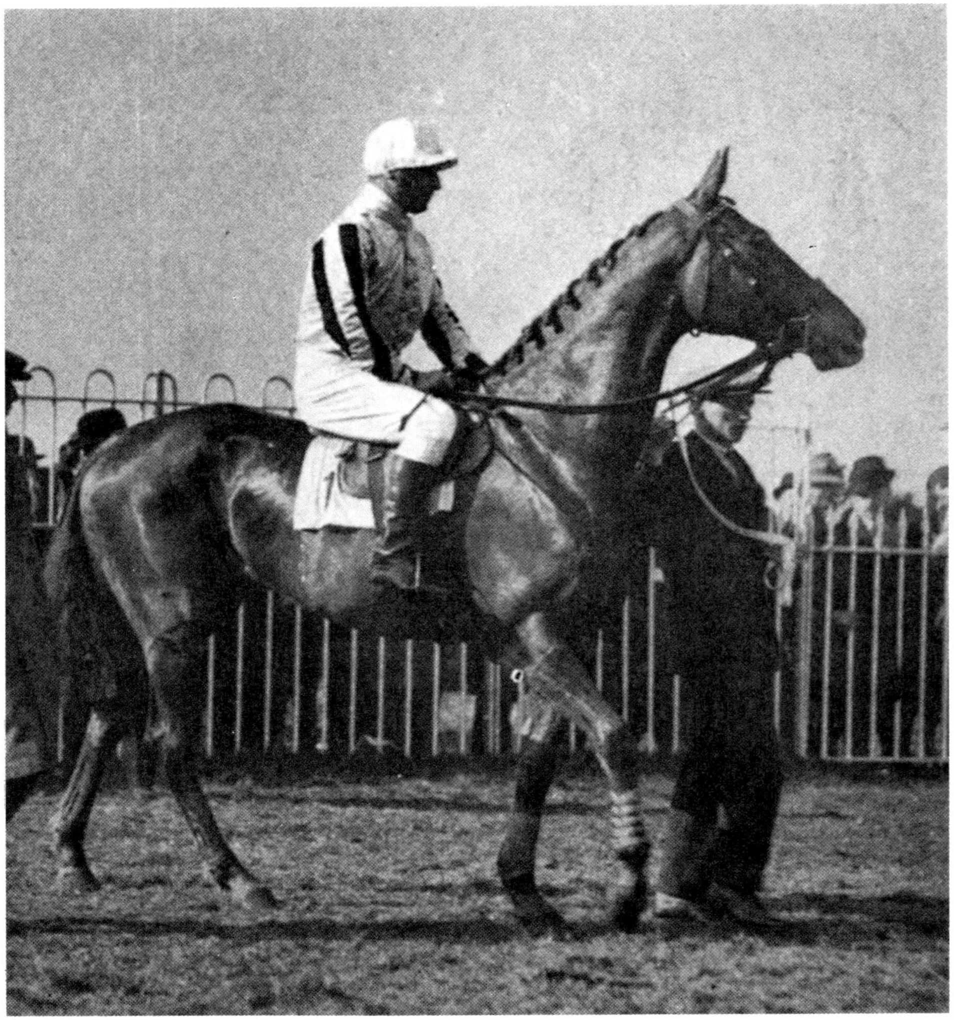

Easter Hero (Dick Rees up)

In the spring of 1925 another equine hero of Snaffles appeared for the first time from Ireland in the form of Easter Hero. At the commencement of his career he was a real tearaway and so impetuous was his jumping that he had difficulty in keeping himself upright and the partnership with his rider intact; and falls were frequent. In fact he fell on his first appearance in England at Cheltenham. But in the hands of Mr. Frank Barbour, a wealthy Belfast linen merchant and clever handler of horses, in the seasons 1926/27 and 1927/28 he was sent out to win nine chases, two of them at Liverpool, on the now defunct Molyneux and Sefton chases, where he astounded onlookers by the speed and boldness with which he tackled the big fences. In the Grand National his brilliance betrayed him. Taking off outside the wing at the Canal Turn, he landed on top of the fence, collapsed into the ditch which was then on the take-off side and, once there, ran up it knocking half the field out of contention.

As a result only nine horses got over the Canal Turn, but coming to the last only two were standing, the American-owned and well-backed Billy Barton and the 66–1 no hoper, amateur ridden, tubed Tipperary Tim. At the last Billy Barton toppled over and Tipperary Tim came home alone. Foinavon at 100–1, when winning in 1967, was also to benefit from a mass pile-up at one fence.

The Canal Turn was one of Snaffles' vantage points for watching the race and picking out its incidents for his illustrations. It must be remembered that much of his work, though it had grown to maturity, was still for periodical publication, at least, at first, before he had worked on it, for that was where his bread and butter lay. Those were the great days of the sporting and social glossies, such as *The Tatler, The Sketch* and, above all, *The Illustrated Sporting and Dramatic News* which were in every club and on every mess table. They eagerly snapped up Snaffles' work paying him handsomely for it. 'The Jostle for the Corner Pew' he called his sketch of the field attacking the Canal Turn before the ditch was filled in, which it was after the Easter Hero debacle. In it he has placed a horse and rider in the ditch, the jockey, as well he might be, looking remarkably apprehensive.

In the following season, 1928/1929, Easter Hero won the Gold Cup with contemptuous ease. The horse was now owned by the wealthy American Jack Whitney who declared him an attended runner for the Grand National. After the previous year's fiasco when only two horses completed the course, one after a fall, the Tophams, the family then controlling Liverpool, increased the entrance money to £100 and increased the forfeits in the hope of reducing the number of runners. The exact opposite happened. The prize money for the winner was calculated to be over £13,000 compared to around £11,000 for that year's Derby. Instead of reducing the field, owners left in any horse with or without a chance, and sixty-six started the Grand National that year, of which only ten finished. Easter Hero went again, this time handicapped to carry the top weight of 12 stone 7 lb. Snaffles was back in position at the Canal Turn for the race and he watched Easter Hero, Sandy Hook and Richmond II, ridden respectively by J. Moloney, J. Fish and

W. Stott, come over it together, second time round in the lead and at full stretch. It was a bright, clear day. The fence and riders could be seen with some ease from the stands and the excitement was intense as the crowd witnessed the sight of these three good horses jumping fast and without error as they took the turn. Easter Hero, on the inside and under the tender hands of Moloney, 'he could ride round Aintree with paper reins', made no mistake this time and landed just in the lead. It was a scene for Snaffles and he captured it. 'Even money on 'em' was how he captioned the picture which appeared in *The Illustrated Sporting and Dramatic News*. Let him describe what he saw in his own words. 'It was worth going a long way last year to see these three horses jumping faultlessly until Sandy Hook made a mistake beyond Valentines, and his place was taken by Gregalach, who robbed Easter Hero of the race. Had it not been for the latter's twisted plate this super horse would most probably have won, for as he passed Valentine's he was flippantly flinging himself, plus 12.7 of ballast, over each fence as it came in his stride and galloping as if he could go on for ever. It seemed as though a top-weight was really going to pull off the National at last.' It was not to be, but it was a supremely gallant failure. Easter Hero struggled gamely into second place beaten by Gregalach to whom he was conceding 17 lb. Richmond II, who was behind him in third place, was receiving no less than 29 lb. After the race it was revealed, as Snaffles records, that Easter Hero had twisted a plate and not only that, it had cut clean through his offside boot and bitten into the flesh.

Easter Hero was not a big strong horse of the fashionable 'Aintree type' so beloved by Snaffles, being all blood and quality. Taking that into account together with the weight he carried and that twisted plate, he must go down as the best horse never to win a National, although Prince Regent, another of Snaffles' heroes and gallant failures must run him close. For the record, Easter Hero won the 1930 Gold Cup, becoming the first horse to do so twice, ridden by the ex-amateur Tim Cullinan; he strained a tendon in the race and was withdrawn four days before the Grand National, leaving Cullinan without a mount but he came in for a spare ride on Shaun Goilin and in a desperate finish won by a head from Melleray's Bell. As well as winning the Cheltenham Gold Cup, he also won the Champion Hurdle on Brown Tony – the only time this tremendous riding treble has ever been achieved.

Easter Hero won a couple of small races in 1931 and again carried 12 stone 7 lb starting a favourite for the National, but he was knocked over by a horse of Dorothy Paget's at Becher's the second time round, when not going like a winner. He was pulled out the next day for the two mile seven furlong Champion Chase and just managed to dead-heat. His owner thought the horse was on the decline so he was retired to his stud in Virginia, where he lived to the age of twenty-eight.

Not only was Easter Hero a great idol of Snaffles probably for his gallant failure in the 1929 National, but the first public idol after the First World War, doing much to help popularise the rising sport of steeplechasing.

Round about 1930 Snaffles produced the pair of point-to-point prints depicting different scenes in the parade ring. The authors, when recording Appendix A, first used in *Snaffles – The Life and Work of Charlie Johnson Payne*, published in 1987, were under the impression that these were published in 1925/1926. However subsequent research leads us to believe that they were probably produced in the early 1930's, as the young lady appearing in 'The One to carry your Half Crown' is also 'The Lovely from a Fashionable Country' which appeared on page 28 of *Red Letter Days* and Snaffles did not start to co-operate with M.J. Farrell for this book until the early 1930's. The other print of this pair is a 'Bona-Fide Fox-Chaser,' which shows a scarlet-coated rider dismounting after winning a point-to-point. It may be of interest to readers that these coats, worn racing, were often made of silk and weighed 1½/2lb.

This is one of the few racing or point-to-point prints where Snaffles has used a hunting remarque

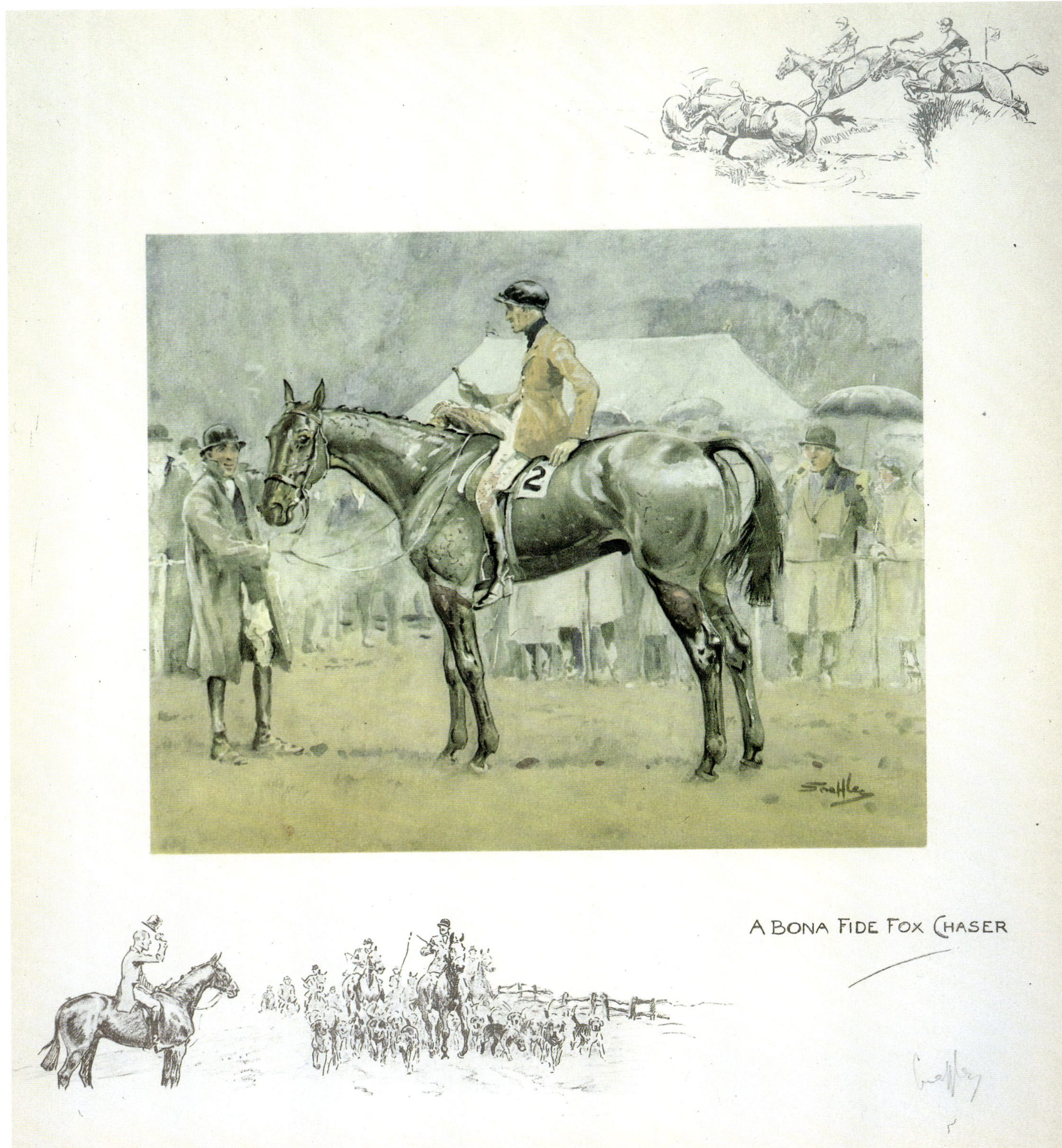

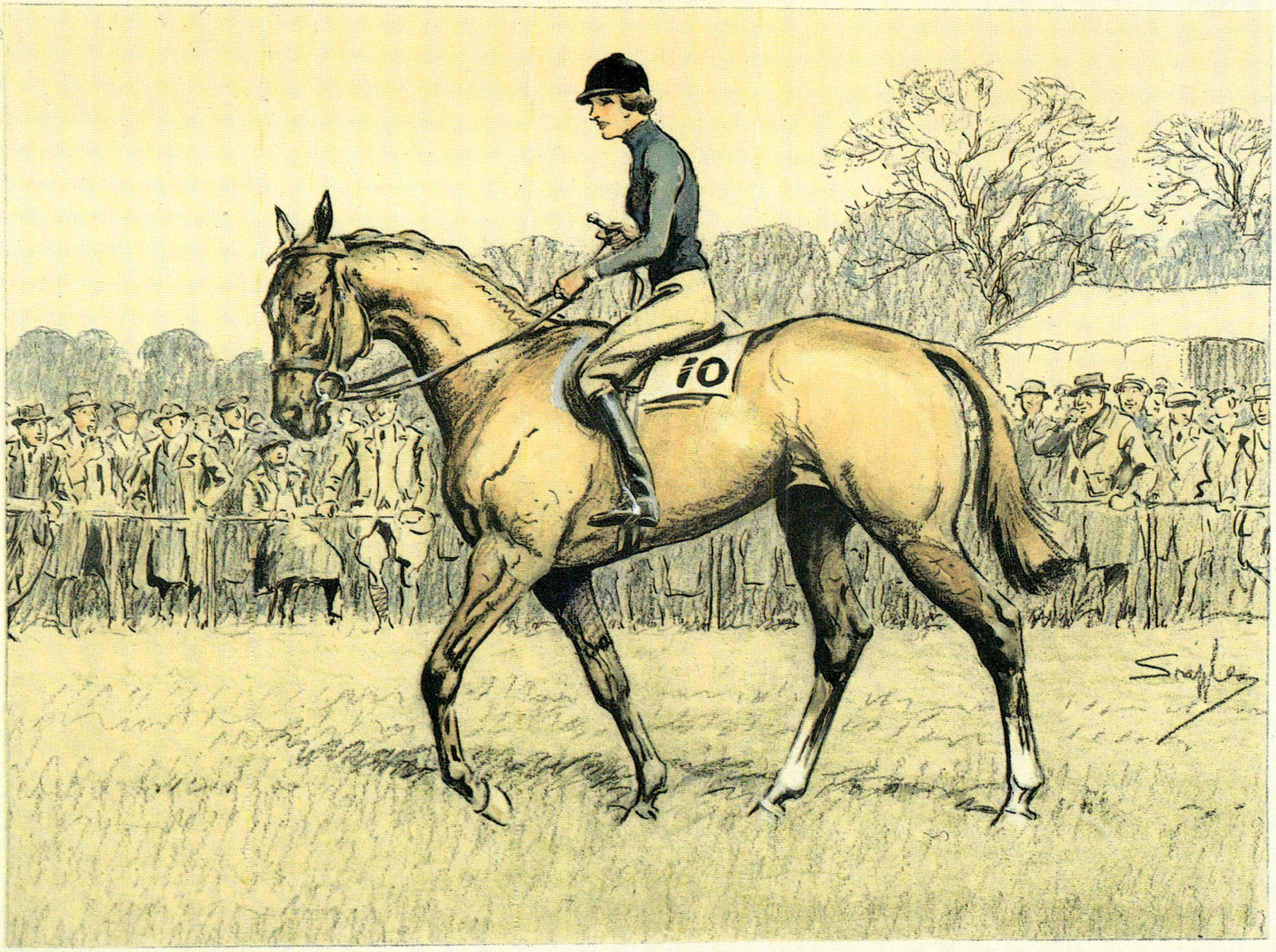

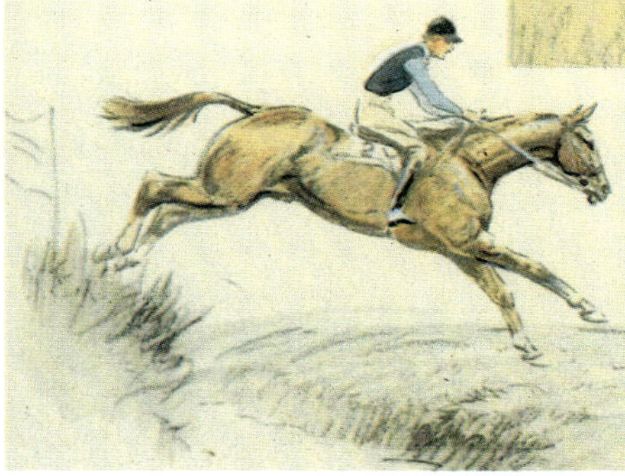

THE ONE TO CARRY YOUR HALF-CROWN.

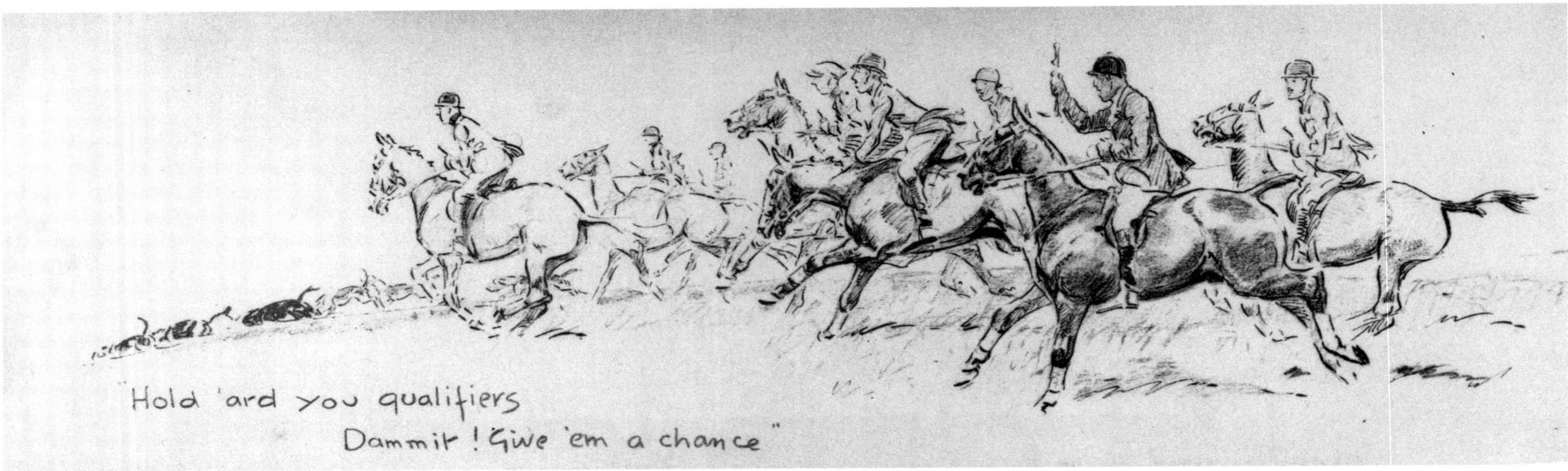

The print of the R.A. Harriers (opposite), executed in 1931, demonstrates clearly how Snaffles completely understood the relationship between the point to pointing and hunting fraternities. We have enlarged the remarque to show how the artist exactly captured the over enthusiasm of the point to point qualifiers incurring the wrath of the field master

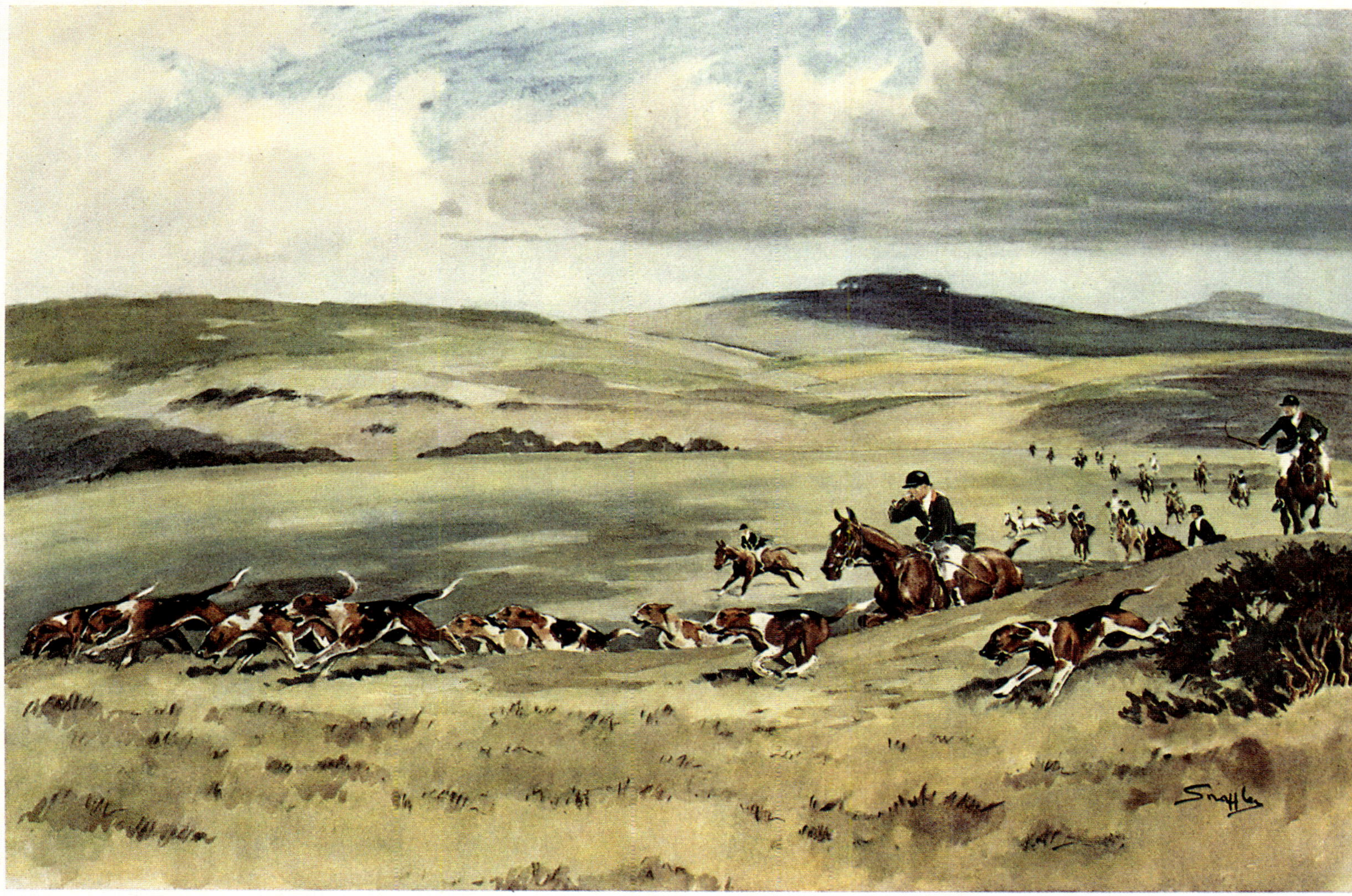

THE R. A. HARRIERS

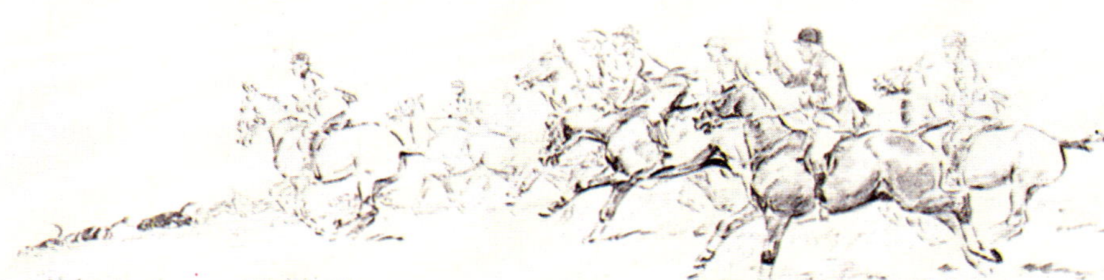

Hold 'ard you qualifiers
Dammit! Give 'em a chance

6 India and Ireland Again

'Much talk there was in the club in Peshawar over the finest view in Europe or Asia', Snaffles was to tell Molly Keane a little later. 'Some said it was in County Meath. Others saw it with the Braunston Vale spread out below them. Some would have it nearer at hand and swore they found no view or moment equal to those when – with the sun coming up beyond the green of the Peshawar Vale and the Khyber Hills rose pink in the distance – hounds are running on over a country of banks and drains, a sure point of four miles in the making and never a sign of wire or a cry of 'War Wheat' '.

Snaffles would have found himself in sympathy with those of the last class he mentioned, although it is true that he was inclined to allow himself to be carried away by his enthusiasms for the place he was at, and the people, in this instance 'the good chaps at Muttra and Meerut and the Masters and Whips of the PVH', with whom he mingled. There is no doubt that India and the field sports of 'the Sahibs and Rajahs' captivated him, for he had, in the words of his favourite poet, ''eard the East a' callin',' and had followed the call on a sporting and sketching tour of India.

Sadly, although he saw much of the amateur racing at Dehli, Meerut and Lucknow on his visit, most of the Indian racing sketches were destroyed in the fires which consumed his stored belongings during the Second World War. However, one or two have survived from *My Sketchbook in the Shiny*, such as the Memsahib's Race at the PVH point-to-point and there is a spirited sketch of the Brigadier of his beloved Horse Gunners 'riding a finish' at a review at Meerut.

The pig-sticking pictures and prints have survived in considerable numbers as have his drawings of 'The Hog-Hunters Cup' a race run after the Kadir Cup 'The Hog-Hunters Grand National' over a ferocious natural country of banks and nullahs. Snaffles' own words, describe the scene of the race as he saw it.

> It was open to the competitors and their horses who had actually ridden after pig at the meeting. The course was just natural Kadir grass. Grass sounds good stuff to gallop over, but this particular form of herbage is more like the top joints of fishing rods than the grass we know and no self-respecting fox-hunter would dare to trot through it.
>
> The obstacles were holes and nullahs, more or less deep – some just small dry beds of streams. There were other hazards to add to the chance of winning, such as the odd buffalo wallow and stampeding cattle getting in front of the galloping horses. But the one I have depicted was a chasm and had to be treated with great respect. With a pig in front to show the way when hunting it was good pig-sticking country. To race over with no pig as pilot was decidedly worrying to both horse and rider as the going was blind underfoot, and no rider was allowed to walk the course beforehand. The distance was about three miles and not flagged, and the conditions were similar to the old-fashioned point-to-point course, except that instead of a church steeple or windmill as a point to ride for, the course was horseshoe in shape and two elephants were sent out across the plain as aids to navigation and marks at which to turn in the vast ocean of grass.

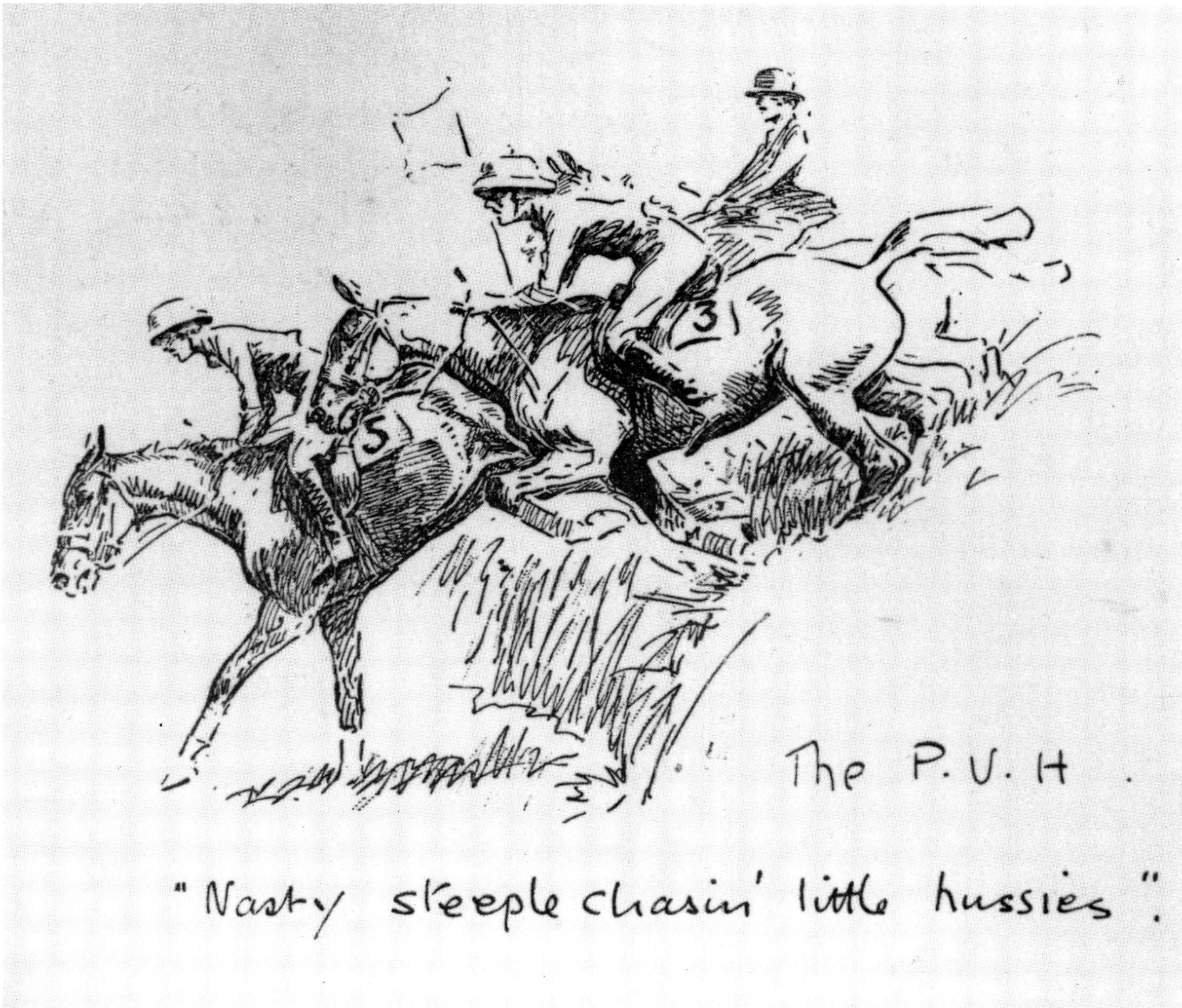
5
3
The P.U.H.
"Nasty steeple chasin' little hussies".

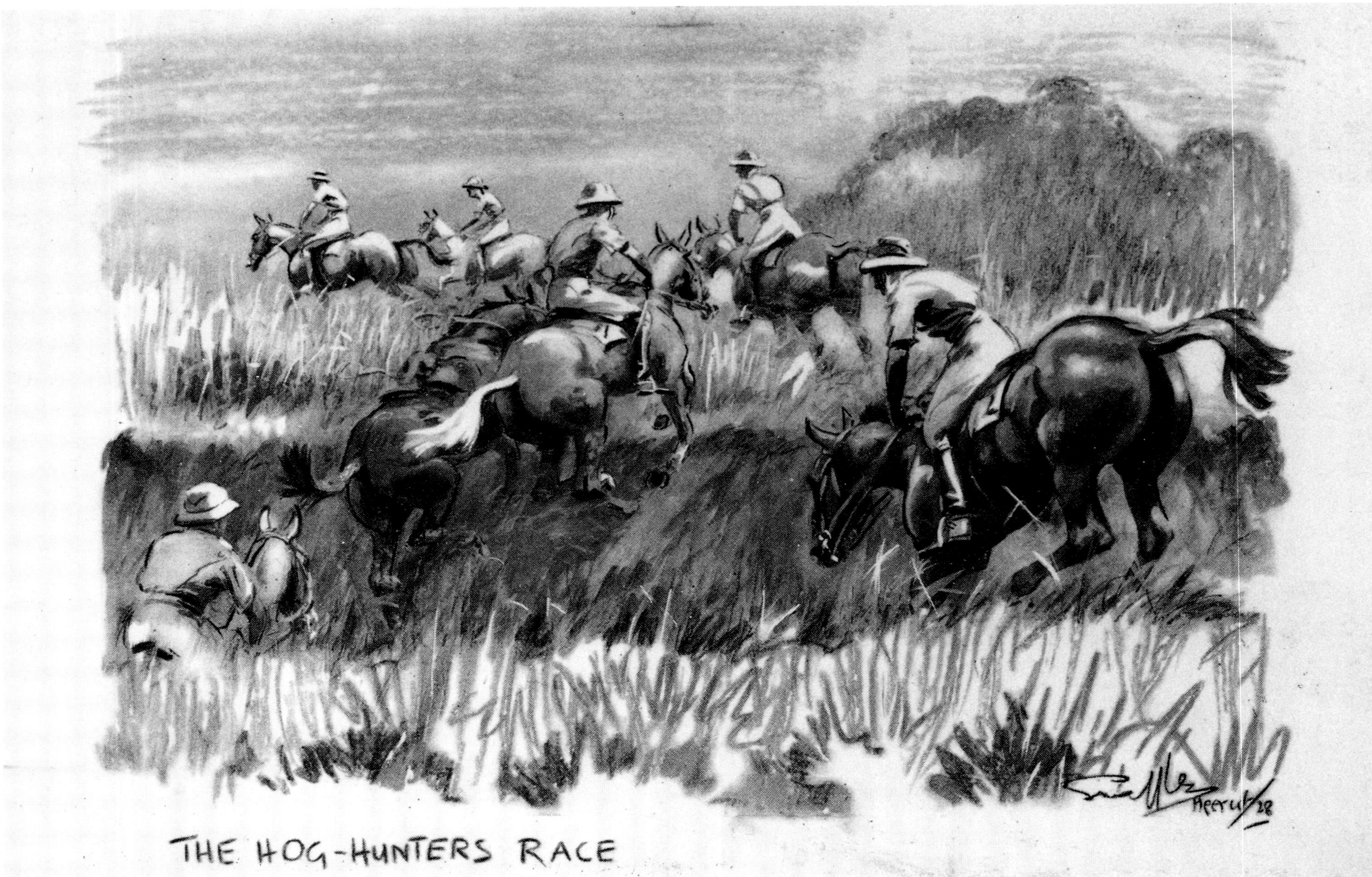

The Hog-Hunters' Cup, run after the Kadir Cup pigsticking meeting, although in theory a flat race, used to result in a large number of falls and visits to the doctor or hospital

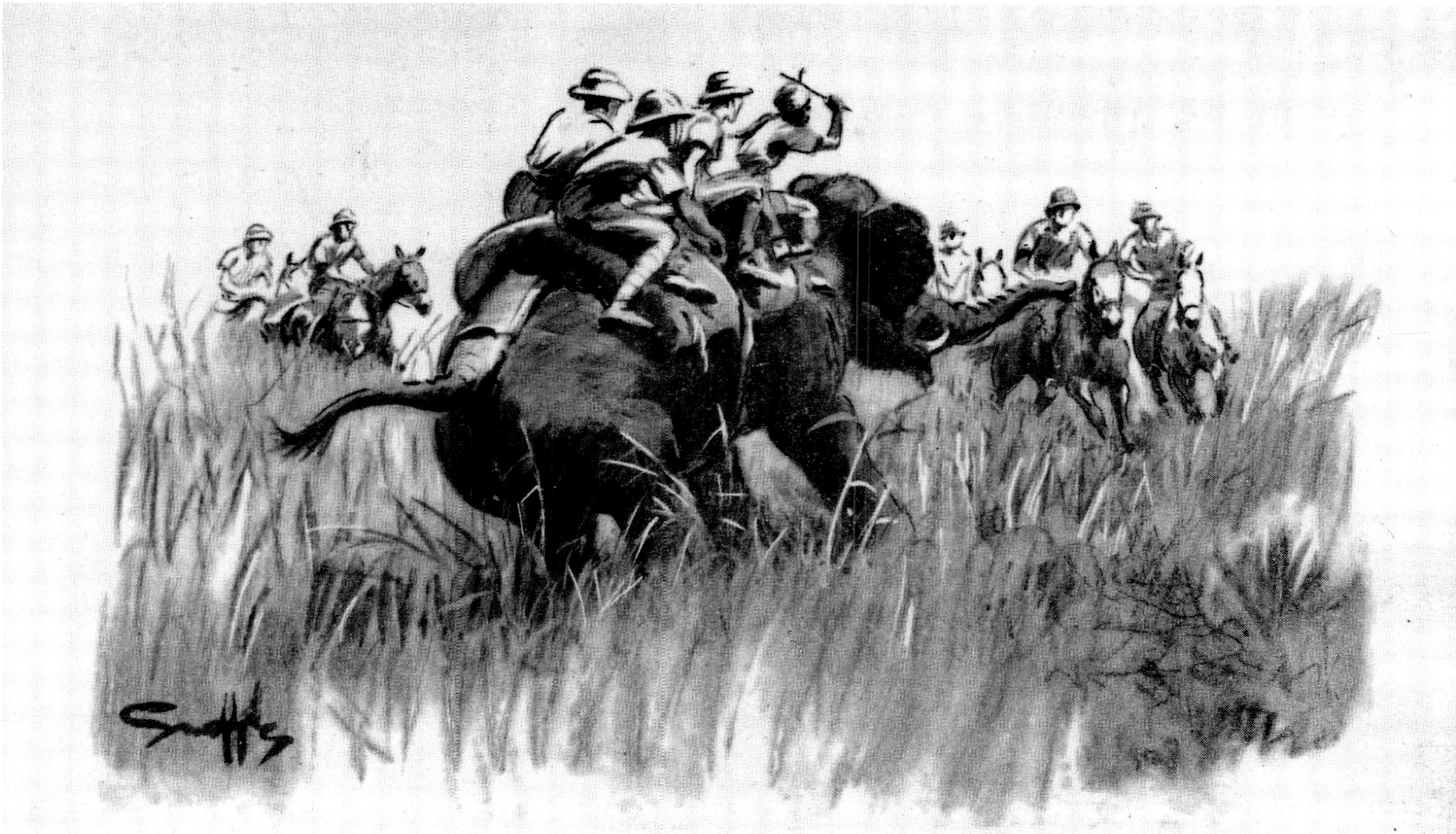

THE MARK HATHI. —— Cutting the corner rather fine.

Snaffles loved elephants. He painted and drew them beautifully

To ride flat out over this country took considerable nerve, a fair degree of horsemanship and above all else tough, old-fashioned 'guts'. It may be of interest to record that HRH The Duke of Windsor, as Prince of Wales, rode in, and won, the lightweight division of this race in 1922; thereby disproving the aspersions then currently being cast on his horsemanship by the media and other wiseacres.

Here, as elsewhere, but especially in his racing and pig-sticking sketches, Snaffles took immense pains to get his details right. Nothing was too much trouble for him nor, it may be said, was he sparing on the demands he made on his models and those who posed for him, as Mrs. Norah Pearson explained in considerable detail to the authors when describing the number of times she was asked to ride Taffy Walwyn's steeplechaser, Viking II and, as Major General Brian Daunt recounted in a letter to John Welcome which reads as follows:

> I first met Snaffles in 1928 when he came up to Landi Kotal which overlooked the Khyber Pass to draw sketches of Mountain Artillery: I was then a subaltern in the 3rd (Peshawar) Mountain Battery, Royal Artillery (Frontier Force) and I spent a very happy morning watching Snaffles making sketches of the Battery coming over a col not far from the Battery Mule Lines ... Knowing that I was coming home on leave in 1929, Snaff wrote to me saying that he hadn't got the officer's legs right, would I come and pose for him. He was living then near Guildford so putting on breeches and gaiters I posed for him on Leith Hill on a bank holiday! So the legs and feet are definitely mine.
>
> After lunch he asked me to pose again, this time standing on my head in an armchair with my legs waving in the air. You can see them in Snaffles' *Sketchbook in The Shiny* – opposite the Sha Alan Regatta picture there is another entitled 'Decanted' those legs and backside are mine though I was never in fact decanted in the Sha Alan.

The activities described in Major General Daunt's letter took place back in England after his return from India when he was re-working and perfecting the sketches of his trip. He eventually produced twelve or fifteen prints, a remarkable visual record of sporting India, the like of which will never again be seen.

On the home front, Snaffles was to produce the hunting print 'R.A. Harriers' in 1931. This shows Major Laynard in full cry with his hounds across the Wiltshire Downs. To this print Snaffles was to use a remarque with a point-to-pointing annotation of an irate field-master trying to control a field of qualifying soldiers by screaming 'Hold hard you qualifiers, dammit give 'em a chance'. Tidworth, on the centre of Salisbury Plain, along with Woolwich, was one of the strongholds of 'Gunnerdom', and Snaffles spent much time there sketching and portraying the soldiers at work and play. He often attended the regular bona-fide military meetings held at Windmill Hill. Using the 1936 Formbook once again as reference, one sees that there were four meetings held there: the Second Cavalry Brigade, the R.A. Harriers, the Salisbury Plain Military and the Tedworth Hunt.

Soon after his return from India, Snaffles received an invitation from Colonel Kerans, a friend he had made while hunting with the Peshawar Vale. The invitation was eagerly accepted and the ensuing trip was responsible for the great series of Irish prints in 1933/35.

It was some twenty years since Snaffles had been in Ireland. His first visit had resulted in such splendid prints as 'An Irish Point-to-Point' and 'The Tiger', and immediately on his return there, he knew that Ireland and its sports were made for him. The next few years when he was visiting Ireland on a regular basis were some of Snaffles' happiest. He loved everything about Ireland and is still remembered there with great affection.

Snaffles' first hunt was in Galway on a horse loaned to him by Major Bertie Waller. Once hounds ran he finally confessed that he was 'distinctly and definitely over-horsed', and the events of the day which were described in considerable detail in the first book of this series would certainly appear to confirm this. In his account of this day's hunting he called his mount 'Jimmy the One'. In fact Jimmy the One was Daddy Two, standing just 15 hands, whom Major Waller rode in cobs races, a feature of Irish point-to-points in those days.

Cobs were defined as standing at 15 hands or under and many were the arguments which took place as to whether or not a horse was qualified to run. These were only settled by the production of a measuring stick and an assessment of height made under the supervision of the course vet – and indeed they were not always even settled then! Major Waller won a succession of these races on Daddy Two and on one occasion such were the arguments that Daddy Two's shoes had to be removed before he would go 'under the stick'.

Horses who have been hunted over banks comparatively slowly, and who are then galloped over them racing, invariably become hotted up when reverting to the hunting field. It is therefore no wonder that Snaffles, on Daddy Two, found himself, when hounds ran, on a 'veritable stag of a horse' and would echo the words of an adviser at the meet that, over the country he was about to face, he would be 'saysick wid leppin'.

The result of all these excitements and falls only served to increase his enthusiasm. He was to depict himself in one of his two great Irish hunting prints, 'The Biggest Walls in the Counthry was in it', on Daddy Two that day riding at an enormous wall with a stream at the other side, virtually unjumpable. They also gave him, too, more humorous material for his sketching hand, while his receptive ear captured the idiom of the country people more surely than any other Englishman has ever done. In all this he was assisted by the magic pen of 'M.J. Farrell', the name under which Molly Keane then wrote, when he went with her, at the invitation of Colonel George Hudson-Kinahan, to portray an Irish point-to-point in the Island Country of County Wexford. His sketches and colour plates were included in the ever popular sporting book *Red Letter Days* that memorable evocation of a sporting Ireland which has vanished never to return.

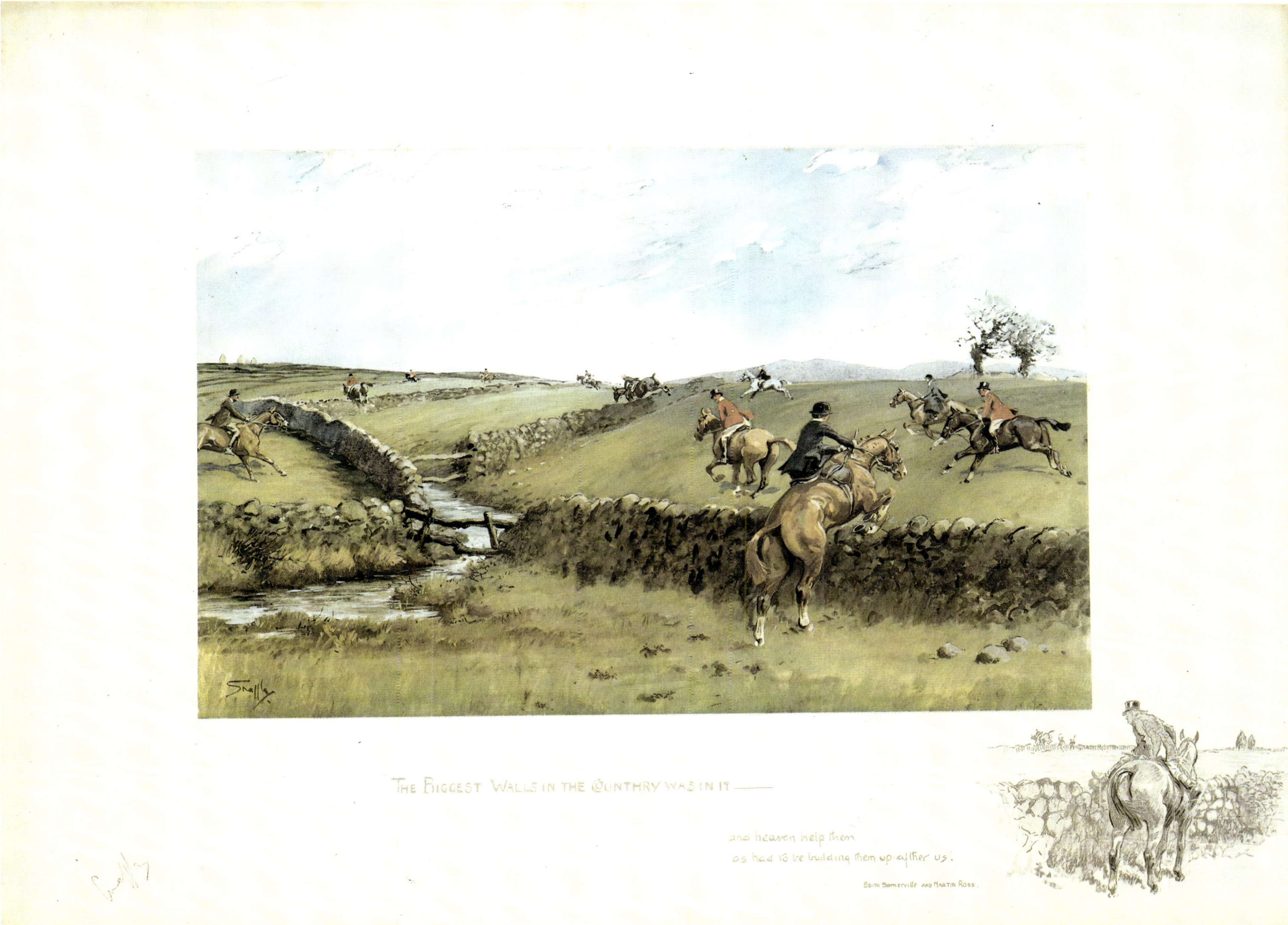

In this print Snaffles is the figure on the left, mounted on a successful point to pointer called Daddy Two, who was under 15 hands and had won cobs' races

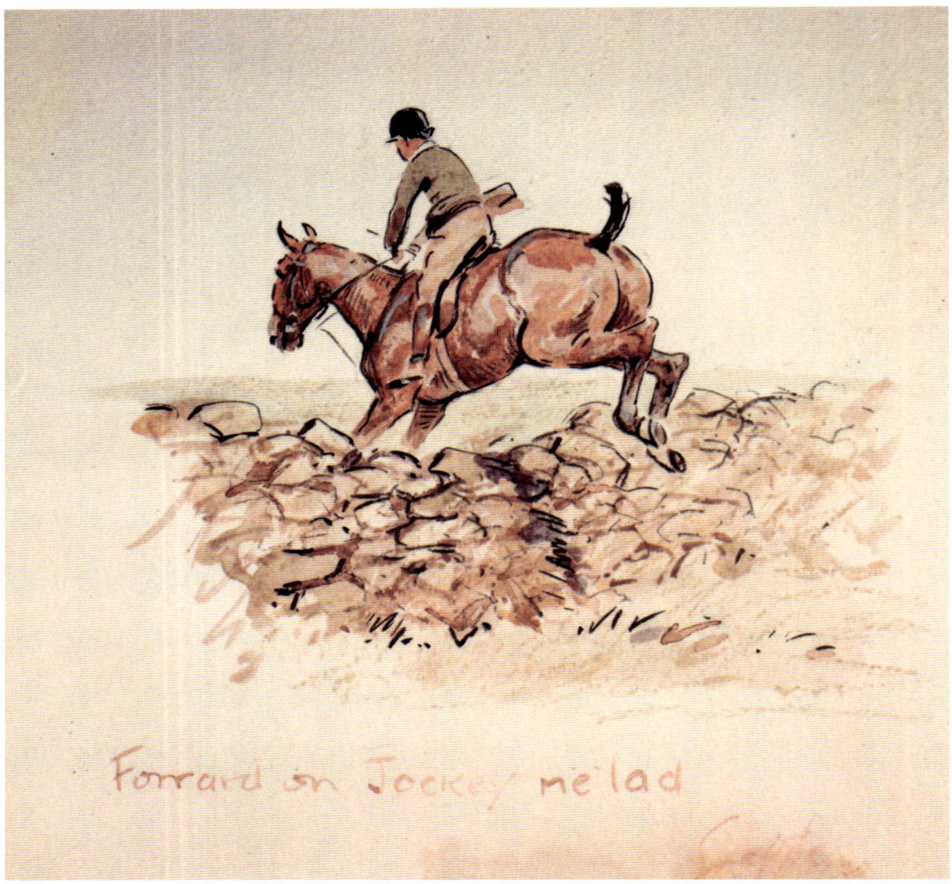

Snaffles did this watercolour of the Wallers' Daddy Two, with their son, Obby, riding him over a wall. He titled it 'Forrard on Jockey me lad' before giving it to Obby's mother

M.J. Farrell chronicled the racing from start to finish with words, while Snaffles depicted the scenes throughout the day with his pencil and watercolours, commencing with a scene in the paddock where the priest surveys a runner and gives his comments. Actually this painting, a watercolour (Snaffles never seemed to use oils) which first appeared as a colour plate in *The Illustrated Sporting and Dramatic News*, was a continuation and elaboration of a sketch he had first made at the East Galway point-to-point and of the same priest, or at least one very similar and in a very similar attitude, watching the saddling. Before it appeared in its final form in *Red Letter Days*, Snaffles had worked on it, as he normally did with his early sketches, to improve it and bring out the salient points. It is of interest to compare the two to show how Snaffles toiled on a regular basis at his pictures, eliminating a detail here and adding another there. In this instance the saddling tent in the background is added, the tilt of the rider's head and the colour of his cap altered, the lady beside the shawled figure on the rails has changed, one hunt servant disappears altogether and there are many other minor changes. It is of interest to observe how meticulous Snaffles was to be exact in every detail, capturing the fact that the rider's breeches were laced not buttoned, his boots were worn low on the leg and, as the painting finally appeared, he has altered and strengthened the rider's expression. In these sketches Snaffles has caught not only the fun, the informality and the spirit of the whole thing, but also the characters who made it. 'The Queen of the Bogs', 'The Lovely from the fashionable country', the running of the race right up to the splendid drawing, 'Got it Won', and the objection to the winner of the Farmers' Race in the tent afterwards. These drawings showed Snaffles at his informal best, lovely, enjoyable pieces of art in their own right, but with his captions they become pure magic. They were, of course, the result of sketches which he had done on his visits to point-to-points in County Wexford where he stayed for lengthy periods, and not pure illustrations such as the work he did for Geoffrey Brooke's *Horse Lovers*. The difference is immediately visible.

Once again Snaffles was to visit Punchestown and there were more sketches of 'thim jockey lads' in action. It was a Punchestown much changed since his previous pre-war visit. Gone were the top hats, the regimental tents for entertaining, the finery, which had now been replaced by tweed. But the spirit in which it was all taken was the same. The big bank was still there and the Conyngham Cup was still run, so there was much to delight him and provide him with material.

Back in England Snaffles grew quite lyrical about Brown Jack's sixth consecutive victory in the Queen Alexandra Stakes at Royal Ascot in 1934. Sadly Snaffles' background picture of this great stayer in his humorous sketch of 'The Only Enthusiastic Admirer' being apprehended by the Police appears to be the sole example of his drawings of Flat racehorses to have survived. Snaffles would of course have been familiar with Brown Jack's owner, Colonel Sir Harold Werner, one of the legendary masters of the Fernie, a pack with whom Snaffles had hunted.

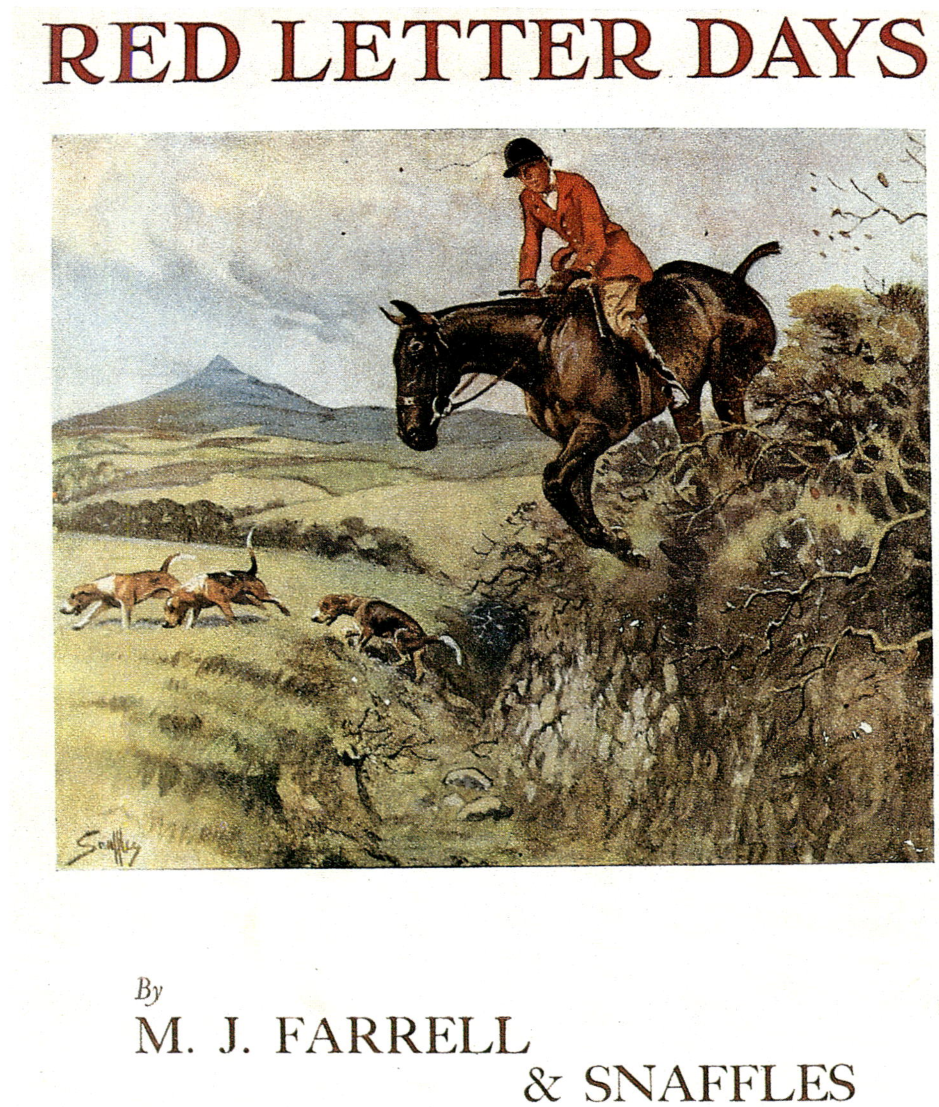

Snaffles' dust wrappers were, without exception, highly successful

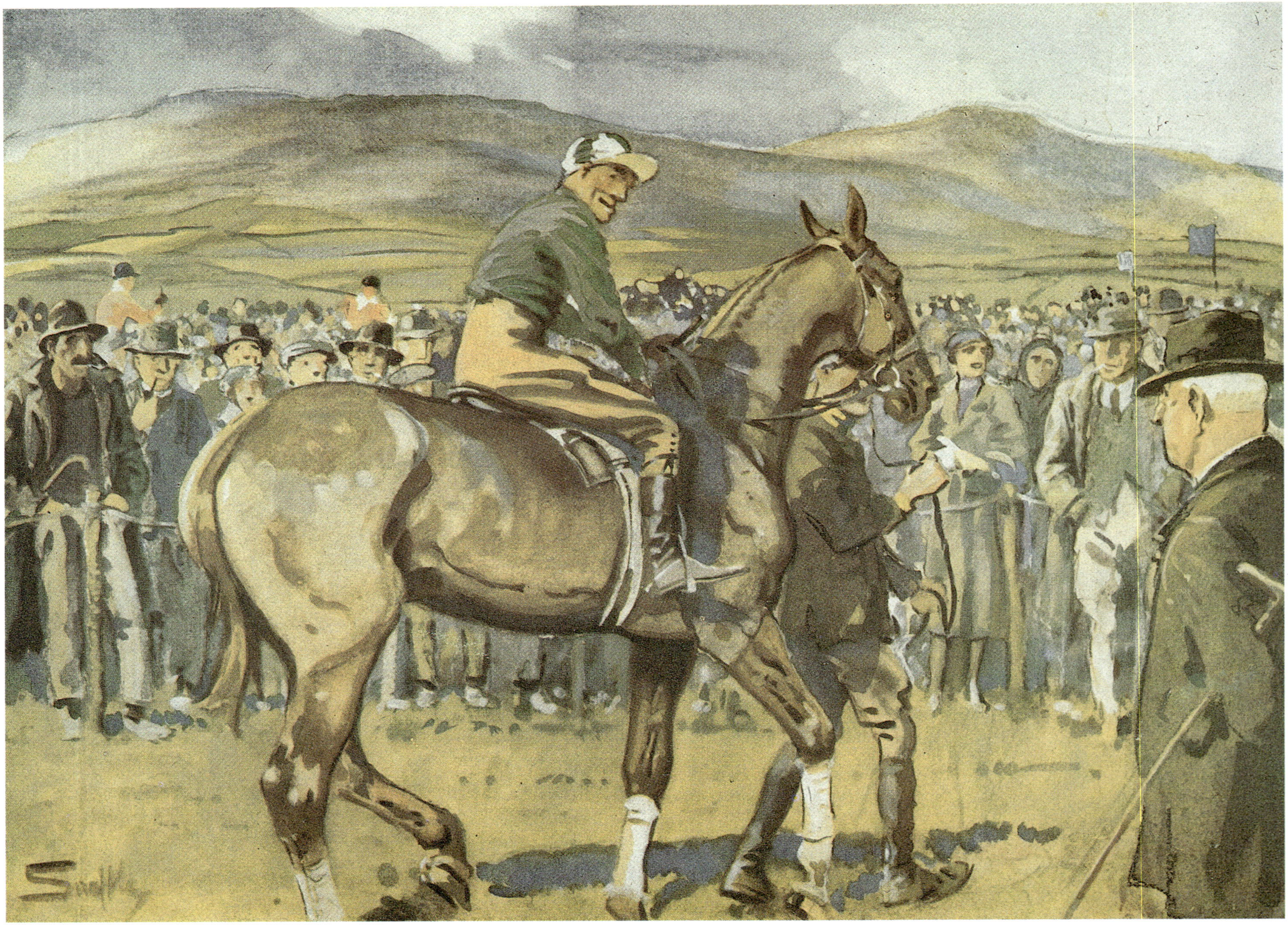

This illustration first appeared in the *Illustrated Sporting and Dramatic News*

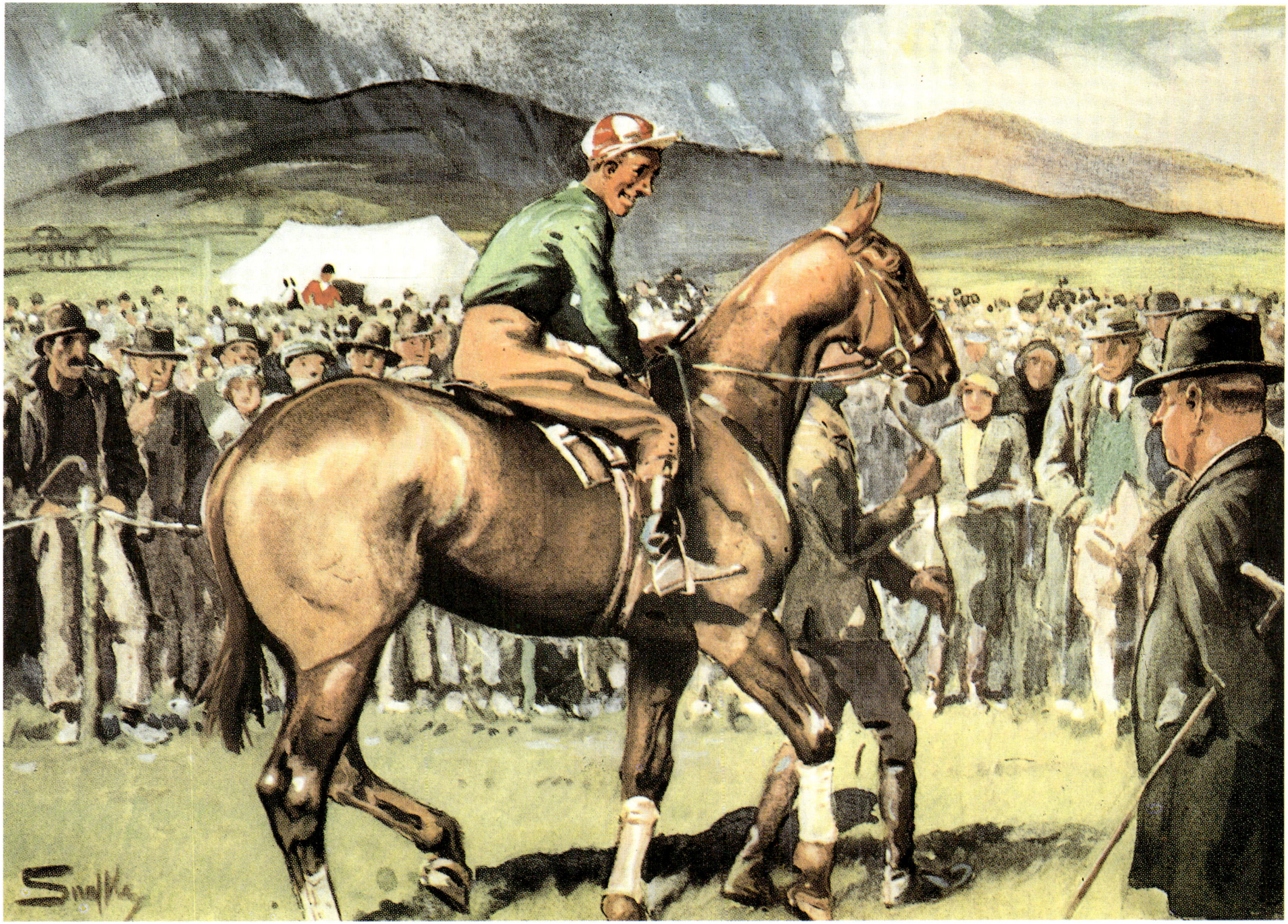

Snaffles has done a considerable amount of reworking his original sketch for his illustration in *Red Letter Days*. Note in this picture a tent, one hunt servant in place of two, different colour cap, seat of jockey, carriage of horse's head, etc.

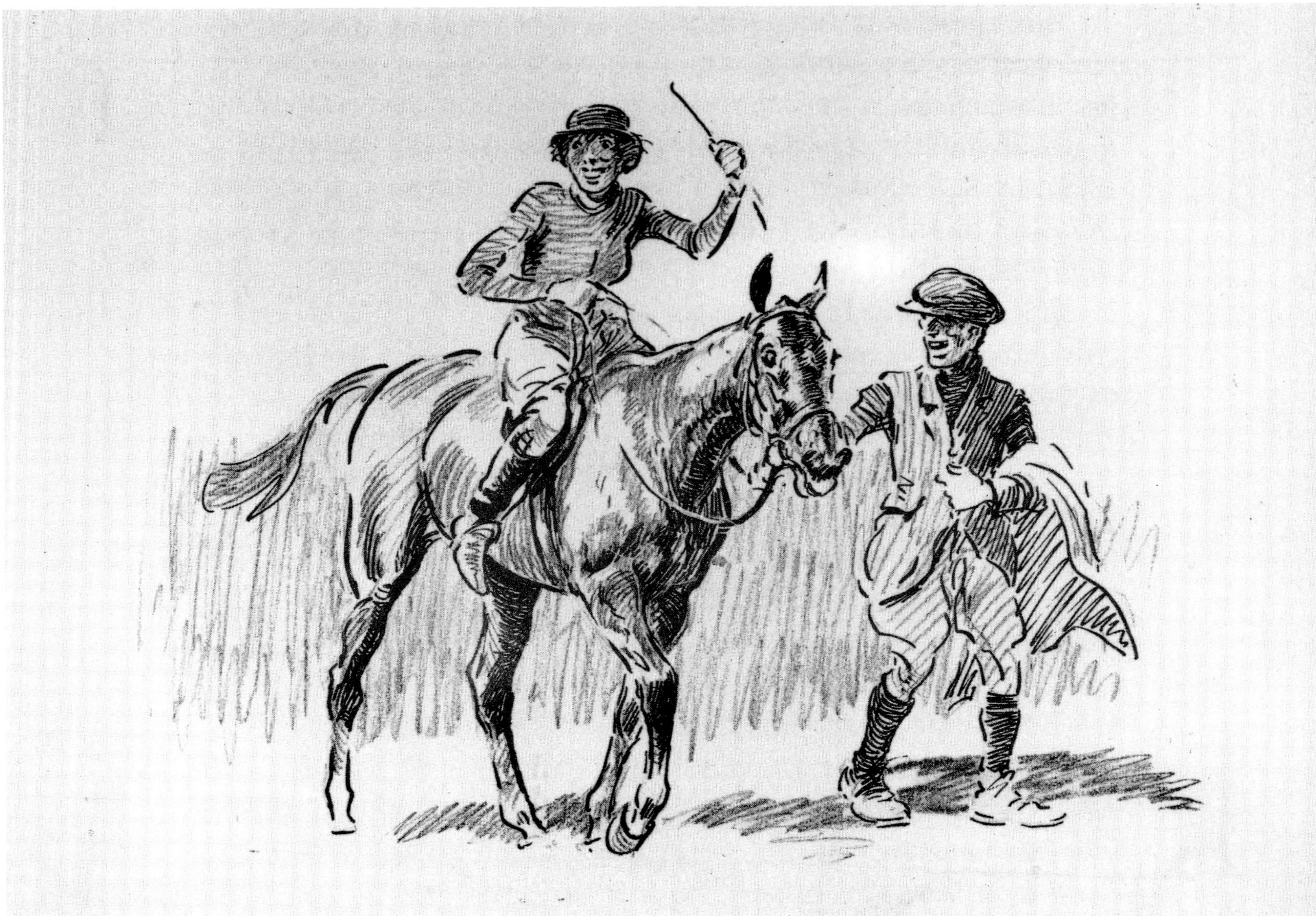

The Queen of the Bogs

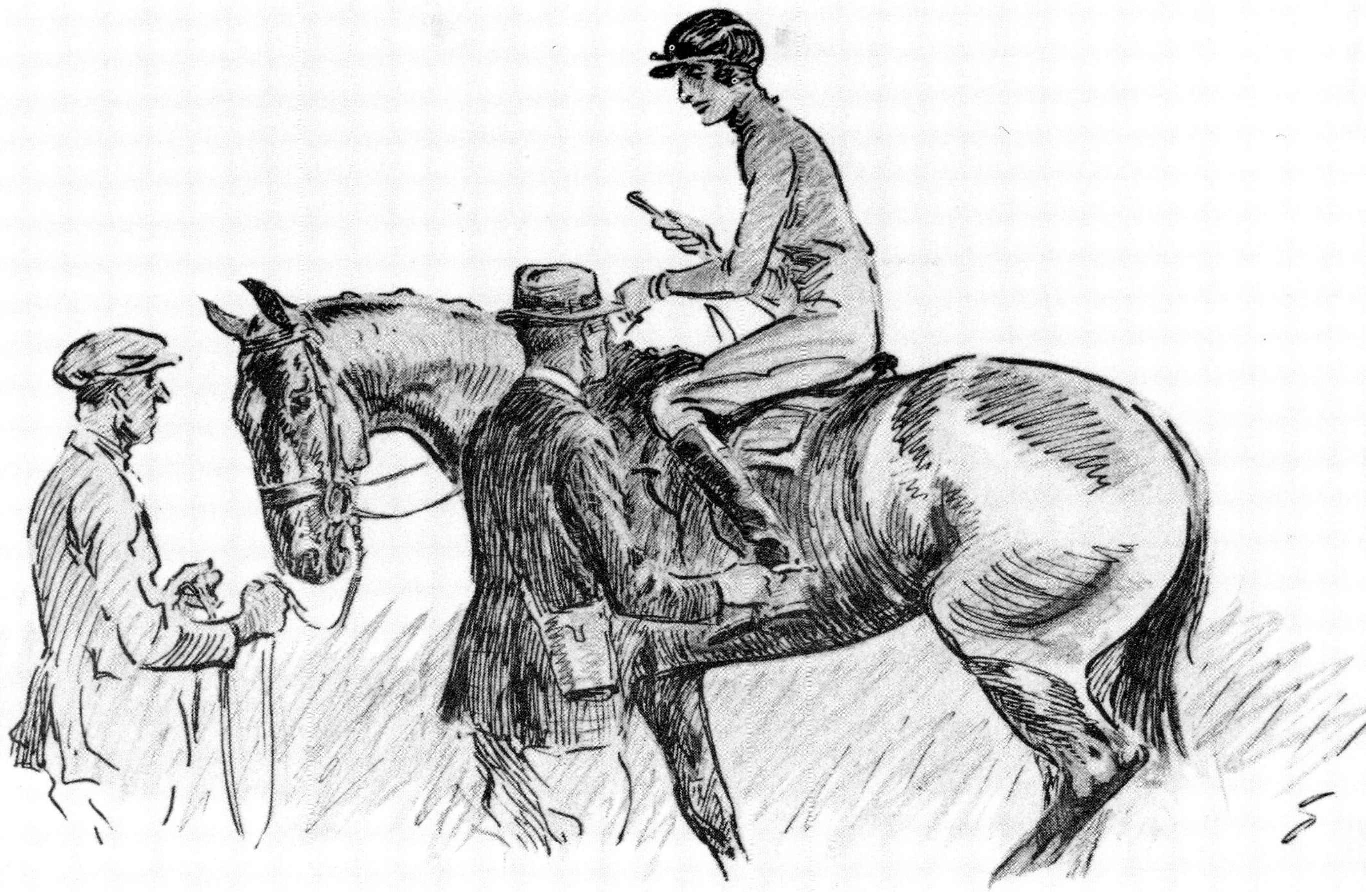

The Lovely from a fashionable country

The illustrations on the previous pages and here are from *Red Letter Days*, a marvellous book, reprinted, we are pleased to say, in 1987

Snaffles had an understanding and feeling for Irish hunting, racing and point to pointing in all its facets, seldom achieved, certainly never surpassed, by any other twentieth century sporting artist.

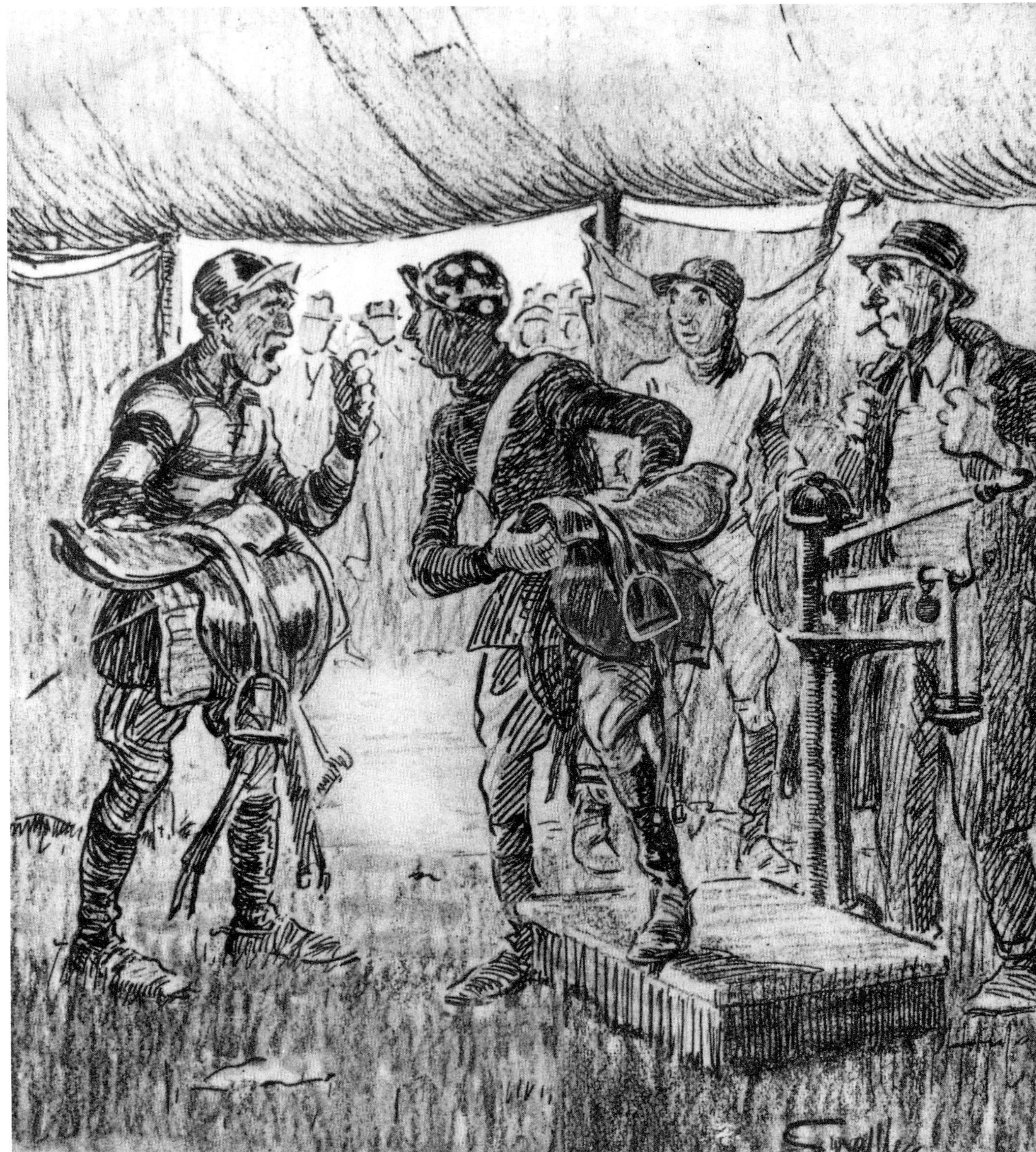

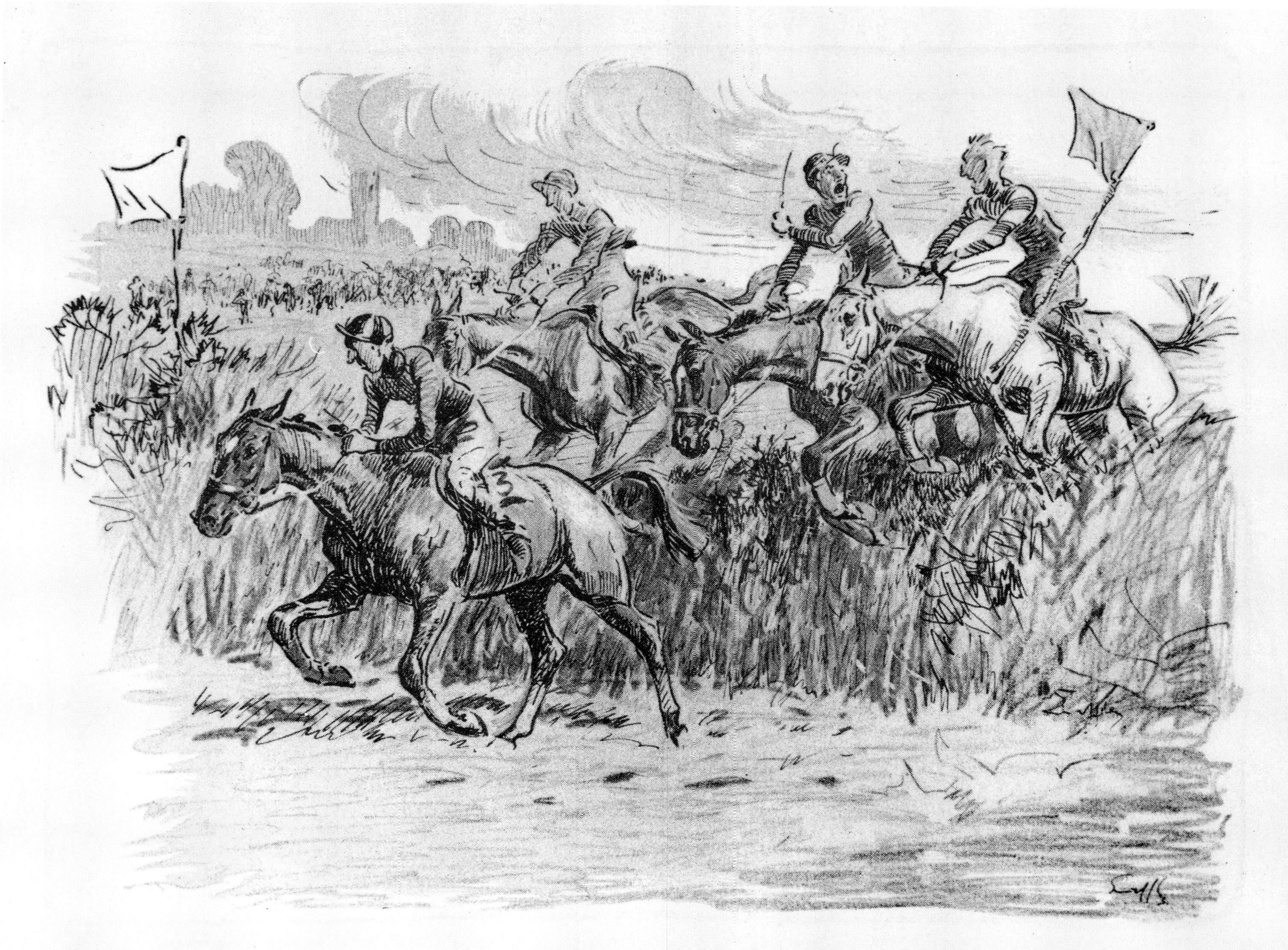

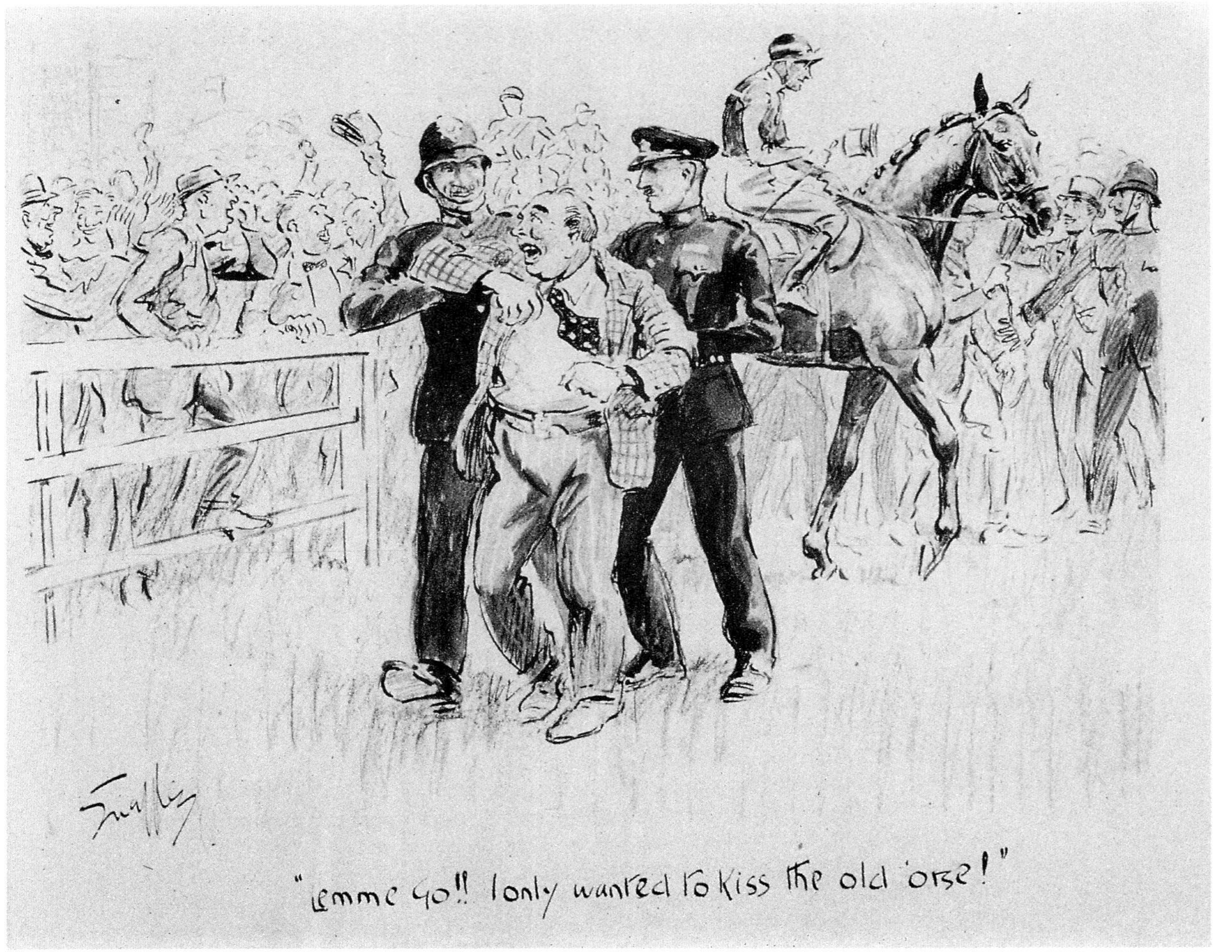

Brown Jack certainly caught Snaffles' imagination. The loss of his sketch books in two fires during the Second World War deprived future generations of a wealth of similar material. It is probably that Snaffles was with Lionel Edwards at Ascot in 1934 to see the great horse win his sixth Queen Alexandra Stakes

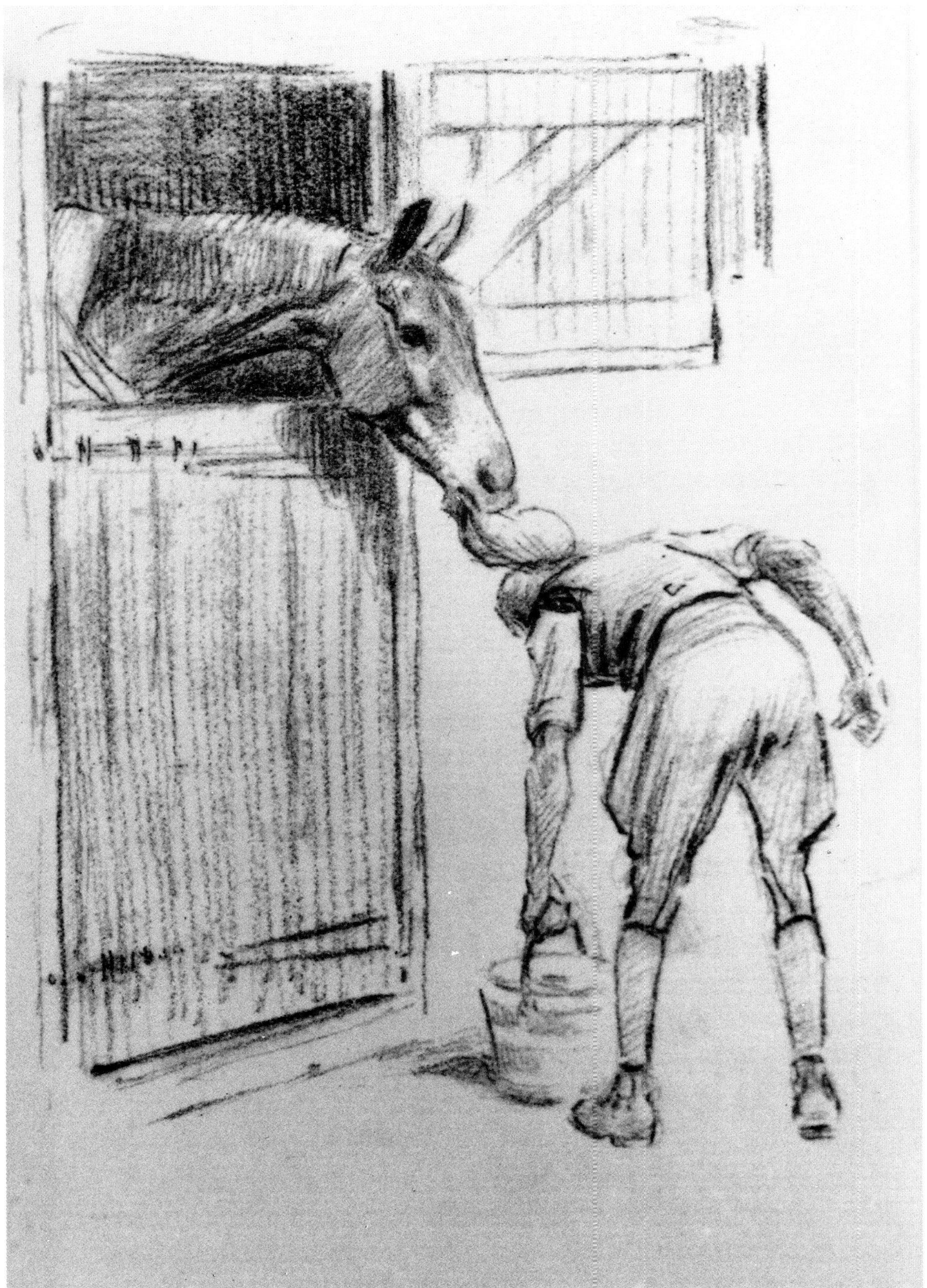

Stealing Alfie's Cap

This little drawing of Brown Jack in a playful mood is by Lionel Edwards

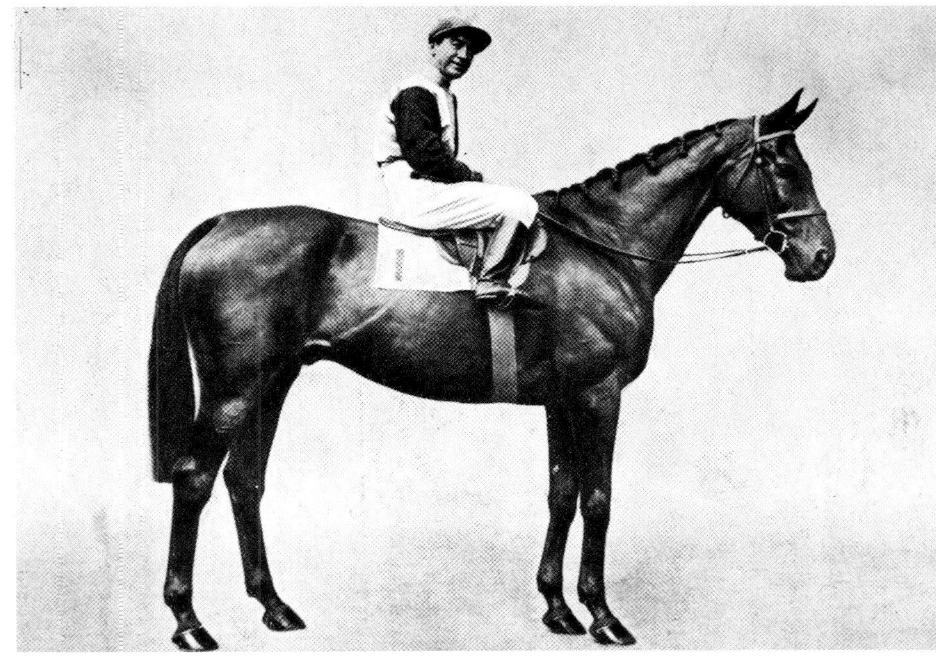

The combination of Brown Jack and Steve Donoghue was the most popular horse and jockey combination on the flat between the wars

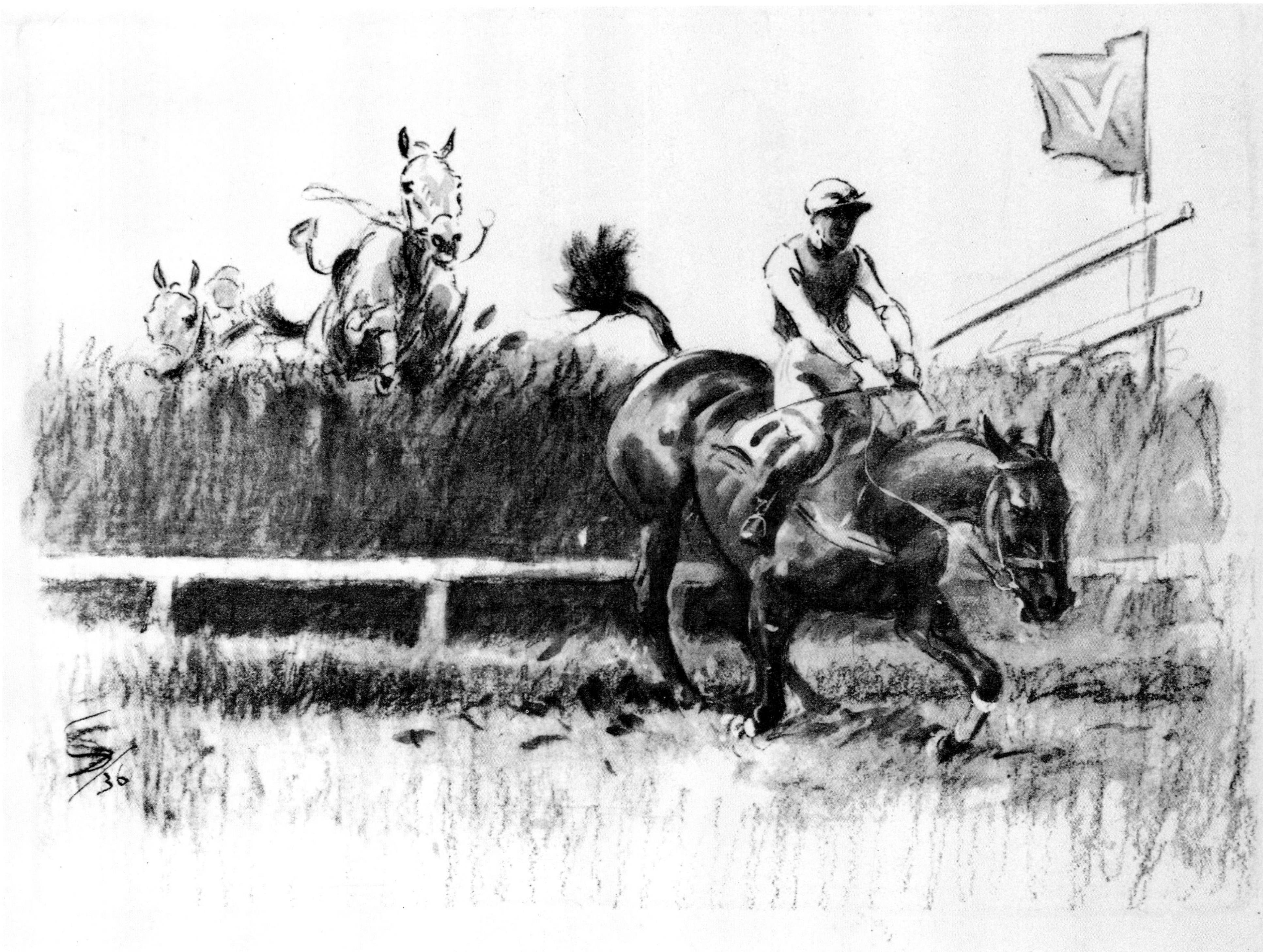

'Reynoldstown giving his backers a shake the second time round at Valentines. But by the superb horsemanship of Fulke Walwyn he was kept on his legs and galloped on to win his second Grand National'

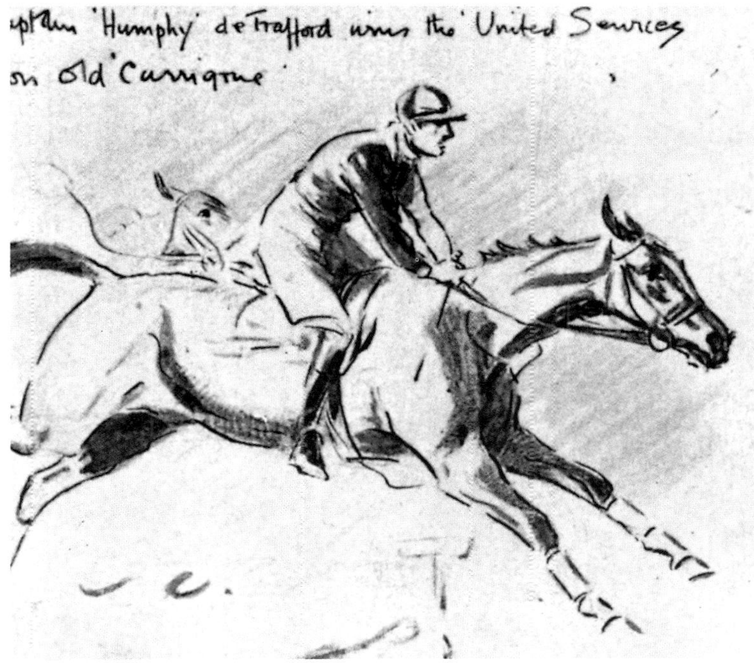

Captain Humphrey de Trafford was a good amateur rider in the 1920s and later became Fulke Walwyn's father-in-law. He owned the Derby winner Parthia

That year, too, saw Snaffles produce what may well have been one of his best of his equestrian portraits, that of his friend and fellow artist, Cecil Aldin, jumping a fence at the South Berks point-to-point. Snaffles always preferred to paint horses in action rather than repose and here he has caught exactly the likeness of horse and man in the act of jumping. 'Out for a Jolly' he wrote, before signing it and presenting it to the subject. Cecil Aldin was so enchanted with this watercolour that he used it as a frontispiece for his memoirs *Time I was Dead* which was published in 1934. We have chosen to do the same thing.

The picture of Cecil Aldin, then aged nearly sixty, 'Out for a Jolly' expresses the sporting spirit Snaffles so much admired, and in which Aldin, and others like him rode in point-to-points, as did many in those days for 'a good bump round'; although it must be said that, though there were many Aldins and others bumping round, the standard of point-to-pointing in the Aldershot area at times could be extremely high, especially when the young Cavalry soldiers were 'having a crack'.

If he wasn't in Ireland, Snaffles would have undoubtedly been at the famous 1930 Garth point-to-point run over the Arborfield course when three comparatively unknown amateurs were all to win races and went on to ride winners of Grand Nationals and one of them also trained Grand National winners. The three young riders were: Frank Furlong, who won the 1935 Grand National on Reynoldstown, Fulke Walwyn, who won the 1936 Grand National on the same horse, and the schoolboy, Bobbie Petre, whose victory in the Grand National came in 1946 on Lovely Cottage. Fulke Walwyn is now the well-known Lambourn trainer, who has won every major steeplechase as a trainer, including the Grand National, the Gold Cup and the Whitbread Gold Cup.

It was the Grand National that was always to claim Snaffles' attention. Some years he made the then fashionable day trip by train to Liverpool, accompanied by a combination of Cecil Aldin, Lionel Edwards and Gilbert Holiday; all keen followers of hounds, good artists and friends of each other. Other years Snaffles spent three or four days attending the whole meeting, so he could watch the amateurs take their turn over the Grand National course in the Foxhunters. He was certainly there as normal to witness the great Golden Miller's win in 1934 carrying 12stones 12 lb. in record time and ridden by Gerry Wilson. He was also there in 1935 to witness the tragedy of the Miller going out of the race, which he had won the previous year in record time, for which he had started the shortest priced favourite in the race's history at two to one. What happened is well described by the turf historian, Patricia Smyly; she says Golden Miller 'was never going at any stage of the race and was well behind by the time the field reached the fence before Valentine's. Here he attempted to refuse, but driven on, bucked and twisted through the fence, ejecting the luckless Wilson like a cork from a bottle.' Snaffles drew the much discussed incident, the only major sporting artist, so far as is known, to have done so, captioning his sketch 'The year Golden Miller stuck his toes in at Valentine's – small blame to him for hadn't he won his sixth Gold Cup a fortnight before and was then asked this question?'. It was in fact only four Gold Cups that he had won by that year, and Golden Miller's sum total was five, a record which still stands. As with his quotations, Snaffles was often exuberant with his facts.

As Golden Miller was undoubtedly the greatest steeplechaser to run between the two World Wars and comparable only to Arkle as a steeplechaser, it may be appropriate to consider two parallel enigmas now, fifty years after the facts, before all those who remember the horse and those associated with him are dead. The enigmas are, why did Golden Miller dislike Liverpool so much? and why did his immensely rich owner, the Honourable Dorothy Paget, continue to run him there when he had made plain his dislike? Before we tackle these questions, we have set out below Golden Miller's record at Liverpool and Cheltenham.

Liverpool

Year	*Race*	*Distance*	*Jockey*	*Weight*	*Result*
1933	Grand National	4½m	T. Leader	12.2	U.R.
1934	Grand National	4½m	G. Wilson	12.2	Won
1935	Grand National	4½m	G. Wilson	12.7	U.R.
1935	Champion Chase	3¾m	G. Wilson	12.0	U.R.
1936	Grand National	4½m	E. Williams	12.7	Refused
1936	Becher's Chase	2½m	F. Walwyn	12.0	Second
1937	Grand National	4½m	D. Morgan	12.7	Refused

Cheltenham

Year	*Race*	*Distance*	*Jockey*	*Weight*	*Result*
1932	Gold Cup	3¼m	T. Leader	12.0	Won
1933	Gold Cup	3¼m	W. Stott	12.0	Won
1934	Gold Cup	3¼m	G. Wilson	12.0	Won
1935	Gold Cup	3¼m	G. Wilson	12.0	Won
1936	Gold Cup	3¼m	E. Williams	12.0	Won
1937	Gold Cup abandoned due to bad weather				
1938	Gold Cup	3¼m	H. Nicholson	12.0	Second

From the above it can be seen that from seven starts Golden Miller only completed the course at Liverpool twice; the first time when he won the National in record time carrying 12 stone 2 lb in 1934 and the second time in November 1936 when Fulke Walwyn persuaded him reluctantly to complete the Becher's Chase.

Why did Golden Miller dislike Liverpool so much? There are two major theories. One was that he had not got over the hard race in the 1935 Gold Cup and possibly had been over-galloped in between the Gold Cup and the Grand National; the other theory is that he was unsuited to Liverpool, due to his habit of jumping off the forehand and perhaps he was slightly straight in the shoulder.

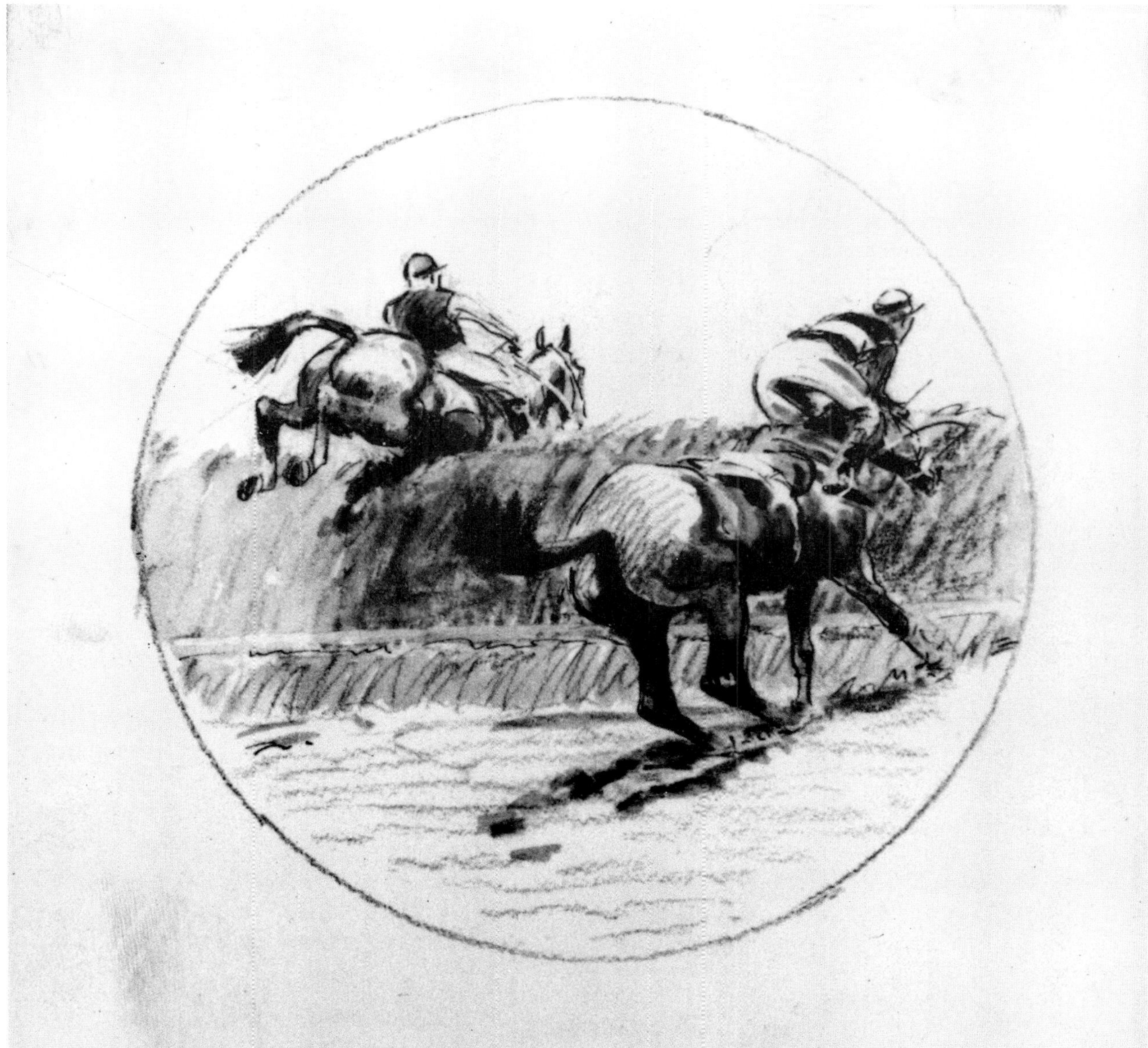

'The year Golden Miller stuck his toes in at Valentines – small blame for him – for hadn't he won his sixth Gold Cup a fortnight before and was then asked this question?'
Some say it was the fence before Valentines, some say it was the fence after; but for Snaffles it was Valentines

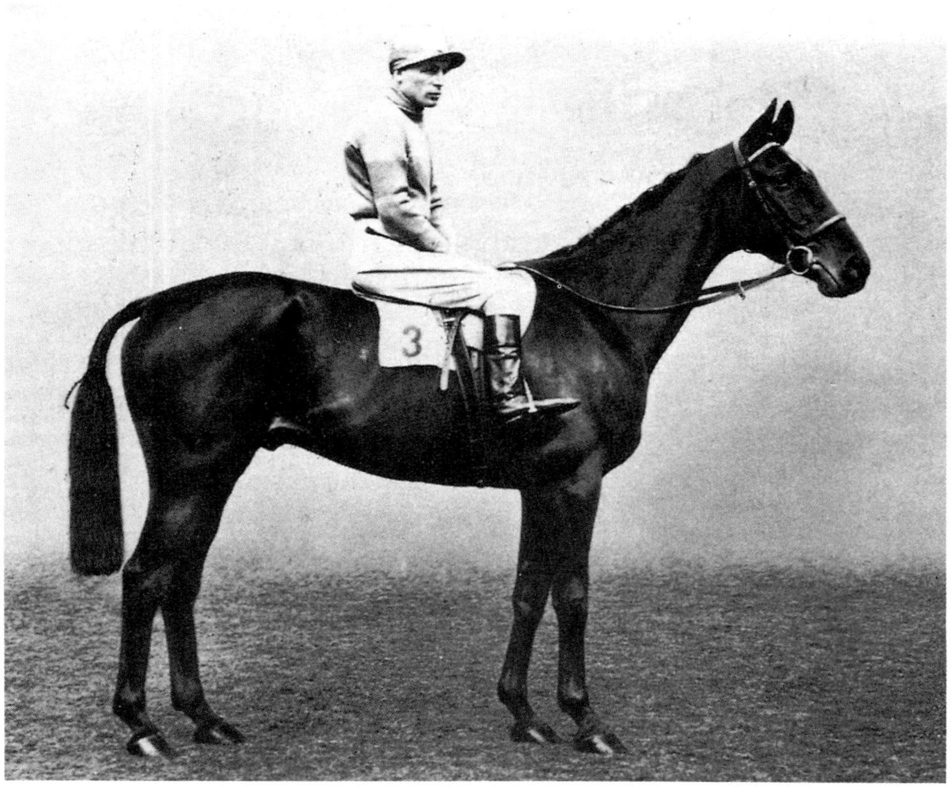

Golden Miller (Gerry Wilson up)

Until after the Second World War, the Grand National was '*the* race' and the Gold Cup a top class National trial, so every trainer aimed to have his best horses at their peak fitness on Grand National day. Therefore his then trainer, Basil Briscoe, did not have the Miller fully wound up for the 1935 Gold Cup due to be run on 14 March, fifteen days before the National.

The Gold Cup that year should have been a nice warm-up race for the Miller to bring him to the boil for the Grand National. The second best horse in the country, Jock Witney's Thormond, was originally aimed at the two miles Coventry Cup, and Briscoe was confident that the Miller would easily account for the rest of the entries. However, after Jock Witney's Rod and Gun won the important National Hunt Chase, Witney had a change of mind and instructed his trainer to run Thormond in the Gold Cup rather than the Coventry Cup; Briscoe was appalled.

The race, watched by a record crowd who had flocked to the course to see the duel between the two best steeplechasers in the country, was run at a tremendous pace from the start. Southern Hero jumped off and set a strong gallop until three fences from home, when Golden Miller and Thormond joined battle. There then ensued one of the greatest races ever witnessed under National Hunt Rules. Two supremely able horses, ridden by two great and fearless jockeys, fought out a never-to-be-forgotten finish. Golden Miller just got home on ground harder than he liked.

When Golden Miller re-appeared fifteen days later at the Grand National, he was a strong favourite at 2 to 1 and there was no question of his jumping ability as he had won the race the previous year in magnificent style and in a then record time. However, the Miller never really strode out, was soon towards the rear of the field and parted company with his jockey as described earlier. The horse was pulled out the next day for the Champion Chase and disaster struck again. It is only in recent years that the Grand National has been run on the last day of the meeting; on a Saturday, rather than a weekday. Golden Miller was a supremely intelligent horse and remembered his experiences of 1935 for the rest of his career.

The other theory put forward for Golden Miller's dislike of Liverpool is that he was a fluent and rather flat jumper round "park courses" jumping off his forehand. Although a beautifully proportioned horse, if he was to be faulted, some people regarded him as slightly straight in the shoulder; and to jump round Liverpool before the changes made to the fences by Brigadier Tony Teacher in the season 1960/1961, two things were essential. The first being a really good shoulder to cope with the drop fences, and the other a horse's ability to 'prop' coming into a fence and jump off his hocks. The fences, before the 1960/1961 season, were much straighter than now and, as a result, horses tended to get too close. Before the changes any horse who jumped off his forehand inevitably got too close to one and paid the penalty. It was only Golden Miller's tremendous athletic ability which allowed him to be the exception to the rule when winning in 1934.

As Snaffles said, when commenting on Jack Horner's 1926 victory, "The Racehorses [thankfully] out of it and the hunters are now putting on a fine show". Jack Horner had spent several seasons as a Blakney Hunt horse before running in chases and had learned the ability to 'prop' when coming into his fences when necessary and jump off his hocks. Jack Horner had once carried a Master of The Blakney in one of the hunt's best ever points of some fourteen miles. It is therefore not surprising that when Snaffles came to choosing a sketch of the Grand National to make into a full blown print, he was to select Jack Horner on his way to win.

Snaffles would have been familiar, for many years, before she bought Golden Miller, with his eccentric young owner, the Honourable Dorothy Paget. She had, at a very young age, inherited a vast fortune from her mother, an American member of the Witney family, so she was a cousin of Jock Witney, the owner of Easter Hero and Thormond. Snaffles would have seen her competing at Olympia and other top horse shows in the twenties' where she had been a highly successful and talented show rider. Later on, he would have seen her at point-to-points as her horses used to run in the Surrey, Sussex and Kent area, where Snaffles did most of his point-to-pointing.

The other question is why did 'Miss P.', as she was commonly known, continue to run Golden Miller at Liverpool? Quintin Gilbey, her perceptive and authorative biographer, who was amongst those who knew her and her entourage as well as anyone, has pointed out two of her salient traits – one was that she gave her affection sparingly, but when she did, she gave it lavishly; and the other was that having been spoiled by an adoring mother who died when she was young, she became deadly obstinate, refusing ever to admit that she might be wrong.

Early in his career, she had conceived a lasting affection for Golden Miller "taken him to her heart' as Gilbey said, describing how she kissed the horse in the unsaddling enclosure after one of his wins and how at this time of her life he took precedence in her affections, even over her then closest companion, Madame de Munn's beautiful daughter Olili. She castigated Briscoe after Miller's poor performance at Liverpool in 1935 and removed all of her horses from the trainer's care straightaway. Thereafter her wilfulness would not allow her to concede that the Miller would not repeat his triumph at Liverpool. She could not bring herself to admit that so far as the Grand National was concerned, her great horse was a fallen idol and, as was her way, she was prepared to follow her inclinations with money. In the 1936 Grand National Golden Miller started favourite at 5 to 1 and in the 1937 race, amazingly, was favourite once more at 8 to 1. These short prices were almost certainly caused by her weight of money. It is worth noting for the record, and odd as it may seem nowadays, Golden Miller's one triumph in the National was worth more than twice his five wins in the Gold Cup.

As soon as it became clear that old age had finally caught up with Golden Miller, early in the 1938/39 season, "Miss P" promptly had him retired to her stud near Stansted in Essex, where every care of him was taken and where she used to pay him frequent visits. Golden Miller lived until the age of thirty.

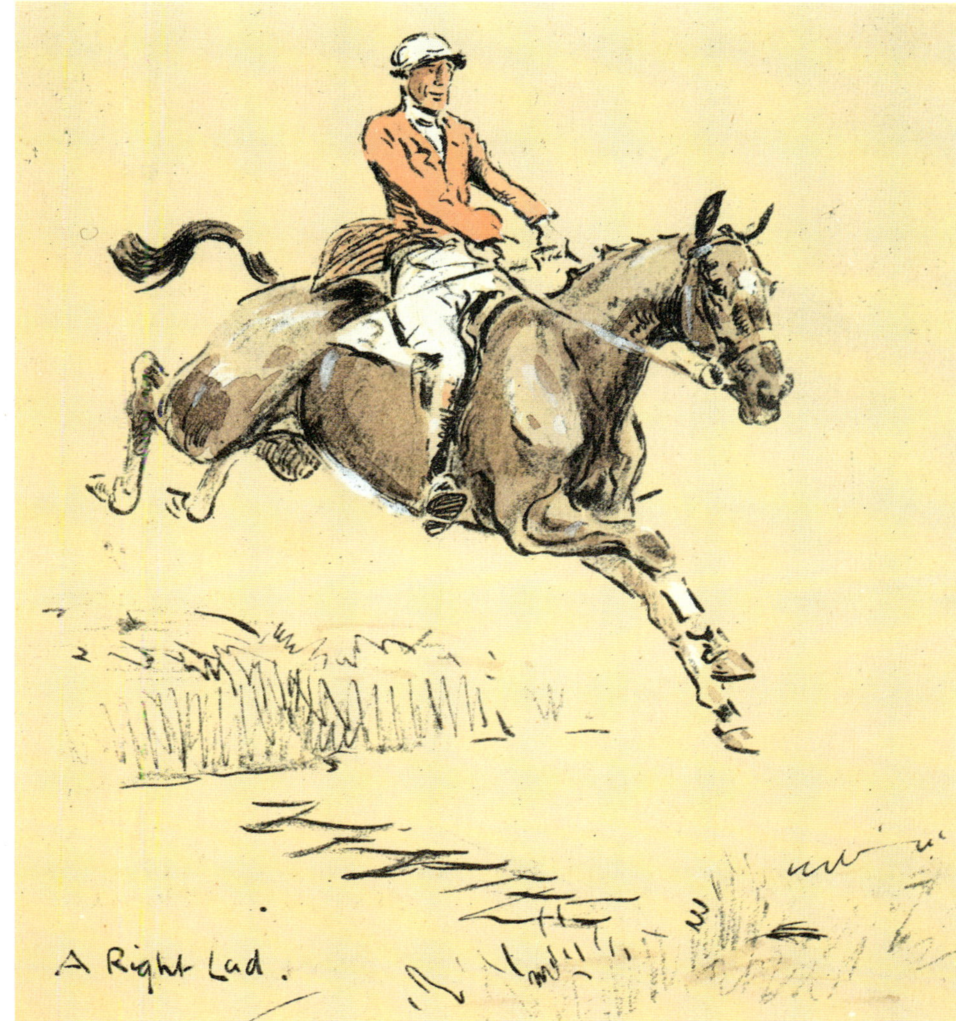

This Christmas card of a horse jumping the water at a point to point was first produced in about 1931

Table D

GRAND NATIONAL

Handicap Steeplechase 4½ miles - Liverpool

(Snaffles saw most of these Races, certainly up to 1939)

1919 Poethlyn (E. Piggott)
Ballyboggan (W. Head)
Pollen (A. Escott)
Loch Allen (J.J. Kelly)
22 ran. Time: 10 min. 8⅖ sec.

1920 Troytown (Mr. J. R. Anthony)
The Turk II (R. Burford)
The Bore (Mr. H. A. Brown)
Sergeant Murphy (W. Smith)
24 ran. Time: 10 min. 20⅖ sec.

1921 Shaun Spadah (F.B. Rees)
The Bore (Mr. H.A. Brown)
All White (R. Chadwick)
Turkey Buzzard (Capt. G.H. Bennet)
35 ran. Time: 10 min. 26 sec.

1922 Music Hall (L. B. Rees)
Drifter (W. Watkinson)
Taffytus (T. Leader)
Sergeant Murphy (C. Hawkins)
32 ran. Time: 9 min. 55⅘ sec.

1923 Sergeant Murphy (Capt. G.H. Bennet)
Shaun Spadah (F.B. Rees)
Conjuror II (Mr. C. Dewhurst)
Punt Gun (M. Tighe)
28 ran. Time: 9 min. 36 sec.

1924 Master Robert (R. Trudgill)
Fly Mask (J. Moylan)
Silvo (G. Goswell)
Drifter (G. Calder)
30 ran. Time: 9 min. 40 sec.

1925 Double Chance (Maj. J.P. Wilson)
Old Tay Bridge (J.R. Anthony)
Fly Mask (E.C. Doyle)
Sprig (T. Leader)
33 ran. Time: 9 min. 42⅗ sec.

1926 Jack Horner (W. Watkinson)
Old Tay Bridge (J.R. Anthony)
Bright's Boy (E. Doyle)
Sprig (T. Leader)
30 ran. Time: 9 min. 36 sec.

1927 Sprig (T. Leader)
Bovril III (Mr. G.W. Pennington)
Bright's Boy (J.R. Anthony)
Drinmond (Mr. J.B. Balding)
37 ran. Time: 10 min. 20⅕sec.

1928 Tipperary Tim (Mr. W. Dutton)
Billy Barton (T. Cullinan)
42 ran. Time: 10 min. 27 sec.

1929 Gregalach (R. Everett)
Easter Hero (J. Moloney)
Richmond II (W. Stott)
Melleray's Belle (J. Mason)
66 ran. Time: 9 min. 47 sec.

1930 Shaun Goilin (T. Cullinan)
Melleray's Belle (J. Mason)
Sir Lindsay (D. Williams)
Glangesia (J. Browne)
41 ran. Time: 9 min. 42⅖ sec.

1931 Grakle (R. Lyall)
Gregalach (J. Moloney)
Annandale (T. Morgan)
Rhyticere (L. Niaudot)
43 ran. Time: 9 min. 32⅘ sec.

1932 Forbra (J. Hamey)
Egremont (Mr. E.C. Paget)
Shaun Goilin (D. Williams)
Near East (T. McCarthy)
36 ran. Time: 9 min. 44⅗ sec.

1933 Kellsboro' Jack (D. Williams)
Really True (Mr. F. Furlong)
Slater (Mr. M. Barry)
Delaneige (J. Moloney)
34 ran. Time: 9 min. 28 sec.
(Record)

1934 Golden Miller (G. Wilson)
Delaneige (J. Moloney)
Thomond II (W. Speck)
Forbra (G. Hardy)
30 ran. Time: 9 min. 20⅖ sec.
(Record)

1935 Reynoldstown (Mr. F. Furlong)
Blue Prince (W. Parvin)
Thomond II (W. Speck)
Lazy Boots (G. Owen)
27 ran. Time: 9 min. 20⅕ sec.
(Record)

1936 Reynoldstown (Mr. F. Walwyn)
Ego (Mr. H. Llewellyn)
Bachelor Prince (J. Fawcus)
Crown Prince (Mr. R. Strutt)
35 ran. Time: 9 min. 37 sec.

1937 Royal Mail (E. Williams)
Cooleen (J. Fawcus)
Pucka Belle (Mr. E. Bailey)
Ego (Mr. H. Llewellyn)
33 ran. Time: 9 min. 59⅗ sec.

1938 Battleship (B. Hobbs)
Royal Danieli (D. Moore)
Workman (J. Brogan)
Cooleen (J. Fawcus)
36 ran. Time: 9 min. 29⅘ sec.

1939 Workman (T. Hyde)
Mac Moffat (I. Alder)
Kilstar (G. Archibald)
Cooleen (J. Fawcus)
37 ran. Time: 9 min. 42⅕ sec.

1940 Bogskar (M. Jones)
Mac Moffat (I. Alder)
Gold Arrow (P. Lay)
Symaethis (M. Feakes)
30 ran. Time: 9 min. 20⅗ sec.

1941–45 No race, owing to World War II

1946 Lovely Cottage (Capt. R. Petre)
Jack Finlay (W. Kidney)
Prince Regent (T. Hyde)
Housewarmer (A. Brabazon)
34 ran. Time: 9 min. 38⅕ sec.

1947 Caughoo (E. Dempsey)
Lough Conn (D. McCann)
Kami (Mr. J. Hislop)
Prince Regent (T. Hyde)
57 ran. Time: 10 min. 3⅕ sec.

1948 Sheila's Cottage (A.P. Thompson)
First of the Dandies (J. Brogan)
Cromwell (Lord Mildmay)
Happy Home (G. Kelly)
43 ran. Time: 9 min 25⅖ sec.

1949 Russian Hero (L. McMorrow)
Roimond (R. Francis)
Royal Mount (P. Doyle)
Cromwell (Lord Mildmay)
43 ran. Time: 9 min. 23⅘ sec.

1950 Freebooter (J. Power)
Wot No Sun (A.P. Thompson)
Acthon Major (R.J. O'Ryan)
Rowland Roy (R. Black)
49 ran. Time: 9 min 24⅕ sec.

1951 Nickel Coin (J. Bullock)
Royal Tan (Mr. A. O'Brien)
Derrinstown (A. Power)
Broomfield (R. Emery)
36 ran. Time: 9 min. 48⅘ sec.

1952 Teal (A.P. Thompson)
Legal Joy (M. Scudamore)
Wot no Sun (D.V. Dick)
Uncle Barney (J. Boddy)
47 ran. Time: 9 min. 20⅗ sec.

1953 Early Mist (B. Marshall)
Mont Tremblant (D.V. Dick)
Irish Lizard (R. Turnell)
Overshadow (P. Taaffe)
31 ran. Time: 9 min. 21⅗ sec.

1954 Royal Tan (B. Marshall)
Tudor Line (G. Slack)
Irish Lizard (M. Scudamore)
Churchtown (T. Taaffe)
29 ran. Time: 9 min. 32⅘ sec.

1955 Quare Times (P. Taaffe)
Tudor Line (G. Slack)
Carey's Cottage (T. Taaffe)
Gigolo (R. Curran)
30 ran. Time: 10 min. 20⅗ sec.

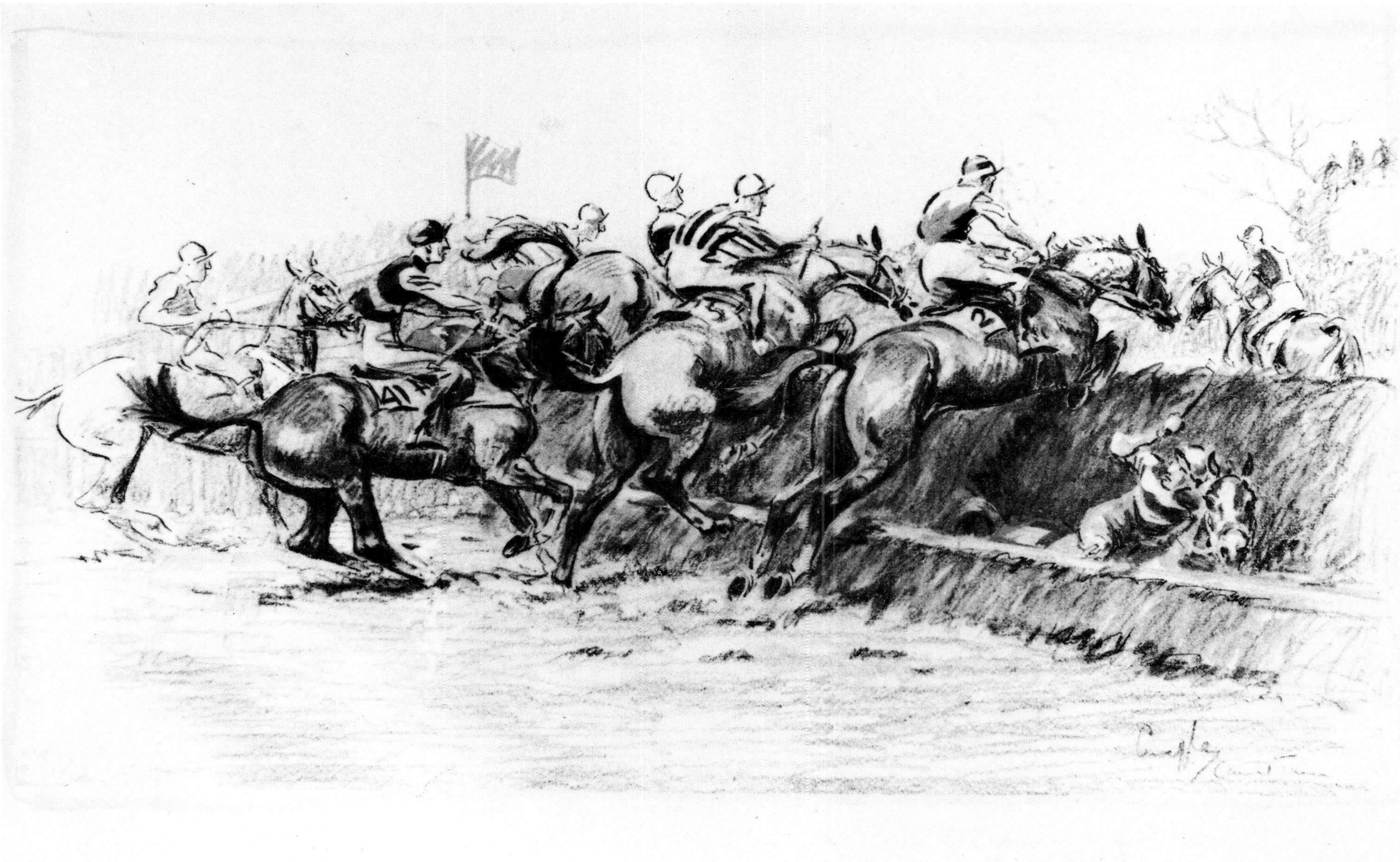

The Canal Turn

The jostle for the corner pew

The 1935 Grand National in which Golden Miller ejected Wilson 'Like a cork from a bottle' was won by Reynoldstown, owned and trained by Major Noel Furlong and ridden by his son Frank. 'Wasn't it wonderful, I bred both of them!' Mrs. Furlong exclaimed to the press as she led in the winner, in one of the most famous of all involuntary exclamations made in the heat of victory. Next year Reynoldstown won again, ridden this time by Mr. F. Walwyn – Mr. Furlong could not do the weight.

Mr. Walwyn's father, Major F. Walwyn, a Master of the Monmouthshire Hounds was one of Snaffles' closest friends. He was a brother of the distinguished amateur rider, Taffy Walwyn. Reynoldstown carried 12 stone 2 lb, the top weight, and set a new record in his victory, defeating Golden Miller's record of two years before. He may, however, have been a fortunate winner, for this was the year that the reins of Davy Jones, a 100 to 1 outsider, snapped at the buckle giving no chance to his rider, the Honourable Anthony Mildmay, of preventing him running out when the race was, apparently, at his mercy. Anthony Mildmay, as Lord Mildmay, later was Champion Amateur five times after the Second World War, and was one of the greatest Corinthian riders of all time and immensely popular with the public. The cry, when he was in with half a chance, of 'C'mon m'Lord' was heard on every steeplechase course in the British Isles. No other steeplechase rider, professional or amateur, has ever won the hearts of the racing public, especially in the cheaper rings, so much as Anthony Mildmay.

Whether Mildmay would have won the National if his reins hadn't come apart is questionable, but Reynoldstown's second win was a courageous one and owed much to his rider since he had made a bad mistake at Valentine's, second time round, where it mattered most. It was the sort of blunder which would have unshipped most jump jockeys, but Mr. Walwyn sat tight, kept himself in the saddle and his horse on its feet. With the sort of uncanny instinct he had for being in the right place in a race at the right time, Snaffles witnessed the incident and, because he so admired good horses and good horsemanship, recorded it for posterity. It is odd that those two great horses, Golden Miller and Reynoldstown, never really fired Snaffles' artistic inspiration, or gave him the urge to portray them again and again in action as Sergeant Murphy and Easter Hero had done.

Between the two wins of Reynoldstown, Snaffles had made yet another trip to India and published a highly successful book in *More Bandobast*. The years 1937 to 1939 were devoted mainly to work on his Indian material and then, once again, all was turmoil in the autumn of 1939 with the outbreak of the Second World War.

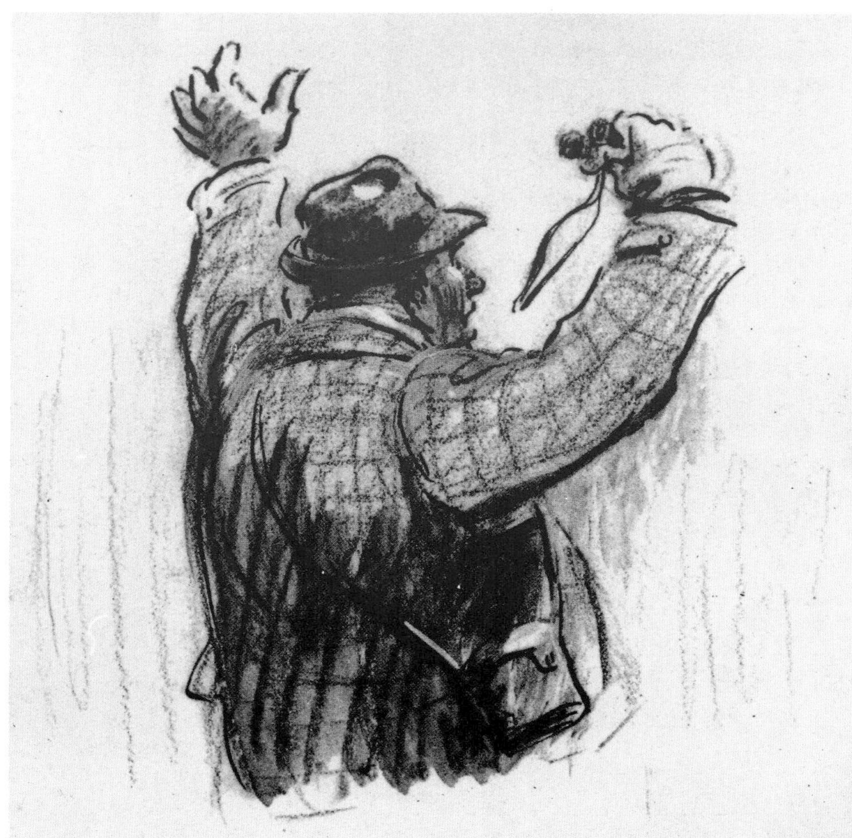

'Oh! Strewth! There goes me Rolls Rice and me yacht at Brighton'

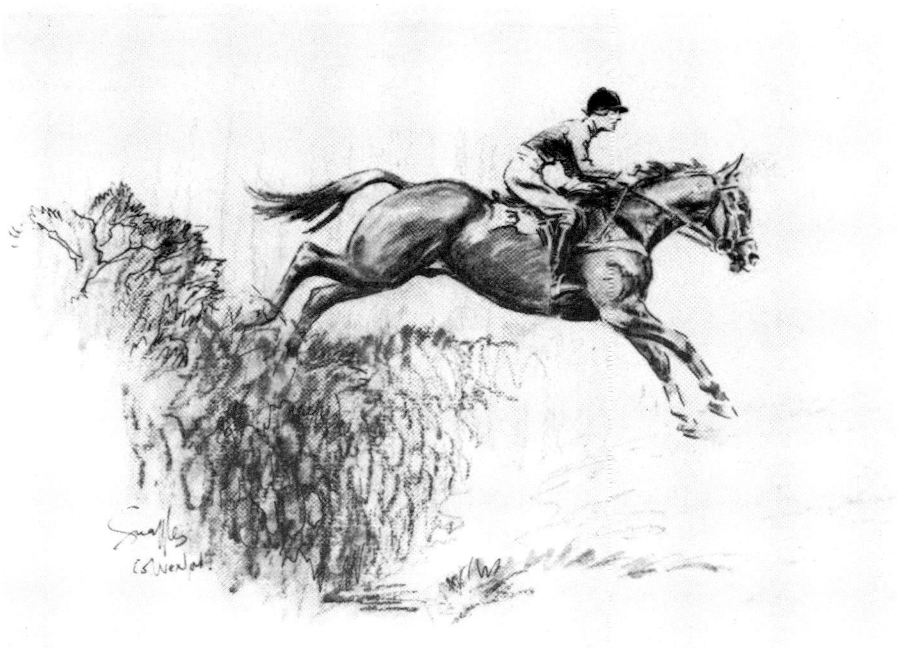

This drawing, used as a book illustration and a Christmas card, presents problems. One would assume that the print 'The one to carry your half crown' (see p101) was an English scene. However this is clearly the same horse and girl as in the remarque, and it is marked 'Wexford'

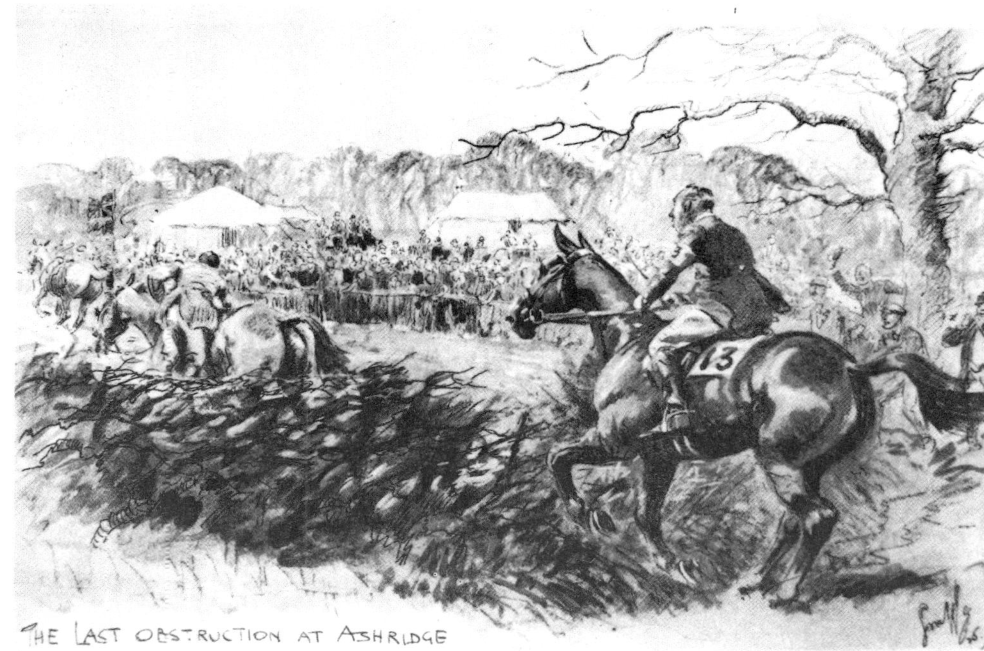

Another book illustration which was also used as a Christmas card. Sometimes Snaffles hand coloured them when he sent them out. More often he did not

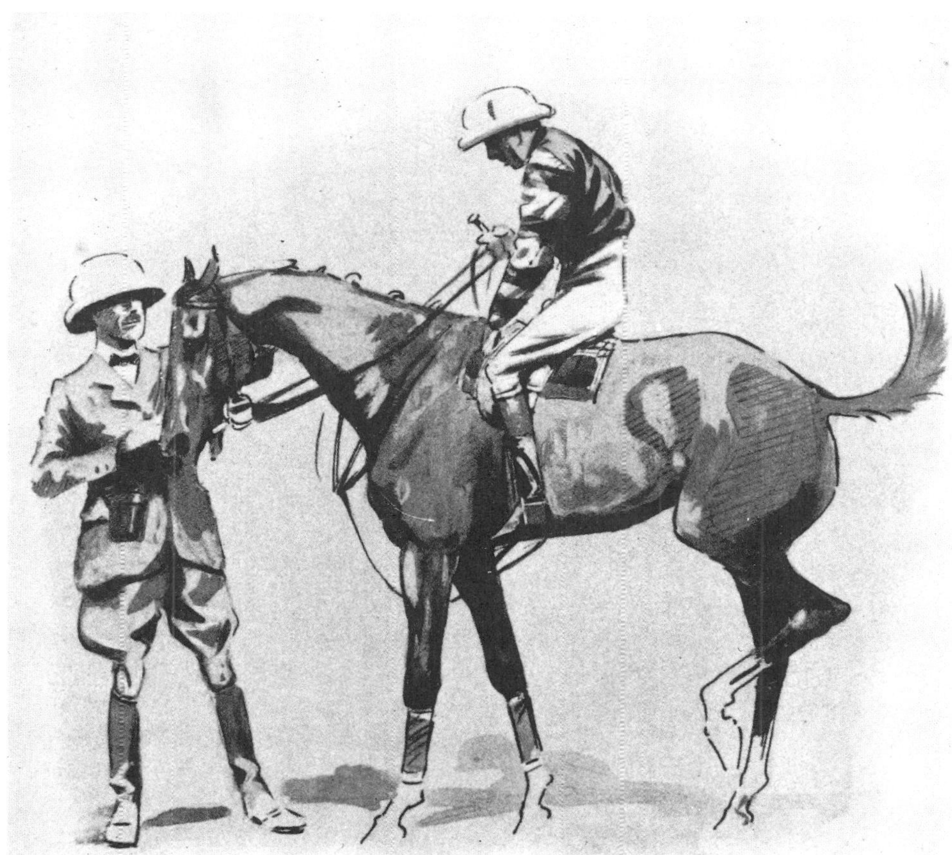

Snaffles saw much amateur racing in India, but few examples of his drawings are still in existence

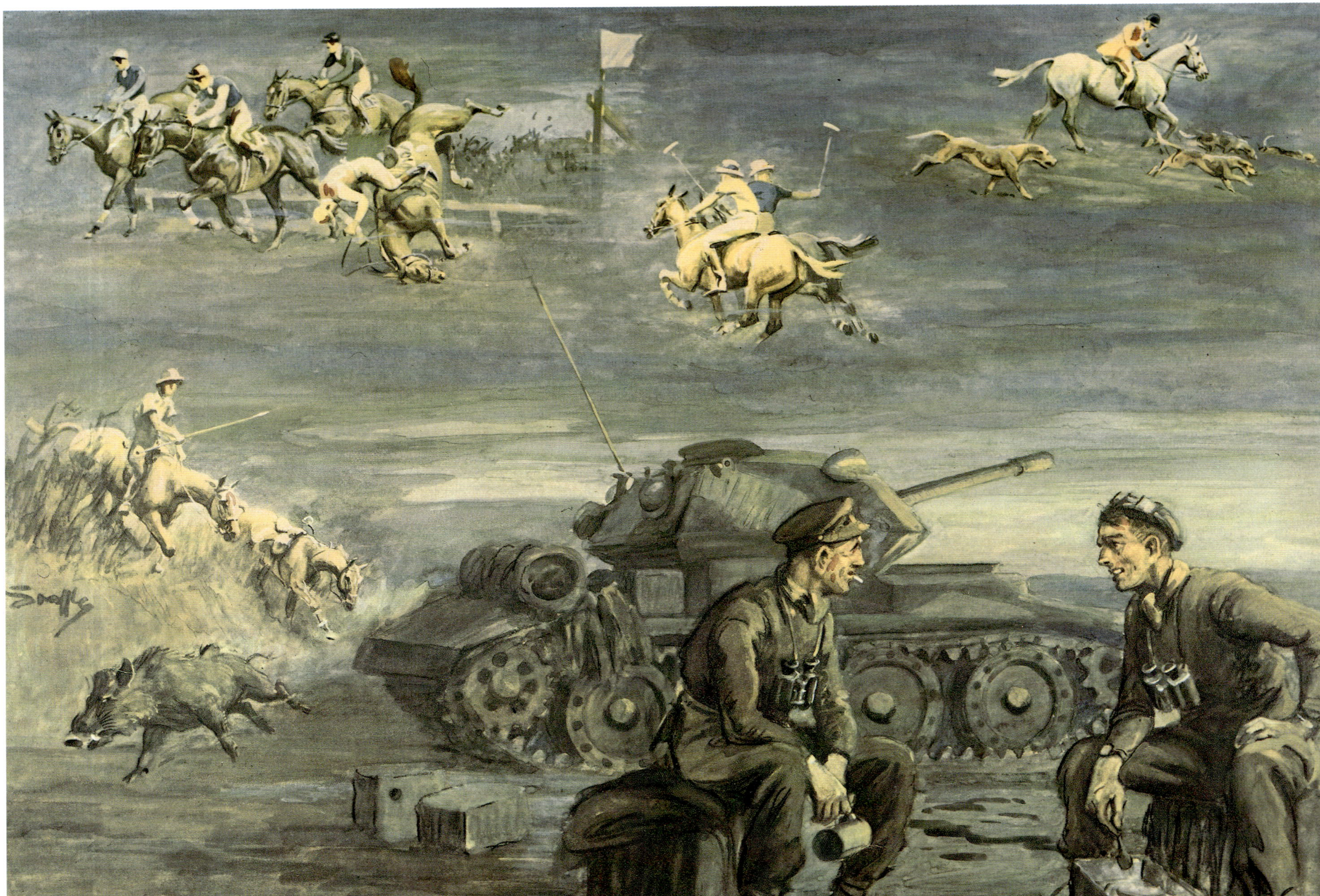

Once upon a time

7 The Second World War and The Finish

At the outbreak of the Second World War, Snaffles was in his fifty-sixth year and none too robust. Flat racing was curtailed, steeplechasing virtually abandoned and Snaffles' brush, so far as racing was concerned, was still. The next six years were very trying times for Snaffles. He moved from his cottage near Guildford to the West Country and worked on camouflaging aerodromes; but his health, much to his chagrin, would not stand the rigours of the Home Guard and he spent most of the war years working on the land. This was the time that he was to produce his two famous farming prints of heavy horses; 'Enjoyin' yerselves aren't yer' and 'Forrard on me lads and hit 'em hard'. He was, of course, very much reverting to his output in the First World War, once again using heavy horses as his subject. During the whole war he only produced seven prints. In the First World War his output had been at least five times that amount.

Around 1943 Snaffles did produce a print of Brigadier Scott Cockburn, one of his pigsticking friends and mentors, sitting on his tank and dreaming of days past, which included a scene of steeplechasing, as well as polo and hunting. This too was a reversion to his output during the First World War and in spirit is not at all unlike the print 'That Far, Far Away Echo' which shows a soldier in the trenches dreaming of hounds and hunting. Lionel Edwards always thought 'That Far, Far Away Echo' was one of Snaffles' best works.

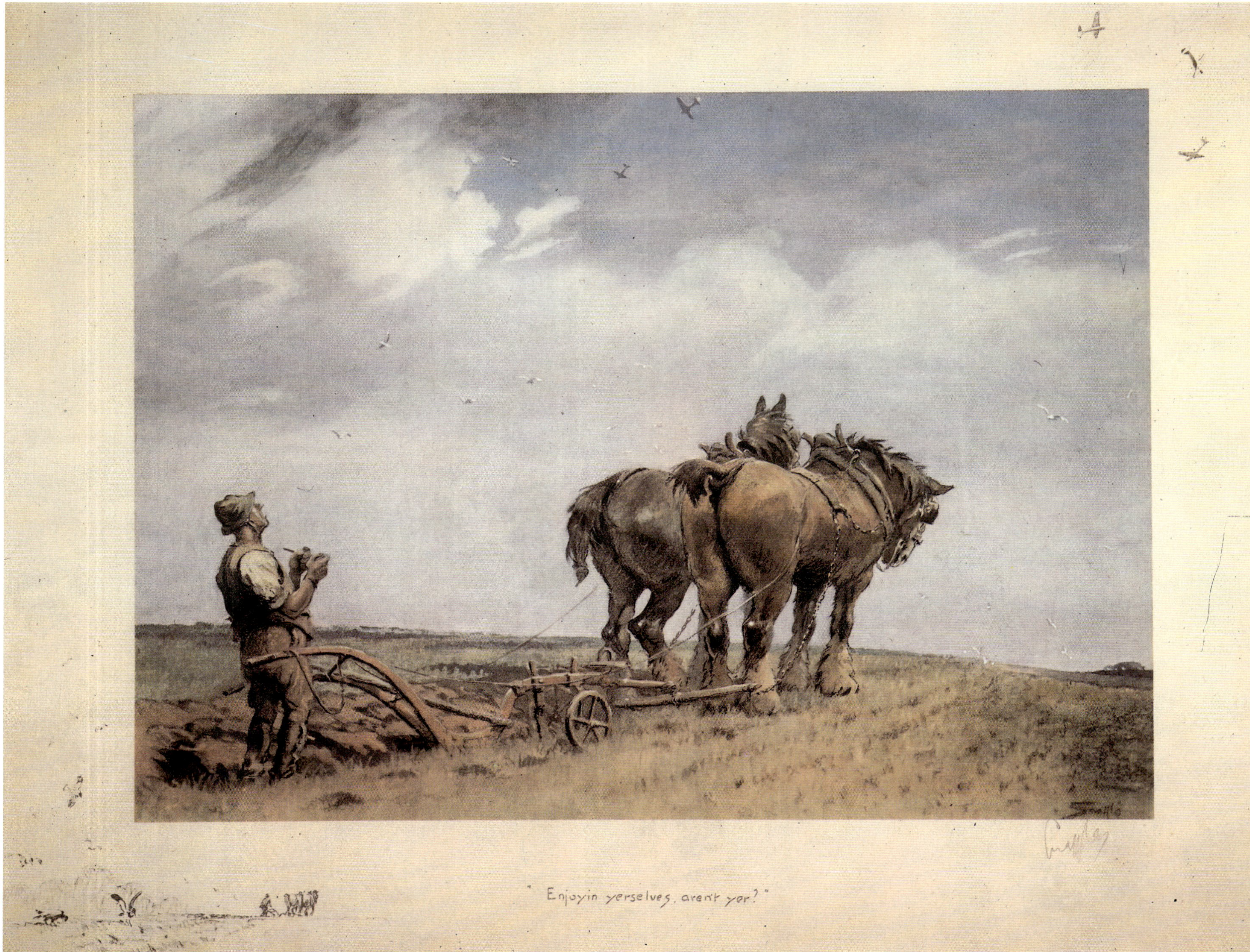

During the Second World War Snaffles drew heavy horses on the land rather than military horses

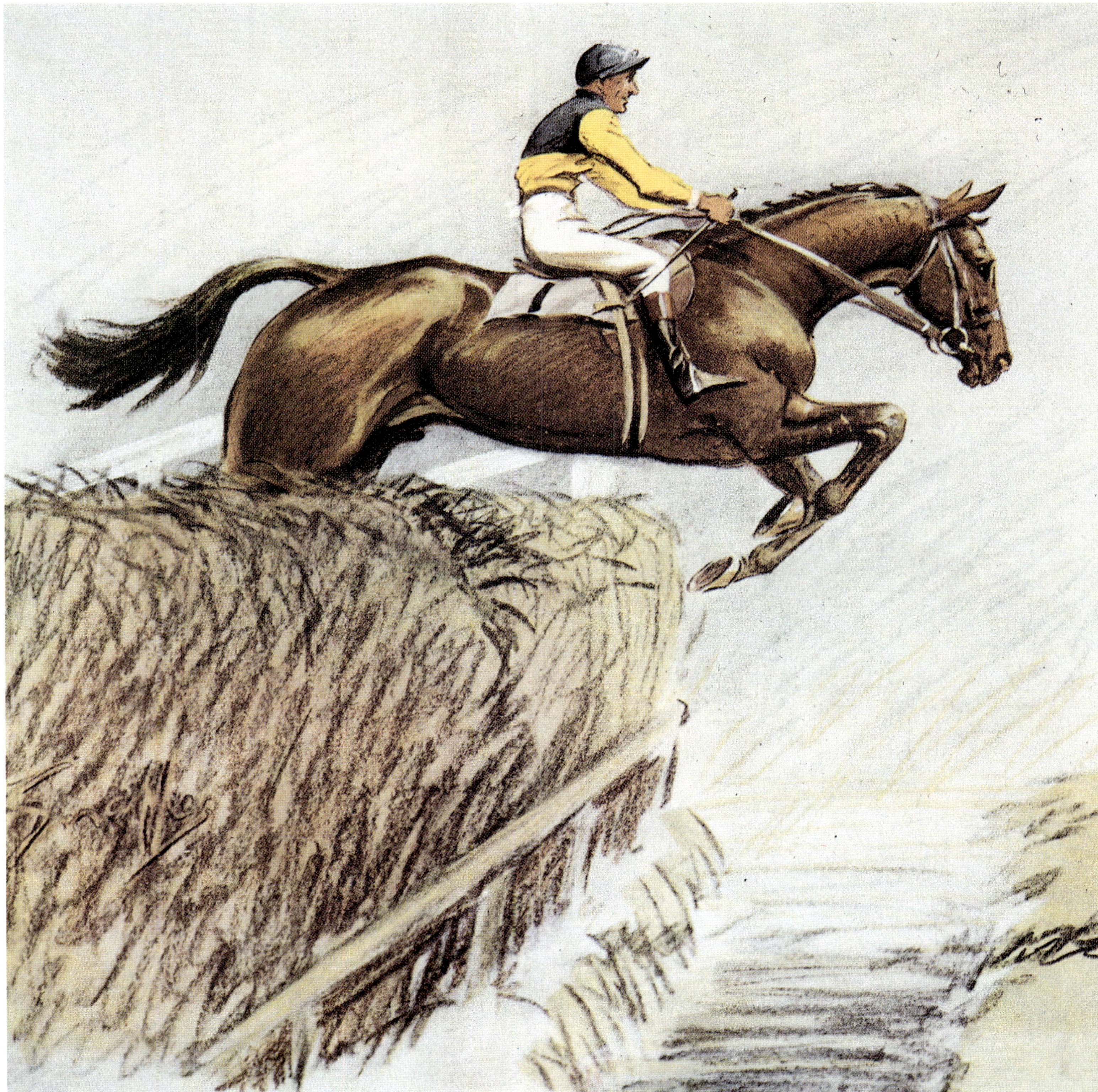

Prince Regent

The last of Snaffles' dream horses

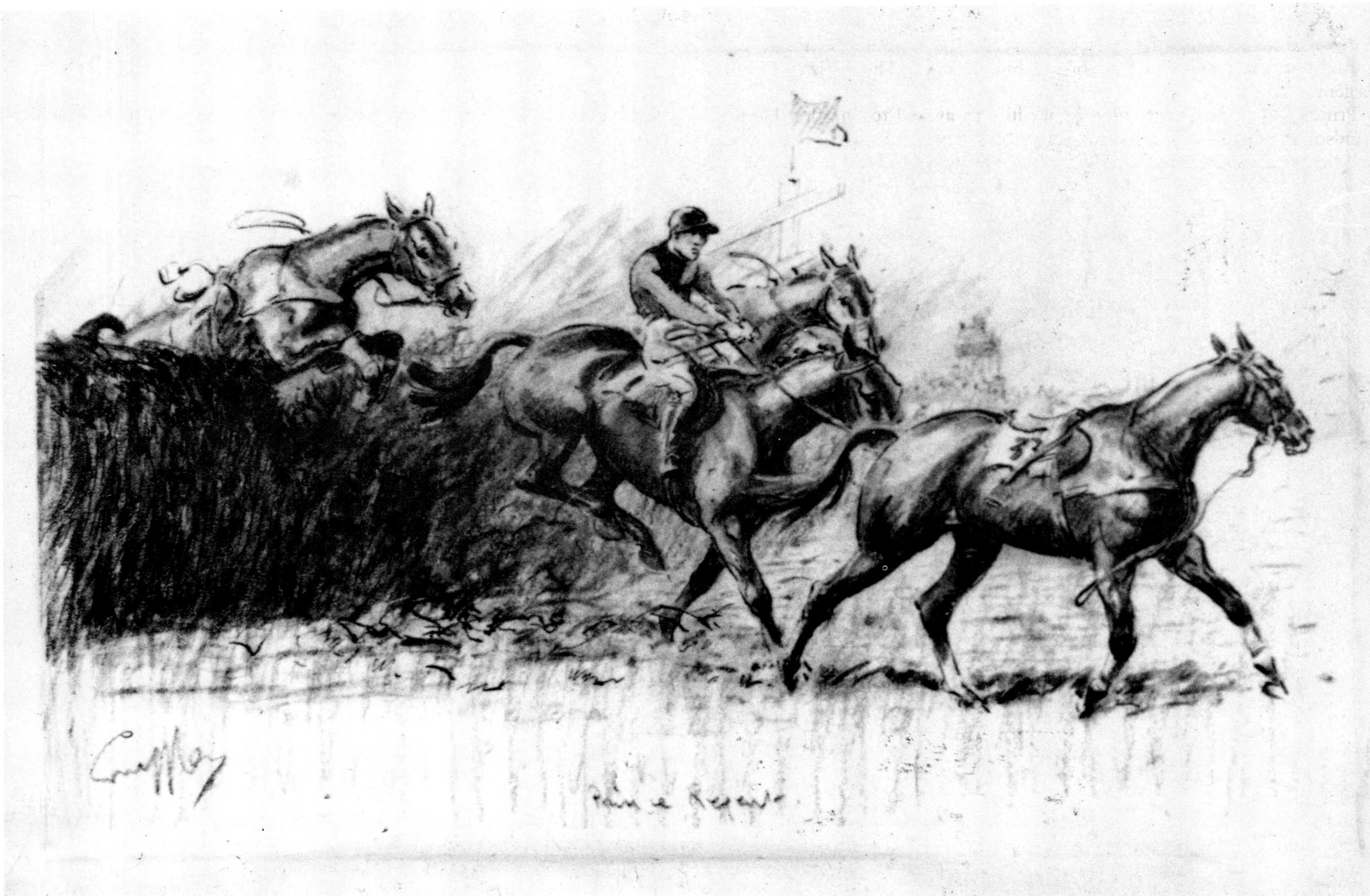

Prince Regent really was an unlucky loser of the 1946 Grand National, as is shown in Snaffles' drawing which shows the champion surrounded by loose horses which impeded him badly over the last few fences

However, there was, waiting in the wings, a champion who was to become possibly the greatest of the artist's equine heroes, although he had to wait until the end of hostilities before he saw him in action. The horse was Prince Regent.

Prince Regent had everything about him to appeal to Snaffles. He was handsome, and great hearted; at the peak of his career in Ireland he was handicapped to give penal burdens of weight away and did it successfully. Above all towards the end of his racing days, when he had passed his prime, he was the sort of gallant failure which always struck chords in Snaffles' romantic nature. He won twelve races in Ireland between 1941 and 1945, including the 1942 Irish Grand National, carrying 12 stone 7 lb.

Prince Regent was a living legend in Ireland and when he came to England his first appearance created great excitement. The public had been starved of steeplechasing; here was a horse whose reputation was every bit as good as Golden Miller's, the last horse to catch the public imagination. It was at Cheltenham in 1946 that Snaffles first saw Prince Regent, before the Gold Cup and instantly placed him amongst his heroes. Prince Regent was then eleven years old, but his looks conquered the knowing crowd who congregated around the rails to pass judgement on the horse that had won everything Ireland could offer during the war years. 'I remember', wrote Snaffles, 'the first time I saw him in the paddock at Cheltenham comporting himself like the perfect gentleman he is. I heard Jack Lawrence, who had hunted the Heythrop for ten years, exclaim 'what a horse! Damned if I wouldn't ride him round Aintree if they would let me have a martingale strap to hang on to'. It was his superlative make and shape that attracted Jack and everybody else who knows what a good horse is. In fact he was the most beautifully made and balanced horse I have ever seen, and no equine artist could possibly flatter him.'

Prince Regent duly won the Gold Cup, but not with quite the authority he would have shown in his prime. 'It took me a minute or two to beat that fellow, Tom', Tim Hyde his rider, warned his trainer, Tom Dreaper, as he dismounted in the winner's enclosure. This did not deter the public from making him the raging favourite for the Grand National, nor did the fact that the handicapper had alloted him top weight of 12stone 5 lb, only 2 lb less than the weight which, together with his injury, had already defeated Easter Hero, and Easter Hero was two years younger.

The effort Prince Regent made was, like Easter Hero's, supremely gallant, but it was unavailing. The ground was like a morass and he did not have any luck in running, being impeded by loose horses for much of the second circuit. Hyde said afterwards that he had to ride three finishes to keep in the race at all. Despite these factors, he landed over the last in front, but that long run in was to prove fatal for him. Lovely Cottage, in receipt of 25 lb, came and caught him and in the end he only finished a tired third.

It was the sort of defeat which thrilled Snaffles' heart. As he says 'it was worth going a long way to see him as he came in to view the second time round, leading a mob of loose horses over Becher's'. There he was, striding along, and carrying his 12 stone 5lb as though it was a bag of straw... they [the two lightweights] caught and passed their leader a few lengths from the Judges' Box – and Lovely Cottage snatched the laurels from my hero. Had it not been for the five years of the war, when Prince Regent was in his prime, better judges than I say no other horse, or even the heaviest handed handicapper, would have deprived this magnificent animal from winning the Grand National two or three years in succession'.

As will be seen, Snaffles' romantic and enthusiastic view of his 'heroes' had not been diminished with the years and it is indeed worth remarking that Tom Dreaper, the wise and vastly experienced trainer of Prince Regent, once said of the mighty Arkle, that it took the second of that great horse's victories in the Gold Cup to convince him that Arkle was the Regent's equal. Snaffles left his testimony to Prince Regent's greatness and his memories of him in the shape of a magnificent colour plate showing him 'Romping over his Fences, as if they had been of no consequence', together with sketches of the Grand National depicting the great horse's jumping and the difficulties he encountered. Ageing as Snaffles was, he still showed that he had lost none of his sure touch when it came to the spirit of the race and those who rode in it.

The period after the Second War was a time of austerity and the demand for sporting prints was at its lowest under the strongly doctrinaire socialist government. Luckily for Snaffles, and for us, he was asked to illustrate a book, *Mixed Bagmen*, for J.K. Stanford. Stanford had written a best seller in the war entitled *The Twelfth*. Snaffles' efforts at illustrations this time were entirely successful and he was able to draw on his retentive memory for scenes from his past for *Mixed Bagmen*. The book, produced by Herbert Jenkins, was well reviewed and Snaffles' illustrations extremely well received. As a result, Snaffles then sat down to write and illustrate his memoirs in three charming volumes; *A Half Century of Memories*, published in 1949; *Four Legged Friends and Acquaintances*, published in 1950; and *I've Heard the Revelly*, published in 1953. They were all illustrated with his own sketches and pictures of good horses and good men whom he had seen during a long lifetime of the best of companions on horse and foot. As always the humour of it all was to the fore and throughout these three volumes he showed how very close to his heart steeplechasing and point-to-pointing were.

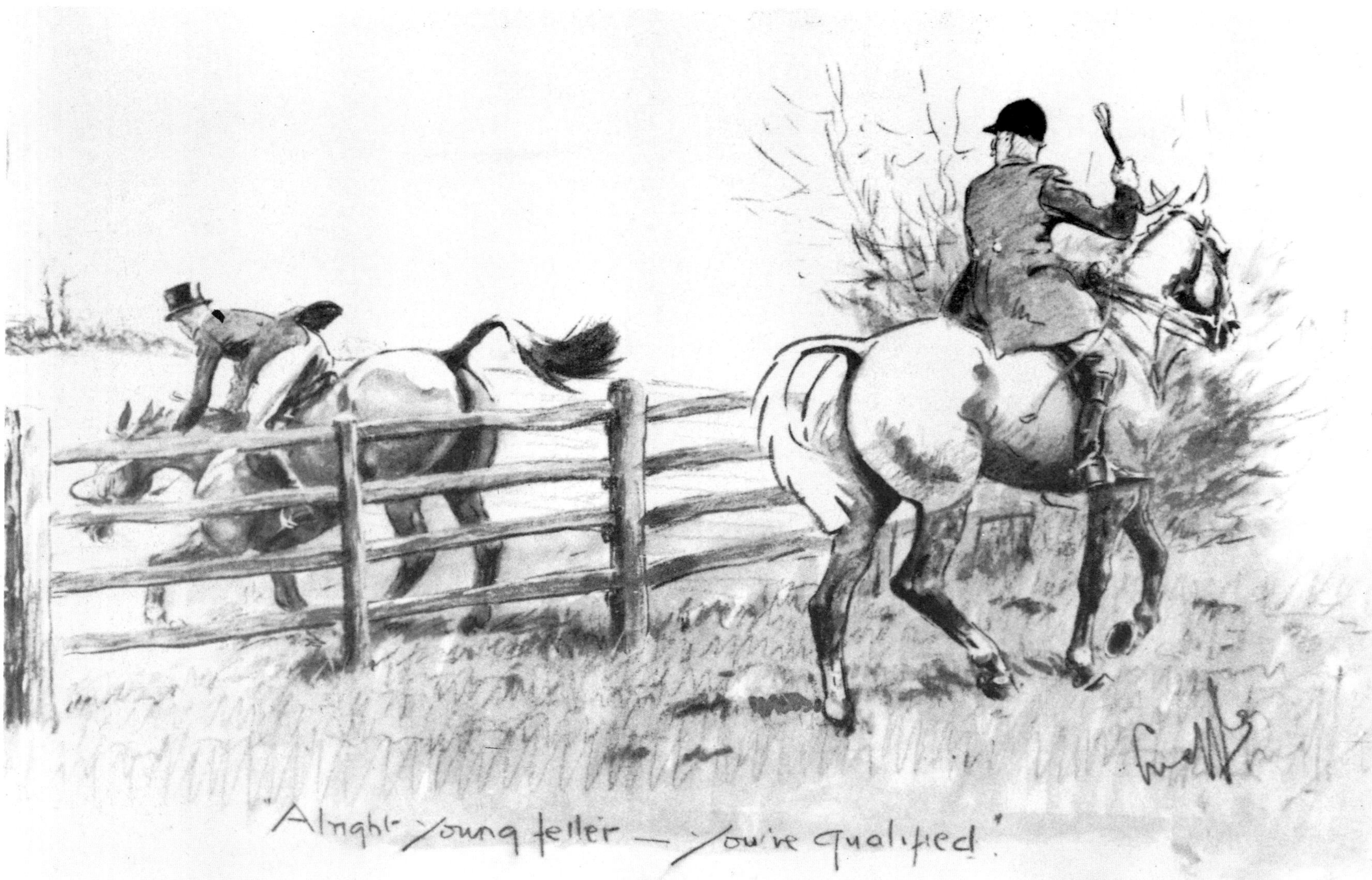

An amusing incident from the 1930s. A young soldier asked the Master for a hunters certificate and was told he could have one if he would give the Master a lead over particularly hazardous posts and rails. He duly did so, only to see the Master walk up fifty yards and go through a gap in the hedge

In 1950 Fores were to publish a truly wonderful pair of point-to-point prints – 'Oh! To be in England now that April's there' (Robert Browning), showing three men riders mounting in a point-to-point parade ring, and 'A Sight to Take Home and Dream About' showing three lady point-to-point riders clearing a fence and brook. These prints are commonly known as 'The Men's Point-to-Point' and 'The Ladies' Point-to-Point' and they make one of Snaffles' greatest pairs of prints, to equal 'The Finest View in Europe' and 'The Worst View in Europe', or 'The Biggest Walls in the Counthry was in it' and 'Great Banks there were below in the fields'.

The watercolours on which these prints were based were completed by Snaffles at the height of his powers around 1936/1938 and then luckily lay undisturbed in Fores' Bond Street premises for over ten years before being turned, with a remarque and wording, into the prints as we know them. As we have previously noted, Snaffles lost most of his possessions in two fires in, or just after, World War II so we are fortunate to have these prints. The Men's Point-to-Point was republished with a different remarque under its original title, 'Oh! To be in Ireland now that April's there' in 1952. That print was Snaffles' last.

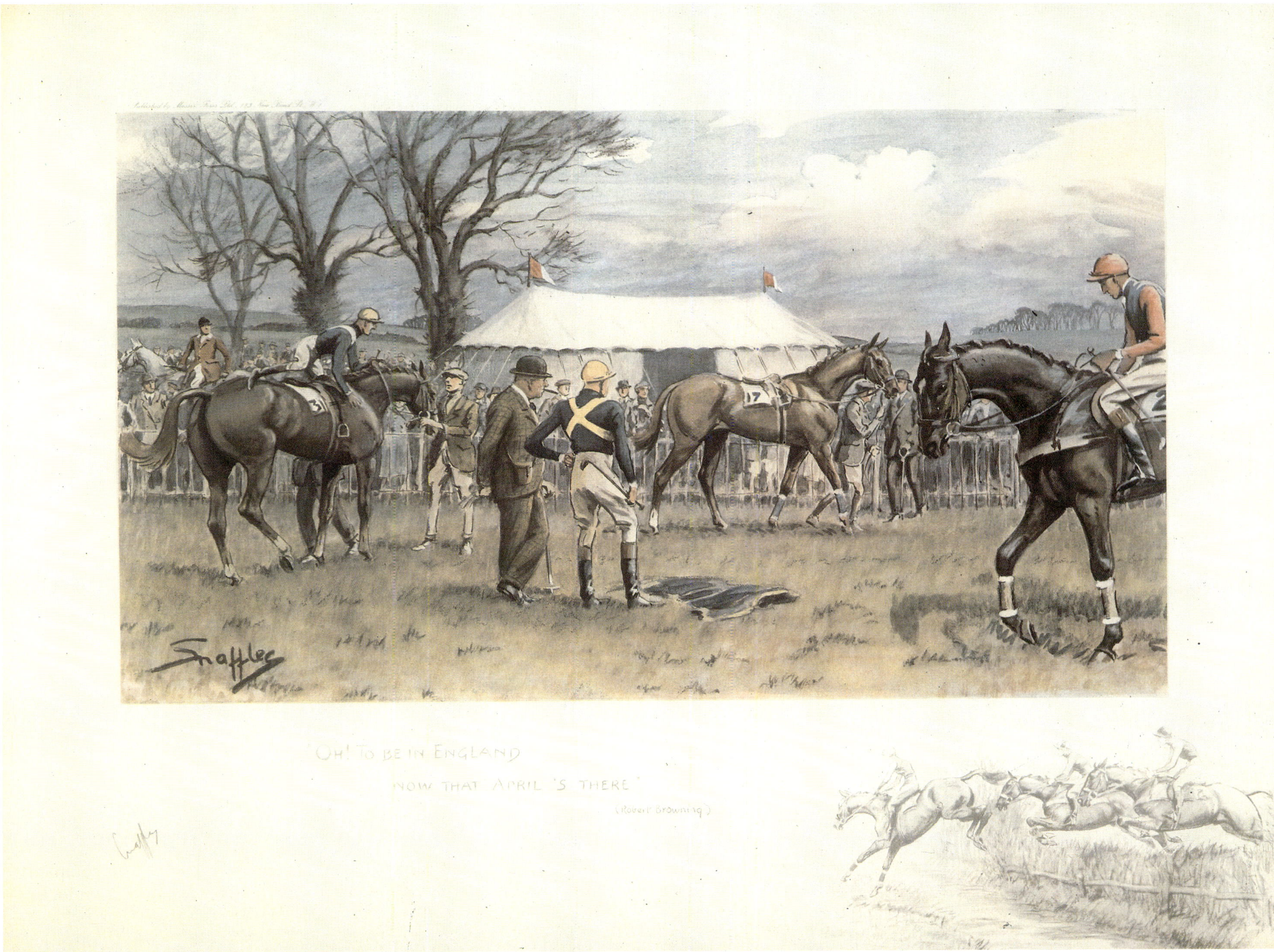

The Men's Point to Point

This drawing was probably conceived in the late 1920s when Cecil Aldin was working on his very successful illustrations for Masefield's book, *Right Royal*

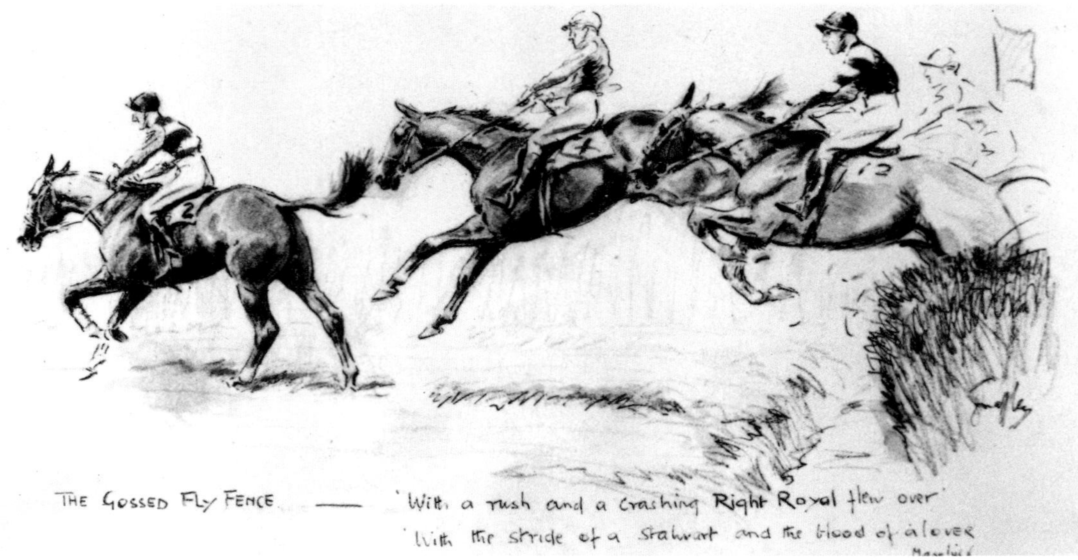

Over more than forty years as a depicter of the point-to-point scene, Snaffles not only produced a good number of prints enjoyable purely as works of art, but also of historical interest, showing the development of point-to-pointing. The best are; the 1914 'The Sojer Hossifer' showing an officer riding truly across country fences, 'Soldiers' 1922, which shows how, after the First World War, although the fences were natural, they had been strengthened and doctored; the pair 'A Bona-Fide Fox-Chaser' and 'The One to carry your Half Crown' of around 1930 clearly indicating considerably more professionalism than in the 1914 or 1922 prints; and, finally 'The Men's Point-to-Point' and 'The Ladies' Point-to-Point' of the late 1930's when the horses were normally 'in the book' and in most places racing was over smaller versions of regulation National Hunt birch fences like we know today.

On the racing front, Snaffles leaves us one of the greatest prints of all time of the Grand National in 'The Canal Turn 1926'. He has really caught the spirit of the era and conveys to us the toughness of horse and rider that was necessary before the fences were modified. Many good artists have managed to do wonderful paintings of racing at Liverpool and Cheltenham, but no-one has ever come close to catching the atmosphere at Sandown before or since Snaffles' print 'Sandown', published sixty years ago in 1928. It was at Sandown that Snaffles got his start as a racing artist and it was to be his favourite racecourse for the rest of his life. So it is right and proper, with his feel for atmosphere, that he should produce one of the few really successful paintings or prints ever done of this course.

After Snaffles completed his book *I've Heard the Revelly* his professional work as an author or artist came to an end, although for the rest of his life he always carried a sketchbook and pencil in his pocket and continued to sketch away right until his last days, whether sitting peacefully by the lake at Fonthill, or wandering around the horseboxes at a point-to-point. He continued to go racing at Sandown, to the Grand Military and the Royal Artillery meetings for another four or five years, but by the end of the fifties he had become increasingly frail and the long trip to Sandown and the crowds became too much.

From around 1958 onwards Snaffles' racing was confined to point-to-points in the Wiltshire and Dorset areas; he and Lucy had moved to Tisbury soon after the Second World War. On these outings he was often accompanied by the great sporting painter Lionel Edwards, who did not live too far away. They had certainly known each other since the early 1920's, if not before, and on numerous occasions had gone in the same party to the Grand National. Prior to the Second World War Snaffles and Lionel Edwards could not have been termed close, in the way that Snaffles had been close friends with Gilbert Holiday and Cecil Aldin. After the Second World War however, Snaffles and Edwards became intimate friends and Edwards showed considerable kindness in taking Snaffles to point-to-points and other equestrian events. Snaffles built up another close friendship with Peter Biegel who also lived near by, and who was to continue the style of sporting painting developed by Snaffles, Edwards and Holiday in the 1920's and 1930's, right up until the early 1980's, with such success. In the 1960's Snaffles and his work were rather forgotten by the public, but he personally, his advice and companionship, were eagerly sought after by the great painters, Edwards and Biegel. It was only after his death in 1967 that Snaffles' ability as an artist had once again become so widely recognised and his work so collected.

Snaffles truly loved a good horse, a good race and a good loser and he has left behind, as a lasting testament to all of these things, a true picture of the development of steeplechasing and point-to-pointing during a period of rapid development and change from around 1907 to 1953. Above all else, Snaffles captured the humour and the spirit of these great sports. His work has stood and will continue to stand the test of time.

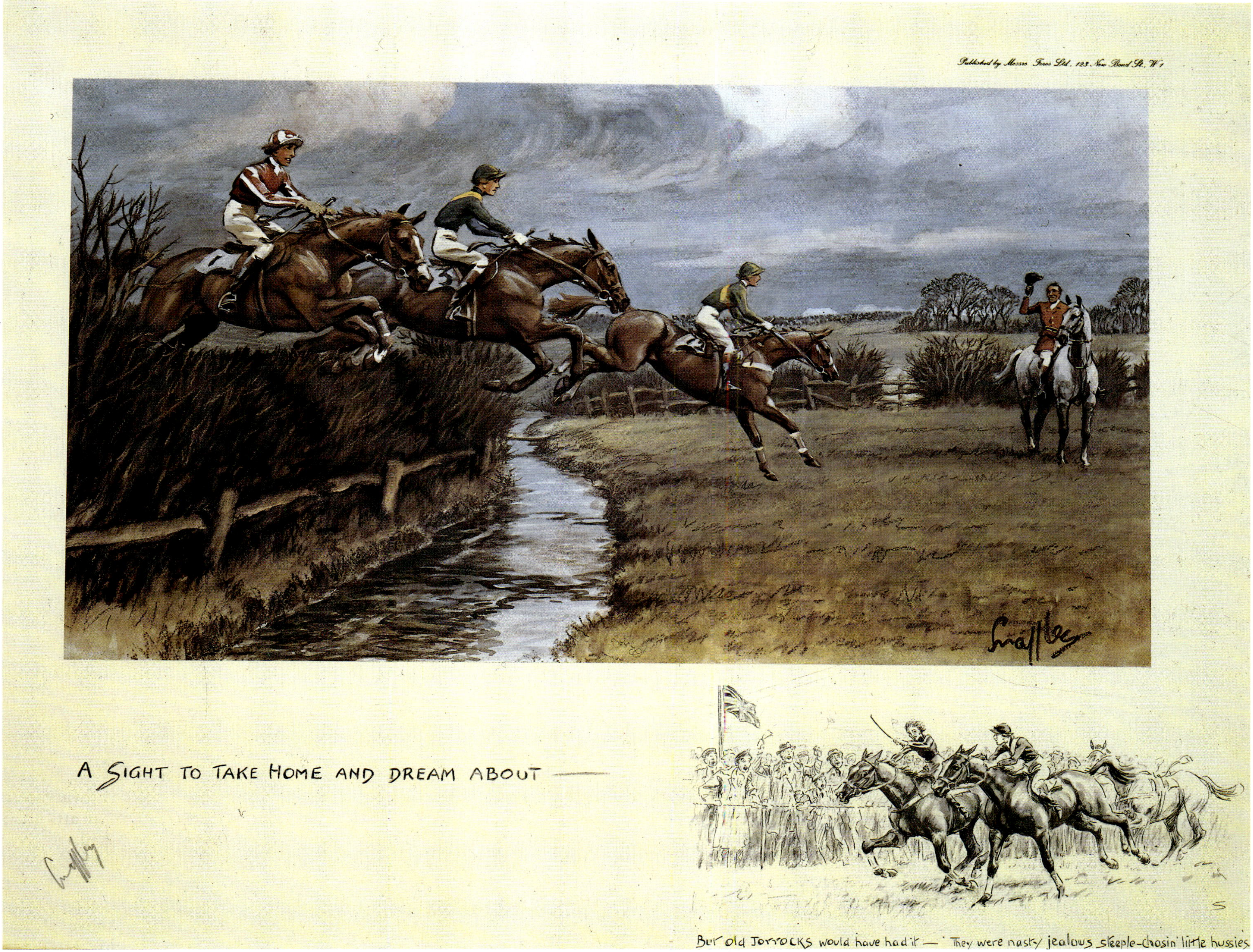

The Ladies' Point to Point

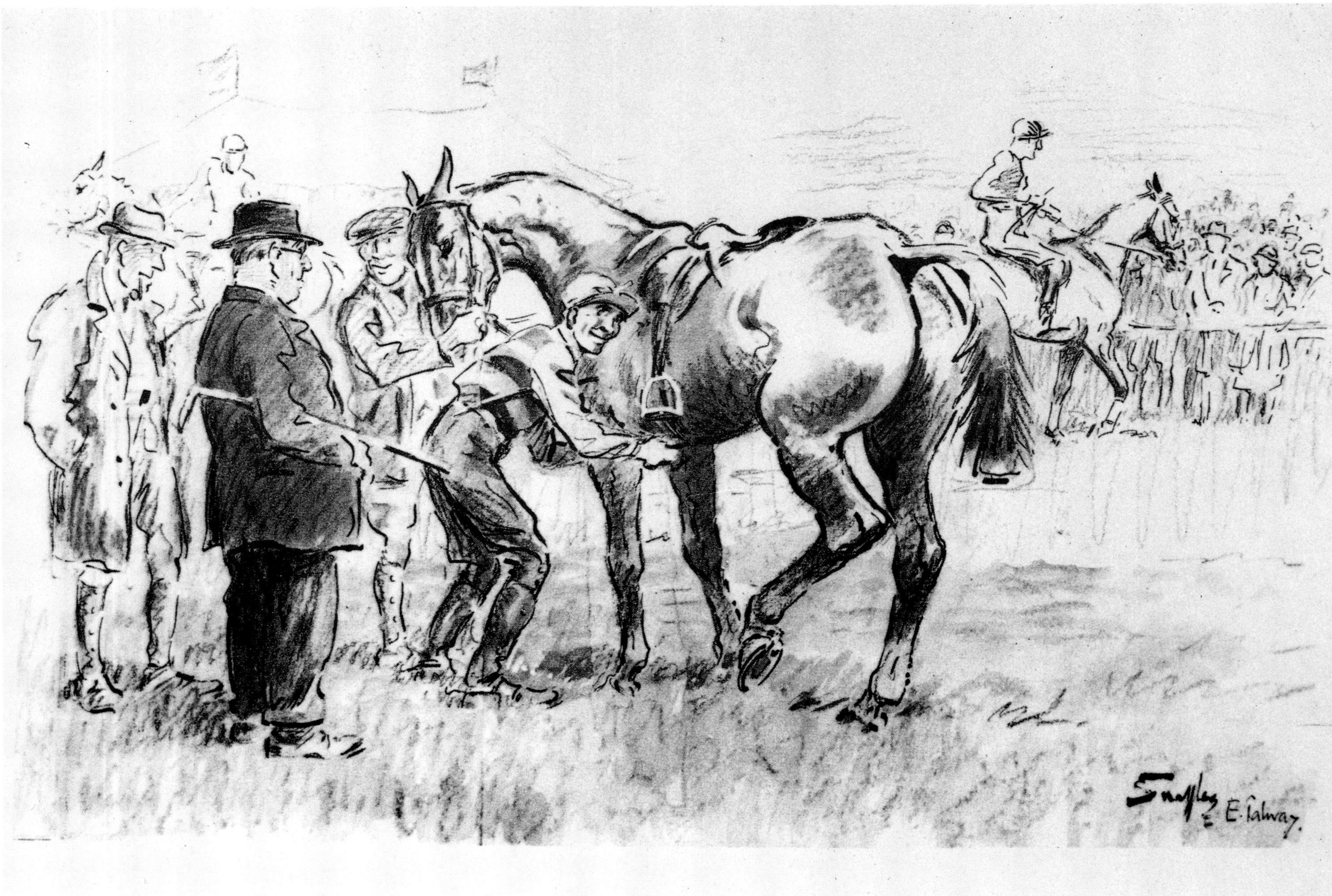

In the last years of his working life, point to pointing was one of Snaffles' main sporting occupations. Although this drawing was done in the late '40s or early '50s, it is clearly based on Snaffles' reminiscences of the early '30s at the East Galway point to point. By now he had lost his notebooks in the fires of World War Two, but the scene was obviously firmly implanted in his photographic memory

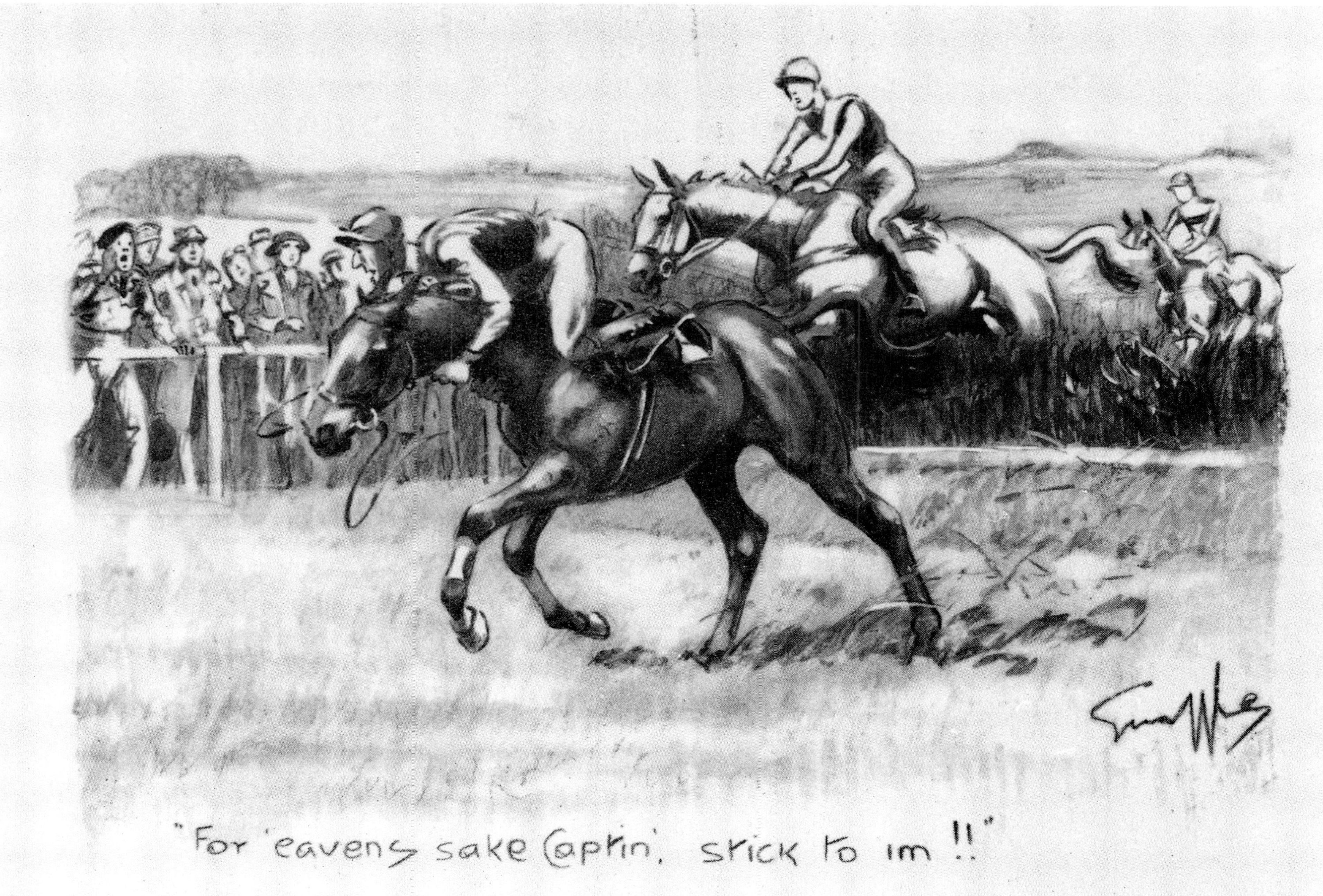

This drawing is of an incident at Larkhill, after the Second World War

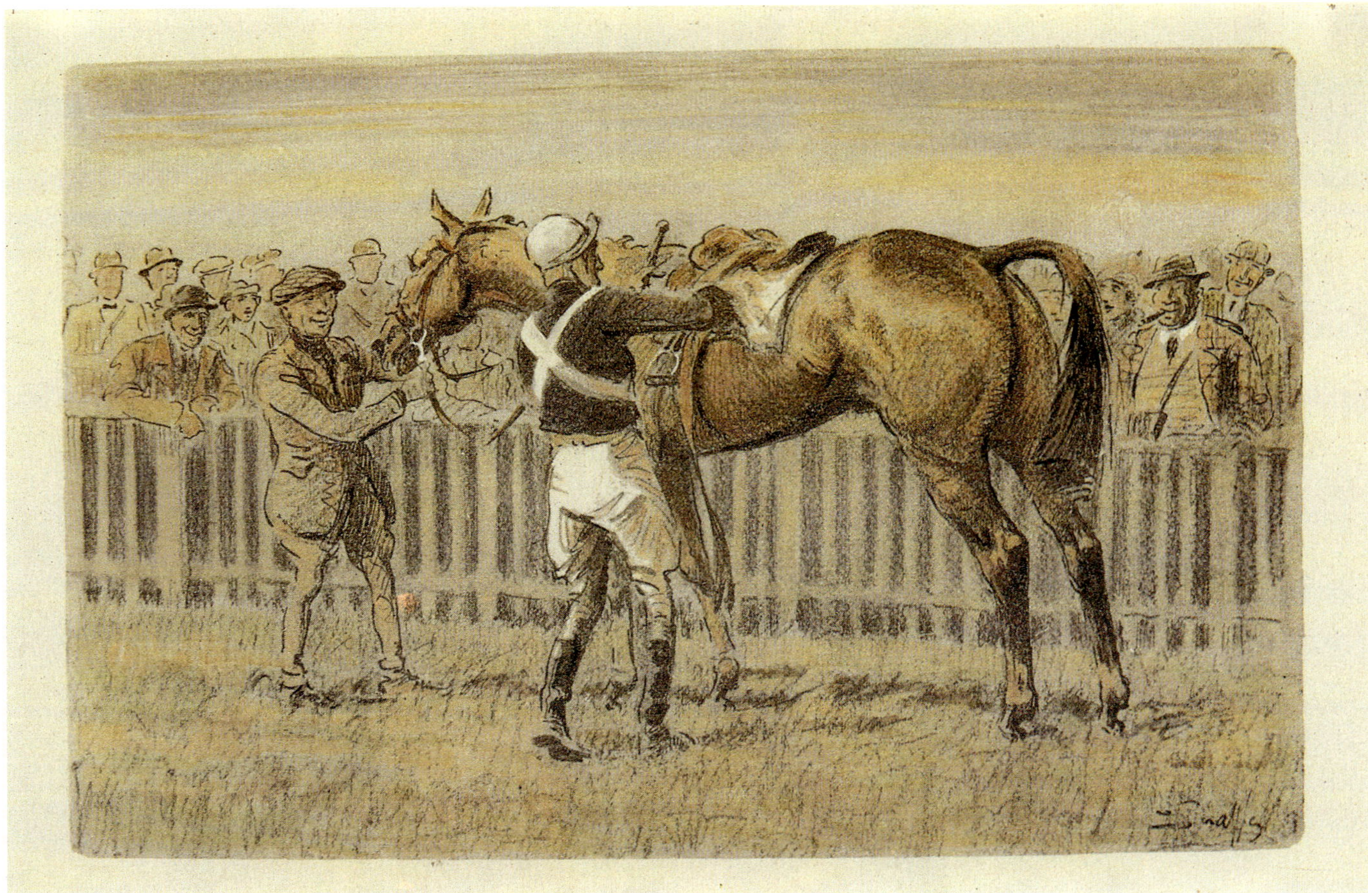

This Christmas card was first sent out in 1946/47. It is almost certainly done from pre-war reminiscences, as it was some time before point to points got back in full swing. As we commented in the first book, this was probably Snaffles' most successful racing Christmas card

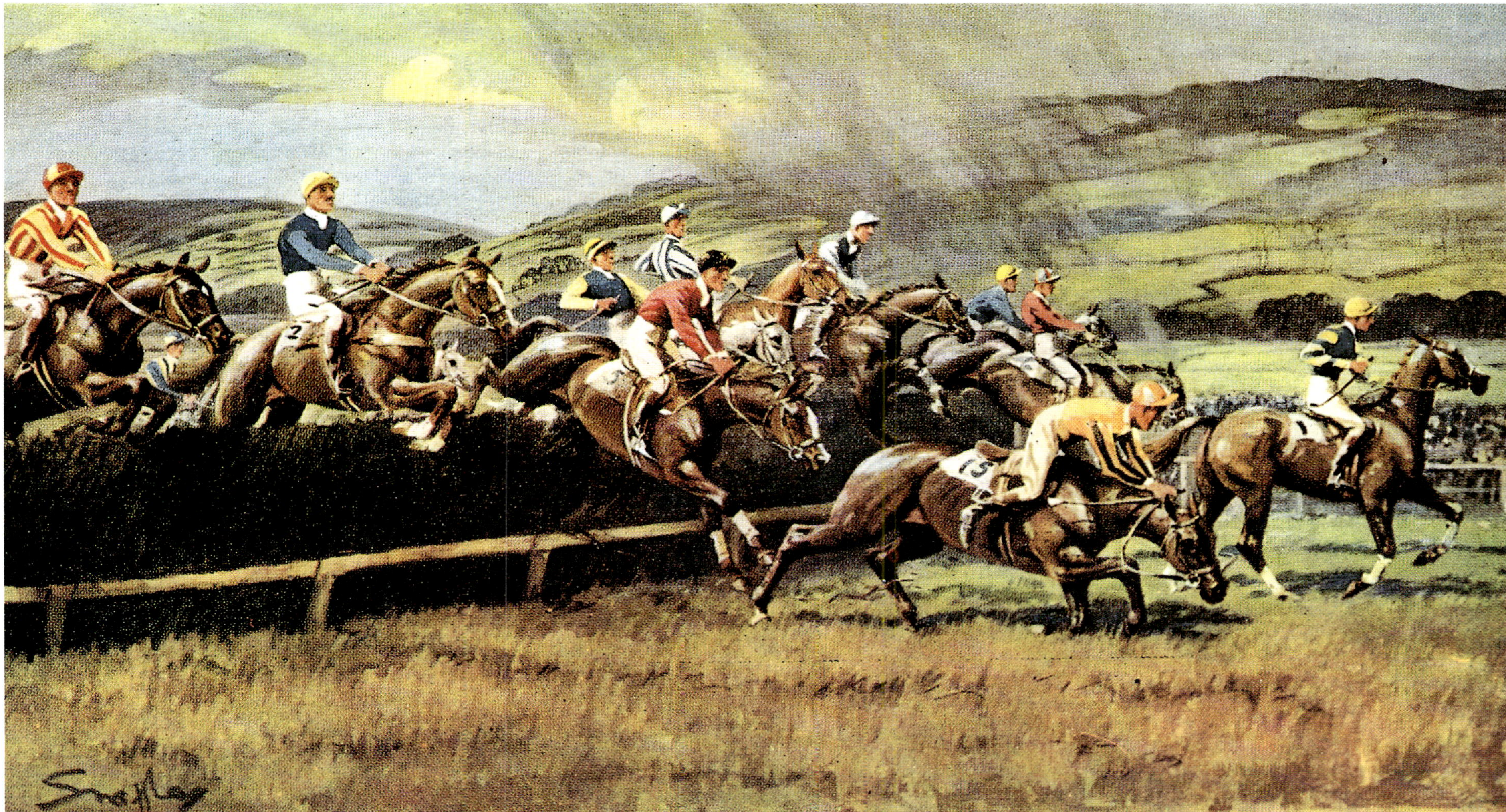

'Gentlemen Bumpers out on The Spree' (R.K. *Transcribed*)

Only in the last few years of his working life have we any record of Snaffles doing a painting at Cheltenham. This is of the National Hunt Chase. It was fitting that his last great racing painting was the only one on which he used a quotation from his favourite author

Appendix A

Listed are the majority of the prints Snaffles produced over a period in excess of forty years. Unless otherwise specified the publishers were Fores of Bond Street or Snaffles himself.

The prints are basically listed in chronological order, but for the sake of clarity where possible we have listed them in obvious sets, or by subject matter. We have also, with a view to clarity, listed prints once only, although in many cases they were issued in two, three or four different versions with a wide variety of remarques or vignettes. There was more uniformity after the First World War when the centre colour-piece was printed in considerable numbers by the printing house of Bemrose in Derby, while the remarque boards continued to be printed in small numbers, almost certainly under the supervision of Snaffles, mainly at Gale & Polden in Aldershot. We have noted in our descriptions where similar images appeared in periodicals and it is our opinion that normally an image appeared in a periodical first and was then worked up into a formal print.

By each entry we have noted its number in the catalogue resonné produced by the British Sporting Art Trust to coincide with their exhibition of Snaffles' work in 1981 (**ISBN: 0 9507794 0 7**).

First set of five small prints (1–5)

Various editions, early ones hand-coloured, later ones colour printed

1 Top o' the Season/Morning etc. 1908

Terrierman standing in a gateway with two terriers, raising his cap. The inscription is personalised, i.e. 'Top o' the morning, m'lady/Major/Judge &c.'
8¾ × 6¾ ins *41*

2 Whatever Ye De, Keep T'owd Tamboureen A-Rowlin' 1908

James Pigg, whip in hand, stands drinking ale. In later editions he has a champagne glass.
11½ × 7½ ins. *36 & 37*

3 Tell Me a Man's a Foxhunter and I Loves 'im at Once 1908

John Jorrocks, M.F.H., sits proudly astride his old horse. Horn in his right hand.
11½ × 12½ ins. *38*

4 I Knows No More Melancholic Ceremony than Takin' the String Out o' One's 'At at the End of the Season 1908

Mr Jorrocks stands, hat in hand, looking forlorn.
11½ × 7½ ins. *35*

5 Ar Never Gets Off 1908

James Pigg leaps a fence head on leaving the field behind.
Many editions.
A variant jumping side on.
12¼ × 9½ ins. *39*

6 Spats and Sporrans c1908

Scenes from a highland tattoo.
8½ × 15½ ins. *Not listed in catalogue*

7 A Point-to-Point 1909

The first fence – slap at it for the honour of hit-'em-an'-hold-'em shire.
In the first edition the horses in the centre are going from right to left. In the other editions (at least five are known up till 1922) they are going from left to right.
Typical vignettes are:
(i) Toss'd about like an old 'at
(ii) Leppin' powder
(iii) The more mud the more glory
(iv) The Wreckers
(v) The Glutton
(vi) Back to the land
(vii) The last fence, tucked up
18 × 26 ins. *25, 26 & 115*

Four Hunting Types (8–11)

Published by Lawrence and Jellicoe. After publication they all appeared in the IS&DN 22.10.10.
Normally printed in colour but there are a few which were hand-coloured. The many editions include some reprinted in the 1980s.

8 Blood and Quality 1910

Lord Ranksborough, riding a thoroughbred, raises his hat.
No background.
15 × 12½ ins. *1*

9 The Gent with 'Osses to Sell 1910

A dealer in a loud check hacking jacket salutes with his crop.
No background.
15 × 12½ ins. *2*

10 Old Tawney 1910

A rotund foxhunter smoking a cigar sits on a quiet cob.
15 × 12½ ins. *3*

11 'Hogany Tops 1910

A first-class foxhunter wearing a black coat mounted on a useful sort.
Later editions have a fox in the background.
15 × 12½ ins. *4*

12 Gee—Gee c1910

George Grossmith, Jnr. the musical comedy actor, poses in loud check breeches, canary yellow waistcoat, resting on his Whangee stick.
No background.
Sometimes a similar print entitled Gee-Gee Junior.
16 × 11 ins. *5*

A large oblong pair (13 & 14) and companion piece (15)

One set is hand-coloured, another printed in Belgium in strong colours.

13 Thrusters 1911

'ustle your 'osses, 'arden your 'earts.
Fourteen members of the field take a hedge from one grass field to another.
12½ × 21½ ins. *6*

14 Roadsters 1911

'ammer 'ammer 'ammer on the 'ard 'igh road.
The field charges along the highroad – children, parson, gigs etc.
12½ × 21½ ins. *7*

15 The Glad Throng that goes Laughin' Along 1913

The Huntsman on foot followed by assorted field.
39½ × 13¼ ins. *49*

A pair (16 & 17)

16 Bang Tails 1911

The back view of a lean follower of the Warwickshire on a thoroughbred.
14½ × 6½ ins. *8*
IS&DN 4.2.11

17 Bob Tails 1911

The back view of a stout gentleman on a cob.
Variations in coat colour and in title.
14½ × 6½ ins. *9a*

Set of eight large hand-coloured hunting scenes (18–25)

18 Not taking any **1911–13**
Fair Thruster: 'Come on it's quite alright.'
Steeplechase Jockey fox catching: 'No thank you Miss, I don't do that sort of thing for pleasure.'
Jockey mounted out hunting refuses to follow lady over large hedge.
18¾ × 20 ins. *21*
IS&DN 25.11.11

19 An Irish Yawner **1911–13**
Three mounted members of the field clamber over an Irish bank.
Remarque: Farmer running with stick.
19¾ × 26¾ ins. *42*

20 The Bullfinch **1911–13**
Black as yer hat on this side and glorious uncertainty on the other.
One of the hunt staff jumps a difficult place whilst the field ride up and down looking for a safer place.
Remarque: Huntsman landing in a brook.
19¾ × 26¾ ins. *43*

21 The Stone Wall **1911–13**
Solid and tall was the rasping wall.
On the skyline the stone wall being jumped, the huntsman and hounds in the foreground.
Remarque: Fox scrambling over a wall.
19¾ × 26¾ ins. *44a*

22 The Stake and Bound **1911–13**
Send 'em at it – and get well into the next field.
The field jumping a stake-and-bound fence in great style.
Remarque: A fallen horse and rider.
19¾ × 26¾ ins. *45*

23 The Whissendine Brook runs deep and wide **1911–13**
Two leap the rail and brook beyond.
Remarque: Hounds scramble out of a brook.
19¾ × 26¾ ins. *46*

24 The Oxer **1911–13**
Go at it – or go home
Whilst two clear the oxer in fine style, a third turns to find an easier line.
Remarque: The man on the grey goes home.
19¾ × 26¾ ins. *47*

25 The Stonefaced 'Narrer Back' **1911–13**
Two members of the field jumping a turf-topped stone wall.
Remarque: Farmer on a horse.
19¾ × 26¾ ins. *48*

26 The Tiger **1912**
Determined jockey winning a point-to-point.
13 × 13½ ins. *Not listed in catalogue*

27 Tom Isaac **1912**
A rum 'un to follow.
The huntsman of the Cottesmore, mounted on a grey, jumps a double oxer.
17½ × 23½ ins. *14*

A true pair (28 & 29).
Both appeared on the same page in the IS&DN 19.10.12

28 The Right Man on the Wrong 'Oss **1912**
The wrong horse sticks its toes in on the edge of a brook.
12¼ × 13¾ ins. *12*

29 The Wrong Man on the Right 'Oss **1912**
A stout man being run away with by a handsome brown horse.
12¼ × 13¾ ins. *13*

30 High Leicestershire **1913**
A lady riding side-saddle jumps a hedge head on. She wears a violet in her lapel.
16¾ × 14¾ ins. *23*

31 Yeomanree Cavalree **1913**
You couldn't spot us at 'arf a mile from the crackest Cavalree.
A group of mounted yeomanry, dominated by an officer on a grey horse in foreground, shamble from right to left.
14 × 16 ins. *55*

A classic pair
Both appeared on the same page in the IS&DN 19.10.12

32 The Spooney **1913**
Who hunts for the ride out and the ride home.
An elegant gentleman in top hat and cutaway pink coat looks at his reflection in a shop window.
12½ × 12 ins. *18*

33 The Sportsman who hunts because he loves it **1913**
A top-hatted follower in a red coat waits patiently at point in terrible weather. Sometimes wears a black coat.
16½ × 15½ ins. *19*

Series of military amateur riders (34–41)
Hand-coloured; very scarce; normally little background.

34 Gay Derg **1911–14**
A mounted jockey wins a point-to-point. The racecourse in the background.
13 × 13¼ ins. *29*

35 The Lancer **1911–14**
Jumping a brush fence in a steeplechase.
8 × 8½ ins. *30*

36 The Springer **1911–14**
Jumping a fence.
8 × 8½ ins. *Not listed in catalogue*

37 Cakes **1911–14**
A jockey gallops by on a horse.
7½ × 9 ins. *31*

38 Pip Hornby **1911–14**
Horse and rider walking along.
8 × 8½ ins. *Not listed in catalogue*

39 George **1911–14**
Brigadier General George C. Paynter galloping by.
7½ × 9 ins. *32*
IS&DN 10.4.15

40 Major Junks **1911–14**
The Major wins holding his stirrup iron in his hand.
28 × 33 ins. *33*

41 Paddy **1911–14**
Paddy Wallace, winner of the Cottesmore Hunt Race 1914 on Mrs Jefferson's Huntstown.
34

42 An Irish Point-to-Point **1911–14**
The field jumping a large ditch and single bank.
Two major versions with many variations published over an eighteen-month period.
Typical vignettes:
(i) Going to the start
(ii) Jockey stranded in the water jump
(iii) Weighing in
(iv) Jockey carrying his saddle
(v) Solitary mounted jockey
(vi) Fallers
(vii) Judge holding an umbrella
(viii) A bookmaker
22 × 29½ ins. *27 & 28*
IS&DN 17.5.1913

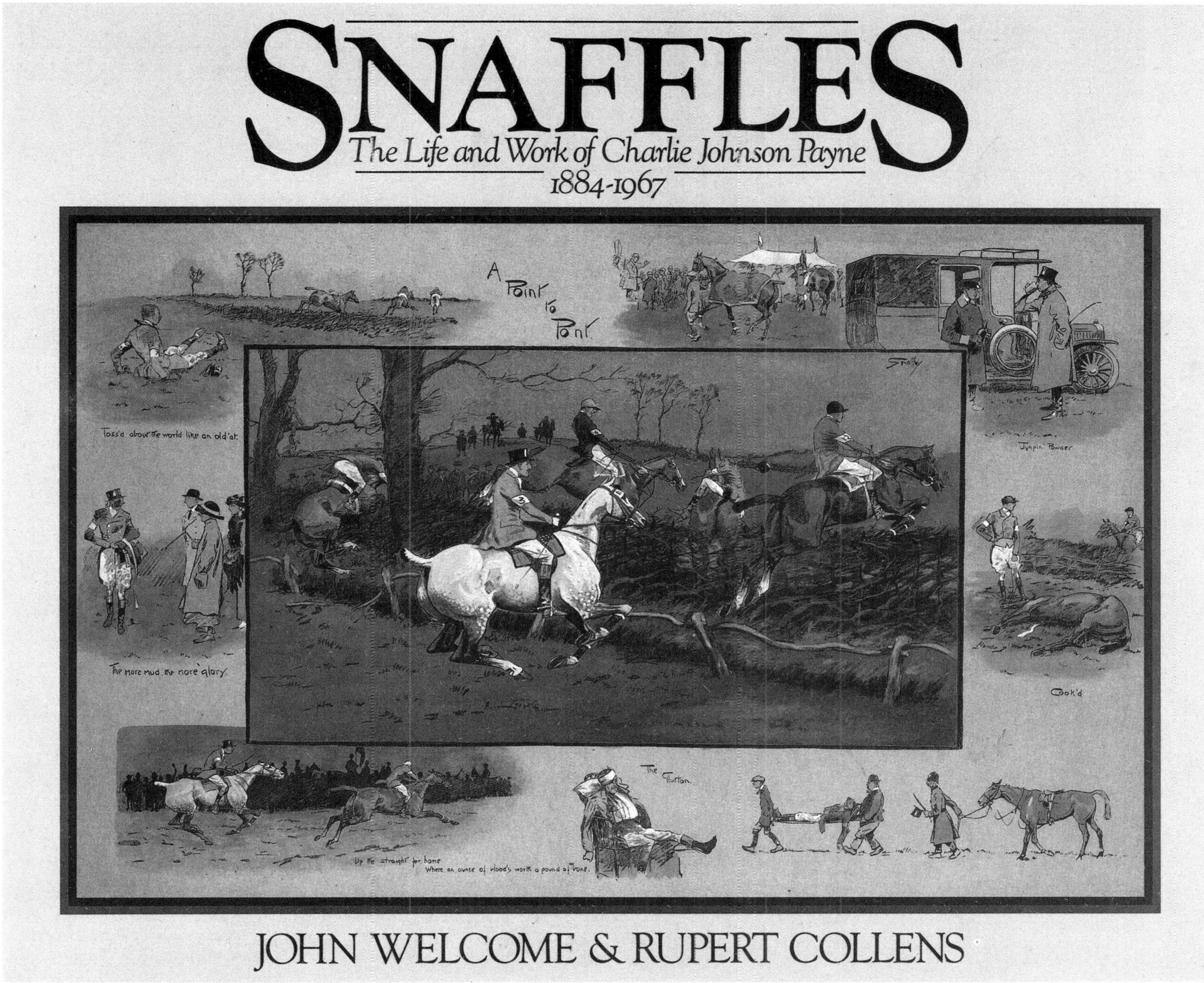

We have frequently referred to 'the first book in this series'. This is the dust wrapper. The foreword was written by Vincent O'Brien, mentioned in this book as being one of the five trainers to complete the Liverpool Grand National/Epsom Derby training double. The first book was a general introduction to the life and personality of Snaffles and to his varied artistic work. Racing and point to pointing represents about twenty-five per cent of his total output

Early Polo (43 & 44)

43 Sport in the Shiny 1913

The game of Sahibs and Rajahs.

A game of polo.
Vignettes:
(i) Stalking
(ii) Steeplechasing
(iii) Buying a horse
(iv) Pigsticking
(v) Polo
(vi) Hunting
24⅞ × 26¼ ins. *51*

44 Game of Sahibs and Rajahs 1913

A polo scene.
Vignette: a mounted Indian.
10 × 17½ ins. *Not listed in catalogue*

Early Indian and African Subjects (45–48)

45 Chasing in India 1913

Wearing topees and silks the field take a fence. The leader has fallen and a riderless horse is in third place.
15 × 20 ins. approx. *52*

46 The Ikonas c1913

I don't know whose darn column I'm in, nor where we're trekking, nor why. (R.K.)

A trooper on a coloured horse, pipe in mouth, the rest of the column silhouetted in the background.
16½ × 15¼ ins. *53*

47 On Trek c1913

Across the veldt two soldiers ride their ponies with rifles in the saddle holsters.
Remarque: Antelope's head and an ox cart.
17 × 24 ins. approx. *54*

48 The Coast c1913

Two Nigerian bearers carry a litter in which lies an Englishman.
15¾ × 24¾ ins. *56*

49 Elegant but a flier c1914

A lady mounted side-saddle on fine grey blood hunter jumps a fence left to right.
17 × 17 ins. *24*
IS&DN 19.10.1918

50 A Bruiser 1914

Top-hatted follower in cutaway red coat tightens his girth.
17¾ × 15¾ ins. *17*
IS&DN 21.2.14

51 The Sojer Hosifer 1914

Nasty steeplechasing beggar.

A rider in a point-to-point jumps a hedge and open ditch.
Also appears as 'The Soldier'.
13¾ × 13½ ins. *15 & 16*
IS&DN 28.2.14

First World War period as special artist in France (52–79)

52 The D.R. 1915

Remarkable close to the old bus's 'ead to let the stuff go by. (Rudyard Kipling with the artist's apologies).

A despatch rider on a motor cycle drives past the dead and a wayside shrine.
Remarque: The rider falling off.
19½ × 17¼ ins. *58*

53 Wipers 1915

A wounded soldier stands in front of the burnt Cloth Hall of Ypres, a German 'pickelhaube' impaled on his bayonet.
Remarque: The dead lying in the mud.
Some minor variations in the ruins.
17¼ × 13¼ ins. *57*
IS&DN 29.5.15

54 A Heilan Lad 1915–1917

A kilted Scottish officer stands ready in trenches with his troops.
Remarques:
(i) Throwing a grenade
(ii) Playing the pipes
(iii) A group of marching soldiers
17¼ × 13¼ ins. *66*

55 The 93rd 1915–17

A Highland officer.
Remarque: A soldier creeps along on his elbows.
17¼ × 13¼ ins. *67*

56 Le 75 1915–17

French artillerymen fire their 75 – the standard French field gun.
Remarque: An observer sits in the branches of a tree.
17¼ × 13¼ ins. *63*

57 Sans Panache 1915–17

French Cavalry 1914.

An unshaven horseless Cavalryman walks past ruins.
Remarques:
(i) A trumpeter
(ii) A galloping horse
(iii) Riding in the peaceful woods of the Vosges
17¼ × 13¼ ins. *59*

58 Le Poilu 1915–17

A wounded French Infantryman.
('Poilu' is French slang for a soldier.)
Remarques: Four sketches of French soldiers, and one study of two soldiers charging.
17¼ × 13¼ ins. *60*

59 That Far, Far Away Echo 1914–15 1915–17

In the trenches a soldier remembers hunting days, in a dream sequence.
Remarque: A horse with its head over the stable door.
17 × 24 ins. approx. *83*

60 Jock (K.I.) 1915–17

A kilted Infantryman stands amongst ruins cleaning his rifle.
Remarque: Two prisoners of war.
17¼ × 13¼ ins. *65*

61 Jock 1915–17

A kilted sergeant lights his pipe.
Little background. Versions exist with different tartans.
Remarque: A solitary piper.
17¼ × 13½ ins. *64a*
IS&DN 5.6.15

62 The Camerons 1915–17

A kilted officer.
Remarque: A charging soldier.
14½ × 10½ ins. *64c*

63 Bon Voyage 1915–17

An English Gunner about to load.
Remarque: Team of six horses and gun.
17¼ × 16¾ ins. *61*

64 Bon Voyage 1915

A French Artilleryman holds a shell.
Remarque: Team of six horses and gun.
17¼ × 16¾ ins. *62*

65 The Bonnie Blue Bonnets frae ower the Border c1915

A single piper leads wounded troops.
Little background.
Remarques:
(i) A soldier in the trench aims his rifle
(ii) A soldier wielding his shovel
17 × 14 ins. *69*

66 **Vimy** c1915
An officer leads an advance from the trenches, other troops in the background.
Remarques:
(i) Dead and dying soldiers
(ii) A maple leaf
$10\frac{3}{4} \times 8\frac{3}{4}$ ins. *71*

67 **The Hairy** 1915
There lay the driver's brother with 'is 'ead between 'is 'eels.
Two of a gun team with heads in nosebags, a trooper standing by.
Remarque: A trooper leaving a dead horse.
$17 \times 16\frac{1}{2}$ ins. *81*

68 **Blighty** 1916
and only five and twenty per cent of the danger.
An officer out hunting jumps a fence to land in front of an irate Master hunting hounds.
Two versions 1916 and 1918.
$20\frac{3}{4} \times 17\frac{3}{4}$ ins. *85*
IS&DN 12.1.18

69 **The Gunner** 1916
Good Hunting! Old Sportsman.
The Gunner looks up at a passing 'plane.
Remarques:
(i) Fighter plane
(ii) Column of guns led by officer on a charger arrive at the gallop
Slightly different versions.
$17\frac{1}{2} \times 9\frac{3}{4}$ ins. *75*
IS&DN 15.1.16

70 **That Far, Far Away Echo 1915–1916** c1916
Similar to No 59 except fox is shown in addition to huntsman and hounds.
17×24 ins. approx. *84*

71 **Hit!** c1916
A soldier lies wounded in the wire.
Remarque: Carried off on a stretcher.
$17\frac{1}{4} \times 13\frac{1}{4}$ ins. *86*
IS&DN 28.10.16

72 **The Bonnie Blue Bonnets frae ower the Border** c1916
Two pipers lead wounded troops through the ruins of a village.
Remarques:
(i) A soldier in the trench aims his rifle
(ii) A soldier wielding his shovel
(iii) A soldier standing wrapped up against the cold
$17\frac{1}{4} \times 16\frac{3}{4}$ ins. approx. *68*

73 **Gunners** c1916
There lay the driver's brother with 'is 'ead between 'is 'eels. (R.K.)
A team of six heavy horses and three drivers wait to limber up. One driver examines a horse's hoof.
Remarque: A team drives past a dead horse.
$13\frac{3}{4} \times 22\frac{1}{2}$ ins. *78*

74 **The Heavies** c1916
Do you say that you sweat with the field guns, by God you must lather with us. (R.K.)
A large number of gunners on foot haul a heavy gun through a wood.
Remarque: A team of horses pulling a gun.
22×29 ins. *89*
The Graphic 11.12.15

75 **Anzac** c1916
An Australian in the trenches of the Dardanelles throws a grenade.
Remarque: A hatless Australian charging.
$17\frac{1}{4} \times 13\frac{1}{4}$ ins. *72*

76 **The Canadian** c1916
A wounded soldier charges through the wire.
Remarques:
(i) Lying on the ground, a soldier aims his rifle
(ii) Head of a soldier
$17\frac{1}{4} \times 13\frac{1}{4}$ ins. *79*

77 **Indian Cavalry (B.E.F.)** c1916
Yi-hai!
A Cavalryman tent pegging.
Remarques:
(i) On a horse he holds a lance aloft
(ii) The head of an Indian
(iii) Another Indian
(iv) Indian with a spade and full pack
(v) Indian sitting sharpening his lance
$15\frac{1}{2} \times 18\frac{1}{2}$ ins. *73*

78 **Faugh-a-Ballagh** c1917
There were lads from Galway, Louth and Neath, who went to their death with a joke on their teeth. (R.K.)
A major hand to hand battle in the trenches.
Remarque: Surrendering Germans.
('Faugh-a-ballagh' means literally 'clear the way'.)
19×19 ins. approx. *74*

79 **The Guns! Thank God! The Guns!** c1917
Ubique means that warnin' grunt the perished linesman knows,
When o'er 'is strung an' sufferin' front the shrapnel sprays 'is foes.
An' as their firin' dies away the 'usky whisper runs
From lips that haven't drunk all day –
The Guns! Thank God! The Guns!
(R.K.)
Along a track in a wood gun teams charge past a group of wounded soldiers.
Different versions and remarques.
Remarque: Medium gun and team pulling up.
$19 \times 27\frac{1}{2}$ ins. *79a*
IS&DN 10.4.15

First World War Royal Naval Air Service and Royal Navy (80–88)

80 **The Sea Hawk** c1917
The Scilly's can say what our road was –
The Hinder she saw where we passed
(with the artist's acknowledgement to Rudyard Kipling).
A seaplane tracking a submarine which in turn is tracking a trawler.
Remarque: A crashed German seaplane.
$21\frac{1}{2} \times 27\frac{1}{2}$ ins. *88*

81 **Gentlemen Unafraid** c1917
Sailors in the bows of a fishing boat aim their machine gun at a submarine.
Remarques:
(i) The Captain speaking from the bridge with a megaphone
(ii) Trawlers fishing
18×26 ins. 90

82 **T.B.Ds** c1917
Captain on the bridge shouting aft through a megaphone.
Remarque: Fleet moving to the right.
18×26 ins. approx. *94*

83 **Punchin' Through It** 1918–20
Looking aft from the foredeck of a small ship.
Remarque: A fleet of ships.
$20\frac{3}{8} \times 16\frac{7}{8}$ ins. *168*

84 **Who Whoop!** c1918
A kill in the open.
A destroyer knocking out a submarine.
Remarque: A fox being accounted for.
18 × 25½ ins. *89*
IS&DN 2.8.19

85 **R.N.R.T.** 1919
An old sailor, in blue uniform smoking a pipe, stands on the bridge of a trawler.
Remarques:
(i) Three heads of fisherman
(ii) Two trawlers
18 × 15 ins. *Not listed in catalogue*

86 **Watching the Sweep R.N.R.T.** c1919
A fisherman in a duffle coat watches from the deck of a snow-covered trawler.
Remarques:
(i) Trawlers
(ii) Engineer 'Tynesider'
(iii) A Shetlander 'Muckle Flugga'
(iv) A Fisherman 'Grimsby'
(v) The head of the captain
(vi) The mate
10½ × 21½ ins. *91*

87 **R.N.R.T.s** c1919
The captain and mate lean over the side of the bridge.
Remarques:
(i) The look-out in the crow's nest
(ii) A trawler
12 × 18 ins. approx. *92*

88 **T.B.D. Shepherding a convoy** c1919
A sketch from the monkey's island of a destroyer. The beef convoy. An oilskin clad captain shouts above the storm through a megaphone.
Remarques:
(i) Captain at voice pipe
(ii) Convoy sailing to the left, one of which has dazzle camouflage
15 × 24 ins. approx. *93*

Two multi-plate sets (89 & 90)

89 **Landing his wager** c1918
Huntsman negotiating a fence, with a fall.
Four plates:
(i) Ten to one ar coomsdown
(ii) A Hundred to one ar coomsdown
(iii) Ar am down
(iv) Owever ar won me bet
Another version featuring only three plates and a grey horse missing (ii).
Each plate 9 × 10½ ins. *95*

90 **A Fire Eater** 1919
A heavyweight negotiating a post and rail.
Three plates mounted together.
(i) Pull that rail out, m'lad
(ii) Now the next
(iii) Look out! Damme I'll get over or under it
Remarque: He takes refreshment from his flask.
11¼ × 33¼ ins. *96*

91 **Swagger** c1919
but a workman.
Pink-coated follower jumps an oxer.
Many editions over 5–10 year period with different remarques.
Remarque: Elegantly sitting on a horse.
100

92 **Jim** 1920
Whatever 'e de keep t'owd tamboureen a rowlin'.
Whipper-in gives a holloa against a background of fields.
Remarque: Huntsman crashes through a fence.
15½ × 16¾ ins. *98*

93 **Ubique Meant** 1920
Bank, 'Olborn Bank – a penny all the way. (R.K.)
A gun team in the tropical sun.
Remarque: A gun carriage and team with palm trees in the distance.
20 × 30 ins. *77*

94 **Tally-Ho Back** c1920
One of the hunt hacks home, pipe in mouth, daydreaming.
In the field a ghostly artillery team passes.
Remarque: Horses in the lines.
16 × 20¾ ins. *86a*

95 **The Bender** c1920
The rider sits vainly pulling to stop the horse.
Sometimes inscribed 'The Nut'.
16½ × 19 ins. *102 & 103*

96 **The Huntsman** c1920
The 'oss loves the 'ounds but I loves both.
The huntsman counts the pack around him.
Remarque: Huntsman blowing 'away'.
Two different versions 1920 and 1923 – the latter more common.
Many variations in remarque.
17¼ × 16¼ ins. *113*
IS&DN 20.10.23

The most famous pair (97 & 98)

97 **The Finest View in Europe** 1921
The picture is presented as if the viewer is mounted on a grey horse which is just approaching a superb cut-and-laid fence. In front is the huntsman and a pack of foxhounds running hard across a Leicestershire hunting field.
Remarque: A fence-layer raises his hand as a holloa.
Many different versions over a ten-year period.
18½ × 29 ins. *104*
IS&DN 27.11.20

98 **The Worst View in Europe** c1922
Oh Murther! The dhrink died out of me and the wrong side of Bechers. Arthur Nightingall on the winner of the 1901 Grand National approaches Bechers in the most unhappy circumstances with a loose grey horse just in front of him and with a horse having a terrible fall at the fence.
Remarque: A First Aid man holds up a flag over a fallen rider whilst a policeman, facing the viewer, holds a horse.
Two main versions of the centrepiece and various versions of the remarque.
16 × 26 ins. *105 & 106*

99 **Soldiers** 1922
Nasty steeplechasin' devils.
In a point-to-point two runners jump a hedge close together.
Remarque: Remounting the far side of a stake and bound.
16¼ × 23¼ ins. *107*
IS&DN 22.4.22

100 **The Gent in Ratcatcher** 1922
I have my man cleaning my 'osses not my breeches.
A foxhunter sits pensively on his horse smoking his pipe.
Two major versions. Different horse and different background.
Remarque: Groom brushing his horse.
16¼ × 14½ ins. 114
IS&DN 25.2.22

101 **Tonnage** 1922

And when hounds really run, can show how sixteen stone should o'er a country go.

Back view of cob and stout rider disappearing through a hedge.
Remarque: Farmer inspects a damaged fence.
16½ × 14½ ins. *101*
IS&DN 10.12.21

102 **A Little Fizzer** 1922

Riding a grey side-saddle, she jumps a hedge and ditch.
Earlier version published without vignette and with a larger image.
16½ × 15 ins. *22*
IS&DN 7.3.14

103 **Foxcatchers** c1923

For the love of it –
For the ride out and the ride home.

A top-hatted follower in a red coat waits patiently at point overlooking flooded marshland.
Remarque: An elegant gentleman looks at his reflection in a shop window.
N.B. This print is a rework into one print of 'The Spooney' (No. 32) and 'The Sportsman' (No. 33)
15½ × 14½ ins. *112*

104 **John Jorrocks, Esq. M.F.H.** c1923

Tell me a man's a Fox'unter and I loves 'im at once.

Jorrocks in all his magnificence sits on his horse, jacket unbuttoned, at a cross road to Handley Cross.
Remarque: Fox leaving covert.
15½ × 16¾ ins. *99*

105 **Seagulls** c1924

A flying boat above the fleet.
Remarque: A flying boat on the water.
21½ × 27½ ins. *87*

106 **Prepare to receive Cavalry** c1924

Four members of a point-to-point field jump a hedge and the Arborfield Ditch. Two fall.
Remarques:
(i) The Starter. 'Are you ready'
(ii) Starter and the departing field, 'Go and heaven be with you'
19¾ × 27¼ ins. *108*

107 **Handing it out to 'em** c1924

A bowler-hatted young woman (now Nora Pearson) clears a post and rail in front of the field.
Remarque: A young lady clears a stone wall.
18½ × 19½ ins. *110*
IS&DN 23.2.29

108 **A Bona-Fide Fox Chaser** c1925

A scarlet-coated rider dismounts from the winner at a point-to-point.
Remarques:
(i) Falling at the water jump
(ii) Taking his hat off as hounds pass
9¼ × 17¼ ins. *111*

109 **The one to carry your half crown** c1926

A young lady point-to-point rider in parade ring.
Remarque: A horse jumping a fence (coloured).
21¼ × 17¾ ins. *117*

110 **If there is a paradise on earth** c1926

It is this! It is this!! It is this!!!

The hounds in full cry followed by the Huntsman and two of the field.
Remarque: Two members of the hunt going home.
18 × 26½ ins. *143*

111 **Happy are they who hunt for their own pleasure** 1926

and not to astonish others.

The field following the hounds in full cry (unseen), while elderly and stout members go slowly through a gateway.
Remarque: Horse and rider have a crashing fall over large timber.
20½ × 31 ins. *118*

112 **The Staff College Drag** 1927

Hold 'em back Rammer.

The Master jumps a fence with the field pressing close on his heels.
Remarques:
(i) Tom Newman in a trap
(ii) 'Yo' over, The Master 1926–27' (Lord Norrie)
(iii) 'Jack with the smell'
(iv) 'That'll larn 'em'. A farmer stands by a stoutly reconstructed fence
(v) 'Tiny' hacking his way through
(vi) 'The Arborfield Brook – asking the Government hairies the question'
(vii) The Pilot 1925/26
21½ × 29½ ins. *119*

113 **The Grand National** 1927

The Canal Turn – A memory to the Old Sergeant and Geoffrey Bennett.

The Canal Turn, second time round in a race won by Jack Horner in 1926. Capt. G.N. 'Tuppy' Bennett, a vet and the leading amateur jockey, rode 'Sergeant Murphy' to victory in 1923. He died as a result of a fall later in the same year.
Remarque: A leaping horse in colour.
21¾ × 33¾ ins. *116*
IS&DN 14.3.27

114 **Merry England** 1927

and worth a guinea a minute (*or* and worth a lakh a minute).

A hunt member gallops on in the rain followed in the distance by a young lady.
Remarque: A fox jumping a full dyke.
Different remarque in later versions showing an officer resting his leg on the arm of a chair in the Indian heat.
17¼ × 15¾ ins. *120*
IS&DN 8.10.27

115 **Sandown** 1928

The last fence at Sandown in a Military Steeplechase. Almost certainly a composite.
Remarque: The Empty Plate – a riderless horse.
20½ × 26½ ins. *146*

Set of Twelve

116 **Sporting Anecdotes for the Twelve Months of the Year** 1928

January: I will do it.
February: You, 'air dresser on the chestnut 'oss, pray 'old 'ard.
Hairdresser: I'm an Officer in the 91st Regiment.
'Then you hossifer in the 91st Regiment wot looks like an 'airdresser – 'old 'ard.'
March: 'Oh my vig, vot a vind. Almost blows the 'orn itself.'
April: 'Confound all Farmers say I wot aren't flattered by 'avin' their fields ridden over.'
May: 'I knows no more melancholic ceremony than takin' the string out of one's 'at at the end of the season.'
June: 'Whoever said winter is the season of our discontent is no sportsman – summer is the season of our misery.'

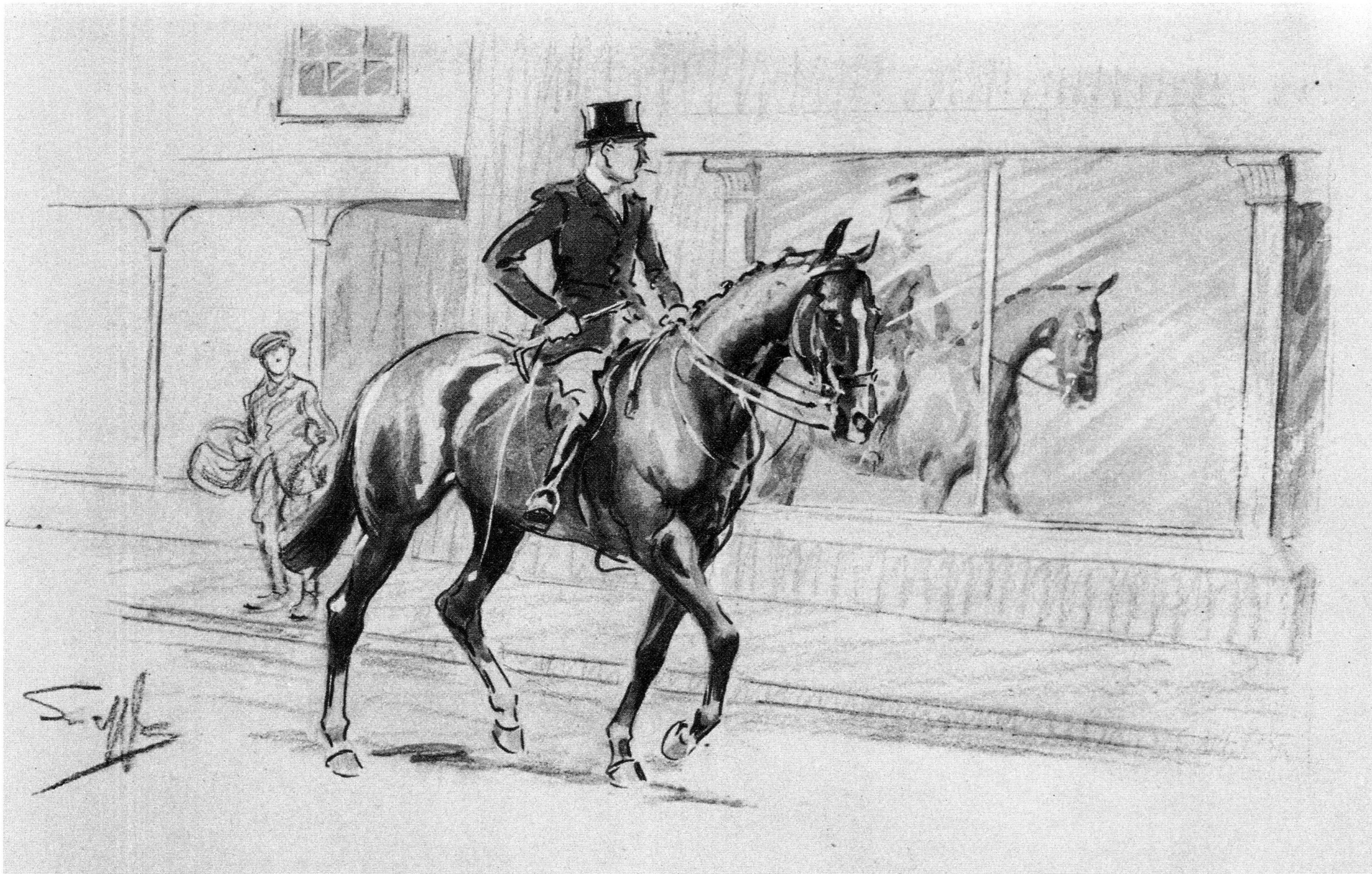

Pride cometh –

Snaffles tells us the smart horse he was riding in this pair of drawings was an ex-hurdler, named The Colonel. According to our research there was no horse running in hurdle races between 1908–14 of that name; so exactly what was the name of 'Flash Harry', as Snaffles nicknamed him, is uncertain

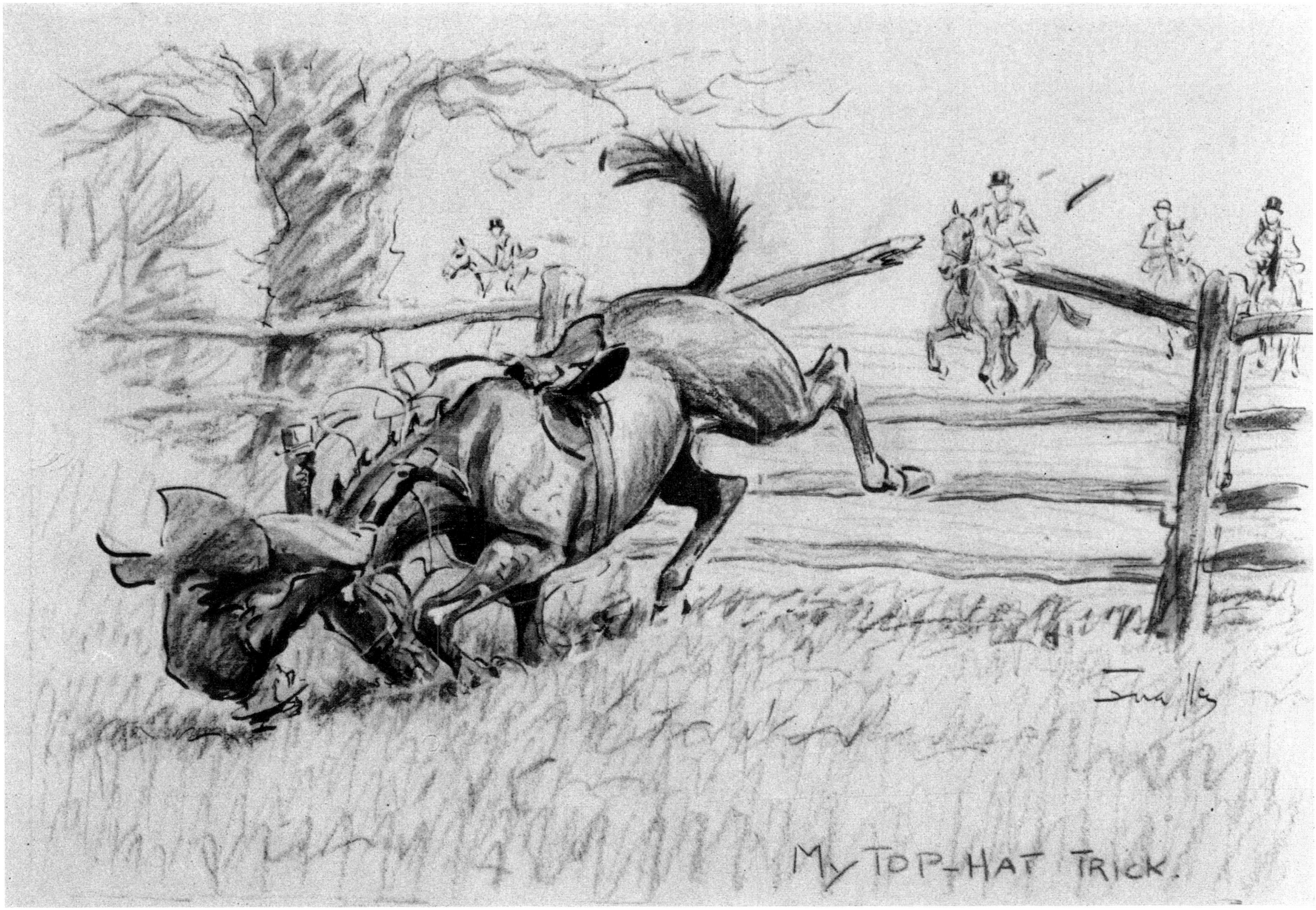

– before a fall.

July: 'Dreadful thought – where's the Brandy.'
August: 'The buyer has need of a hundred eyes – the seller of but one.'
September: 'Dash it, wot a mornin' it is, wot many delicious moments one loses in bed. Dash my vig, if I won't get up at five every morning as long as I live.'
October: 'Hooray! Blister my kidneys. It is a frost! – The dahlias are dead.'
November: 'Dear, Delightful November – the plisantest month in all the year.'
December: 'Tell me a man's a foxhunter an' I loves 'im at once.'

Published by the IS&DN 1928 and offered to sale in hog grained leather case for £1.
6½ × 8¾ ins. *121–132*
IS&DN: 7.1.28.

India (117–127)

117 The Finest View in Asia c1928
Pigsticking; a rider's view of the running pig. The horse was Carclew and the hand is that of Major Scott-Cockburn.
Remarques:
(i) 'Steady Chaps' – give him some rope
(ii) 'One of 'em out of it'
(iii) 'Ride'
18½ × 25¾ ins. *148*
IS&DN 21.4.28

118 The Wet Nalla 1928
What providence sends he takes in his stride.
Pigsticking; a horse and rider plunge head first into a river while another follows the boar up the far bank.
Remarque: Horse and rider leaping into the river.
17 × 25 ins. *149*

119 Pig
There's many a slip 'tween the cup and the pig.
Three wildly chase the pig.
Remarque: A rider falls.
16 × 24 ins. approx. *156*

120 You're bacon to a vast o' Folk and Sportsman to a few c1928
A pig charging.
Remarque: A pig in a sty.
17 × 25 ins. *157*

A set of four pigsticking prints (121–124)

121 The Forward Heat 1930
Three spears wait expectantly by the side of the river waiting to see if it will be their opportunity to go. Captain Head, Captain Catto and Brigadier Scott-Cockburn.
Remarque: The boar leaving a thicket above which the rider's head and shoulders and horse's head are visible.
17 × 25½ ins. *151*

122 The Wet Nalla 1930
A spear jumps down into a wet nalla in fine style – leaning back in the saddle.
Remarque: Similar to the centre piece.
17 × 25½ ins. *150*

123 Getting cantankerous 1930
The pig turns on one of the spears.
Remarque: Pig going between the rider's legs.
17 × 25½ ins. *152*

124 Got yer you old Badmash! 1930
A spear accounts for the pig.
Remarque: A dismounted spear refreshes himself from an Indian water carrier.
17 × 25½ ins. 153

125 The Kadir Bandobast 1930
The field mainly mounted on elephants watches the proceedings of a Kadir Cup.
Remarque: Pigstickers having problems with a jinking pig.
18½ × 28 ins. *154*
IS&DN 30.3.29

126 The Panee 1930
Major R.F. Ruttledge, 1st Whip of the Peshawar Vale, jumping the Arsala Khan.
Remarques:
(i) 'The jumping powder' – Indians sitting in a group
(ii) Riding into the river
19 × 28½ ins. *159*

127 The Peshawar Vale 1932
The gent in the black coat, 'Begad! that would stop them Meath fellers.'
Galloping across the plains and over the Jabkinndda Drain after jackal.
Remarques:
(i) The Meet
(ii) The Finish
13½ × 30 ins. *160*

Modern Polo (128)

128 Carpet Beaters V. Bobbery Wallahs 1930
Central picture of polo with multi-coloured vignettes also of polo.
(i) & (ii) Look out I've got it
(iii) Rattled
(iv) Between chukkars
(v) Get out of it Umpire
(vi) Through! Whoo-op
(vii) Forrard, forrard, forr'd
(viii) A donnybrook along the boards
(ix) A clean and clever one
19¾ × 29¾ ins. *158*

129 R.A. Harriers 1931
Major C.J.P. Layard and his hounds in full cry across the Wiltshire downs.
Remarque: Hold 'ard you qualifiers. Dammit! give 'em a chance.
20 × 26½ ins. *135*

Set of horses (130–134)

Published under the title 'Osses and Obstacles

130 The Timber Merchant 1932
Aye! and owt in the stonemason line does not come amiss to 'im.
The Huntsman jumps a timber fence to be with hounds.
Remarque: Huntsman jumping a stone wall.
18½ × 17 ins. approx. *138*

131 'Andsome is – wot 'andsome does 1932
A dedicated foxhunter on an aged tubed horse.
Remarque: The horse jumps a wide brook.
18½ × 17 ins. *139*

132 A National Candidate 1932
By Goom – Canna that owd chestnut 'oss jump.
Jockey and horse in parade ring.
Remarque: Jumping a fence in the lead.
18½ × 17 ins. *137*

133 The Sparrow Catching Sort 1932
A head like a lady – a farewell like a cook.
Top-hatted, pink-coated follower on fine heavyweight hunter gallops on.
Remarque: Disappearing through a hedge.
18½ × 17 ins. *136*

134 The Pig-Esticker 1932

A groom attends a grey under a mango tree. The spears rests against the tree.
Remarque: A riderless horse jumps a nalla still chasing the pig.
18½ × 17 ins. *155*

Ireland (135–140)

The great pair (135 & 136)

135 The Biggest Walls in the Counthry was in it c1933

and heaven help them as had to be building them up afther us (Somerville & Ross).

The East Galway Hunt in full cry over a fabulous piece of stone wall country.
Remarque: A top-hatted follower lowers a wall by kicking it down whilst still mounted.
20 × 27 ins. 134
IS&DN 28.2.31

136 Great Banks there was below in the Fields c1934

Edith Somerville and Martin Ross.

A composite picture painted by Snaffles as a companion piece to The Biggest Walls to show a fine hunt over a bank country.
Remarques:
(i) A farm labourer, 'Here ye are Meejor – send him along at it'
(ii) The same Irishman fishes the horse out of the hidden dyke
(iii) Returns the horse to its owner
18½ × 27 ins. *133*

137 The Informers c1934

Two donkeys prick up their ears as a fox trots by.
Remarque: In the moonlight a fox climbs a stone wall to view a distant farm yard.
17½ × 22 ins. *140*

138 I would bring such fishes back (Kingsley) c1934

The River Slaney with a bridge over which are crossing a horse and cart.
Remarque: A fisherman and ghillie.
20½ × 21¼ ins. *141*

139 The Stone Faceder c1934

Huntsman, on the famous horse The Doctor, jumps a bank followed by one of the field.
Remarque: A fox.
19½ × 16¾ ins. *109*

140 The Varmint Little Lady c1935

On a wiry little 'oss.

A lady riding astride tightens her girth as a fox steals away from a gorse covert.
Remarque: Jumping a dyke.
19¾ × 35 ins. approx. *142*

Later India and Africa (141–145)

141 The Boundary 1937/39

General Sir Peter St. Clair Ford and the Somali Camel Corps riding across the desert.
18¾ × 24¾ins. *147*

Pair of big game prints (142 & 143)

142 Mister Stripes 1937/39

A tiger stealing through the undergrowth.
Sometimes entitled 'Shere Khan'.
Remarque: A running deer.
21¼ × 18¾ ins. *161*

143 The Dacoit 1937/39

A leopard crouched on a rock in moonlight.
Also entitled 'The Bagheera'.
Remarque: Native boy with goats.
21¾ × 19¾ ins. *163b*

144 Zam-Zammah 1937/39

and the little man himself.

Kim, of the book 'Kim', sitting on a cannon.
13 × 10 ins. *162*

145 Smoking my pipe on the mountings, sniffin' the mornin' cool, I walks in my old brown gaiters along o' my old brown mule (R.K.) 1937/39

A dismounted British Gunner officer climbing the mountains with a dismantled gun on mules.
Remarque: The screw gun going down the mountain.
19¾ × 19¾ ins. 164

Second World War (146–151)

146 The Season 39–40 1940

The hunt passes two parked 4/7th tanks, the soldier salutes, the huntsman takes off his cap.
Remarque: An officer jumping a hedge well up with hounds.
19½ × 28¼ ins. *165*

147 Pass Friend 1940

A fox passes Charlie White of the Home Guard.
9¾ × 14½ ins. *165*
Punch 6.11.40

148 Blimy! Wot a Life c1940

West of Gib, and north across the bay.

A storm looking forrard from amidships.
Remarque: A destroyer in a storm.
19¾ × 25 ins. *167*

149 Enjoying Yerselves aren't yer c1940

A ploughman resting his team of two horses watches planes dog fighting.
Remarques:
(i) Ploughing
(ii) Dog fight
Various captions.
24½ × 30 ins. *170*

150 Ubique Means – (R.K.) 1941

A soldier stands cold and bored in front of a shore battery at Dover.
10½ × 10 ins. *76*
Punch: 24.1.40

151 Forrard on me Lads and hit 'em – 'ard 1942

A farmer, returning home with his horses, waves to a squadron of passing bombers.
Remarque: Huntsman and hounds.
19½ × 23½ ins. *171*
Punch 27.8.41

152 One upon a Time c1943

Sitting by a Vickers light No 6 tank, Brigadier Scott-Cockburn and his driver dream of pigsticking, steeplechasing, polo and hunting.
18 × 24 ins. *172*

Post War (153–155)

153 Oh! To Be in England 1950

now that April's there (Robert Browning).

Jockeys mounting in a point-to-point parade ring.
Remarque: The race over the water jump.
20½ × 26¾ ins. *145*

154 A Sight to take Home and dream about 1950

Three lady point-to-pointers clear a fence and brook.
Remarque: Riding a close finish. 'But old Jorrocks would have had it they were nasty jealous steeple-chasin' little hussies'.
20 × 26 ins. *144*

155 Oh! To be in Ireland now that April's there 1952

As No 153 with different title and a remarque showing jockey jumping a fence from left to right.
20½ × 26¾ ins. *173*

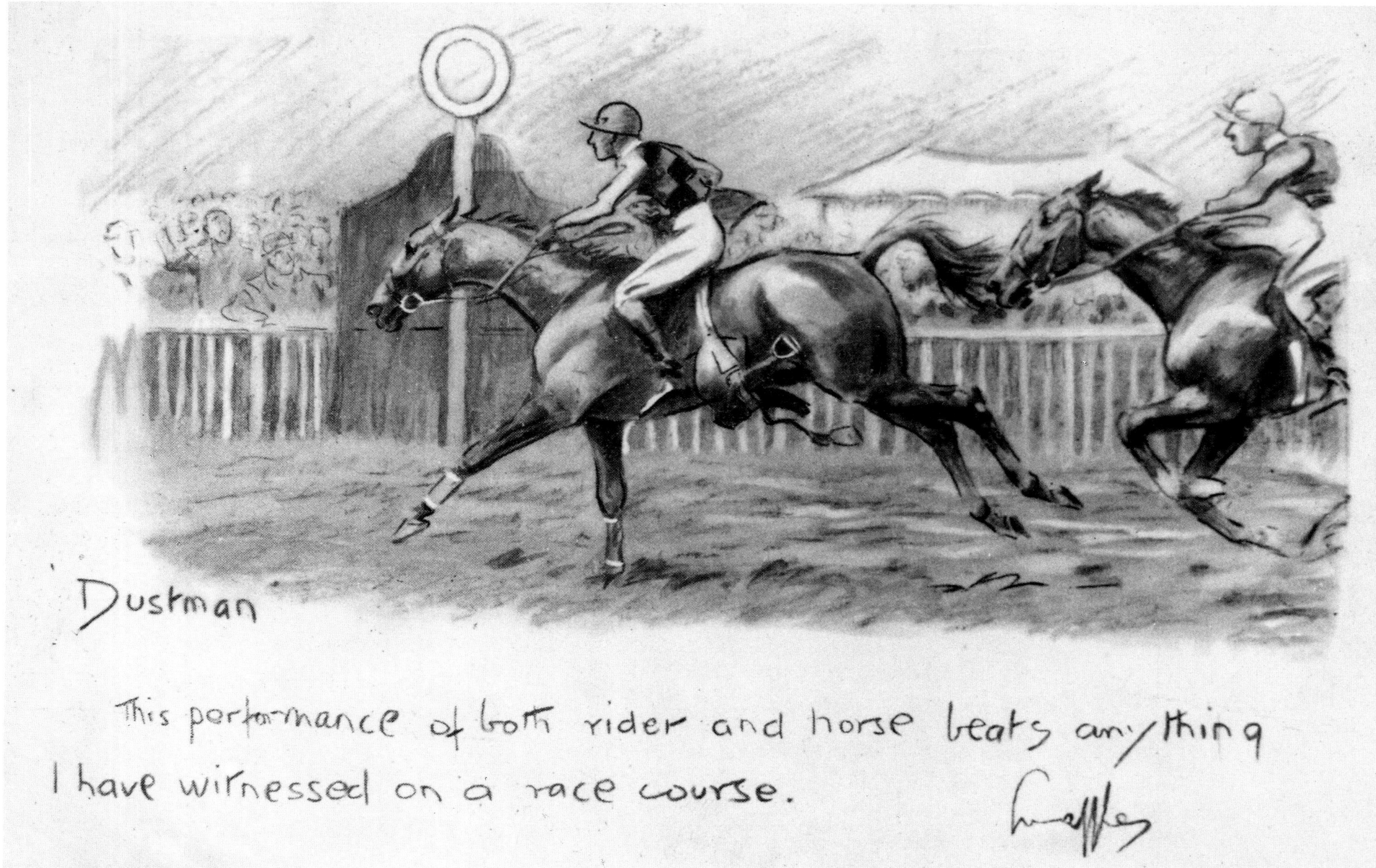
Dustman
This performance of both rider and horse beats anything I have witnessed on a race course.

Appendix B

For nearly forty years Snaffles was a regular contributor to various magazines and annuals including *The Graphic*, *The Illustrated Sporting and Dramatic News*, *The Tatler*, *Punch* and *The Hoghunters' Annual*, starting in 1907 and continuing until well into the Second World War.

He also contributed illustrations to various books such as *In My Opinion*, edited by W.E. Lyon and published in 1928 by Constable which included a colour reproduction of his great painting The Grand National 1925 'Evens on the field at Valentine's the second time round', and contributed black and white illustrations, together with Major M.H. Tulloch, to *The P.V.H.* by Captain G.S. Hurst, MFH, which was published circa 1935 by Gale & Polden; while Cecil Aldin chose to use as the colour frontispiece of his superb memoirs *Time I Was Dead*, Snaffles' watercolour of him at a point-to-point published in 1934 by Eyre & Spottiswoode.

Snaffles was also responsible for all the illustrations in the books listed below:

1928 Geoffrey Brooke's *Horse Lovers* published by Constable
1930 *My Sketchbook in the Shiny* written and illustrated by Snaffles and published by Gale & Polden.
1933 M.J. Farrell's *Red Letter Days* published by Collins.
1935 *'Osses and Obstacles* written and illustrated by Snaffles and published by Collins.
1936 *More Bandobast* written and illustrated by Snaffles and published by Collins.
1947 J.K. Stanford's *Mixed Bagmen* published by Herbert Jenkins.
1949 *A Half Century of Memories* written and illustrated by Snaffles and published by Collins.
1951 *Four Legged Friends and Acquaintances* written and illustrated by Snaffles and published by Collins.
1953 *I've heard the Revelly* written and illustrated by Snaffles and published by Gale & Polden.

Appendix C – Modern Reproductions.

To coincide with this series of books, The Court Gallery, 8 Lancashire Court, New Bond Street, London, and The Marlborough Bookshop & Sporting Gallery, 6 Kingsbury Street, Marlborough, Wiltshire have reproduced a number of Snaffles' most popular prints in high quality Limited Editions. All have facsimile printed signatures, instead of the original pencil signatures, are numbered in pencil and blind-stamped with Snaffles' "Logo". Obviously these prints are unlikely to have the same value as the original editions, but as they sell for between one-tenth and one-quarter of the price of the originals in fine condition, they give the chance for many people to own a Snaffles print or prints.

Furthermore, like many sporting prints published in the 1920's and 1930's by such artists as Lionel Edwards, Gilbert Holiday and, to a lesser extent, Cecil Aldin, certain of Snaffles' prints tend to fade, while the ink and paper used in the modern reproductions is of considerably higher quality and more stable, and it is considered likely that the modern reproductions will have a much longer "life".

The following are currently available or soon will be:

7. A Point-to-Point
43. Sport in the Shiny
97. The Finest View in Europe [*sold out*]
98. The Worst View in Europe
108. A Bona-Fide Fox Chaser
109. The One to carry your half crown
113. The Grand National
115. Sandown
128. Carpet Beaters v. Bobbery Wallahs
132. A National Candidate
135. The Biggest Walls in the Counthry was in it
136. Great Banks there was below in the fields
137. The Informers
147. Pass Friend
153. Oh! To be in England
154. A Sight to take home and dream about
Soldiers at Sandown